Global Cinematic Cities

Global Cinematic Cities

NEW LANDSCAPES OF FILM AND MEDIA

EDITED BY
Johan Andersson and Lawrence Webb

WALLFLOWER PRESS
LONDON & NEW YORK

A Wallflower Press Book
Published by
Columbia University Press
Publishers since 1893
New York•Chichester, West Sussex

cup.columbia.edu

Copyright © 2016 Columbia University Press
All rights reserved

Wallflower Press® is a registered trademark of Columbia University Press

A complete CIP record is available from the Library of Congress

ISBN 978-0-231-17746-7 (cloth : alk. paper)
ISBN 978-0-231-17747-4 (pbk. : alk. paper)
ISBN 978-0-231-85099-5 (e-book)

Columbia University Press books are printed on permanent
and durable acid-free paper.
Printed in the United States of America

Cover image: *Her* (2013) © Annapurna Pictures

CONTENTS

Notes on Contributors — vii

Introduction: Decentring the Cinematic City – Film and Media in the Digital Age — 1
Johan Andersson and Lawrence Webb

TRANSNATIONAL SCREEN CITIES

In the City but Not Bounded by It: Cinema in the Global, the Generic and the Cluster City — 19
Thomas Elsaesser

Traversing the Øresund: the Transnational Urban Region in *Bron/Broen* — 36
Pei-Sze Chow

Neoliberalism, Nollywood and Lagos — 59
Jonathan Haynes

GLOBAL CITY IMAGINARIES

New Urban and Media Ecologies in Contemporary Buenos Aires — 79
Joanna Page

When Harry Met Siri: Digital Romcom and the Global City in Spike Jonze's *Her* — 95
Lawrence Webb

Cinephilia and the City: the Politics of Place in Contemporary Bengali Cinema — 119
Malini Guha

PUBLIC SCREENS AND NEW MEDIA LANDSCAPES

Screen Cultures and the 'Generic City': Public Screens in Cairo and Shanghai 143
Chris Berry

The City as Found Footage: The Reassemblage of Chinese Urban Space 157
Yomi Braester

Remediating the 'Other Half': Planet Slum as Transmedia Project 178
Igor Krstić

NEW NARRATIVE TOPOGRAPHIES

Interstitial Cityspace and the Immigrant Experience in Contemporary French Cinema 201
Will Higbee

Seoul, Busan and Somewhere Near: Korean Gangster Noir and Social Immobility 218
Jinhee Choi

Chase Sequences and Transport Infrastructure in Global Hollywood Spy Films 235
Christian B. Long

Index 253

NOTES ON CONTRIBUTORS

JOHAN ANDERSSON is Lecturer in Urban Geography at King's College London. He is the co-author, with Nick Gallent and Marco Bianconi, of *Planning on the Edge* (Routledge, 2006) and has published articles in journals such as *Antipode, IJURR, Society and Space* and *Urban Studies*. He is the co-editor, with Lawrence Webb, of *The City in American Cinema: Postindustrialism, Urban Culture and Gentrification* (IB Tauris, forthcoming).

CHRIS BERRY is Professor of Film Studies at King's College London. He is the author and editor of numerous books and articles on Asian cinema, screen cultures, and gender and sexuality. His most recent publications include *Chinese Films in Focus* (British Film Institute/Palgrave Macmillan, 2008), *Electronic Elsewheres: Media, Technology, and Social Space* (University of Minnesota Press, 2010) and *Public Space, Media Space* (Palgrave Macmillan, 2013).

YOMI BRAESTER is Byron and Alice Lockwood Professor in the Humanities and Professor of Comparative Literature, Cinema and Media at the University of Washington. He is the author of *Witness Against History: Literature, Film and Public Discourse in Twentieth-Century China* (Stanford University Press, 2003) and *Painting the City Red: Chinese Cinema and the Urban Contract* (Duke University Press, 2010), and co-editor, with James Tweedie, of *Cinema at the City's Edge: Film and Urban Networks in East Asia* (Hong Kong University Press, 2010).

JINHEE CHOI is Senior Lecturer in Film Studies at King's College London. She is the author of *The South Korean Film Renaissance: Local Hitmakers, Global Provocateurs* (Wesleyan University Press, 2010) and the co-editor, with Noël Carroll, of *The Philosophy of Film and Motion Pictures* (Wiley Blackwell, 2005), *Horror to the Extreme: Changing Boundaries in Asian Cinema* (Hong Kong University Press, 2010) and *Cine-Ethics: Ethical Dimensions of Film Theory, Practice and Spectatorship* (Routledge, 2013).

PEI-SZE CHOW received her PhD in Scandinavian Studies from University College London. She is currently preparing a monograph based on her thesis, which examines film policy and representations of the transnational Øresund region on film and television. Her research and teaching focus on contemporary Nordic and European transnational cinema and the cinema of small nations, the aesthetics of space and place, and the relationships between screen media policy and cultural identity.

THOMAS ELSAESSSER is Professor Emeritus at the Department of Media and Culture, University of Amsterdam. He is the author of a wide range of books and articles on film and media studies, most recently *The Persistence of Hollywood* (Routledge, 2012) and *German Cinema – Terror and Trauma: Cultural Memory Since 1945* (Routledge, 2013).

MALINI GUHA is Assistant Professor of Film Studies at Carleton University. She is the author of *From Empire to the World: Migrant London and Paris in the Cinema* (Edinburgh University Press, 2015) and articles in the *Journal of British Cinema and Television* and *Visual Culture in Britain*.

JONATHAN HAYNES is Professor of English at Long Island University in Brooklyn, New York. He is the author of *Nollywood: The Creation of Nigerian Film Genres* (University of Chicago Press, 2016), the co-author, with Onookome Okome, of *Cinema and Social Change in West Africa* (Nigerian Film Corporation, 1995) and the editor of *Nigerian Video Films* (Ohio University Press, 2000) and a special issue of the *Journal of African Cinemas* (2012).

WILL HIGBEE is Professor at the University of Exeter. Amongst other publications, he is the author of *Post-Beur Cinema: North African Émigré and Maghrebi-French Filmmaking in France Since 2000* (Edinburgh University Press, 2014) and the co-editor, with Saer Maty Ba, of *De-Westernizing Film Studies* (Routledge, 2012).

IGOR KRSTIĆ is Postdoctoral Researcher at the University of Reading. He is the author of *Slums on Screen: World Cinema and the Planet of Slums* (Edinburgh University Press, 2016). He is currently assembling an edited collection entitled *World Cinema and the Essay Film*.

CHRISTIAN B. LONG works at Queensland University of Technology. He is the author of *The Imaginary Geography of Hollywood Cinema, 1960–2000* (Intellect, forthcoming) and articles on film and literature in the *Canadian Review of American Studies*, *Senses of Cinema*, the *European Journal of American Culture* and *Post 45*. He is also co-editor, with Jeff Menne, of *Film and the American Presidency* (Routledge, 2015).

JOANNA PAGE is Director of the Centre of Latin American Studies at the University of Cambridge and a specialist in Southern Cone literature and cinema. She is the author of *Crisis and Capitalism in Contemporary Argentine Cinema* (Duke University Press,

2009), *Creativity and Science in Contemporary Argentine Literature: Between Romanticism and Formalism* (University of Calgary Press, 2014) and *Technologies of the Text in a Material Multiverse: Science Fiction from Argentina* (University of Michigan Press, 2016). She is the Principal Investigator for the AHRC-funded international research network 'Science in Text and Culture in Latin America', and a further book is forthcoming on technology and the post-human in the Latin American graphic novel.

LAWRENCE WEBB is Lecturer in Film Studies at the University of Sussex. He is author of *The Cinema of Urban Crisis: Seventies Film and the Reinvention of the City* (Amsterdam University Press, 2014). He is the co-editor, with Joshua Gleich, of *Hollywood On Location: An Industry History* (Rutgers University Press, forthcoming), and co-editor, with Johan Andersson, of *The City in American Cinema: Postindustrialism, Urban Culture and Gentrification* (IB Tauris, forthcoming).

INTRODUCTION: DECENTRING THE CINEMATIC CITY – FILM AND MEDIA IN THE DIGITAL AGE

JOHAN ANDERSSON AND LAWRENCE WEBB

Over the past twenty years, the relationship between screen media and urban space has become one of the most productive interdisciplinary areas of enquiry across a broad intersection of fields, from film and media studies to geography, architecture and visual culture.[1] For film studies, this spatial turn has helped to remap the discipline at different scales, locating film texts, industries and cultures in specific local geographies, while simultaneously reframing and decentring the traditional category of national cinema within global networks of transnational flows. At the same time, urban studies and related disciplines have been refreshed by a new emphasis on the role of audiovisual media in the production of space and the cultural dynamism of urban economies. Yet, somewhat paradoxically, this academic discourse of cinema and the city has flourished at a moment when its key terms have become inherently unstable. Tectonic shifts driven by globalisation and digital technologies have led scholars in both film studies and urban studies to challenge the foundations of their traditional objects of study. As the analytic focus of film studies is questioned by the proliferation of digital media, so the traditional concept of the city is destabilised by rapid urbanisation at a global scale. This collection explores the evolving, mutually constitutive relations between moving image media and the global city, but it does so at a time when profound questions are being asked about the ontological and experiential nature of each. What is cinema and what is a city in the twenty-first century? And how are these categories intertwined in an urban environment increasingly dominated by screens and portable devices beyond the traditional movie theatre?

For film scholars, the shift from celluloid to digital and the perceived displacement of theatrical exhibition by a variety of media platforms has led to a renewed scrutiny of the material basis of film, the specificity of the cinema experience, and by extension, the aims, boundaries and practices of film studies as a discipline. A good deal of scholarship has been preoccupied with the impact of the digital turn, which has brought far-reaching changes to production, distribution, exhibition and promotion, while also disrupting and reorganising traditional forms of audience engagement and interaction. In the first instance, the rapid move to digital production has led theorists to revise our understanding of the medium's relationship to the material world (see Rodowick 2007), while others have investigated the shifting interface between audience and image. Francesco Casetti (2013), for example, argues that the culture of the screen, with its familiar metaphors of window, frame and mirror, has been superseded by that of the display, the emblematic device at the centre of a new media landscape with distinctive modes of interactivity, attention and sociality. Likewise, Steven Shaviro has argued that film has given way to an emerging 'media regime' characterised by digital technologies and a corresponding structure of feeling he calls 'post-cinematic affect' (2010: 1). Though the extent of these transformations might be challenged, they nevertheless present vital questions about the spatial relationships between image and environment, viewer and screen.

For urban scholars, the unprecedented speed of urbanisation in the global South has challenged many preconceptions about urban development, while the intertwined character of physical and digital space has transformed labour markets and the social life of cities. Contrary to the 'death of distance' predictions of twenty years ago, the digital revolution – in tandem with sustainability agendas that have revalorised the concept of dense urban living – have contributed to the continued concentration of the world's population in cities rather than their anticipated dispersal. In this context of urban growth, the headline-grabbing figure of 'over half' of the world's population now living in 'urban areas' – based on a frequently recycled UN report from 2014 – is arguably less interesting than the questions it raises about what 'urban area' means and the extent to which this population pattern actually corresponds to any shared experience of urban life. Scholarly agendas in urban studies have grappled with these issues from multiple and overlapping theoretical paradigms in the past decade (ranging from the resurgence of Marxist urban geography after the financial crisis, to postcolonial and comparative approaches, actor-network and assemblage theories), but the current moment seems particularly focused on epistemological questions about the extent to which the 'city' is still a coherent analytical category (see Scott and Storper 2015).

Questioning the conceptual usefulness of inherited morphological definitions of the city, some theorists view our age as one of 'planetary urbanisation' in which the 'urban' as a process transcends the traditional urban/rural divide (see Brenner and Schmid 2015). Paradoxically, perhaps, such paradigm-shifting declarations dismiss the city as an analytical category, while at the same time valorising the urban as an all-encompassing process. Moreover, the planetary metaphor privileges particular forms of visible change by evoking a perspective from outer space in which the whole surface of the planet looks urbanised (see Merrifield 2013). The current expansion of the 'operational landscapes' of cities beyond their bounded entity, however, is largely facilitated by the invisible infrastructures of communication technologies. To the extent that digital media flows are replacing the stimuli of the crowd – once an integral part of 'the mental life of the metropolis' – new forms of urban consciousness may seem less grounded in place than in disembedded connectivity. At the same time, the explosion in apps with GPS functions underlines the intertwined nature of physical and digital space and suggests that technology is used not as a retreat from particular ways of urban living, but as a means to maximising their potential. Indeed, traditional understandings of cities as dense and diverse sites of encounter, conflict, desire, dreams and myth-making still seem to dominate global popular culture, while many urban cores that suffered post-industrial decline are being repopulated and gentrified.

As these debates show, the spatial relationships between audience, moving image and urban environment are in the process of transformation. In light of these changes, can we still speak of a 'cinematic city'? From one perspective, the rapid transformations we have sketched above suggest a need to reformulate our research agendas, theories and methodologies and challenge us to rethink our approach to contemporary cities and their audiovisual cultures. This collection brings together innovative scholarship on twenty-first-century cinema and media that engages with these questions at a global scale. At the same time, we emphasise continuity as well as change in our accounts of these shifts and stress the importance of placing contemporary cinema and screen cultures within a broader historical field. The feature film format and theatrical exhibition persist, even if the social and aesthetic practices traditionally demarcated by 'cinema' appear to become residual rather than dominant features of our culture. Likewise, while rapid urbanisation at a global scale blurs the conceptual and experiential boundaries of the urban, the notion of 'the city' and the image of individual cities nevertheless retain demonstrable currency and imaginative power for their inhabitants, visitors, governments, policymakers and planners. The city remains a vital framework for orienting our spatial experience, just as the accumulated legacy of the cinema continues to shape our relationship to images, sounds and narratives. This collection therefore argues for the continued relevance of the 'cinematic city' as an object of study and an academic paradigm, while acknowledging a pressing need to update and revise it.

As Barbara Klinger reminds us, films have long been experienced in the domestic setting of the home as well as the public sphere of the theatre. In fact, as Klinger suggests, non-theatrical exhibition has a complex and diverse history, whether one takes into account early home viewing systems or the variety of public spaces used for exhibition, from airplanes and ocean liners to prisons and churches (2006: 3–5). From this perspective, the contemporary explosion in portable screens, public displays, digital streaming and pop-up cinemas extends and amplifies an already-existing relationship between the moving image and urban space that goes beyond the dichotomy of the theatre and the living room. Nevertheless, such a proliferation of films across the blurred boundaries of public and private has reconfigured the cinematic experience in ways that are yet to be fully explored. This dispersal of audiovisual material across multiple screens and sites throughout the urban environment arguably makes the city *more*, rather than less, cinematic. Less bounded in space and time, the moving image inhabits the city in new configurations and patterns. Our continued usage of the term 'cinematic' is therefore intended to situate our intervention within an existing academic literature on cinema and the city, rather than to draw a sharp dividing line between cinema and other media forms. Indeed, the contributions to this book investigate moving images and screens in a variety of contexts, from films to serial television drama, public displays to gallery installations.

As the contributions to this collection demonstrate, the city is a crucial subject, setting and narrative landscape for contemporary cinema, which continues to create new stories and images of urban life while refashioning genres and tropes that have shaped our experience of cities over the twentieth century. The global cinematic city of the twenty-first century is a flexible city of multiple screens and modes of access, a programmable city of festivals, seasons and symposia, and a branded city of transnational media production and film offices. It is in this spirit that we retain the term cinematic city, while cross-pollinating it with the 'global city'.

GLOBAL CITIES, WORLD CINEMAS

The range of geographical contexts considered in this volume is intended to rebalance some of the implicit Eurocentric tendencies of the literature on (post)modernity and the cinematic city, which has tended to focus on paradigmatic European and American cities. The continued reinvigoration of the cinema and the city field is in no small part down to the expansion of the geographical scope of the literature, which now extends firmly beyond Euro-America. Yet with few exceptions (for example, Prakash 2010), the recent decentring of the cinematic city has tended to take the form of journal articles on individual cities or monographs on specific urban contexts (see Mazumdar 2007; Braester 2010; Kuoshu 2010; Conde 2012). By presenting a global constellation of cinematic cities within one volume, this book encourages juxtapositions and comparisons of megacities, urban conurbations and 'ordinary cities' across five continents.

It goes without saying that any book with global aspirations cannot be exhaustive in terms of coverage, but inspired by Dudley Andrew's call for an 'Atlas of World Cinema', we have followed the motto: 'Displacement, not coverage, matters most' (2004: 10). Andrew argued specifically for a 'dynamic and comparative' approach that 'would track a process of cross-pollination that bypasses national directives' (ibid.). This scholarly agenda chimes with the ongoing calls in urban studies for comparative approaches that move beyond paradigmatic case studies in favour of careful analyses of the flows of capital and people that interconnect cities across the globe (see Robinson 2011). The comparative spirit takes many forms and, in this book, ranges from explicitly dual framings that contrast urban contexts to ideas and trends such as the 'composite city', multi-city plots, the recycling and remediation of earlier cinematic and visual cultures, diasporic audiences and the impact of transnational production and distribution contexts on urban imaginaries. What unites these approaches is a sense that neither the lens of national cinema nor single-city frameworks can capture the transnational dynamics of contemporary urban cinema.

In film studies, the idea of the 'cinematic city' emerged from scholarship that situated early cinema within the critical frame of modernity (see Brunsdon 2012; Elsaesser in this volume). However, as other critics have argued, using modernity as a *singular* concept suggests a teleology of Western development and sidelines locally specific encounters with modernity – or *modernities* – in both non-Western and non-metropolitan contexts. While there has been a proliferation of work in recent years that address these Eurocentric biases by exploring modernities in a wide range of geographical contexts, the term's associations with capitalist enterprise and new state formations makes it, in Dipesh Chakrabarty's words, 'impossible to *think* of anywhere in the world without invoking certain categories and concepts, the genealogies of which go deep into the intellectual and even theological traditions of Europe' (2000: 3–4). Indeed, even attempts to provincialise Europe or the US have inadvertently, perhaps, supported a separation of the 'West from the rest'. The affirmative term 'world cinema', for example, has often been defined negatively as everything which is not Hollywood and, therefore, reinforced a binary world-view in 'which Hollywood is the centre and all other cinemas are the periphery' (Nagib 2006: 30).

Similarly, in urban studies, the analytical focus on concepts such as modernity and development has to a large extent separated the study of cities in the global North and South into distinct and incommensurable fields (see Robinson 2011). Current postcolonial research agendas have instead tried to destabilise the South/North division by advocating an epistemological shift 'from the postcolonial as an urban condition to the postcolonial as a critical, deconstructive methodology' (Roy 2011: 308). In this context, the overdetermined prisms of 'formality' and 'informality', often mapped uncritically onto the North/South binary, have been rethought as practices rather than territorial formations (see McFarlane 2012). This conceptual recalibration can also be usefully deployed in analyses of the global film industry where informal production and distribution contexts often intersect with formalised transnational forms of distribution, making the boundaries between the formal and informal economy increasingly porous.

The overarching agenda of thinking across the North and South – without neglecting the uneven legacy of colonialism – is also necessary to capture the interdependent dynamics of exchange, hybridity and circulation of the contemporary cinematic city. Unlike earlier debates about anticolonial resistance to particular forms (the escapism of the Hollywood film and the individualism of European auteur cinema), the emphasis on hybridity and vernaculars in many of the chapters in this collection instead stresses how tropes and genres are re-appropriated in different contexts. For example, several contributors draw attention to the formulaic, but awe-inspiring convention of capturing the city from above in aerial or high angle shots. While the frequent emphasis on tall buildings in these vistas could be seen as a form of as a form of 'Manhattanisation', this imagery of global urbanism is also deployed to challenge discourses of backwardness. Often addressed to the urban middle-class, including particular takes on the 'creative class', these films can be seen to participate in ongoing attempts to move beyond understandings of urbanisation in the global South solely in terms of despair, poverty and dystopia.

To negotiate this terrain, this book adopts the global city as its organising framework, a move that allows both Hollywood and European cinemas to be decentred and repositioned within a world map of economic flows, cultural exchanges and shifting centre-periphery dynamics. Drawing on recent scholarship that has reconceptualised world cinema within the framework of the transnational (Ďurovičová and Newman 2009; Galt and Schoonover 2010; Iordanova, Jones and Vidal 2010), this focus on global – rather than 'world' – cinema enables us to interrogate cinemas and spatialities outside the North Atlantic without neglecting the importance of Europe and the United States (for other significant examples of this approach, see Krause and Petro 2003; Kapur and Wagner 2011). In urban studies, the 'global city' is mainly associated with Saskia Sassen's influential definition in *The Global City: New York, London, Tokyo* (1991), which had a narrow focus on financial services. While Sassen's original analysis contained strong elements of political critique (not least with regards to intra-urban class polarisation), the same cannot be said about the work of the financial consultancies that subsequently appropriated her methods to produce urban league tables. Thus the term's association with rankings – or the terminology of 'core' and 'peripheral' in John Friedmann's related 'world city hypothesis' (1986) – could potentially be seen to reproduce hierarchies and binaries associated with the North/South split. Yet since Sassen's initial intervention, the world has grown more polycentric: in 1990, five per cent of the world's five hundred largest corporations were based in emerging regions, while in 2010 the figure had reached 17 per cent and research by the McKinsey Global Institute (see Dobbs *et al.* 2012) inspired by Sassen's methodology suggests it could reach 45 per cent by 2025. These economic figures are matched by the rising cultural and cinematic importance of emerging cities and urban regions, which now compete with long-established hubs of film production and cultural prestige such as Los Angeles and Paris.

From an industrial perspective, film production is increasingly mobile on an international scale. While city and state governments worldwide compete for the global traffic of location shooting, the digital workflow of post-production, especially visual effects, is also outsourced and dispersed across national borders (Miller *et al.* 2005). However, these interactions do not take place on a smooth and undifferentiated world map, but rather on one with competing centres of gravity and concentrations of power. Production patterns are shaped by state and city incentives as well as the presence of major studio complexes which trade on their relationship to local film industries, infrastructure, built environments and natural resources. As Ben Goldsmith and Tom O'Regan (2003) have shown, studio complexes are not, therefore, 'anywhere but nowhere' but rather 'anywhere and somewhere' – that is, their location and connection to place is a highly significant part of their strategic importance. Though many of these complexes have traditionally been in Western settings – especially the US, Canada, Europe and Australasia – centres such as Qingdao Oriental Movie Metropolis are creating new regional hubs. Expanding beyond film production into other creative industries such as fashion, design and architectural services, such complexes become clusters of activity that mirror the film festival at the other end of the consumption chain.

These intensified flows of transnational production are created and attracted by global cities that Michael Curtin designates 'media capitals'. As Curtin's research demonstrates, cities such as Bombay, Cairo or Hong Kong now 'represent centers of media activity that have specific logics of their own; ones that do not necessarily correspond to the geography, interests or policies of particular nation states.' (2003: 203). Curtin's analysis explicitly draws on Sassen, though as he suggests, her work and that of other economists and geographers frequently downplays cultural forces in their analysis of the global city. Just as geographies of film production have been uneven, so have the distribution of narrative settings. For example, Hollywood's economic hegemony has allowed it to export an Americanised view of urbanism for global consumption. Preceding recent discussion on the 'generic city' (Koolhaas 1995) – a term several contributors in this book deploy – Fredric Jameson noted early in relation to postmodern cinema the tendency to represent urban space *everywhere* as if it were New York or California (1982: 116). In contrast with this homogenisation, Giuliana Bruno's influential analysis of *Blade Runner* (Ridley Scott, 1982) stressed an eclectic urban hybridity as she highlighted how the film is set in a city 'called Los Angeles, but it is an LA that looks very much like New York, Hong Kong, or Tokyo' (1987: 65). What these two seemingly contradictory – but not incompatible – trends of global homogenisation and local hybridisation have in common is that they challenge place-specificity. For many commentators, this perceived crisis of the particularity of place – frequently held up as a hallmark of our current round of globalisation – has been intensified by the digital revolution, which is also seen to disembed social relations from physical locations.

As numerous scholars have argued, however, this narrative has frequently been overstated: in fact, place specificity and the embeddedness of urban cultures and economies may matter more, rather than less, in the context of these globalising forces (see Massey 1994; Sassen 2005). Revising our understanding of cinema and space in the contemporary conjuncture therefore requires attention to this complex imbrication of the material and the immaterial, the global and the local. One aspect of this reconfiguration is the extent to which the digital turn has threatened the indexical link to geographical place – a persistent theme in discussions of the cinematic city. Following Siegfried Kracauer's emphasis on film's affinity for 'the street' and the camera's capacity to record and reveal its material reality, the ontology of the location has underscored the conceptual link between medium and place. As John David Rhodes and Elena Gorfinkel argue, this 'very natural seeming predisposition of the moving image toward an indexical recording of place' (2011: xvi) provokes important questions about the way that place is embedded in the effects of the cinematic apparatus. In the digital era, such questions are equally important but may need to be reformulated. From a conceptual perspective, the digital camera and the endless manipulability of the image weaken or even break the photographic bond to the profilmic location, while the studio has become a virtual as well as a physical space.

However, this account becomes problematic if one takes a more pragmatic view. Just as soundstage work and special effects processes were carefully integrated with location footage in the past, behind-the-scenes reels from contemporary VFX houses have shown just how much of a film's *mise-en-scène* can be manipulated and redesigned in post-production in ways that are consonant with audience expectations of authenticity. Both traditional studio production and contemporary filmmaking practices produce space by integrating heterogeneous materials with varying levels of perceived realism. Though more research remains to be done to investigate the nature of these shifts, it seems premature to suggest that the link between viewer and place has been severed.

Indeed, despite recent media debates about the over-use of CGI and audience demands for greater authenticity, the experiential relationship between cinema and place appears as strong as ever. Even Hollywood's most CGI-heavy franchises can become powerful engines of movie tourism, and there is little evidence to suggest that audiences are less interested in the relationship between film and place, which if anything, appears to be intensifying. For a major release, shooting locations are frequently recorded on the Internet Movie Database before a film hits cinemas, their coordinates plotted and digitally mapped, and their relation to 'real' places debated and dissected by bloggers, fans and local media. Mapping movie locations, once the preserve of fans and scholars, has now become part of the everyday practice of film consumption, and the paratextual materials that have proliferated in the digital era frequently operate in ways that could be considered spatial or cartographic. We might also consider Intellect's burgeoning World Film Locations series, a semi-scholarly list currently at forty volumes and counting, whose titles read like an airport departure board or a chart of popular city break destinations; in this sense, being viewed as 'cinematic' might be understood as a necessary precondition for global city status.

OVERVIEW

The book's opening section focuses on evolving patterns of production, distribution and exhibition. In the first chapter, Thomas Elsaesser advances the international film festival as a model for revising our understanding of both the 'cinematic city' and European cinema. Our concepts of the cinematic city, Elsaesser argues, must be reworked in the era of the post-industrial or global city, which has seen a fundamental reconfiguration of urban societies and their relationship to cinema as culture, institution and economic agent. For Elsaesser, film festivals provide the clearest way to remap these relationships while revising our understanding of European cinema as part of an encompassing notion of 'world cinema'. Simultaneously global, regional and urban, this is a European cinema of the cities appropriate to the age of cultural capitals and city branding initiatives. In navigating this field, Elsaesser draws on two modalities of the global city – the generic city (Rem Koolhaas) and the cluster city (Michael Porter) – each of which help to illuminate the role of the film festival within contemporary cinema and cities. This focus on the film festival enables us to understand the cinematic city as institutional fixture as much as representational trope. Kant's paradox of world citizenship – the paradigm of 'unsocial sociability' – becomes a way to recast apparently oppositional relationships (for example, between Hollywood and international art cinema) as systems of productive feedback and what Elsaesser defines as 'antagonistic mutuality'. The film festival therefore emerges as an emblematic phenomenon of the global, 'progammed' city and a key nodal point in the global/local dynamics of contemporary cinema.

In the second chapter, Pei-Sze Chow develops this transnational theme, examining television production and media policy in the Øresund city region (encompassing Copenhagen and Malmö). How do city regions impact on media production and can narrative forms give shape to new urban-regional identities? Focusing on the crime thriller *Bron/Broen* (2011–), a Swedish-Danish co-production, Chow outlines the industrial and institutional contexts for transnational programming. As she argues, *Bron/Broen* is not only a product of regional policy, but also self-consciously addresses the construction of a new regional identity. Yet this transnational imaginary is harder to assemble than the region's planners and technocrats might wish it to be: the faultlines of the Øresund come to the surface in the show, which uses the long-form possibilities of the serial drama and the transnational 'Nordic Noir' aesthetic to explore the fractures between city, region and nation.

Mapping out new industry dynamics and production trends in the Nigerian film industry, including expansion from Lagos into locations such as Asaba and Onitsha, Jonathan Haynes's chapter examines how Nollywood has been shaped by the distinctive experience of neoliberalism in West Africa. Yet this highly embedded national industry is also being transformed by the role of transnational corporations, which are seeking to formalise distribution via satellite and streaming services such as Netflix, not least to target crucial African diasporic audiences globally. As Haynes's close reading of recent films reveal, the narrative themes of Nollywood also reflect these audience maximisation strategies. *Lagos Cougars* (Desmond Elliot, 2013), for example, is divided between an affluent neighbourhood in Lagos and the prosperous Nigerian community in Houston, Texas, while the corporate style of *Last Flight to Abuja* (Obi Emelonye, 2012) challenges the trope of Africa as backward in order to appeal to both domestic and expatriate pride.

The three chapters in the second section engage with Buenos Aires, Los Angeles and Kolkata, focusing on films that revise or repurpose the traditional screen image of those cities. Drawing on contemporary spatial and media theories, these chapters stake out ways in which cinema engages with gentrification, globalisation and digitisation in the global city. For Joanna Page, *Medianeras* (Gustavo Taretto, 2011) is representative of a new wave of films that move beyond familiar cinematic images of Buenos Aires as a city of poverty, exclusion and marginalisation. In contrast, *Medianeras* inhabits the world of a relatively affluent, professional class of post-industrial workers whose city is saturated by digital media. This highly mediatised environment is established through a heterogenous audiovisual language that features techniques more often associated with architectural animation and television advertising. Drawing on recent work on media ecologies, Page shows how the film and its reflexive participation in the aesthetics of intermediality invokes the city as a place in which the virtual and the material, the human and nonhuman encounter each other in complex ways.

This exploration of post-human subjectivity and the digital city continues in Lawrence Webb's analysis of *Her* (Spike Jonze, 2013) and its projection of human/operating system romance in near-future Los Angeles. Viewing Jonze's film as a hybrid of romantic comedy and science fiction, Webb discusses its repurposing of genre conventions in the context of the digital turn, the creative class, and the hybridisation of the global city. While the film's use of Shanghai locations makes a new intervention into the urban imaginary of Los Angeles, its debt to *Blade Runner* and *Metropolis* (Fritz Lang, 1927) shows how the digital city is nevertheless figured through the representational tropes and legacies of the cinematic city.

Malini Guha's chapter turns to Kolkata's 'middle of the road' cinema and a cycle of films for, and about, the city's middle class population. As she argues, films such as *The Future of the Past* (Anik Dutta, 2012) and *Maach, Mishti and More* (Mainak Bhaumik, 2013) deploy cinephilic references to Bengali film history – especially the work of Parallel Cinema auteurs such as Satyajit Ray and Ritwik Ghatak – as a central strategy in their engagement with Kolkata's rapidly changing urban environment. Mapping cinephilia onto the concept of topophilia, Guha shows how the city's cinematic legacy has become intertwined with contemporary discourses about Kolkata's postcolonial transformation. As Guha argues, the cinephilic gestures of these films are frequently topophilic, evoking nostalgic longings for the particularity of place in the face of globalisation. Considering the ambivalent politics of these films, Guha questions what is at stake in this cinephilic and topophilic mobilisation of the urban past and its relation to the city's projected future.

The third section expands the book's focus beyond cinema to contemplate the broader relationship between the global city, screens and new media. Chris Berry takes a comparative view of public screens in Shanghai and Cairo, questioning how the post-cinematic screen culture of the glance relates to the contemporary global city. Contesting received ideas about the ubiquity of media in the city and notions of the generic city, Berry's research outlines the local specificity of urban screens and their uses. The case studies of Shanghai and Cairo demonstrate that screens are far from ubiquitous, and their patterns of use attest to diverse and specific local cultures rather than homogeneity. Ultimately, these local cultures and their experiences and appropriations of public space provide an optimistic view that neoliberal screen culture, and its encroaching commodification of urban space, might yet be challenged.

Yomi Braester argues that the contemporary urban environment is defined by two forms of the moving image, surveillance videos and found footage. Rather than view these in opposition, Braester suggests that they are complementary, blurring boundaries between public and private spheres, spontaneous and designed images, and between material and virtual spaces. Braester examines these interlinked phenomena in the People's Republic of China, analysing selfies and self-made videos alongside contemporary video art by Tan Tan, Li Juchuan and Ai Weiwei. As these examples show, citizens are not simply subjects of surveillance or masters of their own visual representation. Rather, the interaction between subjects, screens and cameras is mutually constitutive – a process that redefines and reconstitutes public space and urban citizenship. Like Joanna Page, Braester invokes the notion of a new media ecology, conceptualising the city as a 'visual ecosystem' that functions both as 'watching eye and as a visual *objet trouvé*'.

Igor Krstić analyses the photographer Jonas Bendiksen's transmedia work *The Places We Live* (2008) and its engagement with slums in Mumbai, Caracas, Nairobi and Jakarta. This project, which began as a photo book and later developed into an interactive web documentary and immersive touring installation, can be seen as a process of remediation in two ways. As Krstić shows, it refashions earlier representations of slums, notably Jacob Riis's *How the Other Half Lives* (1890) and other spectacular images of urban poverty from the nineteenth century. At the same time, Bendiksen's work 'remediates' in the sense of reform, in its attempt to provide positive counter-narratives to the dystopian notion of a 'planet of slums' popularised by Mike Davis and others. By unpacking the different experiences of this project as photography, interactive documentary and panoramic installation, Krstić questions whether this remediation of slum imagery can provide a critical edge, or if it is just the latest and most hypermediated example of slum tourism for Western audiences.

The final section is concerned with the narrative topographies and spatial trajectories of contemporary cinema. Will Higbee shows how recent films have moved beyond established narrative spaces and representational tropes associated with the immigrant experience in France. Whereas the *beur* cinema of the 1980s and the *banlieue* films of the 1990s represented housing estates on the urban periphery as an emblematic space of social exclusion, recent films have deployed settings that Higbee calls 'interstitial cityscapes' outside the global cities of Paris and Marseilles. Drawing on the work of Hamid Naficy, Higbee argues that films such as *Dernier Maquis* (Rabah Ameur-Zaimeche, 2008), *La Graine et la mulet* (Abdellatif Kechiche, 2007) and *Rust and Bone* (Jacques Audiard, 2012) are set in spaces characterised by multiple points of identification, which problematise the relationship between place and ethnic belonging/exclusion. Similarly, Jinhee Choi's chapter maps the urban spaces in contemporary South Korean gangster films by appropriating Edward Dimendberg's conceptual typology of centripetal and centrifugal space in relation to Seoul and Busan. As Choi argues, the spatial trajectories of these gangster and noir films in which characters often trespass both vertical and horizontal boundaries underline tensions around social immobility in South Korean society. Adding an industry dimension to her analysis of the settings in these films, Choi also draws attention to a shift from Seoul to Busan as a key location in the 2000s as a direct result of the local government's efforts to attract filmmaking to the city.

Finally, the Hollywood film industry is, of course, still hegemonic in terms of economic power, cultural influence and market saturation. Yet, though the industry remains firmly anchored in the management, design and production complex of Southern California, its operational logic has become increasingly decentred through the need to attract global audiences, especially in rapidly expanding markets such as China. Hollywood production practices have long been internationally mobile, though their global strategies continue to evolve. Christian Long tackles this topic via one of the key modalities of Hollywood blockbuster urbanism: the city-hopping itineraries of the global spy thriller. As Long argues, the tendency for the spy film to shoot chase sequences in the megacities of the global South is motivated not only by cheap labour but also by a complex mesh of generic requirements and logistical strategies. Going beyond purely economic accounts of runaway production, Long shows how the built topography and transport infrastucture of a city such as Tangier or Manila offer fresh possibilities for staging action. The global megacity thus becomes an infrastructural resource for Hollywood, binding together economics and aesthetics, ideology and geopolitics.

NOTE

1   The literature is now extensive. In film studies, the idea of the 'cinematic city' emerged from scholarship that situated early cinema within the critical paradigm of modernity (see Hansen 1991; Bruno 1993; Gunning 1994; Charney and Schwartz 1995; Donald 1999). The first generation of edited books on cinema and the city, which appeared in the late 1990s and early 2000s (see Clarke 1997;

Shiel and Fitzmaurice 2001; 2003), were genuinely interdisciplinary attempts to merge insights from the humanities and social sciences and drew inspiration from the modernity/modernism debates as well as an interdisciplinary literature on postmodernity and postmodern urbanism (see Jameson 1984, 1992; Harvey 1989; Davis 1990; Soja 1996; Bruno 1987; Deutsche 1996). These anthologies have been followed by many important contributions to the field, including surveys of urban cinema (see AlSayyad 2006; Mennel 2008), studies of individual cities (see Brunsdon 2007; Braester 2010; Shiel 2012), in-depth analyses of genres, cycles and periods (see Dimendberg 2004; Prakash 2010; Wojcik 2010; Corkin 2011; Webb 2014), theories of cinema and space (see Pratt and San Juan, 2014) and edited collections with varying emphases (see Konstantarakos 2000; Webber and Wilson 2008; Braester and Tweedie 2010; Rhodes and Gorfinkel 2011). See also Brunsdon (2012) for a detailed genealogy of this scholarship.

REFERENCES

AlSayyad, Nezar (2006) *Cinematic Urbanism: A History of the Modern from Reel to Real.* New York: Routledge.

Andrew, Dudley (2004) 'An Atlas of World Cinema', *Framework: The Journal of Cinema and Media*, 45, 2, 9–23.

Braester, Yomi (2010) *Painting the City Red: Chinese Cinema and the Urban Contract.* Durham: Duke University Press.

Braester, Yomi and James Tweedie (eds) (2010) *Cinema at the City's Edge: Film and Urban Networks in East Asia.* Hong Kong: Hong Kong University Press.

Brenner, Neil and Christian Schmid (2015) 'Towards a New Epistemology of the Urban?', *City*, 19, 2/3, 151–82.

Bruno, Giuliana (1987) 'Ramble City: Postmodernism and *Blade Runner*', *October*, 41, 61–74.

____ (1993) *Streetwalking on a Ruined Map: Cultural Theory and the City Films of Elvira Notari.* Princeton: Princeton University Press.

Brunsdon, Charlotte (2007) *London in Cinema: The Cinematic City Since 1945.* London: British Film Institute.

____ (2012) 'Attractions of the Cinematic City', *Screen*, 53, 3, 209–27.

Casetti, Francesco (2013) 'What is a Screen Nowadays?', in Chris Berry, Janet Harbord and Rachel O. Moore (eds) *Public Space, Media Space.* Basingstoke: Palgrave Macmillan.

Chakrabarty, Dipesh (2000) *Provincializing Europe: Postcolonial Thought and Historical Difference.* Princeton: Princeton University Press.

Charney, Leo and Vanessa Schwartz (eds) (1995) *Cinema and the Invention of Modern Life.* Berkeley: University of Los Angeles Press.

Clarke, David (ed.) (1997) *The Cinematic City.* London and New York: Routledge.

Conde, Maite (2012) *Consuming Visions: Cinema, Writing, and Modernity in Rio de Janeiro*. Charlottesville: University of Virginia Press.

Corkin, Stanley (2011) *Starring New York: Filming the Grime and the Glamour of the Long 1970s*. Oxford and New York: Oxford University Press.

Curtin, Michael (2003) 'Media Capital: Towards the Study of Spatial Flows'. *International Journal of Cultural Studies*, 6, 2, 202–28.

Davis, Mike (1990) *City of Quartz: Excavating the Future in Los Angeles*. London: Verso.

Dennison, Stephanie and Song Hwee Lim (2006) *Remapping World Cinema: Identity, Culture and Politics in Film*. London: Wallflower Press.

Deutsche, Rosalyn (1996) *Evictions: Art and Spatial Politics*. Cambridge: MIT Press.

Dimendberg, Edward (2004) *Film Noir and the Spaces of Modernity*. Cambridge: Harvard University Press.

Dobbs, Richard, Jaana Remes, Sven Smit, James Manyika, Jonathan Woetzel, and Yaw Agyenim-Boateng (2012) 'Urban world: The Shifting Global Bus-iness Landscape', McKinsey Global Institute; http://www.mckinsey.com/global-themes/urbanization/urban-world-the-shifting-global-business-landscape

Donald, James (1999) *Imagining the Modern City*. Minneapolis: University of Minnesota Press.

Ďurovičová, Natasa and Kathleen E. Newman (eds) (2009) *World Cinemas, Transnational Perspectives*. New York: Routledge.

Friedberg, Anne (1993) *Window Shopping: Cinema and the Postmodern*. Berkeley: University of Los Angeles Press.

Friedmann, John (1986) 'The World City Hypothesis', *Development and Change*, 17, 1, 69–83.

Galt, Rosalind and Karl Schoonover (eds) (2010) *Global Art Cinema: New Theories and Histories*. Oxford and New York: Oxford University Press.

Goldsmith, Ben and Tom O'Regan (2003) *Cinema Cities, Media Cities: The Contemporary International Studio Complex*. Sydney: Australian Film Commission.

Gunning, Tom (1994) 'The Whole Town's Gawking: Early Cinema and the Visual Experience of Modernity', *Yale Journal of Criticism*, 7, 2, 189–201.

Hansen, Miriam (1991) 'The Mass Production of the Senses: Classical Cinema as Vernacular Modernism', *Modernism/Modernity*, 6, 2, 59–77.

Harvey, David (1989) *The Condition of Postmodernity*. Oxford: Blackwell.

Iordanova, Dina, David Martin-Jones and Belén Vidal (eds) (2010) *Cinema at the Periphery*. Detroit: Wayne State University Press.

Jameson, Fredric (1982) 'On *Diva*', *Social Text*, 6, 114–19.

____ (1984) 'Postmodernism, or The Cultural Logic of Late Capitalism', *New Left Review*, 146, 59–92.

____ (1992) *The Geopolitical Aesthetic: Cinema and Space in the World System*. London: British Film Institute.

Kapur, Jyotsna and Keith B. Wagner (eds) (2011) *Neoliberalism and Global Cinema:*

Capital, Culture, and Marxist Critique. London and New York: Routledge.

Klinger, Barbara (2006) *Beyond the Multiplex: Cinema, New Technologies, and the Home*. Berkeley: University of Los Angeles Press.

Koolhaas, Rem (1995), 'The Generic City', in Rem Koolhaas, Bruce Mau, Jennifer Sigler and Hans Werlemann (eds) *S, M, L, XL*. New York: Monacelli, 1248–64.

Kuoshu, Harry H. (2010) *Metro Movies: Cinematic Urbanism in Post-Mao China*. Carbondale: Southern Illinois University Press

Konstantarakos, Myrto (ed.) (2000) *Spaces in European Cinema*. Bristol: Intellect.

Krause, Linda and Patrice Petro (eds) (2003) *Global Cities: Cinema, Architecture, and Urbanism in a Digital Age*. New Brunswick: Rutgers University Press.

Massey, Doreen (1994) *Space, Place and Gender*. Minneapolis: University of Minnesota Press.

Mazumdar, Ranjani (2007) *Bombay Cinema: An Archive of the City*. Minneapolis: University of Minnesota Press.

McFarlane, Colin (2012) 'Rethinking Informality: Politics, Crisis, and the City', *Planning Theory and Practice*, 13, 1, 89–108.

Mennel, Barbara (2008) *Cities and Cinema*. London and New York: Routledge.

Merrifield, Andy (2013) 'The Urban Question Under Planetary Urbanization', *International Journal of Urban and Regional Research*, 37, 3, 909–22.

Miller, Toby, Nitin Govil, John McMurria and Richard Maxwell (2005) *Global Hollywood 2*. London: British Film Institute.

Nagib, Lúcia (2006) 'Towards a Positive Definition of World Cinema', in Stephanie Dennison and Song Hwee Lim (eds) *Remapping World Cinema: Identity, Culture and Politics in Film*. London and New York: Wallflower Press, 30–7.

Porter, Michael (1998) 'Clusters and the New Economics of Competition', *Harvard Business Review* 76, 6, 77–90; https://hbr.org/1998/11/clusters-and-the-new-economics-of-competition

Prakash, Gyan (ed.) (2010) *Noir Urbanisms: Dystopian Images of the Modern City*. Princeton: Princeton University Press.

Pratt, Geraldine and Rose Marie San Juan (2014) *Film and Urban Space: Critical Possibilities*. Edinburgh: Edinburgh University Press.

Rhodes, John David and Elena Gorfinkel (2011) *Taking Place: Location and the Moving Image*. Minneapolis: University of Minnesota Press.

Robinson, Jennifer (2011) 'Cities in a World of Cities: The Comparative Gesture', *International Journal of Urban and Regional Research*, 35, 1, 1–23.

Rodowick, David N. (2007) *The Virtual Life of Film*. Cambridge: Harvard University Press.

Roy, Ananya (2011) 'Conclusion: Postcolonial Urbanism: Speed, Hysteria, Mass Dreams', in Ananya Roy and Aihwa Ong (eds) *Worlding Cities: Asian Experiments and the Art of Being Global*. Chichester: Wiley-Blackwell, 307–35.

Sassen, Saskia (1991) *The Global City: New York, London, Tokyo*. Princeton: Princeton University Press.

____ (2005) 'The Global City: Introducing a Concept', *Brown Journal of World Affairs*, 11, 2, 27–43.

Scott, Allen J. and Michael Storper (2015) 'The Nature of Cities: The Scope and Limits of Urban Theory', *International Journal of Urban and Regional Research*, 39, 1, 1–15.

Shaviro, Steven (2010) *Post Cinematic Affect*. London: Zero Books.

Shiel, Mark (2012) *Hollywood Cinema and the Real Los Angeles*. London: Reaktion.

Shiel, Mark and Tony Fitzmaurice (2001) *Cinema and the City: Film and Urban Societies in a Global Context*. London: Blackwell.

____ (2003) *Screening the City*. London: Verso.

Soja, Edward W. (1996) *Thirdspace: Journeys to Los Angeles and Other Real-and-Imagined Places*. Oxford: Blackwell.

Webb, Lawrence (2014) *The Cinema of Urban Crisis: Seventies Film and the Reinvention of the City*. Amsterdam: Amsterdam University Press.

Webber, Andrew and Emma Wilson (eds) (2008) *Cities in Transition: The Moving Image and the Metropolis*. London: Wallflower Press.

Wojcik, Pamela Robertson (2010) *The Apartment Plot: Urban Living in American Film and Popular Culture, 1945–1975*. Durham: Duke University Press.

TRANSNATIONAL SCREEN CITIES

IN THE CITY BUT NOT BOUNDED BY IT: CINEMA IN THE GLOBAL, THE GENERIC AND THE CLUSTER CITY

THOMAS ELSAESSER

MODERNITY AND THE CITY

For the past thirty years or so, references to the city, to the metropolis and to urban life have created one of the densest semantic fields for joining technology and capitalism to the human body and the senses, while putting the cinema at the heart of some of the most crucial processes of social transformation. One general name for this rich semantic field is 'Modernity'. In fact, modernity has become the big tent for all those forces unleashed in the wake of industrialisation and the rise of an urban middle class between 1848 and 1914. 'Modernity' means speed and dislocation, new modes of transport and communication, along with such diverse disciplinary regimes of the body, as standardising time and regulating working hours, introducing sports as spectacle and fingerprints as forensic evidence. Modernity brought an unprecedented expansion of leisure and consumption, and it made women enter the industrial labour force in large and indispensable numbers. It created the masses of the urban poor, but also the white-collar worker, with upwardly mobile social aspirations. It fostered the proud militancy of the working class, but it also invented the blasé intellectual with an aristocratic disdain for bourgeois self-discipline and the virtues of hard work.

Charlotte Brunsdon (2012) made a forceful argument not only about how this concept of modernity, and the attendant trope of the cinematic city came about, but why both notions may have come to the end of their useful intellectual life. She advocated, if I understand her correctly, a return to the basics of film studies, the study of genres, if we want to explore the relation of films to political life and social space, and a return to close textual reading if we want to understand the meaning of films as autonomous works. I agree with much of what she says, yet I want to put forward a number of alternatives that might revive the trope of the cinematic city, without necessarily rescuing it from the need to radically rethink it.

In the conceptual trope that Brunsdon described, the 'cinematic city' is very much modelled on the European metropolis, or at any rate, Western cities, whose industrial, commercial or colonial heyday was between the middle of the nineteenth and the middle of the twentieth century. The fact that its chief theorists wrote in the 1920s and 1930s reinforces this point. And indeed, there is no shortage of sociological writing and historical research that has replaced the classic 'metropolis' both in concept and in practice with the post-industrial or the Global City: among many others, Rem Koolhaas (1978), Manuel Castells (1989), David Harvey (1989) and Saskia Sassen (1991) come to mind, but so does Fredric Jameson, with his iconic description and analysis of a revamped and retrofitted downtown Los Angeles, epitomised by John Portman's Bonaventure Hotel. In fact, the term Jameson is now best-remembered for, namely 'postmodernism', is also a first attempt to give a name and some theoretical purchase to the post-industrial urban environment, as laid out in his essay with the programmatic title 'Postmodernism, or the Cultural Logic of Late Capitalism' (1984).

THE GLOBAL CITY

But what is the global city, as opposed to the modernist and the postmodern city? Generally credited to Sassen's book *The Global City: New York, London, Tokyo* from 1991, the term refers to cities that, due to a number of distinct factors, have become important nodes in the global economic system. The idea of the global city therefore implies thinking of the world in terms of networks that come together at certain points, usually in cities whose reach and reference go beyond a single nation, thus suggesting transnationality or post-nationality. Some of the key networks converging in a global city are *economic*: global cities tend to be financial hubs, meaning they are the home of the corporate headquarters for multinational companies, they have a stock exchange that trades globally and they have all the specialised services and dependent suppliers – from law firms, accountants, bankers, traders to fancy restaurants and overpriced real estate. The *political characteristics* of global cities are that they are home to all kinds of behind-the-scenes agencies, like think tanks, lobby groups and other influence peddlers; global cities also impact international events and world affairs, often by hosting the headquarters for international organisations, such as the United Nations, the World Bank, NATO headquarters or UNESCO. The *demographic characteristics* of the global city are besides a large population of typically several million inhabitants, the fact that these populations are ethnically diverse, that they live in agglomerations that are separated, if not segregated according to social status, income, race, and that the transportation infrastructure allows for a high degree of mobility both within and between global cities. Culturally, global cities offer attractions and amenities, such as internationally renowned museums, orchestras, sports teams; they cater for different tastes and needs, across the high culture/popular culture divides, and they are often major tourist destinations by their very size and diversity, as well as by their extreme contrasts between rich and poor, privileged and marginalised. The global city is also an interstitial city: criminal subcultures arise in the gap between the relative 'freedom' and entrepreneurialism of the postmodern metropolis, and they graft themselves onto the pockets of traditional family and tribal structures, themselves necessary buffer-zones to protect the weakest and most disadvantaged in times of rapid transition and change.

As to architecture, one could argue that, since the 1980s, it is the global city that has inherited the trope of the 'cinematic city'. Through the work of Bernard Tschumi, Rem Koolhaas, Robert Venturi and many others, the urbanist discourse of postmodernism was invigorated by cinema, leading to the mantra that architects must 'learn from Las Vegas', from theme parks and the cinema, implying that the built environment benefits from narrative and fantasy. In other words, architects should be able to articulate the sense that buildings, too, have to be dynamic and responsive to the movement of people, of goods and ideas typical of the global city, by making the dimension of time and memory, of story-telling and life-cycles, also enter into buildings, streets and neighbourhoods.

But the global city is also heir to the cinematic city insofar as New York, London, Tokyo, as well as Manila, Seoul, Rio de Janeiro or Istanbul usually testify to a vibrant film culture: they attract media productions of all kinds, including for the cinema, and in many instances, are home to an international film festival. Yet there are also differences between the metropolis of modernity and the global city of postmodernity: whereas in the former case, the cinema both mimetically reproduces and therapeutically compensates the effects of the city on the body, in the latter case, this relation of subject and space articulates itself differently – across what has been called new forms of sociality or sociability.

For one thing, as one would expect, films typical of the global city are concerned with demographic diversity and disparity, that is to say, they highlight the pressures exerted by multicultural communities on urban space, as split loyalties and divided identities break up families and tear apart individuals, across the generations and between the sexes. This is especially true of European global cities: the Paris of *La Haine* (Mathieu Kassovitz, 1995) and *La Graine et le Mulet* (Abdellatif Kechiche, 2007), the London of *Dirty Pretty Things* (Stephen Frears, 2002) and *Bend it Like Beckham* (Gurinder Chadha, 2002), the Amsterdam of *Amsterdam Global Village* (Johan van der Keuken, 1996) and *Shouf, Shouf Habibi* (Albert ter Heerdt, 2004), or the Hamburg and Istanbul of *Gegen die Wand* (Fatih Akin, 2005) and *Auf der anderen Seite* (Fatih Akin, 2008). The old metropolis turned global city is the one where the Third World has come to sit right in the heart of the First World, opening up circuits of exchange and mutual interdependence that run from drugs to sex, through human trafficking and organ transplants. The old metropolis turned global city is also the one haunted by its colonial past, which in the second and third generation suddenly turns out not to be past at all, but insists on returning in the shape of angry entitlements and violent militancy, if only to demand a share in the recognised status of victimhood, retroactively claimed on behalf of grievances suffered by ancestors several decades or even centuries ago.

Elsewhere, it is the contrast between rich and poor, generated by the global city that captivates filmmakers, as in the favela films like *City of God* (Fernando Meirelles, 2002), *Elite Squad* (José Padilha, 2008) and *Line of Passage* (Daniela Thomas and Walter Salles, 2008), where guns and crime signal the presence of consumer goods and aspirations forever out of reach, or where it is the sheer sense of scale and numbers, as in the Mumbai of *Slumdog Millionaire* (Danny Boyle, 2008) and *Still Life* (Jia Zhangke, 2006), set in Fengjie, a vast Sichuan Province mining town, that draws attention to a new kind of non-synchronicity between the rhythms of individual human lives and the pace of change that overcomes the urban environment. The global city may shock us with its a-symmetric power-relations, virulent at all levels of society and poisoning interpersonal relationships; films may depict in sharp emotional colours the contrasts and inequalities, the surreal effects of different faiths, beliefs and values, or of hot resentment existing side by side with heroic aspirations for the better life. But in another sense, it is no longer the shock and trauma of Benjamin's city. There, the psyche and the sensorium had to adjust to (or protect itself from) the violent dislocations of traditional ways of life. Determining the exchange between subjectivity and the city, it was these dislocations that the cinema was called upon to give narrative body to and thus to manage and contain. In the global city of today, it is savvy street kids, moving seemingly without effort between rubbish dumps and night clubs, whose psychic make-up is over-adapted to the unpredictable in the flow of events, and who inhabit the non-places of urban redevelopments. Their gym-toned bodies can stand as the living physiognomy of what in the 'modern city' used to be the crowd but now fused with the *flâneur*. For them, the flare-up of a spontaneous riot, street barricades of upturned vehicles or the acrid smoke plumes of burning tires have replaced the demonstrations once led by political parties, suffragettes and trade unions or anti-war protest marches by hippies and peaceniks.

The most typical cinematic genre of the global city, however, may well not be films about a global city per se, or about social contrasts and ethnic hatred and strife. Especially if we think of the key characteristic of the global city, namely that it is a point of intersection within and between networks, then the global city finds itself perhaps more palpably present in the so-called multi-strand, forking path or network narrative films, where lives become intertwined in fortuitous and fatal ways, as in all those interlaced stories set in Los Angeles, such as *Short Cuts* (Robert Altman, 1993) and *Timecode* (Mike Figgis, 2000), *Magnolia* (Paul Thomas Anderson, 1999) and *Crash* (Paul Haggis, 2004). What such films demonstrate, through the dramaturgical devices of car crashes or earthquakes, marital infidelities or television game shows is on the one hand, a different sense of the precariousness of life, however outwardly protected and risk free one seems to live it: a precariousness paradoxically highlighted by the interconnectedness of everyone with everyone else, rather than mitigated by proximity producing a sense of belonging. On the other hand, this interconnectedness as a consequence of accident, coincidence or sheer contingency, rather than on the basis of ethnicity, family or nation, raises crucial issues of moral responsibility, in the form of guilt or shame. Films like Alejandro González Iñárritu's *Amores Perros* (2000), *21 Grams* (2003), *Babel* (2006) and *Biutiful* (2010) ask, however obliquely and indirectly: on the strength of what values or choices can a human community survive, and on what commitment or solidarity can a viable social contract be based, when it is chance that brings us together, and unintended consequences that rule over our lives? Besides Iñárritu, it is Wong Kar Wai, in *Chungking Express* (1994) and *In the Mood for Love* (2000) who has given us some of the most poignant, most aesthetically daring, but also the most ethically challenging films of this global city in the past decades.

EUROPEAN CITIES AND THE FILM FESTIVAL NETWORK

And this brings me to one of the problems, in the shift from the Cinematic City of modernity and the European metropolis, to the Global City of post-industrialism or hyper-modernity: virtually all the films I have mentioned as exemplifying the global city *at the level of form* – be they fractal forking path narratives, or narratives of time-space compression and the floating world – rather than *in respect of content* (such as those dealing with multiculturalism and its victims and discontents) are *made in Hollywood* and feature Los Angeles; they are from *Latin America* and feature Mexico City and Rio; or they come from *Asia*, whether Hong Kong, in the case of Wong Kar Wai, Taipei, as in the films of Edward Yang and Hou Hsiao-hsien or Jia Zhangke's Mainland China mega-cities.

It raises the question of where to situate the *European cinema* in this paradigm shift? My tentative answer is threefold:

We need to think of Europe as not only a Europe of nation states or a Europe of the regions but also a Europe of the cities. The European Capitals of Culture initiative is a good if symptomatic example of a reorientation of urban geography, and of the post-national cultural topography. As the sociologist and urbanist Allen Scott has pointed out in his study *On Hollywood: The Place, The Industry* (2005), what typifies the twenty-first century in this respect is not merely that the majority of the world's population will live in cities, but that as never before, almost all economic activity carries a cultural component, be this in the form of a 'brand' which advertising saturates with signs of personal well-being, ideals of beauty or embedded social aspirations, or be it in the form of sponsorship and patronage which the global economic players extend to cultural institutions, such as museums, individual artists, sports events, festivals and opera. There is no need to point out that in this context the cinema plays a significant role as cultural lubricant and multipurpose promotional tool, even if patronage may more often come from the various branches and levels of government, or the EU institutions, rather than from corporate sponsors or wealthy philanthropists.

Second, we need to see European cinema within world cinema. I have argued the case for this elsewhere at some length, so I will not repeat my reasons here, except to offer one brief remark about the definition of 'world cinema' (Elsaesser 2005: 485–513). It is, I know, a contested term, but I am retaining it here, largely because the alternatives pose similar problems. Transnational Cinema, Global Art Cinema, Multicultural Cinema, Peripheral Cinema, Hyphenated filmmaking, Contemplative Cinema, Diasporic Cinema, Accented Cinema have all been put forward, and without going into the pros and cons of each definition, I simply want to note the *general problem in these acts of naming*: are these labels meant to be descriptive ('global art cinema'), self-assigned (contemplative cinema), self-empowering (diasporic cinema), analytical, part of a wider discourse (e.g. post-colonial, multi-cultural), metaphoric ('accented'), geographic-topographic ('peripheral'), or even opportunist ('world cinema' might be said to borrow from the success of 'world music')? An additional issue is that the term 'world cinema' used to connote 'the rest' (in the formula 'The West and the rest'), but, once we give up the Eurocentric bipolar opposition 'Europe-Hollywood', we also can no longer assume world cinema to be a fixed entity, and have to accept that 'world cinema' is a relational term, which I see as an advantage. What I mean by 'relational' is that rarely anybody sets out to make 'world cinema', and few want their films to be world cinema: mostly it is a label given to a film by someone else, i.e. it is not a self-assignation (or identity marker), but an other-designation, implying a self-other relationship, always indicative of covert, asymmetrical power-relationships. Furthermore, the only world cinema in the literal sense, i.e. with world reach, is Hollywood, but 'Hollywood' is exactly the antinomic term to what we usually understand by world cinema. Underpinning 'world cinema' is often a semantic cluster that encompasses terms like resistance, opposition, difference, diversity, alterity, independence, counter-cinema, where the dominant is – depending on the context – mainstream, Hollywood, commerce, cultural imperialism, hegemony. My use of world cinema nuances or even challenges this oppositional-antagonistic paradigm, paying closer attention to models that are *relational and context-dependent*, that understand the dynamics of confrontation and cooperation of systems in terms of feedback loops, interdependence and forms of what I have called 'antagonistic mutuality'.

Thirdly, in order to grasp this relationality, world cinema needs to be seen within the force-field of film festivals and their various asymmetries as part of the logic of film festival networks, meaning that festival networks have a physical dimension of place, a temporal dimension of the annual cycle and a virtual dimension as permanent online presence (see Iordanova 2013). Film festivals have their origins in the cities of Europe, initially sited in summer resort towns such as Venice, Cannes, Karlovy Vary or Deauville, needing to fill spare hotel capacity during the off-season months of the year. During the cold war political considerations determined the decision to site a film festival in the divided city of Berlin, as well as the creation of showcases in cities of Communist countries such as the festivals in Moscow and Leipzig. Since the 1970s formerly industrial cities have used film festivals to rebrand themselves, one of the best-known examples being Rotterdam, although there the connection between a conscious use of architecture to promote a certain self-image has been going hand in hand with an equally purposive media policy ever since the 1920s, making Rotterdam an ideal case study for tracing the transitions between the metropolis of modernity and the postmodernity of the global city, around the strategic use of cinema and audiovisual media (see Paalman 2011).

Thus while one might see the subsumption of the formerly national cinemas under the label 'European cinema' and the inclusion of European cinema in world cinema as a demotion and a loss of status, the fact that the film festival is a European invention that has been successfully adopted all over the world would indicate that the emphasis on cities in the way Europe thinks about cinema puts it in the vanguard of other significant global trends and developments. Indeed, film festivals are one of the global phenomena of urban mutation par excellence. Every day of the year, there is a film festival somewhere on the globe, and film festivals have become one of the favourite means for even medium or small cities to change their image, their infrastructure and amenities, in order to attract a better class of tourists, even when they are not seaside or mountain resorts with spare capacity during the off-season. Hosting a film festival, in other words, like hosting trade fairs and corporate conventions, is the cheaper and less fiercely competitive alternative to hosting the World Cup or the Olympic Games, but from a political urbanist perspective, entirely within the same paradigm of city branding, urban renewal and competitive positioning.

My initial intention when doing research on festivals was to extend the primary purposes of a festival – such as agenda setting for the non-Hollywood film community, or adding value to individual films and cultural capital to independent filmmakers by conferring on them the distinction of being recognised as an auteur – to also go beyond these branding functions of the festival, by suggesting that they ideally constitute a kind of alternative public sphere, an extension into the realm of sounds, images and narratives of the work of NGOs, calling film festivals the agoras of a new politics and the mobilisation base for new kinds of citizenship. I would now see such claims to have been somewhat over-ambitious and premature.

THE GENERIC CITY

Yet very much in the same spirit – that is, putting the conjunction of film festivals and cities at the heart of a repositioning of European cinema, and giving them a measure of political significance which is not only that of resisting and opposing, nor that of branding and promotion – I am convinced that the trope of the global city as introduced earlier on, also needs to be revised. This is why I am proposing to add to the global city two further modalities of the contemporary city, what I shall call the generic city and the cluster city.

What do I mean by 'generic city'? It is a term coined by the Dutch architect and urban theorist Rem Koolhaas, whose earlier book, *Delirious New York* already in the 1980s proposed an alternative to the Paris-Baudelaire-Poe-Benjamin formation. Here is Koolhaas on the generic city:

> People can inhabit anything. And they can be miserable in anything and ecstatic in anything. More and more I think that architecture has nothing to do with it. Of course, that's both liberating and alarming. But the generic city, the general urban condition, is happening everywhere, and just the fact that it occurs in such enormous quantities must mean that it's habitable. [...] Architecture can't do anything that the culture doesn't accept. We all complain that we are confronted by urban environments that are completely similar. We say we want to create beauty, identity, quality, singularity. And yet, maybe in truth it is the generic cities that we have desired all along. Maybe their very characterlessness provides the best context for living. (In Heron 1996)

The generic city is one where high modernist boxes reign triumphant, and where an overhead shot of a cityscape looks no different from the circuit board of a computer, but also one that you access not by its topography of built space, but by a combination of its transport systems, institutional portals and security zones, as one traverses them in hotels and airports, corporate headquarters and government buildings, but also as they extend into suburban housing and gated communities. In *Up in the Air* (Jason Reitman, 2009) George Clooney plays a businessman whose job it is to sack people on behalf of corporations and who spends his time mainly in these spaces, but whose routines of access he has turned into elegant ballets of motion and composure. Corresponding to his lifestyle of repetition, habit and routine are *Up in the Air's* frequent bird's-eye shots (that function as punctuation marks) of looking down on cities in the Midwest with colourful names, full of historic associations, like St Louis or Dallas, Tulsa or Kansas City, but whose layout and skyline are uniform and identical. 'The Generic City is a fractal,' Koolhaas writes, 'repeating its shape from laptops up to skyscrapers down. The city has no history, save for one or a few districts where all history has been concentrated. Therefore, in the Generic City everybody is a tourist. Hotels have everything you need – there's no reason to ever leave' (cited in Guimond and Cook 2011).

Koolhaas' generic city combines Paul Virilio's *Overexposed City* (1986) (a pulsating and dynamic city, whose appearance and aspect is being continually refreshed by electronic screens) with Bruno Latour's *Invisible City* (1998), where access, understanding and even the best overview may be via a doorman's visitor log or the timetable of a minister, rather than the view from the top of the Eiffel tower or from the hills of Montmartre. Virilio's main concern is with the dematerialisation of the city induced by the impact of information technologies, notably through security and surveillance, altering perception by shrinking time to the instant and turning distance into dead space. Latour's *Invisible City* is above all meant to wean us from thinking that to see is to know, and to appreciate a different logic from that of sight and visuality (the modernity trope) by introducing us to corridors and waiting rooms, outer offices and idling chauffeurs, child-minders and grandmothers – all actors in networks that are vital to a city's life but which usually escape the horrified or enchanted gaze of the *flâneur*, as well as the number-crunching sociologist poring over governmental statistics.

But why, one may ask, do I need the generic city for my retooling of European cinema in the image of film festivals, and film festivals as the ambiguous emblems of new forms of citizenship? First of all, the generic city is a bracing reality check and a kind of system re-boot, on a hundred years of urbanist fantasies both utopian and dystopian, both ecstatic and catastrophic, jointly entertained by architects and planners, cultural theorists and comic book writers, blockbuster studio productions from Tim Burton to Christopher Nolan and Ridley Scott to Michael Bay, as well as auteurist cinema from Michelangelo Antonioni to Wim Wenders, Francesco Rosi to Eric Rohmer.

Second, the generic city gives us a model of the city that moves without hiatus from the built environment and the grown urban fabric, to the bureaucratic abstractions and time-space logistics that determine decision making above and beyond democratic accountability, but which also recognises the contribution we as citizen make to such changes by our easy acceptance of convenience capitalism in the form of data-mining and ubiquitous surveillance, i.e. the easy way we use electronic communication devices and join social networks and virtual communities, without much regard for either privacy or intimacy. 'Generic' suggests a point beyond resistance and strife, but also beyond the opposition visible/invisible, by indicating that now it is acceptance and habit that has entered the body in the global city, in stark contrast to the shock and trauma that once entered the body in the modernist city.

Such may be the negative virtues of the generic city, but as system reboot they also offer opportunities. These can be summed up, for my purposes, in Immanuel Kant's paradox of world citizenship. When Kant in 1795, under the impact of the French Revolution, thought about how people might be bound to each other, when race, religion and tribal ties no longer prevailed, he came up not only with the idea of cosmopolitanism, but also with the paradox he called 'die ungesellige Geselligkeit des Menschen', 'man's unsocial sociability'. From what I have said so far, one of the qualities of the cinematic city of and for the twenty-first century – not as a representational trope but as an institutional fixture Europe has given to the world – should be its ability to serve as a new model of the social contract under the specific conditions of the film festival, but now seen as paradigmatic for a whole range of local effects, enacted, embedded and extended on a scale and in contexts that are global. Key to this social contract is Kant's unsocial sociability considered as an asset and a resource, rather than a paradox or a predicament. Unsocial sociability mediates – in our classic understanding of the city – between the tribalism of neighbourhoods, i.e. the faith- and race-based blood-loyalty of self-enclosed communities on the one hand, and the blasé *flâneur* with his eroticised chance encounters on the other hand, while also included is the urban dweller of gated communities who pays for the privilege of his or her security through either taxes or sporadic acts of philanthropy. The generic city ideally allows for this unsocial sociability to evolve into other forms of the social 'we', if only by way of a radical rethink of public space. This public space is conceived with and after surveillance, rather than against surveillance, which is to say, it necessarily combines our online lives with the increasingly information rich urban environments into one seamless ambient space, which is why both the overexposed and the invisible city are part of the concept of the generic city.

If I were to name a film that is emblematic of the generic city and how it interacts with its inhabitants as both monads and nomads, it would be Spike Jonze's *Her* (2013), which smoothly modulates between a blandly generic Los Angeles (morphed and blended with Shanghai), a pale and self-isolated loner and a husky-voiced digital assistant, whom he takes on hikes and to bed, and who is so much more pliably alluring than his real-life ex-wife or female friend could ever be.

THE CLUSTER CITY

It is time to introduce my final city concept, that of the cluster city, as both a contrast and a complement to the generic city, and in response to the challenges of the global city. In order to do so, I have to briefly recapitulate in what ways a film festival – my improbable reference point for mapping these city concepts on what I started with, i.e. reconfiguring the now obsolete trope of the cinematic city – has traits in common with the global city. Film festivals are a global phenomenon, but each festival prides itself of its local distinctiveness and unique character. Diversity in uniformity is thus one of its characteristics. Second, the unresolved tension between a high degree of mobility and intense locatedness is typical of both the global city and the festival network, raising the possibility that these two vectors are in fact not antagonistic but belong to a single paradigm which it is the purpose of this chapter to identify, even if it may not yet be able to name it. Third, global cities and festivals have in common that they combine in an apparently antagonistic but in truth mutually sustaining fashion the world of commerce and finance, and the world of art and culture. But festivals are comparable to the generic city, not least because they partake in the ad-hoc sociability of surveillance, which, as argued, has become the default value of any form of contemporary urban living. Generic cities are thus wired cities, both internally monitoring themselves through surveillance and feedback loops, and in constant contact with the outside world, just like the festival, where journalists are as much on the phone or hunched over their laptops as they are looking at the movie screen. The security protocols, access codes and accreditation rituals of festivals are as complex as in any airport or corporate fortress. One might even go so far as to say that film festivals are paradigms of information rich environments, or augmented reality, because of the different types of expertise present at a festival, across the various actors in Bruno Latour's sense, but also in the sense of the kind of parasite host relationships typical of co-evolved ecologies. Festivals, as I have tried to show elsewhere, are in fact systems with an especially high degree of antagonistic mutuality.[1]

However, there are of course also considerable structural and typological differences, which prompts me to supplement the idea of the global and the generic city with the concept of the cluster city, a term I borrow from the economist Michael Porter. In a by now famous essay entitled 'Clusters and the New Economics of Competition' from 1998 Porter argues that '[t]oday's economic map of the world is characterised by clusters: critical masses – in one place – of unusual competitive success in particular fields. Clusters are a striking feature of virtually every national, regional, state, and even metropolitan economy, especially in more economically advanced nations. Silicon Valley and Hollywood may be the world's best-known clusters. Clusters are not unique, however; they are highly typical – and therein lies a paradox: the enduring competitive advantages in a global economy lie increasingly in local things – knowledge, relationships, motivation – that distant rivals cannot match' (Porter 1998: 78).

Porter goes on to explain how clusters affect competition in three broad ways: first, by increasing the productivity of companies based in the area; second, by driving the direction and pace of innovation; and third, by stimulating the formation of new businesses within the cluster. Geographic, cultural and institutional proximity provides companies with special access, closer relationships, better information, powerful competitive incentives and other advantages that are difficult to tap from a distance. The more complex, knowledge-based, and dynamic the world economy becomes, the more this is true.

Porter names Hollywood and Silicon Valley as typical clusters, but he might have gone back to Florence around 1470, Venice in the 1500s and Amsterdam in the Golden Age, each a typical cluster city that not only initiated complex empires based on trade, transport and communication. In the case of Florence and Venice, it also gave us the Renaissance in the arts and sciences, and in more general terms, it was the North Italian city states, to whom we owe the modern conception of the bourgeoisie, as well as the modern banking system. Contemporary Europe of the cultural capitals has made a success of the city as cluster idea, not least thanks to information technologies, media industries and artists – a conjunction I have elsewhere described under the heading of *Tatort/Standort* (site of action/location advantage), i.e. the use of a location advantage in combination with narrative or spectacle potential, including the potential of rebranding a nation's catastrophic history (such as Germany's after World War II and the Holocaust) as narrative and spectacle (see Elsaesser 2014).

CLUSTER CITY BERLIN: TATORT/STANDORT

A specific example of the dynamics of *Tatort/Standort* would be Berlin: bankrupt by all conventional economic standards, it has made culture its business, living off museums, universities and other institutions providing education, art and learning at the interface between industrial decay and gentrification, in a post-industrial ecology where 'struggling' artists are needed like some kind of biological organism or earth-worms, their restlessness and precarious existence providing the momentum that aereates and turns over the urban soil, in preparation of the new crop: chic neighbourhoods with overpriced real-estate. In the Berlin districts of Kreuzberg, Mitte, and Prenzlauer Berg artists' studio spaces and lofts have displaced small corner shops, East Berlin working people and large Turkish families, but they will in turn be displaced by developers of luxury apartments. Such cultural cluster formations evidently need regular exhibitions and festivals as part of their natural metabolism. At the same time, films like *Run Lola Run* (Tom Tykwer, 1998), *Wings of Desire* (Wim Wenders, 1987), *Good Bye Lenin!* (Wolfgang Becker, 2003) and *The Bourne Supremacy* (Paul Greengrass, 2004) have put Berlin on the cinematic map as a place of action and fantasy, of danger and desire.

My argument is that, in the field of European cinema, film festivals are like *cluster cities on the move*, both in space and in time, bringing together different types of expertise in one location, if only for a limited period. But given their evident network dynamics, what constitutes effectiveness and productivity in the case of cities sponsoring festivals and festivals reinforcing the cluster effects of cities may well have to be studied by criteria other than either critical success of an individual film or the accumulated reputation of an auteur. There may be surplus values that they deliver, perhaps even in unintended or unexpected ways. Thanks to festivals more generally, the contemporary urban fabric and architectural space is complemented with a temporal dimension, and the built city is doubled by the programmed city. In this endeavour, major temporary exhibitions and recurring festivals are a key ingredient in structuring the succession of city events across the calendar year. Among the kinds of seasonal events, an international film festival, both cost effective, by attracting local residents and visitors from outside, and helping develop an infrastructure of sociability appreciated by locals and tourists all the year round, has often pride of place. Festivals compete with each other over the most desirable dates in the years and the most promising films or artists of the season, while complementing each other in several respects. Competition raises standards and adds scarcity value to the individual films, but competition also invites comparison, which ensures that festivals in their organisational structure resemble each other – their generic character makes for easy navigation – at the same time as each festival emphasises its local peculiarities, individual traditions and the personal quirks of the festival director, obliged to develop a marketable personality, like the Berlinale director Dieter Kosslick, whose trademark is a red scarf, worn on all occasions, and who tried to brand his festival – to compensate for the bad February weather that dogs the film festival every year – with the slogan 'Berlin – cold but cool'.[2]

For filmmakers the world over the annual festival calendar is now as crucial for their production plans as holiday release dates are for Hollywood blockbusters. To reinforce the many points of contact of the festival circuit and Hollywood, no independent film enters film distribution or the DVD market without displaying the name of one of the prestigious festivals, carried as prominently on poster or sleeve as a Hollywood film displays the studio logo – effectively making the festival the 'producer' of the film, rather than, as in the old days, a country that sent its 'national' films into festival competition. It means that films are henceforth made to measure and to order, that is, their production schedule, their premieres, their financing and marketing is closely coordinated with the festival that has a stake in this or that film or filmmaker, showing remarkable similarities to the post-Fordist production model for niche markets and just-in-time suppliers and outsourced or subcontracted labour.

FESTIVAL CITIES, SOCIAL NETWORKS

While the analogies I have drawn between the programmable cinematic city of festivals, based on the ideas of generic-ness and clustering, and the new unsocial sociability, based on the productivity not of shared, but conflicting interests, may not as yet have progressed much beyond a belief in the urgency of rebuilding a sense of shared public space beyond the now untenable divide between private and public, I want to conclude by sketching how the cluster model of joining culture and economics, and the calendar city that makes festival resemble temporary cities, might redefine the roles and functions of some of the most significant actors in the independent film business. For instance, putting the film festival at the centre of the institution cinema, requires a fresh look at the old division of the film industry into production, distribution and exhibition sector, not least because festivals are often the sole outlet for films being produced all over the world, so that the window of attention festivals provide determines whether a film ever reaches the cinemas, gets acquired by television or finds an online outlet. As production reverts to small-scale niche production, and major festivals commission films the way galleries and curators commission artist's work to specification, so distribution and exhibition move closer together, re-allocating executive power and creative agency in the process.

The old question – whether cinema is defined by its products, i.e. the films as physical objects, or by its services, i.e. as slice of time spent with friends or partner, in the imaginary company of beautiful people or sharing a make-believe world – is also once more on the agenda, but now with an additional possibility: that festival cinema is neither product nor service, but functions more like a platform, an interface or dispositif, allowing for very different input-output relations. Festivals immerse films into several mutually interdependent systems, whose logics of means and ends, of main event and supplement are indeterminate and often reversible. How, for instance, does the branding of cities connect to the intersection of different knowledge streams and competing personalities, or how do the protocols of access and the power-play of the selection process help us understand what kinds of formal or informal markets a festival entails: is it a bazaar or an auction house? Is it a stock exchange of cultural capital that is trading in futures? Or is it negotiating the attention value of certain social issues and hot geopolitical topics?

Thinking of the festival circuit as a series of platforms opens up comparison with the Internet platforms of social networking. As we know, over the past decade, the most significant development has not only been the rise of sites like Wikipedia, Facebook and YouTube – which, by managing content provided by its users, have been celebrated as the triumph of convergence culture – but equally significant has been the closure of the cyberspace frontier, in that the Internet is more and more dominated by what look like multinational corporations, such as Microsoft, Apple and Google; except they do not behave as such, because they, too, blur the distinction between products and services on the one hand, and by seeming to give away so much for free, they turn themselves into neutral facilitators, even benefactors to humanity, providing the tools and means for others to define, trade or display goods and services. One is seeing the beginning of a debate, whether firms like Facebook, Google or Apple should be considered not companies in the traditional business sense at all, but as acting more like governments, understood as providers of platforms, utilities and frameworks within which actors constitute markets and determine social action (see Dannen 2009; Knapp 2014). While certainly not claiming any pertinent analogies between Cannes or Rotterdam on the one hand and Google or Apple on the other, I am nonetheless sufficiently intrigued by the business model of Internet platforms and the business models of cluster cities and festivals, not least because they confirm the proposition by Allen Scott referred to earlier: 'One of the defining features of contemporary society … is the conspicuous convergence that is occurring between the domain of the economic on the one hand and the domain of the cultural on the other. Vast segments of the modern economy are inscribed with significant cultural content, while culture itself is increasingly being … produced by private firms for a profit under conditions of market exchange' (2005: 1).

The implication I draw from these observations on the cinematic city in the twenty-first century, which have been focused on the international film festival as a site both part of and emblematic for the global, the generic and the cluster city is that such a comparison or alignment may help us chart a new path through Kant's 'unsocial sociability'. Then as now we humans seem to have the paradoxical need of being separate and together, of asserting our singularity as well as our sense of community, or to put it in more philosophical terms: of affirming our *Da-sein* (being) next to our *Mit-Sein* (belonging). As more and more of the world's population is living in cities – cities not like London, Munich or Paris, but more like Lagos, Manila or Porto Allegre – old forms of belonging (family, tribe, nation) strain and buckle, and new modes of community-in-contiguity have to be invented.[3] These include the ad-hoc communities of social networks (Facebook, Twitter, Linked-in) as well as other online fora, from city guides to dating sites, from e-Bay to Craigslist, and from Uber to Airbnb. In this apparently so chaotic, conspiratorial and confusing, but also electrifying, exhilarating and euphoric landscape, the presence of the built environment, and the history of physical spaces and located places serve as necessary correctives. Cluster cities (from Renaissance Florence to California's Hollywood), the metropolis (of Georg Simmel, Walter Benjamin and Lewis Mumford), the global city (from New York to Tokyo) and the generic city (of Rem Koolhaas and Bruce Mau) are both reminders and potentialities of how human beings organise their coexistence as social animals and urban dwellers. If the metropolis knew social contrasts, but ordered its urban topography around class and status plus work and leisure, the global city has exacerbated the gap between rich and poor, but – given its dependence on immigrants and their labour – lets race and ethnicity more than class be the markers of exclusion and belonging; it furthermore criss-crosses the divides with communication and transport networks, while making culture and commerce the recto and verso of each other (see Graham and Marvin 1996). Within this scenario, the generic city is the great leveller: 'The Generic City is the city liberated […] from the straitjacket of identity.[…] It is the city without history. It is big enough for everybody. It is easy. It does not need maintenance. If it gets too small it just expands. If it gets old it just self-destructs and renews. It is equally exciting-or unexciting-everywhere. It is "superficial" – like a Hollywood studio lot, it can produce a new identity every Monday morning' (Koolhaas and Mau 1995: 1249). And because it is like a Hollywood studio lot, the generic city needs the cinematic city in its currently most iconic emblem and most telling allegory: the international film festival. Considered as a network in time and space, covering the annual calendar and spanning the globe, festivals do indeed 'produce a new identity every Monday morning', that is, they renew their members and citizens laterally, from place to place, and horizontally, from event to event, and thus provide one possible set of coordinates for the communities to come.

NOTES

1   For a detailed description of a film festival's antagonistic mutuality both internally, and in relation to Hollywood, see Elsaesser (2005: 82–107).
2   The slogan 'Berlin – cold but cool' is in direct response to the city's other marketing slogan, thought up by its then mayor KlausWowereit: 'Berlin – arm aber

sexy' (Berlin – poor but sexy). See Neate (2014).

3   Even among European cities, however, there are differences. As Rem Koolhaas points out: 'The stronger identity, the more it imprisons, the more it resists expansion, interpretation, renewal, contradiction. […] Paris can only become more Parisian – it is already on its way to becoming hyper-Paris, a polished caricature. There are exceptions: London – its only identity a lack of clear identity – is perpetually becoming even less London, more open, less static' (Koolhaas and Mau 1995: 1248).

BIBLIOGRAPHY

Brunsdon, Charlotte (2012) 'The Attractions of the Cinematic City', *Screen* 53, 3, 209–27.
Castells, Manuel (1989) *The Informational City*. Oxford: Blackwell.
Dannen, Chris (2009) 'Facebook: Stop Acting Like a State', February 27; http://www.fastcompany.com/1188814/facebook-stop-acting-nation-state
Elsaesser, Thomas (2005) *European Cinema: Face to Face with Hollywood*. Amsterdam: University of Amsterdam Press.
____ (2014) *German Cinema – Terror and Trauma: Cultural Memory since 1945*. New York: Routledge.
Graham, Stephen and Simon Marvin (1996) *Telecommunications and the City: Electronic Spaces, Urban Places*. London: Routledge.
Guimond, Michele and Jennifer Cook (2011) 'Resonating Space: Space, People, Experience, Data'; https://resonatingspace.wordpress.com/page/5/
Harvey, David (1989) *The Condition of Postmodernity: An Enquiry into the Origins of Cultural Change*. Oxford: Blackwell.
Heron, Katrina (1996) 'From Bauhaus to Koolhaas [Interview with Rem Koolhaas]', *Wired* (4 July); http://archive.wired.com/wired/archive/4.07/koolhaas_pr.html
Iordanova, Dina (2013) *The Film Festival Reader*. St Andrews: St Andrews Film Studies.
Jameson, Fredric (1984) 'Postmodernism, or The Cultural Logic of Late Capitalism'. *New Left Review*, 146, 59–92.
Kant, Immanuel (2006) *Toward Perpetual Peace and Other Writings on Politics, Peace, and History*, ed. Pauline Kleingeld. New Haven: Yale University Press.
Knapp, Thomas L. (2014) 'Google Is Acting Like an Arm of the Surveillance State', August 7; http://www.alternet.org/civil-liberties/google-acting-arm-surveillance-state
Koolhaas, Rem (1978) *Delirious New York: A Retroactive Manifesto for Manhattan*. London: Thames and Hudson.
Koolhaas, Rem and Bruce Mau (1995) *S, M, L, XL*. New York: Monacelli Press.
Latour, Bruno and Emilie Hermant (1998) 'Paris: Invisible City'. http://www.

bruno-latour.fr/virtual/EN/index.html

Neate, Rupert (2014) 'Berlin's 'poor but sexy' appeal turning city into European Silicon Valley', *The Guardian*, 3 January; http://www.theguardian.com/business/2014/jan/03/berlin-poor-sexy-silicon-valley-microsoft-google

Paalman, Floris (2011) *Cinematic Rotterdam: The Times and Tides of a Modern City*. Rotterdam: nai010.

Porter, Michael (1998) 'Clusters and the New Economics of Competition', *Harvard Business Review*, 76, 6, 77–90; https://hbr.org/1998/11/clusters-and- the-new-economics-of-competition

Sassen, Saskia (1991) *The Global City: New York, London, Tokyo*. Princeton: Princeton University Press.

Scott, Allen J. (2005) *On Hollywood: The Place, The Industry*. Princeton: Princeton University Press.

Virilio, Paul (1986) 'The Overexposed City', trans. Astrid Hustvedt, *Zone 1-2*. New York: Urzone, 14–31.

TRAVERSING THE ØRESUND: THE TRANS-NATIONAL URBAN REGION IN *BRON/BROEN*

PEI-SZE CHOW

> OK, you h Redvall ave a bridge, but that does not make it a region unless it ends up in people's minds. (Pedersen 2004: 86)

In September 2011, the first episode of the crime series *Bron/Broen* (2011–; translation: *The Bridge*) was aired on Danish and Swedish television, transmitting grim images of the Øresund bridge bathed in the murkiness of the night into living rooms and on to laptop and mobile phone screens across the two countries. Over the course of its first two seasons, audiences have watched as Swedish detective Saga Norén and her Danish counterpart Martin Rohde traverse the bridge between Copenhagen and Malmö episode after episode in pursuit of murderers and criminal masterminds, while at the same time managing their fragile personal relationships on either end of the bridge. Their investigation takes them – and the viewer – to all manner of locations across the two cities: in one moment the detectives are in Denmark, and in the next scene they are already in Sweden.

Bron/Broen is set in the Øresund region, a transnational conurbation comprising, in the main, the cities of Copenhagen in eastern Denmark and Malmö in southern Sweden.[1] Lying between the two cities is the Øresund, also known as 'the Sound' in English, the marine strait from which the region derives its name. Supported by structural funds through the European Union Interreg programme, the Øresund region formally and materially came into existence on 1 July 2000 with the opening of the fixed link between the two nations, known by its hybrid Danish-Swedish name, Øresundsbron (Øresund Bridge).[2] The statement at the beginning of this essay, uttered by a representative from Wolff Olins, a consultancy tasked with managing the place-branding of the Øresund region, addresses a challenge faced by policy-makers and planners of the cross-border urban metropolis: to make the region economically and socially viable, Danes and Swedes have to subscribe to and internalise the idea of a new regional identity, specifically an Øresund identity.

Indeed, a large part of the work that fell on regional planners at the beginning of the Øresund project was to engage in the processes of marketing the region – that is, to talk it into existence (see Shotter 1993; Tangkjær 1999).[3] With the physical infrastructure now in place, it remains the task of the cultural industries to coax the region's inhabitants into identifying with and participating in a social dynamic similar to Benedict Anderson's concept of an 'imagined community' (2006). In other words, culture, especially audiovisual media, plays an important role in cultivating this new social identity. This set of circumstances raises the following questions: what does this new transnational community and space look like? And how is the new urban region imagined through an audiovisual lens? In exploring the ways in which a popular television series participates in the construction of the imagined space of the Øresund region, this chapter seeks to address how popular audiovisual texts and, in particular, the long-form television serial format, mediate the spatial and cultural complexities of the transnational Øresund imaginary.

My argument is that *Bron/Broen*, while a tangible product of the political and planned vision of a transnational region, is at the same time paradoxically critical of the Øresund imaginary of borderlessness and integration. On the one hand, the television series is a manifestation of a wider regional production context, a product of a bilateral co-production venture that emerges from the rhetoric of transnational Danish-Swedish collaboration in the Øresund region. This rhetoric in the production conditions translates directly onto the plot of the series that mirrors the aspirations of the region. Yet, on the other hand, its representation of the region through the lens of 'Nordic noir' paradoxically and critically foregrounds the region's fault lines and tensions in medium-specific ways.[4] Through the episodic nature of the television drama format, *Bron/Broen* articulates images of the transnational urban region as a fractured place that is composed of fragmented, albeit imbricated, spaces that emphatically contest the euphoric utopian vision of binational collaboration and cross-border urban energy invoked by Øresund planners in the late 1990s (see Löfgren 2000: 29). Furthermore, I contend that the series portrays a critical and prescient representation of the region's current difficulties in sustaining this vision, especially in light of an announcement made by Copenhagen authorities that the Øresund region will be rebranded as 'Greater Copenhagen and Skåne' from January 2016 (see Crouch 2015; Laasby 2015).

As the lead Danish actor Kim Bodnia remarks in an interview, *Bron/Broen* is 'a symptom of something real' (in Nimbus Film 2013). Developed and broadcast in the first ten years since the 'birth' of the region, *Bron/Broen* registers some of the anxieties of spatial transformation in the post-industrial region, where newfound mobilities across a transnational urban space are projected through the narrative lens of the Scandinavian television crime genre and infused with the audiovisual aesthetics of the Nordic Noir wave that combines the subdued lighting and pronounced use of shadows typical of its American forebear with recognisably Nordic phenomena, climate and seasonal conditions, light and language(s) (see Waade and Jensen 2013: 192). *Bron/Broen* is the first major televisual production to specifically address, represent and reimagine transnational, intercultural encounters in the Øresund region, as well as the implications of new spatial experiences initiated by the bridge. It is my contention that the series, at both the production and narrative levels, articulates the difficulties and contradictions in fostering a sense of a coherent Øresund identity.

In this chapter, I first discuss the screen-industrial conditions in which the series was produced, a context in which both state-led and commercial interests work in tandem to foster audiovisual culture in the region. To this end, I briefly outline the constellation of policies, institutions and transnational production funds that give rise to the conditions of what Mette Hjort (2009) calls 'affinitive transnationalism' in the Danish and Swedish audiovisual industries. Following this, I show through a close reading of textual features how the series constructs the imagined space of the Øresund region and simultaneously articulates its fault lines in medium-specific ways. Finally, I address the funding and production contexts of *Bron/Broen*, detailing the material ways that that the region is performed on-screen (and off-screen) to domestic and international audiences and showing how aspects of production further complicate the projection of a transnational urban region.

A POST-INDUSTRIAL REGION: GEOGRAPHY AND ECONOMICS

As a result of several wars between the two kingdoms in the seventeenth century, contact across the Øresund diminished and the body of water came to be perceived by politicians in the late nineteenth and twentieth centuries as an iron curtain rather than a space to be traversed (see Löfgren 2008: 198). This perspective has changed since the 1950s, and the strait, previously regarded by the populace as a 'blue wall' and a barrier representing the strict national borders and unused economic potential, is now a porous and liminal body that connects the two lands (see Pedersen 2004: 81; OECD 2003: 76; Olshov 2010: 51). Linked by the iconic Øresundsbron, the economic and political activity of the region is centred on Denmark's capital, Copenhagen, and the former shipbuilding city of Malmö sitting on the periphery of Sweden.[5]

From the 1970s until the late 1980s, the two cities separately faced similar problems: widespread unemployment, a declining population, competition from abroad, and the demise of the manufacturing and shipping industries. In Europe, the late twentieth century saw the push for supra-national and inter-regional integration dominate the political and economic stage, reflected in the several cross-border development projects in the European Union, from which the Øresund project draws funding and political support. Prompted by stagnating economies on both sides, the plan to physically connect the two cities by the Øresund Bridge brought the assurance that the larger Øresund project and associated new infrastructure under the Trans-European Transport Network (TENs-T) initiative would open up the domestic, regional and national markets to the wider European and consequently international market (see Bucken-Knapp 2003: 66–8; Baeten 2012: 28). Since 1996, structural funds have been made available through the EU Interreg programmes that focus on stimulating inter-regional cooperation.

Malmö's transition from an industrial to post-industrial city has been the more salient of the two cities. This transformation has happened within the larger context of the regionalisation of Swedish politics and governance since the 1990s and which continues into the present. Subsequent prestige-laden, 'starchitectural' (see Ponzini and Natasi 2011) urban development projects such as the Turning Torso (completed in 2005), the tallest skyscraper in Scandinavia, and the complete overhaul and gentrification of the Västra Hamnen (Western Harbour) district in Malmö are material and highly visible manifestations of the city's development strategy of moving away from industrial decline and modifying its shipbuilding image and heritage, ultimately shifting to a knowledge-based economy focusing on scientific research, culture and sustainable development (see OECD 2003: 77).

FILM POLICY IN A BINATIONAL REGION

The political rhetoric of regional reorganisation, combined with the shift in economic priorities toward transnational integration and culture-building has had an impact on national film policy and the gradual internationalisation of Danish and Swedish production practices. As Ib Bondebjerg and Eva Novrup Redvall note, Scandinavian audiovisual cultures and national institutions are shifting away from essentialist conceptions of national culture toward a more transnational agenda as a means of grappling with the changing realities of production and consumption in a globalised era (2013: 138). *Bron/Broen* is a manifestation of the Danish and Swedish film industries' reactive strategies that adopt co-production and collaboration as a means of ensuring their survival, a motivating rhetoric that echoes the drive behind the formation of the Øresund region. In this section I will summarise the current conditions of production and support that have been developing since the 1990s, and that form the film-political context in which *Bron/Broen* emerges.

From the perspective of the modern Scandinavian welfare state, film policy is an essential part of the development of national culture, particularly support for developing artistic diversity in filmmaking.[6] In Denmark and Sweden, a high level of state involvement in film culture is necessary to ensure its survival and sustainability, especially where the two small national cinemas not only face significant challenges from Hollywood's globalising imperative, but also limitations with regard to wider circulation beyond national borders (cultural, linguistic, etc.). Before 1999, the Øresund region, to a certain extent, already possessed the conditions for 'affinitive transnationalism' to flourish, in that the existing linguistic, cultural and even ethnic affinities between Denmark and Sweden make possible the cross-border networks and platforms for audiovisual collaboration and co-production (see Hjort 2009: 17). Despite this, a more concerted effort to encourage co-production at a regional level has only come into focus since 2010.

SUPPORT FOR TRANSNATIONAL CO-PRODUCTIONS

Structures of funding and support for film and television drama productions are closely intertwined in Denmark and Sweden, where state broadcasters Danmarks Radio (DR) and Sveriges Television (SVT) – who are both co-producers of *Bron/Broen* – as well as commercial broadcasters are obliged to contribute to funds for national audiovisual production as part of the respective national Film Agreements. In turn, these funds are distributed by the national film institutes to co-fund productions that span film, television and other screen-based media. Due to the small size of the domestic markets and talent pool, it is also not uncommon to find professionals such as producers, actors, technical crew and production companies regularly working on both film and television projects, marking a high level of cross-over in the audiovisual industry (see Redvall 2013: 198).

What is significant to this present essay is the dynamic of transnational coproduction in the Scandinavian context.[7] Through the late 1990s and into the 2000s, the Danish and Swedish audiovisual industries saw a marked rise in transnational co-productions, and since the 2000s, cross-border production and distribution have been more significant in television drama compared to film (see Bondebjerg and Redvall 2013: 128). This has been facilitated by the availability of funding from both public and private sources. Under various schemes, the Danish Film Institute offers funding of up to 60 per cent of the Danish share of production costs (see Danish Film Institute 2012: 7). The Swedish Film Institute contributes a maximum of 80 per cent of the Swedish share (see Swedish Film Institute 2012), providing a subsidy of up to SEK 2 million for eligible Swedish drama series projects (see Swedish Film Institute 2013). In any case, television in the Scandinavian context has long had a strong collaborative dimension, where most productions are co-funded by state broadcasters and also facilitated on a pan-Nordic level by the Nordic Film & TV Fund, created in 1990.[8]

Driven by a social-democratic ethos, the public service imperative of both Danish and Swedish television places a focus on ensuring a broad offering to all members of society, with a particular focus on producing high-quality programmes that reflect the diversity of the entire country, as the Swedish Ministry of Culture asserts in its broadcasting charter (see Sveriges Television 2012). Similarly, Section 10 of the Danish Radio and Television Broadcasting Act states:

> Programming shall ensure that the general public has access to important information on society and debate. Furthermore, particular emphasis shall be placed on Danish language and culture. Programming shall cover all genres in the production of art and culture and provide programmes that reflect the diversity of cultural interests in Danish society. (Danish Ministry of Culture 2010: 3)

Notably, these are aims that may seem to be emphatically concerned with notions of the national. Yet when taking into account the transnationalising strategies of the film institutes since the late 1990s – i.e. support for cross-border co-productions in both film and television – we find a more open attitude toward the understanding of what constitutes a 'Danish' or 'Swedish' production in the contemporary era, which is alluded to in the idea of the 'diversity' of the nation in current film policy. For instance, productions qualifying for state support no longer have to be made by Danish citizens, feature only Danish actors, nor focus exclusively on Danish issues and traditions. Joshua Oppenheimer's *The Act of Killing* (2012) illustrates this expanded notion of a 'Danish' production: the Danish/Norwegian/British documentary about Indonesian mass murderers was directed by an American based in Copenhagen, received funding from the DFI, and has won top honours in numerous domestic and international festivals.

REGIONAL AUDIOVISUAL PRODUCTION

This shift towards transnational co-productions in the 'regional turn' in film policy and the rise of regional film funds such as the Copenhagen Film Fund and Film i Skåne, are important developments in this regard, particularly in relation to a television production so specifically focused on a transnational region like *Bron/Broen*. Sweden's Stockholm-centric film policy before the 1990s had meant that peripheral regions possessed very little in terms of infrastructure and film talent (see Blomgren 2008: 6). This changed with the gradual regionalisation of the Swedish political landscape that began in 1974 and that gained steam in the late 1990s, fuelled by Sweden's entry into the EU in 1995. Being an EU member allows regional production centres direct access to EU development funds, whose aims were to create economic regions that would develop new industries and employment opportunities (see Hedling 2010b: 335; Stenport 2013: 86). According to the programme priorities of the EU's Interreg programme, one of the aims is to 'strengthen a common identity in the region' (Interreg IVA 2014: np). The role of culture, particularly film and television, in spurring regional development and fostering a sense of identity has thus been given high priority in Swedish national policy in more recent years (see Statens Offentliga Utredningar 2009: 9).

In the wake of the international success of *Bron/Broen*, Region Skåne, the administrative body of the region, and its subsidiary Film i Skåne released a five-year regional strategy plan for film and moving image in early 2015, detailing a more coherent vision of and commitment to the development of the audiovisual industry and the importance of audiovisual culture to the identity of the region (see Region Skåne 2015). This is a significant milestone for Skåne and a timely one, as there had been much debate prior to this about the direction in which the industry was heading and the potential for the film sector to be a vital part of the region's development (see Marklund 2011; Mathieu 2013). The regional film production centre Film i Skåne is a co-producer of *Bron/Broen* and is responsible for the development of film culture in the Skåne region, and one of its strategies is to pro-actively fund productions that employ local talent and are filmed in Skåne and the Øresund region. This new confidence, I would argue, is in part due to the high-profile success of *Bron/Broen*, which has not only contributed to a growth in film tourism in Skåne, but also drawn much attention to the production capabilities and talent in the region, influencing shifts in policy-making and thus feeding directly into the making of the region's cinematic ambitions. Similarly, Susanne Eichner and Anne Marit Waade remark that Region Skåne has used the series as a success story to market its own ambitions and success (2015: 13), where images of and references to the series are peppered across its website. According to Olof Hedling, film and television production in regions such as Skåne is used specifically to strengthen regional identity on top of serving as a source of employment and rejuvenating the regional economy: for instance, 'territorialization clauses' (2010a: 72) are included in the contracts with producers to ensure that film shoots take place in specific locations or studios in the relevant region. In addition to the economic benefits, the region is also given wider international exposure, benefiting from place marketing via media exposure and tourism.

On the other side of the Sound, Copenhagen already boasts a high level of cultural and political capital being the nexus of national film production, and it is now focusing on improving economic relations within the wider Capital Region, other sub-national regions within the country, and in the Øresund. This is achieved through a binding agreement with the Danish Cultural Ministry (Kulturministeriet) titled *Kultur Metropol Øresund* (KMO) that aims to establish and support cultural collaborations over a four-year period within the region (2012–15). In addition, the Danish Cultural Ministry has announced that an annual budget of 2.5 million kroner will be earmarked for television productions made in collaboration with regional film funds (see Kulturministeriet 2014). The Copenhagen Film Fund, which has established a major stake in *Bron/Broen* from the third season on, operates out of the KMO with the remit of driving the economic stimulation of the local film and television businesses in the nine municipalities of the Capital Region.

It was in this climate of cross-border capital and policy and increased co-operation at national and regional levels that *Bron/Broen* emerged. Being of dual nationality, where all aspects of production and even plot are split equally, *Bron/Broen* indeed reflects the commitment to expanded definitions of 'national' audiovisual work that acknowledge the transnational nature of contemporary film and television production. That the series is partly supported by regional film funds is also significant as it demonstrates a material link, through territorial clauses for instance, between funding sources and the representation of particular locations in the region on screen. In the following sections I turn to the ways the series specifically constructs and negotiates the region at the textual level and through its production context.

TRAVERSING THE REGION THROUGH TELEVISION

Andrew Nestingen writes that there is 'a good reason to turn to crime narratives as a means of examining Scandinavia' (2008: 14); his claim is that popular crime fiction texts use crime to engage with debates concerning national identity, society and transnational relations. In the case of *Bron/Broen*, it is the Øresund region that is under examination, and according to producers Bo Ehrhardt and Anders Landström, the drama intentionally projects the region as a single metropolis: 'the boundaries between Malmö and Copenhagen were to be blurred' (in Söelund 2013: 14). Indeed, without verbal or visual cues, it is not always clear whether a particular scene is taking place in Copenhagen or in Malmö. That the Danish and Swedish characters largely speak to each other as though the two languages are mutually intelligible – barring some misunderstandings in the first two episodes – is also one of the ways cultural-linguistic boundaries are blurred.[9] Ostensibly, *Bron/Broen* is a crime drama series that foregrounds the working relationship between two cops with clashing personalities, but this is played out against the landscape of a transnational metropolis, portrayed as a paradoxically fractured yet seamless urban space that must be traversed to stop the perpetrators. As the Swedish ethnologist Orvar Löfgren remarks, 'the Øresund rhetoric rests heavily on the magic of movements', of people crossing borders (2000: 53); by tracing Saga and Martin's navigation of the region from scene to scene, a sense of region-building emerges. A larger part of the drama

Fig. 1 Title shot of the second season of *Bron/Broen*.

is therefore mediated through the detectives' practices of mobility – physical and linguistic – across the Øresund region, and a sense of the region only comes into being through this movement across borders.

The opening credits sequence announces the start of each episode of *Bron/Broen*, beginning with a travelling shot from inside a car looking towards the night-time sky. As the viewer presumably 'drives' across the Øresund Bridge, streetlights pass and we begin to get a glimpse of the bridge's cables. This is our entry into the world of *Bron/Broen*, of beginning *in medias res*, as it were, and the viewer is placed directly in the fictional world through the camera's perspective, in the midst of crossing a boundary. The first shot then fades into shorter aerial establishing shots of the Øresund Bridge against a pitch-black sky while the title song 'Hollow Talk' by Danish band Chorus of the Young Believers plays. In a minor key, the music opens with the singer's mumbled strain laid over a dirge-like repetition of a single note on the piano, conjuring an atmosphere of anticipation while the montage rolls through the rest of the major urban landmarks in the region (Turning Torso skyscraper, streets of the two city centres, Rigshospitalet, Malmöhus Windmill, the Little Mermaid), all devoid of human activity but with visible light trails of moving vehicles on the city streets, navigating the region. Les Roberts writes that 'different architectures and practices of mobility produce specific renderings of the city-in-film' (2012: 12), reflecting a broader sense of place. Here, the Øresund strait is a significant locus of meaning for the characters in the drama, whose movements on and across the body of water motivate the action of the narrative – the start of both seasons involve bodies colliding on and into the bridge. Except for the first and last shots, the opening sequence is composed of a series of clips that have been sped up and that frame the city spaces in such a way that the dark sky takes up more than half of the image. The steady, imposing darkness is juxtaposed against frenzied movement in the city that is made visible by the head- and tail-lights of vehicles zipping down the darkened city streets, as though panic-stricken.

In a study of literary noir representations of Malmö in the 1990s and 2000s, Ann Steiner notes that the post-industrial social transformations in the city are typically depicted in terms of urban anxiety:

> The new Malmö is described as a place of crime and despair. The middle-class town is bleak, desolate and commercial, and the segregated, suburban poor areas are full of immigrants, drugs and social problems. (2010: 369)

In the context of a television series, the visual imagination of Malmö and Copenhagen in *Bron/Broen* matches the tone Steiner lays out in her study. The drama, mediated in a realistic style, depicts the region and its urban spaces such as the bridge as conduits for the anxieties of spatial and social change. Through the noir lens, life in the region is depicted as a broken and fragmented society where danger not only lurks on city streets, urban parks, and in the uninhabited countryside, but also in places typically

Fig. 2 Regionauts: an aerial shot from the title sequence showing a car crossing the bridge.

perceived as 'safe' such as the school and the home.

The entire Øresund region is represented as one big crime scene that is marketed to audiences worldwide. Aesthetically, it follows all the visual conventions of the Nordic noir trend: the wintry urban landscape is always cloudy or shot in the darkness of night (see Gray 2014: 76; Creeber 2015: 26). The colour palette of the entire series is in washed-out, muted tones of grey, blue and green. Establishing shots between scenes feature the bridge filmed from various perspectives that emphasise awe and fascination, as well as fear – the bridge is a conduit for transnational crime. What is distinct about the spatial representations in the series is that there is little indication in most scenes whether they are in Sweden or in Denmark, except via verbal cues from the characters, or through visual cues such as landmarks, street signs and other banal objects. In fact, to the non-Danish/Swedish viewer familiar with neither city, their landmarks and the languages spoken, the drama could well have just taken place in a single city. This, of course, is one of the intentions of the writers – to create a narrative and visual space where the sense of a geographical border is erased. In doing so, *Bron/Broen* not only works within Nordic noir conventions, but also renews the genre by introducing transnational, cross-border relations as a translatable plot premise and multilingualism as a feature of the performance.

To borrow a term coined by Tom O'Dell, our detectives are the 'regionauts' of the imagined cross-border metropolis (2003: 38), effortlessly traversing the two national territories to explore and investigate transnational crime. Their investigation takes them – and us – from the middle of the bridge to hospitals, docks, warehouses, city streets, offices, homes, abandoned structures, parks and the zoo. For a few minutes between scenes, the detectives are shown in Saga's car driving across the bridge, reaching their next destination directly in the next shot. The fluid mobility across vast locations created by the editing neglects borders and compresses the space of the region into a fractured topology of crime scenes, criminal hideaways, police headquarters and the detectives' own homes, sutured together by cutaways and establishing shots of unspecified urban locales and, above all, the bridge.

Just as the detectives journey from location to location across the region in every episode, the narrative similarly travels between a variety of characters and sub-plots over the course of each season, providing a kind of patchwork of social life in the Øresund, albeit one marked by crime. On the one hand, the serial format on television allows room for multiple narratives to be developed over extended screen time in a way that would not be feasible in a feature film. On the other hand, in a series of ten episodes, plenty of characters enter and exit the narrative episode by episode, and their actions and experiences drive the central story forward even as sub-plots are resolved within individual episodes. What this presents to viewers is a multiplicity and simultaneity of perspectives – subjective experiences of the region through each of these minor characters who typically come from diverse social groups and whose depictions are emphatic comments on topical welfare-state issues pertinent to modern day Denmark and Sweden: mental illness, homelessness, domestic abuse, child labour, ethnic minorities, journalism and the media and eco-terrorism.

In other words, while the main narrative focuses on the crime, other storylines are also incorporated in what is known as a 'three-plot structure' in which politics and the private lives of characters are also given equal narrative weight (see Redvall 2013: 172–3). This mix of narratives woven into the main plot reflects what Peter Billingham describes a 'multi-vocal narrative structure' that can 'expose and reveal a refracted, kaleidoscopic "sense of the city"', where 'the politics of location is inextricably interwoven with the politics of identity' (2000: 1). Underneath the crime narrative lies a more complex social mapping and characterisation of the Øresund: real and current socio-political issues are not just referenced in each episode, but rather they motivate the central narrative arc. Take, for example, episode six of the first season, where the question of police brutality, multi-racial integration and the negative perceptions of immigrant Muslim communities in Copenhagen form the crux. To reiterate, the episodic and serial nature of the drama series make possible the inclusion of many different and simultaneous stories and therefore holds the potential to present multiple perspectives that each depict different segments of Øresund society. In a transnational context, this interweaving of multiple stories works to 'write' the region into existence, bringing the voices and spaces of two nations into a single televisual space. We can thus perceive the detectives' repeated crossings over the bridge in terms of a stitching movement, in that by moving back and forth across the bridge the characters bear with them 'the power of unification' (O'Dell 2011: 15), which of course crime then seeks to tear apart.

Furthermore, the series depicts the spaces of the Øresund region as inevitably connected to larger global forces – after all, the Øresund is a region with global aspirations. For example, the narrative of the second season is especially provocative in its evocation of a larger transnational political space beyond the geographical context of the region. Claiming responsibility for the various crimes, a group of eco-terrorists

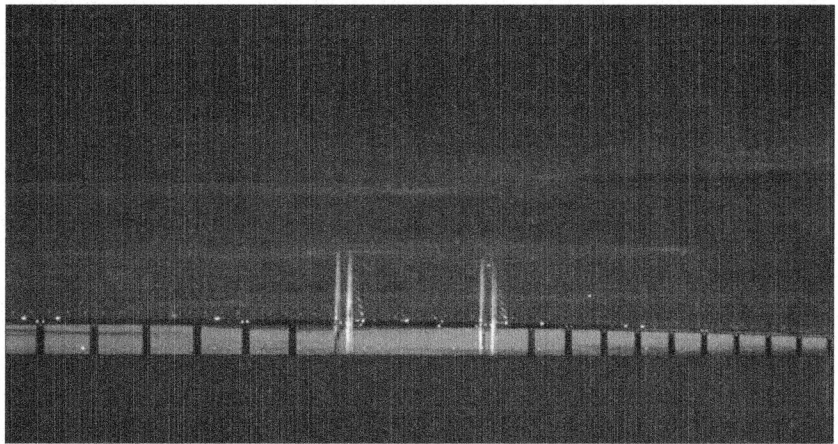

Fig. 3 The end credits of *Bron/Broen* appear against a long shot of the bridge surrounded by a dark sky.

disseminate their demands through YouTube videos and communicate by Internet chat early in the season. Through acts of terror, their challenge to society at large is to rethink one's complicity in the destruction of ecological resources. Through the kind of collective violence and action they have undertaken, the group seeks to disrupt what they perceive as the blind adherence to neoliberal ideals of individual profit over collective and ecological good. The severity and geographical impact of each successive crime grows with every episode on a scale from 'local' to 'regional' to 'global'. The final action of the second season hones in on an EU summit on the environment where shots of protesters gathering outside the venue recall familiar scenes of street protests at G7 summits while a deadly virus threatens to spread globally through the interconnected conduits of air travel.

NAVIGATING THE REGION THROUGH DIGITAL PARATEXTS

Another way by which the series generates a sense of moving through the region is in the mapping of the events in the narrative on the official series website. As Jonathan Gray (2010) has explained, paratexts perform multiple functions for the audience, shaping their interactions with the audiovisual text through ephemera such as promotional trailers, merchandising and official websites. On DR's official website for the series, a customised Google Maps representation of the geographical region shows a constellation of 'pins' across different parts of Copenhagen and Malmö (see DR1 2013). Each pin represents a key location featured in the series and clicking on a pin brings up screenshots and brief contextual information relating the location to a character or event, such as 'Saga's flat' or 'Martin stayed in a hotel here'.

The spectator is positioned in the role of a criminologist-navigator, although the extent of her crime-mapping activity is limited to pointing, clicking, dragging and zooming in and out. The spectator of *Bron/Broen* is offered a more 'active, creative mode of vision' (Verhoeff 2012: 13) through her navigation of the space via this interactive Google Maps interface. Indeed, this interactive map, as a paratextual resource, is not only intended to lend credence to the fiction of geographical fidelity in the series, but also to orient the spectator in the imagined space of the metropolis. In other words, this online paratext, available to a global audience, serves an orientation strategy to help viewers make sense of the region, the distances traversed by the characters, and the geographical relationship between locations and events in the story (see Mittell 2015: 262). In some ways this particular website plays an instructional role in guiding viewers (domestic or international) in the names of places and of the geography of the region. Where the televisual text compresses space – and time – through editing, online digital cartography opens up possibilities of traversing the space of the Øresund, here with the fictional narrative as a frame and the map of the actual Øresund region as a canvas.

Indeed, the larger aim is to draw viewers closer – and connect them – to the narrative universe of the series by enhancing their emotional and spatial experience of the region, akin to what Kjetil Sandvik calls a process of *augmentation*: 'an emotional enhancement of our sense and experience of place by means of mediatisation' (2010: 140). The online map works similarly by inviting viewers to investigate the region cartographically. For viewers of *Bron/Broen*, the actual location of the Øresund region has become augmented. The narrative fiction of *Bron/Broen* forms another layer on top of the cartographical representation of the Øresund, which mediates and remediates the region through multiple layers upon the televisual text, allowing the viewer to further engage with the story and make sense of the space of the region by navigating its geography via the Google Maps interface. Taking into consideration also the changing ways by which audiences access the text and its paratexts, the traditional 'flow' of television is now interrupted and fragmented further onto different screens, a result of television's increasingly close relationship with internet-enabled channels of distribution. There is thus a shift in the agency that contemporary viewers possess alongside expanded access to televisual content that enable them to 'look beyond their regions or nations, accessing the world from outside a viewing position long controlled by national institutions and transnational industries' (Uricchio 2011: 31–2). The map is not only a compressed version of a vast geographical region shrunk into a 'bite-sized' representation, but the expanded nature of a digital map allows viewers to explore and create their own journeys through the region beyond the limited gaze of the camera's perspective.

Thus far, I have examined how *Bron/Broen* mediates and constructs the Øresund as an ambiguous and multi-faceted urban space where, although boundaries between the two countries are blurred and the two national spaces appear sutured together, the region is portrayed as internally fragmented and its imagined transnational coherence is distorted by the noir treatment. A closer look at the production processes of the series reveals a yet more contrary picture of how *Bron/Broen* simultaneously articulates the transnational regional project and unsettles it.

BRON/BROEN AS TRANSNATIONAL PROJECT(ION)

The assignment from our producers was to:
1. Create a show that was equally set in Denmark and Sweden. And
2. It had to be a thriller.

That meant detectives. From two countries. (Rosenfeldt 2014)

Since the broadcast of the first season, there has been much discussion in the media about the unique production conditions behind the series, with much attention paid to the dual nationality of the series. A Danish-Swedish team of writers, Hans Rosenfeldt, Nikolaj Scherfig, Måns Marlin and Björn Stein began work on developing *Bron/Broen* in 2006, writing and developing the storyline and screenplay for a further five years until funding was confirmed and the final phase of scriptwriting was completed (see Scherfig 2012).

What is distinctive about the funding of *Bron/Broen* is that it resembles the financing of a feature film rather than a conventional television project that is mainly spearheaded, financed and developed by state broadcasters, as was the case for *Forbrydelsen* (*The Killing*, 2007–12) and *Borgen* (2010–13), alongside most other series produced by DR or SVT. The fact that the production team behind *Bron/Broen* comprises two companies that mainly work with film – Filmlance International and Nimbus Film – also demonstrates a high level of crossover between the film and television industries in the region. As Eva Novrup Redvall similarly notes in reference to Nimbus Film, *Bron/Broen* is 'an example of how Danish production companies that have traditionally been working with film are looking still more into also producing high-profile television drama' (2013: 198). That it is a product of the commercial production context is also significant here as the production team developed the series with minimal creative input from (yet is primarily funded by) state broadcasters DR and SVT. The implication here is that the producers of the series therefore hold very little obligation to fulfil particular public service values (see Waade and Jensen 2013: 195), specifically those that insist on some measure of representing 'themes of the nation' (see Hjort 2000) or region beyond setting and film location. In other words, one would contend that what *Bron/Broen* reflects about the region is largely uncoloured and unfettered by the policy demands of any one national production culture.

Even so, it must be acknowledged that this relationship is complex and the national still has a bearing on aspects of the production process, which inevitably affects the series' portrayal of its fictional milieu. In relation to this, we must also consider implicit pressures from funding sources and the effect of administrative hurdles such as different national tax regimes and employment regulations. For instance, the changing funding sources of the production across the first to third seasons have played an increasing role in dictating visual elements such as shooting locales. This territorial stipulation has a clear implication on production and, as I argue, on the subtle articulation of national boundaries within the Øresund region in the series.

For instance, according to Anders Landström, a producer on the series, Filmlance has officially been the lead partner in the production and all of the crew and cast are employed under Swedish law and regulations (see Abbott 2015). This has meant that most of the filming has been done in Skåne instead of equally on both sides of the Øresund. In the narrative universe of the series, Copenhagen and Malmö are depicted as one borderless metropolitan region. Aside from established and more easily recognisable places such as the respective Copenhagen and Malmö police headquarters and other specific urban landmarks, most scenes are shot in 'neutral' locations that have few distinguishing national traits that mark whether the action is taking place in Denmark or Sweden. In practical terms, the cost of moving the entire fleet of trailers, technical equipment and personnel between Copenhagen and Malmö limited the extent to which actual border crossing took place in the production. Consequently the production team made the decision to film several exterior scenes in 'neutral' locations such as meadows or deserted industrial areas in Skåne, or, where street scenes were filmed, replacing visible identifiable Swedish elements such as road signs with Danish equivalents. Ultimately, according to the executive producer Thomas Nilsson, it did not matter where the crew were shooting because modifications could easily be made to make Denmark look like Sweden and vice versa; interior scenes such as those taking place in apartments were similarly flexible in that the spaces were fitted with the appropriate furnishings to look either Danish or Swedish depending on the scene (see Bock 2015).

However, this Swedish emphasis sits in tension with another statement regarding the extent to which the series' Danish partners are involved. The Copenhagen Film Fund (CFF), having newly invested a large sum in the production, announced in 2014 that the third season of *Bron/Broen* will be 'more Danish' than before (see Copenhagen Film Fund 2014). This is indeed a provocative statement and a surprising shift in the production and marketing of the series, especially as one of the unique selling points of the first and second seasons was the shared, 50/50 Danish-Swedish involvement in the crafting of the series. The CFF's financial involvement means that a larger portion of the production crew will be Danish, 'thereby securing more Danish jobs' and bringing more of the series' production to Denmark. By strategically investing in an internationally successful series like *Bron/Broen*, and, through this money, having a say in the production process, the CFF is ensuring that the Danish film industry benefits not only economically, but also from the higher visibility to international audiences. In an interview, the lead writer Hans Rosenfeldt remarks that the first season had to include Denmark because of Danish funding (see Hall 2012), and even now, that the producers of the third season are reiterating the same motivation shows that a project's source of funding plays a consequential role in determining particular territorial aspects of a production – in this case, location and setting. Here, issues of funding and practical considerations relating to administrative matters still register a separation along national lines, thereby complicating the shared, transnational claims of the text.

CONCLUSION

By way of conclusion, let me briefly draw attention to yet another police-procedural crime drama, *The Team* (2015–), which I argue is a manifestation of the legacy of *Bron/Broen*. In late February 2015, the first episode of *The Team* simultaneously premiered on Danish, Swedish, Austrian, German, Belgian and Swiss television. With a screenplay developed by a Danish team of writers, the crime drama focuses on a tri-national team of investigators from Germany, Denmark and Belgium who work together to solve the murders of three Lithuanian women in Berlin, Copenhagen and Antwerp. As in *Bron/Broen*, the lead actors each speak German, Danish and Flemish in their separate native contexts, but instead of mutual comprehension, they use English to communicate with each other when they have scenes together – English is also used whenever there are encounters with other European characters such as the Lithuanians. The series is co-produced by eleven media organisations from eight member states and is screened in the six countries whose state broadcasters were involved in the production. It is also part-funded by the EU's Creative Europe programme.

Directly inspired by the success and international appeal of *Bron/Broen* and *Borgen*, it seemed clear to one of the lead producers of *The Team*, the European Broadcasting Union (EBU) – responsible for the Eurovision Song Contest – that 'language is no barrier to the international success of "Made in Europe" fiction' (Banks 2015: np). I do not want to overstate the novelty of this sort of multi-national European televisual collaboration since it is not a new development unique to the post-2000 period. Yet *The Team* is a bold experiment in multi-lingual and multi-cultural representation in a pan-European television co-production between several national producers and broadcasters. In a similar way to *Bron/Broen*, which filters the spatial and cultural imagination of the Øresund region through crime, *The Team* uses the genre as a way of reimagining as well as problematising territorial boundaries and transnational movement within the Schengen area, and, to a certain extent, the notion of European cooperation and a sense of transnational affinity. It is in this vein that the trend of realistic, multi-lingual television dramas created via cross-border co-production, as manifested by *Bron/Broen* and in concert with the growing success of DR writing teams, has had a noteworthy impact on the European production landscape.

In this essay I have sketched the constellation of film-cultural policies that have shaped audiovisual production in the Øresund region since the 1990s and shown how these conditions negotiate a sense of the transnational through bilateral coproduction strategies. As a televisual event that emerges from this milieu, *Bron/Broen* has been relatively successful in being circulated to over 150 countries, as well as spawning two remakes focusing on the UK-France and US-Mexico border regions. *Bron/Broen* has not only engendered a greater awareness of the Øresund beyond its own geographical borders as it imagines and projects the region in medium-specific ways, but also speaks to the problems and complexity of spatial experience in cross-border regions in the twenty-first century.

What is distinctive about how the series portrays the transnational urban region in the Scandinavian context is the way it directly engages with, harnesses, and yet contests the political rhetoric of the Øresund project at the production, funding and narrative levels through the medium of long-form television drama. Indeed, the fact that the series is named after the central architectural landmark of the region foregrounds this engagement. The producers of the series have traded on the bi-national production context being the first of its kind in the Scandinavian region – a creative and financial set-up where Danish and Swedish joint involvement is split 50/50 – and this noteworthy aspect regarding the making of the series feeds into the fictional story of Danish and Swedish police collaboration across a cross-border region. The story of the collaboration between Saga and Martin and the ways they navigate their transnational relationship is in many ways the story of the Øresund project, a narrative in which the Danish and Swedish languages are mutually intelligible and intercultural differences are easily overcome. Yet upon closer examination, I have argued that *Bron/Broen* registers the critical difficulties of representing the contemporary televisual city(-region) in an age of transnational flows and boundaries that are continually shifting. On both the textual and production levels, not only does the noir lens disrupt visions of cross-border collaboration to offer a counter-narrative of the Øresund imaginary, but the national also resolutely asserts itself in various ways, destabilising and fracturing the transnational imaginary.

NOTES

1 It should be noted that the geographical boundaries of the Øresund region are still disputed, and there are multiple official definitions of different scales. My interest in this essay is the core urban area comprising the two cities. Elsewhere, a broader definition would include the two Danish regions of Sjælland (Zealand) and Region Hovedstaden (Capital Region) and the Swedish county of Skåne (Scania) (see Berg and Löfgren 2000: 9–10).
2 'Øresund' is the Danish spelling, while 'Öresund' is the Swedish. For consistency, I have elected to maintain the use of the Danish spelling throughout this essay.
3 Shotter emphasises that socio-political concepts relating to society, the individual or citizenship take shape through our *talk* about them: 'We make them "make sense" in the course of our arguments about them', relying extensively on clarification and persuasion rather than being 'proved' in empirical terms (1993: 154).
4 Paula Arvas and Andrew Nestingen state that 'Scandinavian crime fiction', as a literary genre, has become a well-known brand in Europe and in North America since the 1990s (2011: 1), and the term continues to be used not just

by literary but also film and television scholars (see Nestingen 2008; Agger and Waade 2010). The emergence of 'Nordic noir' in English-language critical writing, however, is a more recent trend (see McCabe 2011; Agger 2012; Waade and Jensen 2013; Peacock 2013, 2014). Ultimately, the term 'Nordic noir' is used to denote the sub-genre of televisual crime thriller fiction from the Nordic countries that has a characteristically bleak visual style layered over a wintry, Northern European setting and a specific sensibility that tends towards uncertainty and pessimism (see Forshaw 2013; Waade and Jensen 2013; Peacock 2014). Waade and Jensen (2013) and Creeber (2015), in particular, discuss Nordic noir production values using *Bron/Broen* as a case study.

5   Pundits argue that Malmö has since become the unofficial 'capital' of Southern Sweden (see Olshov 2010: 77), a statement that is significant in the light of the regionalisation of Swedish politics since the late 1990s. Region Skåne, as the county administration is known, now has greater agency in policy-making in the cultural sphere.

6   One thing to note is that state film policy in the Scandinavian context necessarily includes both the film and television milieux: the term 'film' in policy discourse therefore covers television drama as well as the conventional formats of feature-length, short and documentary film.

7   A more comprehensive overview of the reasons for this within the Danish context can be found in Brandstrup and Redvall (2005).

8   While the terms 'Scandinavian' and 'Nordic' are sometimes used interchangeably in the English-speaking world, each term communicates specific meanings in 'the North' and in academic scholarship. The Nordic region refers to the five sovereign nations of Denmark, Finland, Iceland, Norway and Sweden (including the territories of Greenland, the Faroe Islands and Åland), that together form the geo-political forum called the Nordic Council; 'Scandinavia' is defined in topographical and socio-linguistic terms as Norway, Sweden and Denmark based on the close cultural, historical, and linguistic links between these nations (see Hilson 2008: 11–13).

9   For reasons of space I will not be discussing language in detail in this chapter, but it is worth mentioning that the primary audience for the series is its Danish and Swedish viewers. Both languages are used equally throughout the series, and I would suggest that this mode of address seeks to foster an imagined televisual community of Øresund spectators, as it were.

BIBLIOGRAPHY

Abbott, Dennis (2015) 'Creative Europe Backs Scandinavian Crime Saga – The Bridge', *Creative Europe*, March 19; http://ec.europa.eu/programmes/creative-europe/news/2015/bridge_en.htm

Agger, Gunhild (2012) 'Nordic Noir on Television: The Killing I-III', *Cinéma & Cie: International Film Studies Journal*, 12, 19, 39–50.

Agger, Gunhild and Anne Marit Waade (eds) (2010) *Den skandinaviske krimi: bestseller og blockbuster*. Göteborg: Nordicom.

Anderson, Benedict (2006) *Imagined Communities: Reflections on the Origin and Spread of Nationalism*. London: Verso.

Arvas, Paula and Andrew Nestingen (2011) 'Introduction: Contemporary Scandinavian Crime Fiction', in Andrew Nestingen and Paula Arvas (eds) *Scandinavian Crime Fiction*. Cardiff: University of Wales Press, 1–20.

Baeten, Guy (2012) 'Normalising Neoliberal Planning: The Case of Malmö, Sweden', in Tuna Tasan-Kok and Guy Baeten (eds) *Contradictions of Neoliberal Planning: Cities, Policies, and Politics*. Dordrecht: Springer, 21–42.

Banks, Martin (2015) 'EU Crime TV Show Launched to "Bring Together" a Divided Continent', *The Telegraph*, February 2; http://www.telegraph.co.uk/news/worldnews/europe/eu/11384701/EU-crime-TV-show-launched-to-bring-together-a-divided-continent.html

Berg, Per Olof and Orvar Löfgren (2000) 'Studying the Birth of a Transnational Region', in Per Olof Berg, Anders Linde-Laursen and Orvar Löfgren (eds) *Invoking a Transnational Metropolis: The Making of the Øresund Region*. Lund: Studentlitteratur, 7–26.

Billingham, Peter (2000) *Sensing the City Through Television: Urban Identities in Fictional Drama*. Bristol: Intellect.

Blomgren, Roger (2008) *Cultural Industry from Threat to Salvation: Film Production from Art Policy to Regional Development*. Trollhättan: Högskolan Väst.

Bock, Terezia (2015) 'Nu Avslöjas Hemlisen I Tv-Serien "Bron"', *Kvällsposten*, February 20; http://www.expressen.se/kvp/noje/nu-avslojas-hemlisen-i-tv-serien-bron/

Bondebjerg, Ib and Eva Novrup Redvall (2013) 'Transnational Scandinavia? Scandinavian Film Culture in a European and Global Context', in Manuel Palacio and Jörg Türschmann (eds) *Transnational Cinema in Europe*. Zürich: LIT Verlag, 127–45.

Brandstrup, Pil Gundelach and Eva Novrup Redvall (2005) 'Breaking the Borders: Danish Cooperations in the 1990s', in Andrew Nestigen and Trevor G. Elkington (eds) *Transnational Cinema in a Global North: Nordic Cinema in Transition*. Detroit: Wayne State University Press, 141–64.

Bucken-Knapp, Gregg (2003) 'Shaping Possible Integration in the Emerging Cross-Border Øresund Region', in James Anderson, Liam O'Dowd and Thomas M. Wilson (eds) *European Studies: Culture and Cooperation in Europe's Borderlands*, 19. Amsterdam: Rodopi, 55–80.

Copenhagen Film Fund (2014) 'The Bridge III Will Be More Danish than the First Two Seasons', October 8; http://cphfilmfund.com/en/the-bridge-iii-will-be-more-danish-than-the-first-two-seasons/

Creeber, Glen (2015) 'Killing Us Softly: Investigating the Aesthetics, Philosophy and Influence of Nordic Noir Television', *The Journal of Popular Television*, 3, 1, 21–35.

Crouch, David (2015) 'Denmark Wants to Rebrand Part of Sweden as "Greater Copenhagen"', *The Guardian*, March 5; http://www.theguardian.com/world/2015/mar/05/denmark-wants-to-rebrand-part-of-sweden-as-greater-copenhagen

Danish Film Institute (2012) 'Terms for Support to Feature Films Valid from 1 October 2012'; http://www.dfi.dk/~/media/Sektioner/English/Vilk%C3%A5r%202012/dfi-vilkaar-spillefilm-2012-english.ashx.

Danish Ministry of Culture (2010) *The Radio and Television Broadcasting Act.*

DR1 (2013) 'Punkter', *Broen*. October 6; http://www.dr.dk/DR1/Broen/kort.htm

Eichner, Susanne and Anne Marit Waade (2015) 'Local Colour in German and Danish Television: Tatort and Bron//Broen', *Global Media Journal*, 5, 1, 1–20.

Forshaw, Barry (2013) *Nordic Noir: The Pocket Essential Guide to Scandinavian Crime Fiction, Film & TV*. Harpenden: Pocket Essentials.

Gray, Emily (2014) 'In/between Places: Connection and Isolation in *The Bridge*', *Aeternum: The Journal of Contemporary Gothic Studies*, 1, 1, 73–85.

Gray, Jonathan (2010) *Show Sold Separately: Promos, Spoilers, and Other Media Paratexts*. New York: New York University Press.

Hall, Eva (2012) 'Masters Series Interview: "The Bridge" Creator Hans Rosenfeldt on Writing Great Crime Drama', *Irish Film & Television Network*, September 27; http://www.iftn.ie/news/?act1=record&only=1&aid=73&rid=4285399&tpl=archnews&force=1

Hedling, Olof (2010a) 'A Film Friendly Town? Assessing a Decade at a Small Swedish Production Centre', *Film International*, 8, 6, 70–8.

____ (2010b) 'The Regional Turn: Developments in Scandinavian Film Prod-uction', in Mariah Larsson and Anders Marklund (eds) *Swedish Film: An Introduction and Reader*. Lund: Nordic Academic Press, 334–45.

Hilson, Mary (2008) *The Nordic Model: Scandinavia Since 1945*. London: Reaktion Books.

Hjort, Mette (2000) 'Themes of Nation', in Mette Hjort and Scott MacKenzie (eds) *Cinema and Nation*. London: Routledge, 95–110.

____ (2009) 'On the Plurality of Cinematic Transnationalism', in Nataša Ďurovičová and Kathleen Newman (eds) *World Cinemas, Transnational Perspectives*. New York and London: Routledge, 12–33.

Interreg IVA (2014) 'Programme Priorities', *Interreg IVA: Öresund – Kattegat – Skaggerak*; http://www.interreg-oks.eu/en/Menu/About+the+programme/Programme+priorities.

Kulturministeriet (2014) *Mediepolitisk Aftale for 2015–2018*.

Laasby, Gitte (2015) 'Frank Jensen vil indlemme Skåne i Storkøbenhavn', *Ekstra Bladet*. March 6; http://ekstrabladet.dk/nyheder/samfund/frank-jensen-vil-indlemme-skaane-i-storkoebenhavn/5470155.

Löfgren, Orvar (2000) 'Moving Metaphors', in Per Olof Berg, Anders Linde-Laursen and Orvar Löfgren (eds) *Invoking a Transnational Metropolis: The Making of the Øresund Region*. Lund: Studentlitteratur, 27–53.

____ (2008) 'Regionauts: The Transformation of Cross-Border Regions in Scandinavia', *European Urban and Regional Studies*, 15, 3, 195–209.

Marklund, Anders (2011) 'Utvärdering av Region Skånes filmkulturella verksamhet', Kultur Skåne; http://www.skane.se/Public/Kultur/Utredningar%20och%20 rapporter/Utvardering_RS_filmkulturella_verksamhet_2012.pdf

Mathieu, Chris (2013) 'En Förstudie Om Behovet Av En Strategi För Det Regionala Filmområdet I Skåne'. Sociologiska institutionen, Lunds universitet. http://www.skane.se/Public/Kultur/Utredningar%20och%20rapporter/Forstudie_ filmstrategi_2013.pdf

McCabe, Janet (2011) 'Dark Nordic Saturday Nights on BBC4', *CST Online*, 25 March; http://www.cstonline.tv/cst-blog-3

Mittell, Jason (2015) *Complex TV: The Poetics of Contemporary Television Storytelling*. New York: New York University Press.

Nestingen, Andrew (2008) *Crime and Fantasy in Scandinavia: Fiction, Film, and Social Change*. Seattle: University of Washington Press.

Nimbus Film (2013) *The Bridge Season II – Behind the Scenes*. YouTube video; http://www.youtube.com/watch?v=BA_Q4I9Swlo.

O'Dell, Tom (2003) 'Øresund and the Regionauts', in James Anderson, Liam O'Dowd, and Thomas M. Wilson (eds) *Culture and Cooperation in Europe's Borderlands*. Amsterdam: Rodopi, 31–54.

____ (2011) 'Mobility and the Stitching Together of Everyday Life Experiences in the Oresund Region', in Mark Vacher, Tom O'Dell, and Laura Schollert Hvalsum (eds) *Spatial and Temporal Modalities of Everyday Integration*. Lund/Copenhagen: Institutionen för kulturvetenskaper, Lunds Universitet & SAXO-Instituttet, Københavns Universitet, 13–22.

OECD (2003) *Öresund, Denmark/Sweden*. OECD Territorial Reviews. Paris: OECD Publications.

Olshov, Anders (2010) 'Denmark-Sweden Øresund Mega-City Region and the Øresund Bridge', in *Sustainable Transport Development Strategy of the Mega-City Region in Europe and China*. The Emerging Cross-Border Mega-City Region and Sustainable Transportation, 50–81.

Peacock, Steven (ed.) (2013) *Stieg Larsson's Millennium Trilogy: Interdisciplinary Approaches to Nordic Noir on Page and Screen*. Basingstoke: Palgrave Macmillan.

____ (2014) *Swedish Crime Fiction: Novel, Film, Television*. Manchester: Manchester University Press.

Pedersen, Søren Buhl (2004) 'Place Branding: Giving the Region of Øresund a Competitive Edge', *Journal of Urban Technology*, 11, 1, 77–95.

Ponzini, Davide and Michele Natasi (2011) *Starchitecture: Scenes, Actors and Spectacles in Contemporary Cities*. Turin: Allemandi.

Redvall, Eva Novrup (2013) *Writing and Producing Television Drama in Denmark:*

From The Kingdom to The Killing. Basingstoke: Palgrave Macmillan.

Region Skåne (2015) 'Strategi för film och rörlig bild 2015–2020', Region Skåne.

Roberts, Les (2012) *Film, Mobility and Urban Space: A Cinematic Geography of Liverpool*. Liverpool: Liverpool University Press.

Rosenfeldt, Hans (2014) '*The Bridge*: Writing My Favourite Scenes', *BBC – TV Blog*. January 24; http://www.bbc.co.uk/blogs/tv/posts/The-Bridge

Sandvik, Kjetil (2010) 'Crime Scenes as Augmented Reality: Models for Enhancing Places Emotionally by Means of Narratives, Fictions and Virtual Reality', in Britta Timm Knudsen and Anne Marit Waade (eds) *Re-Investing Authenticity: Tourism, Place and Emotions*. Bristol: Channel View Publications, 138–53.

Scherfig, Nikolaj (2012) 'Broen til suksess', *Rushprint*, December 6; http://rushprint.no/2012/12/broen-til-suksess/

Shotter, John (1993) *Conversational Realities: Constructing Life Through Language*. London: Sage.

Söelund, Emilia (2013) 'Sofia Helin: Back at the Scene of the Crime'. *Øresund Magazine*, 11–15.

Statens Offentliga Utredningar (2009) 'Report of the Swedish Committee of Inquiry on Cultural Policy', SOU 16. Stockholm.

Steiner, Ann (2010) 'Town Called Malmö: Nostalgia and Urban Anxiety in Literature from the 1990s and 2000s', in Erik Hedling, Olof Hedling, and Mats Jönsson (eds) *Regional Aesthetics: Locating Swedish Media*. Stockholm: Kungliga Biblioteket, 359–76.

Stenport, Anna Westerståhl (2013) '"We Train Auteurs": Education, Decentralization, Regional Funding, and Niche Marketing in the New Swedish Cinema', in Mette Hjort (ed.) *The Education of the Filmmaker in Europe, Australia, and Asia*. New York: Palgrave Macmillan, 85–104.

Sveriges Television (2012) 'The Broadcasting Charter', October 3; http://www.svt.se/aboutsvt/the-broadcasting-charter

Swedish Film Institute (2012) 'Co-Production of Feature Films, with a Swedish Minority Producer', November 22; http://www.sfi.se/en-GB/Our-grants/Funding/Co-productions--feature-films-with-Sweden-as-the-minority-country/

____ (2013) 'Funding for Drama Series', February 6; http://www.sfi.se/en-GB/Our-grants/Funding/Funding-for-drama-series-/

Tangkjær, Christian (1999) 'Performing a Transnational Region: The Importance of "Open House Strategy"', in *Managing the Big City*. Göteborg University; http://openarchive.cbs.dk/bitstream/handle/10398/6352/wp899.pdf.

Uricchio, William (2011) 'The Recurrent, the Recombinatory and the Ephemeral', in Paul Grainge (ed.) *Ephemeral Media: Transitory Screen Culture from Television to YouTube*. London: Palgrave Macmillan/British Film Institute, 23–36.

Verhoeff, Nanna (2012) *Mobile Screens: The Visual Regime of Navigation*. Amsterdam: Amsterdam University Press.

Waade, Anne Marit and Pia Majbritt Jensen (2013) 'Nordic Noir Production

Values: *The Killing* and *The Bridge*', *Akademisk Kvarter: Tidsskrift for Humanistisk Forskning*, 7, 189–201.

NEOLIBERALISM, NOLLYWOOD AND LAGOS

JONATHAN HAYNES

The Nigerian film industry provides a dramatic example of Africa's long history of unequal and unstable insertion into the structures of global capitalism, and a dramatic example of the instabilities of platforms and technologies in contemporary global media environments. 'Nollywood'[1] arose in the early 1990s as a popular art based in the informal sector, which allowed it to flourish at a moment of full economic and social crisis in Nigeria; advances in video technology and the global liberalisation of media environments in this period were other conditions of its existence (see Haynes 2000a, 2011). Rapid developments in the period from 2007 to 2015, tied to the global economy, are reshaping the industry and challenging its original popular, grassroots character as transnational corporations have come to dominate the international distribution of Nigerian films and have begun to produce their own original films and television serials. The direction or directions the film industry will take is unclear, but its whole cultural and ideological character is at stake. The same or parallel global and national developments are also reshaping Nigerian cities. This chapter focuses on how the representation of Lagos has changed as Nollywood explores the city's new neoliberal penumbra.

THE DISASTER

Postindustrialism did not arrive in Nigeria as an organic evolution in its own trajectory of capitalist development – it was the result of the structural adjustment programme (SAP) imposed from without by Nigeria's creditors in 1986. The SAP collapsed Nigerian industry, along with the whole formal sector. The basic institutions of modern society largely stopped functioning, crime and corruption blossomed, and many of the most educated and dynamic citizens left the country. SAP and the subsequent global wave of democratisation following the collapse of the Soviet Union were supposed to normalise Africa as part of the global economic and political system, but the opposite happened in Nigeria. Military dictators did not need democratic support because they controlled enormous oil revenues. Beyond oil, Nigeria's relationship with the world economy became defined by the brain drain and the country's new roles as transhipment point for the international drug trade, home of the fraud known as '419', and exporter of sex workers.

For about two decades, roughly 1985 to 2005, international capitalism lost interest in Africa. It had become too poor to provide decent profits and doing business there was too troublesome. When theories of globalisation emerged, they routinely failed even to mention Africa, as James Ferguson points out. He describes how neoliberal globalisation appears in Africa not as an era but as a force that hops across the landscape, creating isolated nodes of global connection and integration (often related to extraction of minerals) that need to be carefully fenced off from the surrounding poverty (2006: 1–23).

What is special about Nigeria has been the lack of fencing. Successive governments have not been organised enough to run orderly systems of economic apartheid. Even the oil installations of the Niger Delta are spectacularly chaotic: a quarter of Nigerian oil production disappears into an enormous parallel system of illicit refineries and storage facilities, while criminal gangs and impoverished villagers punch holes in petrol pipelines and help themselves. The military regimes of the 1990s did not bother to maintain social order in the cities, either. Even in the wealthiest neighbourhoods violent criminals ranged freely, electricity and water were scarce, and garbage piled up. A lack of effective urban planning meant rich and poor were not rigorously segregated. And deep structures and values of Nigerian society militated against the neat fencing off of classes: these include an incomplete process of class formation; a nearly universal aspiration to become wealthy (at least in the dynamic cultures of southern Nigeria); and extended family structures and patron-client relationships that inherently cut across class lines. Always fundamental, such relationships became crucial for survival when modern formal structures collapsed.

A POPULAR ART

Nollywood was born out of this situation and expressed it. The leading theme of the first video films was 'get-rich-quick' – the scramble for wealth in an anomic environment, shadowed by terror of being thrown out of one's position in the crumbling social order. Prostitution, armed robbery, 419 fraud and drug dealing were prominently featured avenues to quick riches, but the signature instance was the 'money ritual': an occult practice through which wealth is magically produced by sacrificing a human being. Usually a group of cultists is involved. Such rituals, which have a long history in Nigerian cultures, gained new force as a representation of the predatory cabals that were running Nigeria, and – because in Nollywood's version, the cabal frequently requires the sacrifice of the person whom the candidate loves the most – they also represented (in the manner of television soap operas) the strain put on marriages and other intimate relationships by economic hardship and greed. The lurid representation of the attractive fruits of wickedness was coupled with a strong moral reaction that had multiple bases, including the values of village social organisation and indigenous religious traditions, the Manichaean spiritual world of Pentecostalism, and the ideal of companionate Christian marriage introduced by missionaries.

Unlike the American and Latin American soap operas that it in some ways resembles, Nollywood is not mass culture, created by corporations to sell products and train viewers as consumers in a capitalist economy (see Haynes 2000b). Nollywood grew as a popular art for and about a heterogeneous urban audience; the Igbo marketers who have mostly controlled distribution and financing are the same in culture and educational level as their core audience. (The classic essay defining the African popular arts is Barber 1987.) The industry lives through its sensitive commercial relationship with the desires of its audience, and that audience has supported a film tradition given to exploring social problems rather than hiding them (see Barrot 2008). Nollywood began with outraged moral inquiry into the sources of wealth under military rule and continued to be suspicious of wealth as well as fascinated by it, prying under the attractive surfaces for dark secrets and hidden crimes. Like film and television industries everywhere, Nollywood likes showing lifestyles far wealthier than its audience's; but ideologically, the films spoke to and for ordinary Nigerians and tended to keep the larger society in mind if not always in view. The 'family films' of the 1990s often featured upper-middle-class Lagos families ensconced behind their high compound walls and were dedicated to defending the nuclear family, but even these films often addressed challenges to the family from without. Village relatives with their social, cultural and financial demands, occult forces that might also be linked to the village, and everything that came with the severely depressed economy of the structural adjustment era all impinged on the imagination of this genre (see Haynes 2016).

LAGOS, CITY OF DREAMS AND NIGHTMARES

The natural setting for Nollywood's stories was Lagos – natural because the film industry was based and sold most of its films there, and because for Nigerians Lagos symbolises central Nollywood themes and attractions: ambition, glamour, danger and modernity. With a population of about twenty million, Lagos imposes itself on the national imagination. It was never the exclusive setting, though, and from the beginning films often oscillated between Lagos and a village or town from which the characters come, reflecting the mobility of the Nigerian population.

As discussed in a previous essay, 'Nollywood in Lagos, Lagos in Nollywood Films' (Haynes 2007), the representation of Lagos was shaped by basic structures of the industry. Nollywood is a huge industry composed of many small producers working on very small budgets (the first great hit, *Living in Bondage* (1992), was made for $12,000; by 2015 budgets typically ran from $20,000 to $80,000). A consequence of this is that Nollywood has very little infrastructure – no studios or warehouses full of props and costumes. Shooting almost always takes place in borrowed locations over which the filmmakers have very little control. This reinforces the strong tendency (inherited from Nigerian television serials, on which most of the first generation of Nollywood filmmakers had worked) for films to be composed mainly of conversations taking place inside rooms, captured with one camera in simple shot/reverse-shot patterns. It also reinforces what I have described as 'inadvertent realism': even when movies are intent on conveying glamorous lifestyles, the ambient chaos often obtrudes into the images. Because of the social diversity of its audience and personnel, Nollywood was always comfortable in all sorts of neighbourhoods.

Most early Nollywood films were shot in or around Lagos, but Lagos is a difficult, distracting and expensive place to shoot, and beginning in the late 1990s film production shifted towards south-eastern Nigeria (not coincidentally, the home of the powerful Igbo marketers). Onitsha became a strong secondary centre for financing and organising productions. By 2012, about half of all Nollywood films were being shot in and around Asaba, a quiet city across the Niger River from Onitsha. Asaba is good at providing settings for the kind of middle-class life the Nollywood audience generally aspires to: urban but pleasant and relaxed, with abundant greenery and good infrastructure.

But Asaba remains an anonymous location, almost never named and without easily identifiable landmarks. Films made there or in other cities often have establishing shots of Lagos spliced into them. In Nollywood film culture, only Lagos and (to a much lesser extent) Abuja, the political capital, are iconic urban landscapes. The establishing shots that signify Lagos are heavily stereotyped and have changed little over the years. In fact, the same shots are often used in different films. One set of these iconic images are of the imposing modern structures built during the oil boom of the 1970s: the skyline of the Lagos Island business district with its small cluster of tall buildings, and the freeways, especially the elevated one sweeping over the downtown Marina. Another set is high-angle shots (taken from those downtown tall buildings) of the exclusive residential neighbourhoods of Ikoyi (on Lagos Island) and Victoria Island; these also exploit the dramatic and distinctive natural setting of the islands, separated by narrow bodies of water and linked with bridges. A third set features the upscale shopping and entertainment streets of the Lagos mainland neighbourhoods of Ikeja and Surulere.

AFRICA RISING

The title of Vijay Mahajan's book *Africa Rising: How 900 Million African Consumers Offer More than You Think* (2009) became shorthand for a new moment in international capitalism's view of Africa. Suddenly Africa was back on their map. The international business press trumpeted the fact that six of the world's ten fastest-growing economies were in sub-Saharan Africa. Foreign direct investment poured in. For a decade, Nigeria's growth rate averaged seven percent, and in 2014 its economy was declared to have surpassed South Africa's as the largest in Africa.

Many people observed that this announcement did not change the lives of the majority of Nigerians who live on less than two dollars a day. The deep structural problems in Nigeria, stemming from bad governance and insufficient, crumbling infrastructure, were on spectacular display in 2015 as the Goodluck Jonathan administration handed over to the new president Muhammadu Buhari: the treasury was so empty that the government could not pay its employees, electricity generation reached a nadir, and a shortage of petrol left the country largely paralysed. The supply of electricity was so inadequate and undependable at the best of times that all businesses and citizens who could afford it had their own generators, but there was no petrol to run the generators. Radio and television stations had to curtail broadcasting, and cell phone networks – the heart and pride of contemporary Nigeria, which has had the most rapidly-growing telecoms market in the world – threatened to go down.

Still, some things had changed dramatically for the better: the middle class had reappeared, ready to consume, and the number of millionaires rapidly expanded. These changes were displayed most dramatically in Lagos. Successive governors of Lagos State had undertaken to make Lagos a major hub of African development and a node of the global economy. To this end the city's reputation as urban apocalypse

Fig. 1 Lagos as world capital: Establishing shot from *Lagos Cougars*

had to be overcome, and they did what had never been done before: planning to address the infrastructure needs of the whole city (see Gandy 2005, 2006; Haynes 2007). The vast slums had not yet seen much change, but downtown traffic moved better, crime had been radically reduced, and generally the city had become much more liveable. An ambitious project was underway to build a whole new district of business and residential towers on landfill offshore, in the manner of the Persian Gulf Emirates. Large gated residential developments had been built on the outskirts of the city, and fashionable new residential neighbourhoods had sprung up along parts of the waterfront. The Lekki Peninsula, stretching east from exclusive Victoria Island, had become an enormous enclave for the prosperous.

These transformations are informed by other developments. Estimates of the number of Nigerians living outside of Nigeria run up to twenty or even thirty million. This diaspora is largely a product of the brain drain and is very well educated and well off. The expatriates never lost touch with Nigeria and began moving back or shuttling back and forth, making investments, and encouraging their foreign-born children to make careers in the newly booming economy. They are having a strong and highly visible impact. The Lagos waterfront residential developments are associated with them, and a striking number of the younger generation of television announcers, talk show hosts and other media personalities have British or American accents.

And class formation is taking hold. In the first couple of generations after Independence in 1960, it was common, even normal, for professionals to have parents who were illiterate farmers, and the vast majority of the population either lived in a village or had strong connections to one. This is much less true now. People comment on the deculturation of children who grow up hardly speaking the language of their ancestors because they live in a multiethnic city and spend their time in school or plugged into digital media – all environments dominated by English or Pidgin.

Nollywood, in response to these and other influences, has begun to segment. Nollywood was always complex and the segmentation is far from complete, but several distinct kinds of markets and of filmmaking have emerged. 'Asaba films', as they are often called, are the low end of the market and are under the direct control of the marketers in nearby Onitsha. They are cranked out quickly on very low budgets (the average in 2013 was about $25,000) and are sold as video compact discs by small shops and street hawkers with little publicity besides word of mouth.

At the high end of the market is so-called 'New Nollywood' (the name became current around 2010), consisting of independent producer/directors who aspire to make films with larger budgets and of high enough artistic and technical quality to be screened in cinemas and at international film festivals (see Adejunmobi 2014; Haynes 2014). This initiative continues the long-standing desire of the more ambitious Lagos directors to escape from the conditions of the market for discs run by the Igbo traders. These films eventually end up in that market (where they are usually quickly pirated), but first they will have made back most of their budgets from other sources. The new multiplex cinemas that have been built in Nigerian cities since 2004 are a key element. These cinemas are almost all inside new upscale shopping malls and charge what are by Nigerian standards very high prices, restricting their clientele to the elite. Expatriate Nigerian audiences are another indispensable element, reached through cinemas in London, ad hoc screenings in the United States and elsewhere, the sale of foreign DVD rights and the Internet. Broadcast rights are sold to terrestrial, satellite and cable television broadcasters in Nigeria and around the world.

CORPORATE INTERESTS IN NOLLYWOOD

The newest element in the situation is the role now played by transnational corporations. Nollywood grew around networks set up by market traders operating out of tiny shops. Their jealous control of distribution and the opaque, informal character of the industry – little or nothing is written down and piracy and cheating are endemic – kept formal capitalist companies and banks out of the picture, though the industry's huge revenues and potential caught their interest. John C. McCall (2012) argues Nollywood's commercial economy is not properly capitalist at all. An attempt in 2007 by the National Film and Video Censors Board to formalise the industry was bitterly (and successfully) opposed by the marketers (see Obiaya 2012; Bud 2014).

This character of the industry, coupled with the ease of pirating video, meant that Nollywood has never controlled the foreign distribution of its films, even as Nollywood became immensely popular in most countries across the African continent, the Caribbean, and in African expatriate communities everywhere. The films were reproduced and distributed abroad by small-scale entrepreneurs, usually African but often not Nigerian. At first they were almost all pirated (see Jedlowski 2013).

The first important corporate intervention was in 2004 when the South African media conglomerate MultiChoice launched its first Africa Magic satellite channel, broadcasting Nollywood films to 41 countries in Africa. Africa Magic has a huge audience in Nigeria, where many other television channels also show Nollywood films. The sale of discs plummeted: why buy films when they were on TV, 24/7? The derisory payments producers got for television rights did not begin to compensate for the decline in disc sales, leading to a prolonged crisis of profitability in the industry.

Nigeria has a high rate of Internet connectivity, but as of 2015 the Internet was too slow to allow streaming of feature films. But abroad, the Internet became decisive as a distribution platform. At first the situation was anarchic, with fans putting up thousands of films on YouTube for free viewing. Then iROKO Partners, an Internet startup created by a young Londoner of Nigerian parentage, Jason Njoku, set itself up as 'the Netflix of Africa'. Launched in 2011, it quickly dominated the business of streaming Nollywood films. It acquired the backing of international venture capital and by 2015 had a catalogue of five thousand Nollywood films and subscribers in 178 countries.

Both MultiChoice and iROKO Partners have begun producing original films and serial dramas in Nigeria. MultiChoice began in 2008 with *Tinsel*, a serial about the entertainment industry. The most expensively produced programme on Nigerian television, it is produced in Lagos under close supervision by South African executives. In 2013 MultiChoice launched into a novel form of low-budget production that blurs the distinction between film and television.[2] MultiChoice's affiliates Africa Magic and EbonyLife TV commissioned large batches of one-hour films with budgets that were extremely low even by Nigerian standards: about $8,000. The results resemble reality television, the cheapest kind of television programming.

The point of these films is the style, the look. The producers who contracted to make them were given strict instructions that the locations must be glamorous and the actors young and beautiful, speaking clear English (Kenneth Gyang, personal communication). Mo Abudu, the founder and CEO of EbonyLife TV, is explicit about her cultural intentions: she aspires to become the African Oprah and has told her staff their model should be *Real Housewives of Atlanta* (see Tsika 2015).

NOLLYWOOD'S NEW LAGOS: APPARENT AUTONOMY

Lagos Cougars (Desmond Elliot, 2013) is a more substantial Nollywood movie that illustrates parallel cultural tendencies. In March 2015, it was among the first batch of Nollywood films to be streamed by Netflix. Emem Isong wrote, cast, produced and executive produced the film. Isong has been making romantic comedies about young Lagosian urban professionals, strongly influenced by American and British models, since the late 1990s; at first she had this genre nearly to herself, but now it claims a large share of the market. As the film's title indicates, the professional women at its centre are no longer young, and all three have relationships with younger men. The

Fig. 2 *Lagos Cougars*: at home in fashionable luxury.

three friends are differentiated in the manner of *Sex and the City*. One is brazenly cynical in her pursuit of toy boys. Another, innocent and sincere, gets rid of her cheating fiancé in favour of true love with an employee at her fashion house. The third is persuaded to have a fling with a young man who turns out to be her son's best friend; she resolves the resulting dilemma by sacrificing her feelings and desires for the sake of propriety and her relationship with her son. The movie divides its time between Lekki, the posh Lagos neighbourhood described above, and Houston, Texas, home to a large and prosperous Nigerian community. It is remarkably difficult to tell Houston and Lekki apart, especially once we get off the well-manicured streets into the interiors of homes, clubs and restaurants – everything has the same quietly opulent suburban style.

One might compare this film with a genre stemming from Kenneth Nnebue's *Glamour Girls* (1994), the first English-language Nollywood film, which is also about independent women, no longer young, on the hunt for money and sexual pleasure. *Glamour Girls*, embodying a popular perspective, is simultaneously scandalised by women who do not obey conservative social norms and interested in what such women can show about a ruthless and mercenary Lagos where the men are no better than the women. *Lagos Cougars* has no such hard edges or exploratory interest; it is entirely dedicated to sympathetic engagement with the emotional lives of the women and is tightly framed around their comfortable environment.

A striking number of films and television serials deploy a new formula: yuppie women sharing a flat have contrasting personalities, romantic lives and different professions, all of them fashionable and many of them typical of Saskia Sassen's global city of outsourced professionals (1991) or Richard Florida's city of creative communities (2005). The fashion design shop and boutique of *Lagos Cougars* is an example. iROKO's serial *Poisoned Bait* centres on a literary agent and her best friend, a struggling writer. The serial *Classique* (from veteran producer Zeb Ejiro) is about friends who start a talent agency, contrasting one's strict professionalism with another's readiness to try anything that promises money.

Last Flight to Abuja (2012), by the leading 'New Nollywood' director Obi Emelonye, glamorises corporate culture itself rather than capitalism's creative penumbra. A title follows an opening sequence of terror aboard a smoke-filled airplane: 'In 2006, a series of air mishaps rocked Nigeria's aviation industry. This is the story of one of them.' In standard disaster movie fashion, the film then backtracks to give us the stories of various passengers. First we see a staff meeting of an IT company in Lagos. The Chairman, happy with the latest sales report, hands out tickets to Abuja for an all-expenses-paid retreat for relaxation and company team-building. The premonitory terror of one employee's daughter keeps him off the plane, and the pilot's wife's nightmares cause him to change his schedule though, ironically, this puts him onto the doomed aircraft. These premonitions and the general attention to the twists of fate leading up to boarding the plane introduce a characteristically Nollywood fascination with the workings of destiny into the slick international surfaces of air travel.

Fig. 3 From the credits of *Last Flight to Abuja*.

David (Jim Iyke), a sales manager at the company, boards and sits next to Suzie (Omotola Jalade-Ekeinde). She is an Abuja-based executive in a commuting relationship with her fiancé, with whom we saw her talk on the phone as she drove through Abuja's sleek corporate cityscape. He wants her to quit her job, but she is proud of her MBA and doesn't want to be a housewife. She flew to Lagos on the spur of the moment because he sounded unhappy, but there she finds another woman in his bed. So she catches the last flight back to Abuja. She shares all this with David in the next seat. He reveals that he is also a lovelorn workaholic. When the plane fills with smoke, he asks her for a date so they'll have something to live for.

Adesola (Hakeem Kae-Kazim), the company's chief sales manager, is also on board. Flashbacks tell his story. An intern with whom he once had an affair knows he has been shaving money off the company's contracts and is blackmailing him. He accidentally kills her as they fight in a hotel room. He realises on the plane that his company ID fell out of his pocket into a pool of her blood. Auditors are on the trail of his professional malfeasance, and the police are waiting in Abuja to arrest him for murder. In the crash his leg gets caught under a seat (with fatalistic cynicism, he had refused to brace himself as instructed), so he alone is unable to escape before the plane explodes in flames. On the TV news, Suzie's faithless fiancé sees her embracing David in front of the inferno as an emergency rescue crew efficiently goes about its business.

We are shown why the plane goes down: a passenger checked a car battery as luggage and it shorted out, bursting into flames. We also see a mechanic completing a pre-flight inspection, suggesting the blameless competence of the airline. The glamour of air travel is emphasised by a sequence of the pilot sweeping through the terminal with a flight attendant on each arm while people watch admiringly. A woman comments, 'There's something damn crazy about a pilot in uniform.' In the cockpit, before the trouble starts the pilot and female co-pilot carry on a conversation that continues the film's preoccupations with love relationships, fidelity and the gender double standard in the context of demanding careers. If being a pilot makes him sexually glamorous, it seems to destroy her desirability, even though she is beautiful – men find her intimidating, or perhaps suspect she is a lesbian. The whole conversation, especially the male pilot's responsible management of his sexual power (he flirts but keeps to his marriage vows), reinforces the film's adulation of the airlines and its conservative values: competent professionals are in control as they should be, the virtuous natural leaders of society.

Hollywood hasn't felt this way about air travel in decades, and in Hollywood disaster movies there is usually a villain: a terrorist on board, an avaricious corporate executive risking lives by cutting corners, or an elaborate conspiracy of some kind that may express dark suspicions about the nature of the American economy and polity. In *Last Flight*, there is only the battery and the principle of an inherent justice that underlies Nollywood's melodramatic plots. Adesola's misdeeds will be punished by fate before the authorities get to him. Obscure promptings springing from the love of a wife or daughter may save a man. The true lovers Suzie and David, battered by a society of philanderers and gold-diggers, find one another and have their union broadcast.

The film's opening title reminds the audience of the series of 'air mishaps' in 2006, and ends with a dedication 'to the victims of the June 3rd disasters' – a 2012 event in which a plane crashed while approaching the Lagos airport, killing everyone on board and setting a neighbourhood on fire. In the film, the air traffic controller in Lagos wishes he'd gone home before the crisis, but otherwise the film gives no hint, and actually works hard to avoid any suspicion that there might be anything systemic about the crashes.

The facts are otherwise. The film is clearly modelled on an October 2005 crash, which killed not one sinner but all 117 people on board. The authorities did not respond with rapid, competent authority. When the plane disappeared from radar it took hours to locate the crash site, though it was less than twenty miles north of Lagos and a fireball had lit up the night sky. Because the passenger manifest was inaccurate, as they commonly were given chaotic boarding procedures, it took time to determine who had died (see Polgreen 2005). By the time the authorities arrived on the scene, villagers from the area had pillaged the wreck, apparently making off with the black

Fig. 4 *Last Flight to Abuja*: the romance of air travel.

box voice and data recorders. Absent the black boxes and any survivors, the official commission of inquiry could not establish the cause of the crash. It did find that the plane had technical defects and was not following an adequate maintenance regime and so should not have been flying, and that the undertrained and overworked pilot also should not have been flying (see Anon. 2014). Three other spectacular crashes within the next eighteen months killed hundreds more. Outraged protests brought rxfeal reforms and dramatic improvement; Nigerian airspace ceased to be considered the most dangerous in the world, though challenges remain.

Why this weirdly complete and elaborate misrepresentation of the event, even as *Last Flight* explicitly refers to it, exploiting the power of the public's memory?

The film feels like corporate propaganda though it was not financed by an airline or other corporation. The credits and the bonus 'Making of' documentary on the DVD illustrate the resourceful exploitation of personal networks typical of New Nollywood productions. The money came from Emelonye's brother, a businessman, and other 'friends and family'. Emelonye lives in Britain and recruited young Britons as editor, director of photography, co-producer and composer. Emelonye boasts of the film's high budget; they shot in the airport for fourteen days, a conspicuously expensive thing to do. High-end equipment was rented from Hollywood. The casting is a tribute to the drawing power of the Nollywood brand, including Hakeem Kae-Kazim, a British Hollywood actor, and major stars from the Hausa and Yoruba film industries as well as Nollywood.

The film perhaps veers towards corporate propaganda and whitewashes the realities of the crash out of pride in the new shiny corporate dimension of Nigeria – an expatriate's pride (shared with the African diasporic audiences indispensable to New Nollywood projects), concerned to counter racist stereotypes about African backwardness. Perhaps the production was also carried away by its own Hollywood-like ability to simulate the world of air travel and the crash of a jetliner – an unprecedented technical accomplishment for Nollywood.

Last Flight is not the product of Nollywood's integration with corporate capitalism, then, but it demonstrates eligibility for such integration. Emelonye's 2015 film *Thy Will Be Done* was financed by ROC Studios, iROKO Partner's production and financing division, and it premiered at the Southbank IMAX theatre in London amidst publicity about Nollywood taking over the largest, most iconic screen in Britain.

Revelling in the culture of business and success is nothing new for Nollywood, which always catered to its audience's aspirations. Near the beginning of *Last Flight* we hear a radio DJ saying, 'be optimistic and embrace change' – a peppy dose of official ideology for transnational capitalist strivers, but the phrase would have resonated with the young careerists' great-grandparents, market women or farmers turning entrepreneurially to cocoa cultivation for the cash to educate their children. In Lagos, two-thirds of jobs are in the informal sector, but the 600,000 people who move to the city each year are dreaming of something better (see Brown 2015), and they like entertainment that shows their aspirations, not their realities.

But Nollywood mostly did not present wealth in isolation from a bigger picture. What is new is the consolidation of a Potemkin Village version of the country in which the private lives of the privileged fill the screen, their apparently autonomous reality obscuring much of what the old Nollywood knew. Historically, Nollywood has taken the perspective of the nation, not of a class fraction.

IT'S COMPLICATED: OTHER TENDENCIES AND AN UNDECIDED FUTURE

This tendency to move upscale is strong but not dominant. Both the television broadcasters and the Internet companies are, after all, in the business of providing huge amounts of content to suit viewers of various tastes, classes, cultures and nationalities, which should temper the desire to brand themselves in an exclusively glamorous mould. Films from the Yoruba and Hausa branches of the Nigerian film industry do well on these platforms even with audiences not from those ethnic groups (see Ekwuazi 2014), partly (it seems) because the films are more deeply embedded in African culture and less dedicated to chasing after Western lifestyles.

iROKO Partners' first foray into producing an original series was *Festac Town* (2014–), named after a Lagos neighbourhood and created by Mary Remmy Njoku. She is a Nollywood actress, now the chief executive of ROC Studios and the wife of Jason Njoku, iROKO's founder. At that London IMAX premiere, the couple was photographed on the red carpet looking like movie moguls.

But the character she plays in *Festac Town* is the opposite of glamorous. Justina is unemployed and extremely poor, living with her young twin daughters in a single room, pregnant with another child. The show takes a level view of her life, toning down Nollywood's usual sentimentality and melodrama. In early episodes we watch her losing her struggles to find a job, provide for her children, and deal with her

Fig. 5 Establishing shot in opening credits of *Festac Town*

Fig. 5 *Festac Town*: Mary Remmy Njoku as Justina

depression. *Festac Town* captures the human costs of life in Lagos, the constriction of living in small, dilapidated spaces, the desperate strict parenting meant to keep children from being swept away into the ambient wastage of human life, the hope of giving them the education she never had, the brutal demands for overdue rent by a landlord who spews accusations about her sexuality, the failing attempt to keep body and soul together through selling vegetables to her neighbours, the trudging around looking for wage labour, the fervent prayers as her last resort. But her story also shows what keeps people going in these conditions: a warm, open disposition that gives her a place in the fabric of the neighbourhood and secures relationships with benefactors.

Festac Town has a wide social range, firmly anchored at the lower end. The opening credit sequence explores Festac's streets from a moving vehicle, ending at a banged-up apartment building. Inside, a group of prostitutes recurrently quarrel in Pidgin. Nearly the whole show is in Pidgin, the lingua franca of southern Nigeria – the pungent popular speech carefully excluded from EbonyLife TV. Outside on the streets, young men take drugs and drink, the fruits of criminal activities organised by a crime boss who has connections to wealthy men who are themselves linked to powerful politicians. It is through these connections that we work our way up the social scale.

The show picks up the mantle of the enormously popular Nigerian television series of the 1960s and 1970s such as *Village Headmaster* and *Masquerade*, which deliberately created an image of the Nigerian nation as an expansive family or neighbourhood with characters of various ethnicities, ages, classes and educational levels, all contributing to a rich comic play of perspectives and the linguistic stew of the dialogue. *Festac Town*'s astringent realism is much darker; like Nollywood (and like HBO's panoramic urban dramas, a possible model), ROC Studios can take advantage of a freedom never possible on government-controlled broadcast television. The description of the series on the iROKOtv website reads, 'The secret lives of the upper, middle, and lower class living in Festac. Their fears, tears, pains and victories.' This might serve as a thematic summary of all the thousands of Nollywood films: the wide social range, the emphasis on unveiling what is hidden, the primacy of florid emotionality, the deep interest in tribulation and the congenital optimism that promises final victory.

The future direction of Nigerian film and television is profoundly uncertain, then, and their social nature is at stake. The social and cultural stratification of Nigerian society (and Nigerian cities) will clearly continue, and transnational corporations will clearly continue to play a major role in Nigerian media. In one scenario, the corporations quickly become dominant and Nollywood turns into another mass culture industry. In another scenario, Nollywood finds an entirely new platform and economic basis: thousands of small community cinemas in popular neighbourhoods, supplementing the proliferating upscale multiplexes. As of 2015, there was much talk of such community theatres but they did not yet exist (see Haynes 2014). The revenues they generated would restore the clear hegemony of the tastes and desires of a broad popular audience over film production, while New Nollywood directors reached more elite audiences and the corporations controlled international distribution and provided the stability and deep financing for television serials. Nollywood's whole history is of managing to survive in the face of rapidly shifting and apparently impossible circumstances, and of maintaining a vision of a broad social cohesion in spite of all the provocations of recent Nigerian history. So there are reasons for optimism about its future.

NOTES

1. 'Nollywood' is sometimes used to mean the whole Nigerian video film industry, which has three main branches making films in English, Hausa and Yoruba; 'Nollywood' is also used to refer exclusively to the English-language branch located in southern Nigeria, which is how I use it, though much of the following applies to the other branches as well.
2. That distinction has always been exceptionally narrow and permeable in the case of Nollywood, which largely grew out of Nigerian television (see Obaseki 2009). Nollywood films are almost always viewed on television screens, and their aesthetics resemble televisual forms (see Adejunmobi 2003). Many producers and directors move back and forth between film and television.

BIBLIOGRAPHY

Adejunmobi, Moradewun (2003) 'Video Film Technology and Serial Narratives in West Africa', in Foluke Ogunleye (ed.) *African Video Film Today*. Manzini,

Swaziland: Academic Publishers, 51–68.

____ (2014) 'Evolving Nollywood Templates for Minor Transnational Film', *Black Camera*, 5, 2, 74–94.

Anon. (2014) 'Bellview Airlines Flight 210'. Wikipedia; https://en.wikipedia.org/wiki/Bellview_Airlines_Flight_210

Barber, Karin (1987) 'Popular Arts in Africa', *African Studies Review*, 30, 3, 1–78.

Barrot, Pierre (2009) 'Audacity, Scandal & Censorship', in Pierre Barrot (ed.) *Nollywood: The Video Phenomenon in Nigeria*. Bloomington: Indiana University Press, 43–50.

Brown, Ryan Lenora (2015) 'In Nigeria, the Hustle that makes Lagos Bustle', *Christian Science Monitor*, 28 June; http://news.yahoo.com/nigeria-hustle-makes-lagos-bustle-110001264.html

Bud, Alexander (2014) 'The End of Nollywood's Guilded Age? Marketers, the State, and the Struggle for Distribution', *Critical African Studies*, 6, 1, 91–121.

Ekwuazi, Hyginus (2014) 'The Perception/Reception of DSTV/Multichoice's Africa Magic Channels by Selected Nigerian Audiences', *Journal of African Cinemas*, 6, 1, 21–48.

Ferguson, James (2006) *Global Shadows: Africa in the Neoliberal World Order*. Durham: Duke University Press.

Florida, Richard (2005) *Cities and the Creative Class*. London: Routledge.

Gandy, Matthew (2005) 'Learning From Lagos', *New Left Review*, 33, 36–52.

____ (2006) 'Planning, Anti-Planning and the Infrastructure Crisis Facing Metropolitan Lagos', *Urban Studies*, 43, 2, 371–96.

Haynes, Jonathan (ed.) ([1997] 2000a) *Nigerian Video Films*. Athens: Ohio University Press.

____ (2000b) 'Introduction', in Jonathan Haynes (ed.) *Nigerian Video Films*. Athens: Ohio University Press, 1–36.

____ (2007) 'Nollywood in Lagos, Lagos in Nollywood Films', *Africa Today*, 54, 2, 130–50.

____ (2011) 'African Cinema and Nollywood: Contradictions', *Situations*, 4, 1, 67–90.

____ (2014) '"New Nollywood": Kunle Afolayan', *Black Camera*, 5, 2, 53–73.

____ (2016) *Nollywood: The Creation of Nigerian Film Genres*. Chicago: University of Chicago Press.

Jedlowski, Alessandro (2013) 'From Nollywood to Nollyworld: Processes of Transnationalization in the Nigerian Video Film Industry', in Matthias Krings and Onookome Okome (eds) *Global Nollywood and Beyond: Transnational Dimensions of an African Video Film Industry*. Bloomington: Indiana University Press, 25–45.

Mahajan, Vijay (2009) *Africa Rising: How 900 Million African Consumers Offer More than You Think*. Upper Saddle River: Pearson.

McCall, John C. (2012) 'The Capital Gap: Nollywood and the Limits of Informal Trade', *Journal of African Cinemas*, 4, 1, 9–23.

Obaseki, Don Pedro (2008) 'Nigerian Video as the "Child of Television"', in Pierre Barrot (ed.) *Nollywood: The Video Phenomenon in Nigeria*. Bloomington: Indiana University Press, 72–6.

Obiaya, Ikechukwu (2012) 'Restructuring the Nigerian Video Film Industry', unpublished PhD thesis, Universidad de Navarra.

Polgreen, Lydia and Tony Iyare (2005) 'Plane Crashes in Nigeria: All 117 Aboard Are Probably Dead', *New York Times*, 24 October; http://www.nytimes.com/2005/10/24/world/africa/plane-crashes-in-nigeria-all-117-aboard-are-probably-dead.html?_r=0

Sassen, Saskia (1991) *The Global City: New York, London, Tokyo*. Princeton: Princeton University Press.

Tsika, Noah (2015) 'From the Chibok Girls to the Ebola Outbreak: Nollywood's Responsiveness to Current Events'. Paper presented at the Society for Cinema and Media Studies Annual Conference, Montreal, 28 March.

GLOBAL CITY IMAGINARIES

NEW URBAN AND MEDIA ECOLOGIES IN CONTEMPORARY BUENOS AIRES

JOANNA PAGE

Although globalisation and deindustrialisation have triggered profound structural changes in many regions of the world, in the Global North the impact of these has been mitigated by the relative strength of regulatory institutions and a continuing commitment to the welfare state. In Latin America, by contrast, such changes have taken place in a largely deregulated environment and are at least partly responsible for a marked increase in social and economic inequality. In Argentina, the neoliberal policies brought in by the military regime of 1976–83 and pursued relentlessly by President Menem in the 1990s have exacerbated trends evident in post-industrial societies in other parts of the world, such as large-scale privatisation, the incursion of heavyweight multinationals, the curtailing of workers' rights, the proliferation of short-term contracts and significant cuts in social welfare. As Maristella Svampa observes, Argentina has become 'una sociedad excluyente' (an exclusionary society), in which a deep gulf separates the security-obsessed urban elite – participating fully in globalised virtual networks via the Internet, purchasing global brands, living in gated communities and sending their children to private schools – from a much greater proportion of the population who are unemployed or trapped in precarious and low-paid forms of labour, often within the informal sector (2005: 47–9, 149, 151, 169–70).

Argentine cinema of the late 1990s and the first years of the new millennium sought to capture the experience of the marginalised within an inhuman city that offers neither refuge nor hope of a release from poverty and exclusion. As Gonzalo Aguilar suggests, a number of films focus on 'los descartes del capitalismo' (what capitalism has discarded), tracing the erratic itineraries of vagabonds, delinquents and other nomads through Buenos Aires (2006: 42–53). The unemployed youths of

Adrián Caetano and Bruno Stagnaro's *Pizza, birra, faso* (*Pizza, Beer, and Cigarettes*, 1997) roam through an unhomely city, whose fractured spaces are emphasised by the film's aesthetics of discontinuity (see Page 2009: 37–43). Violence and lawlessness characterise the city of Caetano's *Bolivia* (2001) and *Un oso rojo* (*A Red Bear*, 2001), as well as Pablo Trapero's *El bonaerense* (2002).[1] Other films strike a nostalgic key, charting the erosion of social spaces that once resisted the lure of modernisation and commercialisation, such as the *club de barrio* (neighbourhood sports club) in José Campanella's *Luna de Avellaneda* (*Avellaneda's Moon*, 2004), or the old-fashioned local tango bar in Daniel Burak's *Bar El Chino* (2003). Notwithstanding widespread unemployment around the turn of the century, cinema of this period also registers the huge growth in service industries that accompanied the affluent 1990s and continues to sustain the everyday lives of the city's wealthiest inhabitants. Martín Rejtman's films *Silvia Prieto* (1998) and *Los guantes mágicos* (*The Magic Gloves*, 2003) abound in what one character airily calls 'services for the middle class', from massages, health spas, singing lessons, yoga classes and professional dog-walking.

The city of these films is shaped by a faltering and cruelly uneven modernisation that has only increased social inequality and segregation. Although manifestly alienating and dehumanising, this is not the highly rationalised modern metropolis described by Georg Simmel at the beginning of the twentieth century, whose 'intellectualism' and 'calculating exactness' leave no room for the expression of human personality (2002: 12, 13). It is, instead, a divided and dysfunctional city of multiple exclusions, riddled with 'the *black holes of informational capitalism*', in which the 'individualisation' of work leaves workers unprotected and alone, 'to bargain their fate vis-à-vis constantly changing market forces', and destitution leads to the 'perverse integration' of excluded individuals by means of criminal activity (Castells 2010: 167, 74; emphasis in original). If the modern city of Simmel's analysis binds its inhabitants to 'a firmly fixed framework of time' (2002: 13), the contemporary Latin American city seems to be governed by multiple and contradictory temporalities, as the global elite embrace rapid technological advance, leaving vast areas of the city to fall into decline and shantytowns to spring up among the rusting ruins of industrial zones, creating a landscape of oxidised scrap iron that is, as Beatriz Sarlo observes (2009: 81), 'producto del trabajo y de la desaparición del trabajo' (the product of work and the disappearance of work). What unites its citizens is a shared experience of insecurity: even the fortressing of the wealthy in gated communities patrolled by private security guards cannot protect them from crime.

This essay will focus on an alternative vision of the affordances and constraints of the contemporary city as constructed in a more recent film from Argentina, Gustavo Taretto's *Medianeras* (*Sidewalls*, 2011). My reading will draw on the post-human and post-anthropocentric perspectives emerging from studies associated with new materialism, in which human agency is only one of the many agential forces that animate the material world. Extending the complex interactions between the organic and the inorganic described by ecology to the contemporary city throws light on the dynamic relationship between humans and non-humans within the space of the city; it also brings a helpful counterbalance to those discourses of the global city which emphasise virtual experience, wireless networking, transnationalism, and the effects of cultural homogenisation, tempting us to overlook the extent to which our experience of the city remains thoroughly embodied and embedded in the material and the local.

Combining elements of the romantic comedy genre with those of a film essay, *Medianeras* assembles a heterogeneous audiovisual language that features techniques more often associated with architectural animation and television advertising. Taretto had previously worked for an advertising agency for many years, and the use of split screens, animation, simple messages and readily recognisable icons lends a buoyant humour to his tale of two neurotic thirty-somethings searching for love in Argentina's capital city. Focusing neither on the very rich nor the completely destitute, Taretto chooses as his protagonists two members of the expanding 'creative class' which has typically driven economic growth in the post-industrial context.[2] Martín and Mariana live in tiny apartments in downtown Buenos Aires. Martín has lived a hermit-like existence for two years: working from home as a freelance website designer allows him to avoid confronting his fear of public spaces. Mariana, trained as an architect, has yet to find work in that field and makes ends meet by designing shop window displays. After the difficult break-up of a four-year relationship, she too lives alone, with only her mannequins to talk to, bathe and caress.

The representation of Buenos Aires in Taretto's film marks a clear departure in urban cinema in Argentina. While it partially echoes earlier depictions of Buenos Aires as alienating, dehumanising and ungovernable, its purpose is not to denounce social inequality or to lament the plight of Castells's 'Fourth World'. Neither is it, on the other hand, to trumpet the coming of the globalised network city, in which the boundaries of place and the material conditions of urban existence are seemingly overcome and social and cultural experience increasingly move into virtual and mediatised realms. Instead, as I will show, the film adopts an ecological framework for understanding the city as a place in which the virtual and the material, and the human and nonhuman, encounter each other in complex and often unpredictable ways. In this way, it resonates strongly with recent approaches to urban studies that draw on ecological paradigms to understand the nature of interactions between the material fabric and forces that comprise the city and its human inhabitants. This emphasis on material engagement also prompts and informs the film's reflexive treatment of new media ecologies.

The Buenos Aires we are shown in *Medianeras* is not the city redesigned at the turn of the nineteenth century to boast grand Haussmann-inspired boulevards, public parks and broad vistas. Instead, it is an unregulated mishmash of apartment blocks, built without the guidance of a blueprint, a sense of aesthetic coherence, or any thought to the wellbeing of its inhabitants. The voiceover at the beginning of the film, later revealed to be Martín's, blames the city's architects for a whole host of social and psychological ills, from depression to suicide. Crammed into shoebox

Fig. 1 Unplanned growth and heterogeneous architectural styles in Buenos Aires, as depicted in *Medianeras*.

apartments with little natural illumination, the city's inhabitants (both human and canine) suffer from neuroses – agoraphobia, claustrophobia, insomnia – and manifest destructive behaviours associated with over-confinement or over-stimulation in teeming public places. In the densely populated city, the acts of others have an inordinate effect on us: Mariana is driven to rage and then to tears at the sound of her neighbour's piano-playing, and the fatal leap of a suicidal dog from an apartment balcony causes a woman below to have a heart attack and a man to be hit by a car.

Thus far, the experience of the city represented in *Medianeras* recalls Benjamin's notion of shock, as a response to the rush of stimuli in the urban context. The individual moving through the traffic of a large city experiences 'a series of shocks and collisions', writes Benjamin; 'at dangerous intersections, nervous impulses flow through him in rapid succession' (2003: 328). As Ash Amin and Nigel Thrift point out, for both Simmel and Benjamin, overstimulation on the streets of the modern city provokes a 'neurasthenic' reaction, producing fatigue and anomie (2002: 33). Several decades on, in the networked, mediatised city, even homes provide little respite from the frenzy of the street. No distinction is drawn between workspace and living space in *Medianeras*: Martín has effectively converted his apartment into an office, and Mariana's apartment is crammed with architectural models and mannequins in various states of repair. Distinctions between inside and outside are effectively undone: both are embraced in the mediasphere, as the world's tragedies played out daily on television screens and posted within seconds on webpages. As Scott McQuire observes, media technology has brought about 'a profound *de-territorialisation* of the home, insofar as what we see and experience within its walls is no longer contained by their limits' (2008: 10).

The film focuses on the impact of media technology, for good or ill, on subjectivity and sociability in the contemporary city. As we are shown the tangled skeins of overhead cables that betray the improvised, hasty introduction of fibreoptic connectivity in Buenos Aires, Mariana wonders '¿Cuándo seremos una ciudad inalámbrica?

[...] ¿Tantos kilómetros de cables, sirven para unirnos o para mantenernos alejados a cada uno en su lugar?' (When we will be a wireless city? All those kilometres of cables: do they serve to unite us or keep us part, each in their own home?'). The transformation of the home into a media centre, supplied with home entertainment systems and the Internet, multiplies connections between the city's inhabitants and an increasingly transnational network of media advertising, information and culture; at the same time, of course, they may therefore become more isolated, falling back on home entertainment to fill their time in a cycle of consumption that points to 'the almighty role of the cultural industries in advancing the neoliberal project' (Georgiou 2013: 23). Martín does everything online: he banks online, reads magazines, downloads music, listens to the radio, shops for food, watches films, chats, studies, plays games and has sex online. He reflects that 'Internet me acercó al mundo pero me alejó de la vida' (the Internet brought me close to the world but took me further from life). As Sherry Turkle suggests in *Alone Together* – her study of the impact of technology as 'the architect of our intimacies' – our networked existence 'allows us to hide from each other, even as we are tethered to each other' (2011: 1). The characters of *Medianeras* often use communication technologies such as mobile phones to keep each other at arm's length in this way, pretending to be unavailable when it suits them. However, *Medianeras* does encourage us to see the potential in media technologies to create new forms of sociability. Both Martín and Mariana, naturally reserved individuals, share their emotions with much greater ease online in anonymous chatrooms. Mark Deuze reminds us that 'the same media that isolate and divide also heighten people's awareness of others' and that this may lead to the dissolving of the boundary 'between solitude and solidarity' (2014: 208). On more than one occasion, the film cuts between scenes in which each character, enclosed in their apartment, cries over the same film as the other or is uplifted by the same song on the radio, thereby suggesting the role of media in producing a kind of shared affective experience that transcends the boundaries of physical space.

In the media-saturated city, personal relationships become infused with the principles and practices of advertising. Martín, searching women's profiles on an online dating site, reflects that his dates are like McDonalds: the photos are always bigger and more delicious than reality, and he feels the same disappointment on a date as when eating a Big Mac. The pernicious lies sold by online dating agencies – that your perfect match exists out there, somewhere, and can be found by comparing tickboxes of interests and preferences – are underpinned by the same promise as many advertising campaigns, which dupe us into believing that buying the right product, with the right features, will revolutionise our lives. As a film, *Medianeras* could itself be accused of peddling many of the same illusions. On the somewhat dubious basis of their shared loneliness and similarly long list of neuroses, Martín and Mariana are presented as the ideal match for each other, and their future happiness will be secured if only they can find each other. The film's plot is dedicated to orchestrating this encounter, and its frequent resort to parallel editing foretells the inevitable convergence of the protagonists' paths. Cross-cut sequences that show Martín walking from right to left across the screen and Mariana from left to right tantalise us with the possibility that they are just about to bump into each other on the street, and their actions are often mirrored in matched shots, in which one character is seen unknowingly to repeat the gestures of the other. Like most romantic comedies, the film comes to an abrupt end when the couple finally gets together, leaving intact the dream of living happily ever after.

Even expressions of individualism, rebellion and creativity are co-opted by the dominant discourses of commerce in the film. The *medianeras* of the title refer to the sidewalls of apartment buildings, which are left blank and windowless as they adjoin neighbouring blocks. As the film explains, in recent decades they have been converted into 'un medio más para la publicidad' (yet another advertising space), plastered with enormous adverts for retail brands or arrows directing citizens to the nearest fast food establishment. Against all planning regulations, small and improvised windows have been introduced in these sidewalls. Both Martín and Mariana contract someone to knock a window through the wall of their apartments, in order to let in more light. As they lean out afterwards to enjoy the view, a long shot reveals that Mariana's window has been inserted at the end of an arrow in an advert pointing to 'todo lo que estás buscando' (everything you have been looking for) while Martín's peeks out of the crotch panel of a pair of boxer shorts sported by a male model in an advert for the clothing retailer Absolut Joy. As Gisela Castro suggests (2013), the illegal windows introduce 'un elemento anárquico y jocoso' (an anarchic and comic element) in these advertisements. However, their humorous placement also signals the extent to which personal relationships and the business of searching for a partner have become governed by the discourses and practices of the market.

Medianeras openly acknowledges the insertion of its own love story within the market by foregrounding its strategies of transmediation. When Martín and Mariana finally meet and see in each other what they have been looking for, the film cuts immediately to a full-screen shot of the YouTube homepage. The words 'mariana

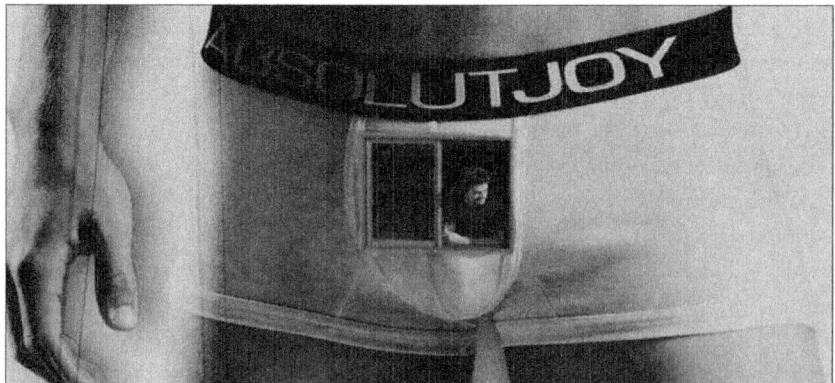

Fig. 2 Improvised sidewall windows.

y martín', typed into the search box, take us to a video recording made by the two actors, in which they mime the words of Marvin Gaye and Tammi Terrell's 1967 hit duet 'Ain't no Mountain High Enough'. The video was uploaded to YouTube to coincide with the film's release in October 2011.[3] Taretto explains that the initial idea had been to end the film after the encounter of the two on the street, with a closing title page simply directing spectators to see the epilogue online on YouTube. In this way he hoped to extend the life of the film beyond the duration of its cinematic screening, ensuring that viewers 'took it home' with them (see Amondaray 2012). The decision to include the YouTube epilogue in the film itself leaves us unsure whether it is part of the narrative or the film's promotional material. Are we watching the characters making a video to celebrate their new relationship or the actors making one to promote the film? By introducing this uncertainty, the epilogue blurs the boundaries between the filmed world and the real one, and between love and advertising.

One of the film's critics (Schmorak Leijnse 2011) finds the ending to be out of keeping with the film's logic, arguing that 'Si la idea era sacar a esa pareja de su encierro cibernético, no tenía mucho sentido hacerlos cantar y bailar en un videoclip casero publicado en YouTube' (if the idea was to rescue the couple from their cybernetic seclusion, it does not make a lot of sense to make them sing and dance in a home video uploaded onto YouTube). The ending becomes much more coherent, however, if we do not read the film primarily as a critique of media-induced isolation – a reading that is not easy to sustain, in any case, given its attention to the potential of media to unite as well as to divide – but as an exploration of the broader relationships between human subjectivity and media, and between different forms of media. The inclusion of the YouTube epilogue definitively converts *Medianeras* into a transmedial object, causing us to reflect on how film absorbs and is absorbed by other forms of digital media and their associated platforms. These colonising strategies are mutual: if part of the film finds its way onto the internet (and indeed, the full version was also available on YouTube at the time of writing), webpages are also inserted into the film on many occasions, filling the camera frame.

Medianeras becomes 'post-cinematic' in the way described by Steven Shaviro in his study of *Southland Tales* (Richard Kelly, 2006), a film that is also supplemented by materials in other media and, in a similar way to *Medianeras*, 'folds the practice of multimedia distribution and dispersion into the narrative of the film itself', to the extent that 'its audiovisual flow is entirely post-cinematic, and of a piece with the video-based and digital media that play such a role within it' (2010: 70). As Richard Grusin argues, 'The conception of film as a distinctive medium is now giving way both conceptually and in practice to film as a distributed form of mediation,' which 'does not end after its closing credits, but rather continues beyond the theater to the DVD, the video game, the soundtrack, the websites, and so forth' (2006: 75, 76). In this 'logic of remediation' we also witness 'the emergence of a visual style and narrative logic that bear more relationship to digital media like DVDs and video games than to that of photography, drama, or fiction' (Grusin 2006: 77–8).

This is clearly the case in *Medianeras*, which often adopts an aesthetic more akin to clip-art, as well as featuring infographics and employing CGI to create collages and animation effects. It is the wholehearted embrace in *Medianeras* of market-led remediation strategies, together with its creative and ludic participation in an aesthetic of intermediality, that compromises any straightforward role of critique for the film in relation to the mediatised city it represents.

The reflexive staging of competition and collaboration between different media regimes in *Medianeras* is evidence instead of the film's interest in exploring the dynamics of what has often been called 'media ecology'. If ecology is commonly defined as the scientific study of relationships between living organisms and their environment, media ecology describes the ways in which media 'function as environments, ecologies, and systems' (Strate 2008: 135). This means, firstly – as Marshall McLuhan saw back in the 1960s – that 'no medium has its meaning or existence alone, but only in constant interplay with other media' (1994: 26) and secondly, that media technologies play a significant role in shaping human subjectivity, such that, as Lance Strate explains, 'particular forms of communication, consciousness, and culture emerge out of particular media ecologies' (2008: 135).

What distinguishes the 'media ecology' approach in theories of media and society is its emphasis on the materiality of media technology rather than the 'content' of media, or any notion of media's erosion of place and embeddedness. This is also placed at the fore in *Medianeras*, which does not focus on the role of media in (re)producing specific ideologies or associate new digital media technologies with some new phase of virtual, placeless, disembodied experience, but often insists instead on the material quality of our interactions with them and how these affect human subjectivity and sociality. The film's interest is not in *mediation* – how media have been used as a medium to communicate specific messages, and the impact of these – but in *mediatisation*, which, as Stig Hjarvard explains, refers most often to long-term structural transformations associated with media, or 'how media, culture and society are mutually implicated in processes of change' (2014: 125). For this reason it does not primarily encourage us to understand media from a social-constructivist position, according to which media play a leading role in the construction of what we experience as social and cultural reality, and often stand between us and what they represent. Instead, it points to ways in which media bind us to the material and sensory world, forming assemblages that bring together the human and the technological in processes of co-evolution. Both characters' moods are intensely coloured by the physiological effects generated by watching films or listening to music, and have come to feel more comfortable expressing solidarity at a distance, across the internet. Sitting at the computer all day (and often into the night) gives Martín pain in his neck and back and is doubtless one of the causes of his insomnia.

Media ecology approaches often bear witness to a broader shift away from the idea of technology as an instrument used at the service of human agency and towards an understanding of the co-evolution of technology, culture and society. Hjarvard enjoins us to consider media as 'technologies and material objects' that are 'both *shaped by* humans and society and *shaping* human interaction and society' (2014: 132, 33). Significantly, *Medianeras* extends this approach to understanding the material environment of the city more generally, in ways that resonate with the interest of new materialist theorists in the agency of matter and its relationship with human agency, and also with a recent return to forms of materialist thinking in design and architecture.

Taretto's film affords us a glimpse of the 'ontological inseparability' that marks the relationship between cognition and material culture for Lambros Malafouris, in his development of new materialist ideas within the field of archaeology. If, as Malafouris argues, 'Thinking is not something that happens "inside" brains, bodies or things; rather, it emerges from contextualised processes that take place "between" brains, bodies, and things', it follows that agency is not bound to either humans or nonhumans, but 'the relational and emergent product of material engagement' (2013: 77, 78). This understanding of agency is very present in *Medianeras*. The material fabric of the city is shown to interact and co-evolve with the lives of its inhabitants in a way that challenges both a simplistic notion of determinism, on the one hand (that we are entirely shaped by our environment), or an illusion of human mastery on the other (that the material environment is a human creation). While the opening sequence of the film casts blame on the city's architects and planners, it immediately suggests some transferral of agency from human designers to the material environment itself, with the attribution of action to Buenos Aires, which 'crece descontrolada e imperfecta' (grows, uncontrolled and imperfect). Similarly, we are told that 'se yerguen miles y miles de edificios, sin ningún criterio' (thousands and thousands of buildings rise up, indiscriminately), as if these have simply appeared as a natural result of organic growth rather than human construction.

Although the film begins with static shots of the cityscape, the immobility of the camera's frame is quickly belied by movements within it, as construction workers walk across the floors of unfinished tower blocks and a window-cleaner sways on a rope harness. But it is not only humans who move. Reflective surfaces animate many of the buildings, formally extending them into the space below, above and alongside them as they capture the movements of cars and chimney ventilators. Their apparent permanence and stasis is continually modulated by the flows of city life. They take on passing forms as the mind might register fleeting images or other stimuli, flashing up before they fade away. On occasion the camera assists by panning across or circling around a glass surface, producing myriad movements and distortions in the building reflected in it, as if both were constantly mutating in shape.

Indeed, the city's buildings are caught up in processes of continual transformation, human and nonhuman: Taretto draws attention to the ways in which the original designs of their architects acquire irony or pathos through their juxtaposition with other styles, or are subject to unprogrammed uses or modifications. Buildings become improbable homes to weeds sprouting from the concrete itself; they bear the imprint of passing time, in the form of pollution, cracks, outdated political graffiti

Fig. 3 Reflective surfaces animate many of the film's buildings.

and scarred surfaces caused by the demolition of neighbouring blocks. The *medianeras* (side walls) also register the changing economic fortunes of the nation, hired as advertising spaces in times of commercial boom but left unemployed – like many of the city's inhabitants – in times of financial crisis.

The human protagonists of *Medianeras* interact in different ways with complex forces at work within the material world of the city, forces that have unforeseen effects, sometimes hampering and sometimes enabling the exercise of their own agency. Objects and systems are shown to follow their own trajectories, intersecting in unpredictable ways with the characters' own, throwing up the myriad encounters (and missed encounters) that characterise city life. This vision accords with Jane Bennett's concept of 'vital materialism,' a term she uses to refer to 'the capacity of things – edibles, commodities, storms, metals – not only to impede or block the will and designs of humans but also to act as quasi agents or forces with trajectories, propensities, or tendencies of their own' (2010: viii). This is most clearly to be seen in a

Fig. 4 The city's buildings are involved in processes of continual transformation, human and nonhuman.

scene that is pivotal to the film's plot, in which Mariana and Martín 'meet' each other in an online chatroom. Such virtual encounters are definitively enmeshed within the material world in *Medianeras*, and indeed a recognisably Argentine one: communications are established via a tangled morass of overhead cables, rather than discreet underground connections, and just as Martín gives Mariana his phone number during their online chat, one of Buenos Aires's recurrent power cuts hurls it irrevocably into the ether, dealing a serious blow to their chances of pursuing a budding internet romance. Ironically, it is this power cut that allows the two characters finally to meet in person, while buying candles at the kiosk in the street below. And if one electrical irregularity stymies their chance of meeting, another helps to bring them together: they are jolted into speaking to each other when a strong electrical charge passes between them as their hands inadvertently touch, perhaps from a torch one of them has carried to light the way to the kiosk.

The electrical blackout is, in fact, one of the cases Bennett explores to demonstrate an agency that is distributed across 'an ontologically heterogeneous field', rather than being solely located in a human body or produced by human effort. If the assemblage that constitutes the electrical power grid involves human actors, it also includes 'some very active and powerful nonhumans: electrons, trees, wind, fire, electromagnetic fields' (2010: 24). Far from a simple machine operated by humans, the electrical grid 'is better understood as a volatile mix of coal, sweat, electromagnetic fields, computer programs, electron streams, profit motives, heat, lifestyles, nuclear fuel, plastic, fantasies of mastery, static, legislation, water, economic theory, wire, and wood – to name just some of the actants' (2010: 25). This understanding of the complex dynamics that allow the electricity grid to function (and occasionally bring about its dysfunction) effectively displaces the human as the sole agent and redistributes power and agency across an extremely broad field of actants, human and nonhuman, abstract and material.

Ecology is a powerful name for such interactions and modifications, and one that is increasingly invoked in urban studies. As Adrian Franklin reminds us, 'all ecologies involve highly complex relationships between a heterogeneous assembly of constituents in such a way that every part is to a degree co-constituted or becomes constituted through its relatings' (2010: 110). I see no need, however, to qualify this approach by suggesting – as Franklin does – that ecology is used in this case as a metaphor (2010: 110, 117). The processes of specialisation, competition, mutation, adaptation that bind humans to their material environment are not 'like' those of biological ecosystems, but form part of such systems. Indeed, with particular relevance for *Medianeras*, 'ecology' derives from the Greek word *oikos*, or 'house, dwelling place, habitation'. Coined by the German zoologist Ernst Haeckel, it was defined in his book *Principles of General Morphology of Organisms* (1905) as 'the science of relations of the organism to the surrounding environment', which specifically included 'organic or inorganic' conditions (cit. Schulze *et al.* 2005: 1).

It might be argued that lending urban growth and social change the implacable force of natural selection in biological evolution effectively downplays and depoliticises questions of city planning. An objection of this kind would fail to take into account, however, that understanding the city as a complex system continually forged by human and nonhuman forces leads us more surely to questions of ethics in urban planning, given the profound effects that small actions may have on the delicate balance of ecological systems. If, as Bennett argues, 'the image of dead or thoroughly instrumentalised matter feeds human hubris and our earth-destroying fantasies of conquest and consumption' (2010: ix) then an acknowledgement that matter may be the source as well as the object of agentic forces puts humans back into their proper place, within (and not above or beyond) matter. Mariana in *Medianeras* articulates something of this perspective when she explains that visiting the Planetarium 'puts her in her place' and reminds her that the world does not revolve around her. As she watches the planets recede into the solar system, which vanishes in turn into the galaxy and then, dizzyingly, into a universe of countless galaxies, she observes that 'Me recuerda que soy parte de un todo, infinito y eterno' (it reminds me that I am part of a whole, infinite and eternal).

The decidedly non-anthropocentric orientation of new materialist thought allows us to approach the flows and contradictions of the city as a system that transcends the will and actions of its creators, becoming, as Franklin indicates, 'more than its human designers could ever intend. It takes on a life of its own and it impacts on the lives of those who live there in the same way that other environmental forces do' (2010: 198). *Medianeras* provides examples of human attempts to shape the city with the aim of expressing or reflecting our own social attitudes and codes: like everything made by humans, Martín observes, buildings are constructed to differentiate us, with different values accorded to higher-floor or lower-floor apartments, with a view to the front or the back. Mariana relates the story behind the Kavanagh Building, Latin America's first skyscraper, which was reputedly built as an act of revenge, to prevent the wealthy Anchorenas from viewing the church they had constructed from their nearby palace. However, it is the unpredicted ways in which buildings, media or other material technologies have come to shape *us* that forms the major focus of the film, which charts the extent to which human subjectivity and forms of sociability are intimately related to the dimensions and affordances of the material city.

Indeed, this perspective provides the basis for a new repoliticisation of the practice of architecture that would anchor it more firmly to broader issues of urban planning. Stan Allen's call on the eve of the twenty-first century for an 'infrastructural urbanism' is a critical response to the semiotic (and postmodern) turn from the late 1960s, which approached architecture as 'a discursive system that expresses, critiques, or makes apparent the hard realities of a world that is held safely at arm's length' and therefore abandoned 'the possibility of ever *intervening* in that reality' (1999: 50). Instead, Allen advocates an understanding of architecture 'as *material* practice – as an activity that works in and among the world of things, and not exclusively with meaning and image' (1999: 52), and which returns to certain ideas of

Fig. 5 Cross-fades between filmed images and architects' sketches connect the virtual and the material.

instrumentality and performance neglected under postmodernism, embedding the practice of architecture thoroughly within the social and economic infrastructure of the city (see 1999: 52–3). Moving away from an understanding of architecture as expression, critique or even 'interrogation (laying bare of the intricacies of architecture's complicity with power and politics)' (1999: 50), Allen promotes one that focuses instead on its capacity to *transform* reality.

The close relationship between image and material practice in architecture is frequently highlighted in *Medianeras*, with the aid of a wide range of techniques. The film's animated sequences often take the form of architects' sketches, traced rapidly on a blank screen, which are then suffused with colour and cross-faded with photographs or film stills. Similar techniques are used to effect transitions between cartoon figures and real characters. These sequences remind us of the traffic between the virtual and the material, the simulated and the real, within the mediatised city, but also within architecture as a practice. This dynamic is also marked by Allen, in his recognition that 'Material practices organise and transform aggregates of labor, materials, energy and resources, but they work through necessarily mediated procedures – operations of drawing and projection, for example – that leave their trace on the work' (1999: 53). Ultimately, in this way, the 'material turn' in philosophy, architecture and many other bodies of thought and praxis does not come to supersede language, semiotics or representation but to re-embed these within material experience.[4] This relationship is given literal expression in the intertitles that divide *Medianeras* into chapters: peeking coyly from behind the branches of a tree, balancing on an overhead cable, or reposing on the terrace of a building, they point to the extent to which the film's story is embedded in the material fabric of the city.

For Franklin, what distinguishes the experience of living in the contemporary city is that 'our concerns now extend into vast global figurations which are dependent upon and are mediated by equally complex socio-technical interfaces and forms of agency that we do not understand, control or predict with any great accuracy' (2010:

Fig. 6 The intertitles in *Medianeras* embed its story in the material fabric of the city.

117–18). He cites a range of 'hybrids of human and non-human agency', including GM crops, carbon emissions and bird flu. As a result, 'The city is confronted as nature and constituted as nature' (2010: 198); we cannot maintain any artificial distinction between the urban environment and the 'natural' one, but instead focus on their co-evolution. It is this understanding, alongside a growing appreciation of the dynamic and turbulent flows that bind human and nonhuman forces together, that identifies the city of Taretto's film as one that is no longer modern, or even postmodern. *Medianeras* resists the regime of 'purification' that is inherent in modernity for Bruno Latour, under which nature-culture hybrids are divided into different ontological zones: human and non-human (1993: 10–11).[5] Moreover, it seeks to explore a human subjectivity that is primarily forged, not through language or discourse, but through material engagement, and gives the lie to the presumed disembedding effects of new media and the rise of the global information society. Moving away from the studies of alienation and marginalisation that have dominated Argentine cinema since the 1990s, *Medianeras* – in its interest in media and urban ecologies – emphasises instead the 'throwntogetherness' (Massey 2008: 160) of the human and nonhuman in the contemporary city, in which new media technologies, with their global reach, do not help us to transcend the material environment so much as embed us more thoroughly, and ambivalently, within it.

NOTES

1. For a very effective discussion of the violence of everyday life in the city and its relationship with neoliberalism in *El bonaerense*, see Scorer (2010).
2. Richard Florida uses the term 'creative class' to describe a burgeoning class of professionals, composed of knowledge-workers, writers, architects and 'people in design, education, arts, music and entertainment, whose economic function is to

create new ideas, new technology and/or creative content' (2002: 8).
3   See https://www.youtube.com/watch?v=CxQHrBrYCiU.
4   For a more extended discussion of the interplay between recent directions in architecture and new materialist thought, see McKim (2014) and Leach (2009).
5   Paradoxically, for Latour, it is this work of purification that both responds to and makes necessary a work of hybridisation, and the central characteristic of modernity is the simultaneous liberation and disavowal of the relationship between these two (1993: 10–11, 34, 50).

BIBLIOGRAPHY

Aguilar, Gonzalo (2006) *Otros mundos: ensayo sobre el nuevo cine argentino*. Buenos Aires: Santiago Arcos Editor.

Allen, Stan (1999) *Points + Lines: Diagrams for the City*. New York: Princeton Architectural Press.

Amin, Ash and Nigel Thrift (2002) *Cities: Reimagining the Urban*. Cambridge: Polity Press.

Amondaray, Milagros (2012) 'El cine bajo la mirada de … Gustavo Taretto', 6 December; http://blogs.lanacion.com.ar/cine/el-cine-bajo-la-mirada-de-el-cine-bajo-la-mirada-degustavo-taretto/

Benjamin, Walter ([1939] 2003) 'On Some Motifs in Baudelaire', in Edmund Jephcott, Howard Eiland, and Michael W. Jennings (eds) *Walter Benjamin: Selected Writings, Volume 4, 1938–1940*. Cambridge: Harvard University Press, 313–55.

Bennett, Jane (2010) *Vibrant Matter: A Political Ecology of Things*. Durham: Duke University Press.

Castells, Manuel (2010) *End of Millennium*, 2nd edn. Chichester and Malden, MA: Wiley-Blackwell.

Castro, Gisela G. S. (2013) '(In)comunicación, consumo y sociabilidad en la escena urbana: Breve reflexión a partir del cine', *Razón y Palabra*, 18, 84; http://www.redalyc.org/articulo.oa?id=199528904022

Deuze, Mark (2014) 'Media Life and the Mediatization of the Lifeworld', in Andreas Hepp and Friedrich Krotz (eds) *Mediatized Worlds: Culture and Society in a Media Age*. New York: Palgrave Macmillan, 207–20.

Florida, Richard (2002) *The Rise Of The Creative Class: And How It's Transforming Work, Leisure, Community And Everyday Life*. New York: Basic Books.

Franklin, Adrian (2010) *City Life*. London: Sage.

Georgiou, Myria (2013) *Media and the City: Cosmopolitanism and Difference*. Cambridge: Polity Press.

Grusin, Richard (2006) 'DVDs, Video Games, and the Cinema of Interactions', in *Ilha Do Desterro: A Journal of English Language, Literature in English and Cultural*

Studies, 51, 69–91.

Hjarvard, Stig (2014) 'From Mediation to Mediatization: The Institutionalization of New Media', in Andreas Hepp and Friedrich Krotz (eds) *Mediatized Worlds: Culture and Society in a Media Age*. New York: Palgrave Macmillan, 123–39.

Latour, Bruno (1993) *We Have Never Been Modern*. Cambridge: Harvard University Press.

Leach, Neil (2009) 'New Materialism,' *Urban Flux*, 1, 26–9.

Malafouris, Lambros (2013) *How Things Shape the Mind: A Theory of Material Engagement*. Cambridge: MIT Press.

Massey, Doreen (2008) *For Space*. London: Sage.

McKim, Joel (2014) 'Radical Infrastructure? A New Realism and Materialism in Philosophy and Architecture', in Nadir Lahiji (ed.) *Radical Philosophy and Architecture: The Missed Encounter*. London: Bloomsbury, 133–50.

McLuhan, Marshall (1994) *Understanding Media: The Extensions of Man*. Cambridge: MIT Press.

McQuire, Scott (2008) *The Media City: Media, Architecture and Urban Space*. London: Sage.

Page, Joanna (2009) *Crisis and Capitalism in Contemporary Argentine Cinema*. Durham and London: Duke University Press.

Sarlo, Beatriz (2009) *La ciudad vista: mercancías y cultura urbana*. Buenos Aires: Siglo Veintiuno.

Schmorak Leijnse, Adriana (2011) '*Medianeras*', *Cinecritic: Revista de Cine*, October; http://www.cinecritic.biz/es/index.php?option=com_content&view=article&id=351:medianeras&catid=1:categorie1cinecritique

Schulze, Ernst-Detlef, Erwin Beck and Klaus Müller-Hohenstein (2005) *Plant Ecology*. Berlin and Heidelberg: Springer.

Scorer, James (2010) 'Trigger-Happy: Police, Violence and the State in *El bonaerense/ The Policeman*', in Cacilda Rêgo and Carolina Rocha (eds) *New Trends in Argentine and Brazilian Cinema*. Bristol: Intellect, 163–75.

Shaviro, Steven (2010) *Post-Cinematic Affect*. Winchester: Zero Books.

Simmel, Georg ([1903] 2002) 'The Metropolis and Mental Life', in Gary Bridge and Sophie Watson (eds) *The Blackwell City Reader*. Oxford and Malden, MA: Wiley-Blackwell, 11–19.

Strate, Lance (2008) 'Studying Media *as* Media: McLuhan and the Media Ecology Approach', *MediaTropes eJournal*, 1, 127–42.

Svampa, Maristella (2005) *La sociedad excluyente: la Argentina bajo el signo del neoliberalismo*. Buenos Aires: Taurus.

Turkle, Sherry (2011) *Alone Together: Why We Expect More from Technology and Less from Each Other*. New York: Basic Books.

WHEN HARRY MET SIRI: DIGITAL ROMCOM AND THE GLOBAL CITY IN SPIKE JONZE'S *HER*

LAWRENCE WEBB

Spike Jonze's near-future, post-human romance *Her* (2013) left a substantial cultural footprint. In addition to numerous reviews, interviews and profiles of key creative personnel, the film inspired meta-critical commentary (see Debruge 2014; THR Staff 2014), listicles (see Patches 2013; Rosen 2013), op-eds and think pieces (see Rosen 2014; Schneider 2014), behind-the-scenes features on production design and cinematography, comedy parodies (including a *Saturday Night Live* skit), and even a fashion line inspired by its distinctive retro costumes. Though a good proportion of this critical commentary and online promotional drive focused on the film's eminently topical themes of digital romance and artificial intelligence, another persistent subject was the representation of the city. In particular, *Her* was widely praised for creating a ground-breaking vision of a near-future Los Angeles. For Manohla Dargis in the *New York Times*, the film offered a familiar yet 'modestly embellished' and 'exquisite' portrait of a city to come (2013: np). The *Guardian*'s Peter Bradshaw dubbed it a 'postmodern pastoral … a techno-perfect Los Angeles of the near future' (2014: np). Emphatically turning away from the city's emblematic sprawl, freeways and automobiles, the film envisioned, for Scott Foundas, 'a society where green living has triumphed' (2013: np). Critics further lauded the film's artful compression of Los Angeles and Shanghai locations to create a 'beautifully imagined yet highly plausible' projection of urban cosmopolitanism (ibid.)

As one might expect, the local press offered the most detailed accounts. The *Los Angeles Times* presented a five-day series on the making of *Her*, including a celebratory online map of the film's shooting locations and key architectural landmarks (see Zeitchik 2013). While this suggests a familiar intersection of civic pride, city branding and movie tourism, other commentators attributed greater import to the film's intervention into the urban imaginary. For architectural critic Christopher Hawthorne, the film positively invoked a world in which 'a benevolent Robert Moses, a planning dictator with a green agenda, had taken over the political realm in Los Angeles' (2014: np). The *Los Angeles Magazine* directly contrasted this image of utopian planning with existing iterations of the cinematic city, particularly *Blade Runner* (Ridley Scott, 1982), noting that *Her* 'dispenses with the dystopian noir to depict a sunny pedestrian technopolis' (Shatkin 2014: np). Such ideas were reinforced by numerous interviews with the film's creative team. The film's production designer, K. K. Barrett, explicitly linked the film's vision of the city to aspirations and dreams about future urban development. 'The myth that we've always been hoping for in Los Angeles,' said Barrett, 'is that this urban center downtown will become something practical, liveable, and enviable. We created that' (in Steffen 2015: np).

As Barrett's comments suggest, the cinematic reimagination of a setting such as Los Angeles is always in dialogue with pre-existing ideas and images of the city, and such a creative revision of the cityscape might be construed – not least by its authors – as a material intervention into urban discourse. Moreover, the repeated discussion of the city in *Her*'s critical and paratextual materials suggests that debate and speculation about the cinematic city and its relation to 'real' issues of development and planning are not scholarly preserves but rather an essential part of the textual flow experienced by audiences.[1] But what is at stake in *Her*'s reinvention of the city, beyond the largely celebratory frame offered by the press? This chapter explores the film's engagement with the city in greater depth, unpacking its distinctive view of Los Angeles within the context of transformative shifts in urban development and discourse that have taken place since the 1990s. As I will argue, the film addresses a number of contemporary concerns – the impact of digital technologies on social interaction and public space, the legacy of downtown redevelopment and accelerated gentrification, and anxieties about homogenisation and 'authenticity' in the global city – by reworking existing genre lineages of the cinematic city.

In particular, I will examine the ways in which Jonze's film revises and updates tropes of the future city by combining the generic frameworks of romantic comedy and science fiction, genres closely associated with the urban present and the urban future respectively. In broad terms, the romantic comedy engages with long-standing concerns about the scale of the city and the possibility of making genuine connections within it. Its account of modernity is fundamentally positive, even utopian, in that it is a genre premised on urban encounter, on the very possibility of finding the 'one' amongst the multitude of the city. In recent years, this relationship between the romantic comedy and urban space has been reoriented by online dating and other technological shifts in cultures of intimacy. At the same time, the genre has arguably become a key cultural manifestation of the downtown revival and an expression of the prerogatives, and anxieties, of the urban professional class. In this context, *Her*'s projection of Los Angeles as a pedestrian city is grounded in the actual transformation of American cities by gentrification and the proliferation of the so-called 'creative class'.

In contrast, science fiction films have long been used as vehicles for projecting urban futures of a dystopian stamp. This has created a space for negotiating anxieties about technological change and the nature of the human condition. In the second half of the chapter, I discuss *Her* in relation to two key precursors: *Metropolis* (Fritz Lang, 1927) and *Blade Runner*. Drawing on the legacy of *Metropolis*, *Her* mediates positive and negative views of technology via the ambivalent figure of the female operating system. As such, the film engages with cultural anxieties that globalisation and digital media might have detrimental effects on the authenticity of the self and urban culture more generally. In doing so, it draws on older tropes – the lonely, atomised city dweller and the gendered fear of technology – that are shaped by the legacy of the cinematic city. Like *Blade Runner*, its vision of the city is also an Asian-American hybrid. Shot on location in Los Angeles and the Pudong district of Shanghai, *Her* seamlessly weaves together a composite global city that avoids the orientalist dystopia of *Blade Runner* while still evoking East Asia as the locus of technological innovation. Yet, while the future cities of *Metropolis* and *Blade Runner* were animated by class struggle, *Her* elides questions of class and politics even as it examines the nature of labour and 'creativity' in the digital city.

Her brings these two generic identities into tension to produce a city that is not reducible to a simple utopia/dystopia binary. As I will argue, the film revises and repurposes these lineages to engage with the emerging realities of the global city in the digital era. In doing so, it demonstrates how our figuration of the contemporary city of digital media, portable screens and constant connectivity is still mediated via the accumulated legacy of the 'cinematic city', its representational tropes and genre logics.

DIGITAL LOVE: HER AS ROMANTIC COMEDY

Her was somewhat playfully marketed as 'A Spike Jonze love story', placing both the notion of romance and the auteur brand above the film's near-future setting and its technological themes. Though the film is not a straight comedy, not least because of its pervasive melancholy tone, critics were nevertheless quick to spot the family resemblance to romantic comedy and in particular, the 'nervous romances' of Woody Allen, with *Slate*'s Dana Stevens dubbing it 'a post-human *Annie Hall*' (see Krutnik 2002; Stevens 2013). Following this thread in the film's reception, viewing *Her* as an off-centre romantic comedy not only helps locate it within a broader generic context but also productively situates the film within a particular tradition of urban representation. *Her* exemplifies how the contemporary romantic comedy has adapted to shifting notions of romance in the digital era, and how it reconfigures its conventions through revising its relationship to its principal narrative space, the big city.

The film's narrative arc shares much of the romantic comedy's DNA. Theodore Twombly (Joaquin Phoenix) works for a firm ('beautifulhandwrittenletters.com') that specialises in composing and manufacturing handwritten letters for customers too busy, inarticulate or emotionally inadequate to do so themselves. Recently separated from his wife, Catherine (Rooney Mara), and with divorce proceedings underway, Theodore lives a lonely, atomised existence in the city, though he craves connection and emotional engagement. The traditional 'meet-cute' arrives with Theodore's installation of the ground-breaking, artificially intelligent operating system, OS1, personalised with a young female voice as Samantha (Scarlett Johansson). Samantha quickly becomes a cross between a virtual companion, personal assistant and life coach. But after an unsuccessful blind date with another woman, Samantha and Theodore become lovers and 'consummate' their relationship. While this diverges from traditional romcom logic, which dictates that sexual gratification must be deferred, it draws on the lineage of post-classical comedies such as *Annie Hall* (1977) in presenting the relationship as an object for scrutiny and introspective reflection. What follows is a gently humorous, if tender and heartfelt exploration of the possibility of love between a human and a disembodied, artificially intelligent operating system.

The film's comic conceit is to work through this scenario by reimagining standard tropes of the urban romance: strolling in the city, people watching, double dating and a trip to the beach. Ultimately, though, Samantha's developing intelligence surpasses the human scale and the authenticity of their connection is, for Theodore, fatally compromised by the revelation that he is only one among Samantha's many partners. Having punctured the bubble of digital romance, the film ends with a more hopeful note of genuine emotional connection between Theodore and his hitherto platonic friend, Amy (Amy Adams), who has also been jilted by her OS lover. The film closes with a panoramic shot of the pair contemplating the skyline from the rooftops – a romantic cityscape that recalls the famous poster image of *Manhattan* (Woody Allen, 1979) and suggests that the resolution of the story may, in fact, be

Fig. 1 The cityscape as romantic panorama in *Her* (2013).

found in the well-worn romcom trope that the 'one' is hidden in plain sight in the form of an existing friendship.

Jonze's speculative notion of a human-operating system romance therefore extends the idea of online dating and virtual courtship via a science-fiction scenario, reworking the romcom for the digital era. In doing so, it engages with issues discussed by Sherry Turkle in her popular books on human-technology interactions. As Turkle explains, digital technologies have impacted not only on our personal interactions but also on the nature of social space. Continuously connected online yet disconnected in the material world, the 'tethered self' exists in a 'world of continual partial attention' (2011: 142). As a result, public space is all but emptied of its collective nature as its users remain in physical proximity yet are constantly drawn away by the lure of the screen. Moreover, for Turkle, the related rise of 'affective computing' – robots, toys and other digital devices created to simulate companionship and love – might even lead to a redefinition of love itself. As she puts it,

> The questions for the future are not whether children will love their robot companions more than their pets or even their parents. The questions are rather, what will love be? And what will it mean to achieve ever-greater intimacy with our machines? Are we ready to see ourselves in the mirror of machines and to see love as our performance of love? (2011: 125)

In this context, *Her* and other contemporary romcoms grapple with a split between traditional notions of romantic fulfilment and emerging ideas about the nature of love and post-human subjectivity.

Yet, as Frank Krutnik has shown, such tensions between tradition and modernity have long been central to the genre's identity. As he puts it, Hollywood romantic comedies are always 'driven by a process of negotiation between traditionalist concepts of heterosexual monogamy and an intimate culture that is constantly in flux' (2002: 130). For recent romcoms, the disruptive influence of online dating sites, mobile apps and social media more generally have reshaped the contours of intimacy and, significantly, the perceived role of virtual and material spaces in courtship and connectivity. As Jeff Scheible has argued, this is part of a wider trend for recent films to apprehend the new digital culture and its affective structures; noting 'Cinema's Year of OS Romance', he suggests that films such as *Her* and *Noah* (Patrick Cederberg and Walter Woodman, 2013) address 'new concerns about the digitally mediated self, the ethical stakes of privacy, corporate surveillance, and net neutrality' (2014: 22). Scheible marks a shift between the 1990s digital utopianism of Norah Ephron's *You've Got Mail* (1998), which suggested that the anonymity of online encounters could enable a new kind of authentic emotional bond, and recent films that express contemporary anxieties about the idea of disembodied romance and the ambivalent nature of the digital self (see 2014: 22–3). Reframing the focus from the 'digital mediascape' to the media city more generally, we might view both *You've Got*

Mail and *Her* not just as digital romances, but also as films about transitions in urban space. As such, *Her* is concerned with the split between embodiment and disembodiment as well as an implicit divide between virtual space and the traditional urban setting of the romantic comedy. Along with other recent entries into this genre, *Her* attempts to reconcile conventional ideas of romance with an emerging digital landscape and the potential loss of the city as a physical space of romantic encounter.

As Deborah Jermyn has argued, the romantic comedy is a characteristically urban genre, although it is New York City not Los Angeles that has provided its most persistent setting in American film;[2] as 'cinema's romantic playground' (2009: 12), New York's urban topography and cultural milieu have been central to the development of the genre from *The Apartment* (Billy Wilder, 1960) and *Breakfast at Tiffany's* (Blake Edwards, 1961) to *Annie Hall*, *When Harry Met Sally* (Rob Reiner, 1989) and *You've Got Mail*. For Jermyn, the narrative patterns and ideological framework of the romantic comedy are rooted in New York's restless dynamism, its emblematic status within the American imaginary as a place of opportunity and migrant aspiration, and its close association with the independent female consumer (see 2009: 14–16). Yet this potentially liberal social context is frequently in tension with the inherent conservatism of the genre's narrative template and its emphasis on the monogamous heterosexual couple as the basis of romantic and personal fulfilment. In comparison, Los Angeles has been a much less frequent setting for Hollywood romantic comedies, despite its centrality to other visions of urban modernity (see Dimendberg, 2010).[3] The sprawling distances of Los Angeles, the city's structural dependence on the car, and its aura of privatisation and segregation have proved less amenable to the genre. Unlike New York, Los Angeles is not primarily figured as a 'melting pot' but rather as a mosaic of diverse and disaggregated fragments, and while Hollywood may seem like the sine qua non of aspiration, it has been routinely fictionalised as a place where dreams are frustrated, debased or commodified. And in contrast to the New York romantic comedy, the characteristic narrative forms of Los Angeles – arguably *film noir* and multi-protagonist 'network narratives' such as *Short Cuts* (Robert Altman, 1993) and *Magnolia* (Paul Thomas Anderson, 1999) – tend to emphasise alienation and disconnection rather than romantic encounter and fulfilment. *Her*'s recuperation of Los Angeles as a love story setting draws on both of these lineages, figuring it as a site of romantic potential as well as a more familiar LA landscape of detachment and anomie.

But in order to refashion Los Angeles as a suitable setting for a romantic film, *Her* needed to reimagine the urban *form* of the city, refiguring it as a high density, walkable space. For a film notionally about the virtual, *Her* is saturated with views of the material, built space of the city as well as its proliferating screens and displays. Scenes in Theodore's apartment are frequently framed to show panoramic views of the city outside, and many of the film's central scenes between Theodore and Samantha are staged in outdoor spaces and public areas. Indeed, one of the key romantic scenes of the film finds a way for Theodore and Samantha to walk through

Fig. 2 Theodore and Samantha walk in the city.

the city, with his mobile device placed in his shirt pocket to provide her with a 'view'. Like Woody Allen and Diane Keaton's characters in *Annie Hall*, they engage in the pleasures of urban *flânerie* and people watching. And after their first sexual encounter, beautiful panoramic shots of the city skyline at sunrise are juxtaposed with the sounds of Samantha's 'orgasm'.

As critics were quick to point out, the film's views of the city present a subtle, though profound, shift in the cinematic representation of Los Angeles. Focusing on high-level walkways and public spaces, and entirely avoiding car journeys, *Her* envisages a city that has turned emphatically away from its automobile-centred past. Jonze also allows an unusual amount of 'shoe leather' time, so that the very act of walking in the city and the physical experience of urban space are emphasised.[4] Much of the narrative takes place within a revived – if somewhat sterile – downtown, and

Fig. 3 Los Angeles as pedestrianised space.

the protagonists traverse the city on foot and by an extended public transit system reaching all the way to the coast. As the *Los Angeles Times* map makes clear, the film's principal locations cluster downtown, suggesting a re-centring of a famously decentralised urban sprawl around a high-density core. Traditional areas of cinematic LA such as Hollywood and Beverly Hills are largely avoided, as are other familiar cinematic landscapes such as that of South Central, most recently seen in *Straight Outta Compton* (F. Gary Gray, 2015). We are left to imagine whether poverty has been eliminated or simply displaced to an unseen periphery. Theodore's immediate surroundings are presented as a relatively segregated and homogenous enclave space – one that is primarily white, as a number of critics have pointed out (unsettling not least because it entirely disavows the presence of significant ethnic communities – nearly half of LA is Latino/Hispanic, for example) (see Renninger 2013).

Landmarks and iconic buildings are used sparingly, but two stand out. One is the Disney Concert Hall (2003), an emblem of downtown regeneration by star architect Frank Gehry. The other is One Wilshire, a building famous for its role as the city's telecommunications hub, which is clearly visible from Theodore's apartment (shot at the Watermarke on 9th and Flower). Whereas the Concert Hall represents the symbolic reworking of the city's *visual* form, One Wilshire is emblematic of the less tangible and figurable aspects of the contemporary city. For Kazys Varnelis, it is One Wilshire, rather than Gehry's concert hall or the Bonaventure Hotel of Fredric Jameson's famous analysis, that is the foremost 'product, index, and generator of contemporary urbanism and the networked economy' (2003: np). While the film reimagines downtown LA, it does so using iconic buildings that mobilise ideas both of city branding and the digital domain.

This split between the visual and the virtual is also explored at the level of form. The city is filled with a multiplicity of screens and displays: the computer terminal, the omnipresent screens in public spaces, the small screen of Theodore's mobile device, and the immersive 3D projection of his video game system. The digital city is, one the one hand, permeated with screens and images on portable devices and public displays; while on the other, it is striated by essentially non-visual informational processes. Sound becomes crucial to figuring this non-visual aspect of this city. In *Her,* keyboards, mice and touch-screens have largely been dispensed with in favour of voice-activated technologies. Making Samantha a disembodied, 'acousmatic' voice creates an intimate and interior link with the audience, while at the same time evoking the potential isolation of the urban experience. As Michael Bull has suggested, the contemporary city is shaped both by the privatising tendencies of post-Fordist capitalism and a concomitant impulse towards proximity and contact, a dialectic that is nowhere more clearly expressed than in the iPod and the practices of auditory mobility; making the love interest a disembodied, technologically mediated voice directly invokes this already existing culture of 'mediated urban isolation' (2007: 4), and the privatised nature of the listening experience for both protagonist and viewer works in tandem with the film's concerns with the social experience of the digital city.

Fig. 4 The city as mediatized space.

As a female character, Samantha is unavailable as object-to-be-looked-at, though the distinctive, husky voice of Scarlett Johansson provides a kind of compensating aural plenitude (the studio's recasting of Samantha Morton with Johansson is telling in this respect).

Her is not alone in its romantic recapture of downtown LA. It adds to a growing number of films, most notably such indie romcoms *In Search of a Midnight Kiss* (Alex Holdridge, 2007) and *(500) Days of Summer* (Marc Webb, 2009), that have represented downtown as a compact space suitable for romantic exploration and amorous encounter. Reinventing near-future Los Angeles as a pedestrian city, these films resonate with concerns of sustainability, ecology and walkable urbanism in recent planning and theory. In doing so, they contribute to a broader trend of Los Angeles filmmaking in creating what Mark Shiel describes as 'low carbon narratives' (2012: 282). Such films are typically low budget and revise the traditional image of Los Angeles as a virtually unmappable sprawl negotiable only by car, creating smaller scale, pedestrian geographies of the city that might, as Shiel optimistically suggests, come to define a 'new urban ecology of the movies' (2012: 283).

For the romantic comedy in particular, this development chimes with a broader reorientation of the genre's geography. Beyond Los Angeles, the romantic comedy has also germinated in diverse urban settings – for example, Philadelphia in *Baby Mama* (Michael McCullers, 2008), *How Do You Know* (James L. Brooks, 2011) and *Silver Linings Playbook* (David O. Russell, 2012), Pittsburgh in *She's Out of My League* (Jim Field Smith, 2010), and Austin, Texas in *Results* (Andrew Bujalski, 2015). This attests to the resurgence of these cities as location shooting destinations, itself a symptom of their redevelopment and reinvention as hubs of cultural production. To put it another way, for a city to become a suitable setting for a romantic comedy indicates a certain repositioning of its public self-image: it has developed – or wishes to develop – an urban form, social environment and taste culture appropriate to the genre's narrative requirements and target audience. To retrofit the city as a suitable setting for the romantic comedy, then, the inner city had to be recovered as a *cinematic* space; in turn, this symbolic, screen reinvention has played an active role in the repositioning or rebranding of urban space.

In this respect, we might consider the ways that the development of the romantic comedy – especially its independent variant – has correlated closely with processes of gentrification and especially the discourse of the 'creative city'. In Richard Florida's influential formulation (2004), the revival and redevelopment of urban centres has been led by professionals in various kinds of 'creative' and cultural industries, from artists and architects to engineers and academics. Though it has been widely critiqued in urban studies (see Peck 2005), this idea of the creative city has retained demonstrable currency beyond academia.[5] In contrast to the conformity of William Whyte's 'organization man', the creative class – at least according to Florida – is defined by individuality, self-expression and openness to difference. Florida explicitly places Whyte in opposition to Jane Jacobs, suggesting that her model urban environment, mid-twentieth century Greenwich Village, provided a prototype for the creative economy in its diversity, dynamism and entrepreneurial spirit (see 2004: 41–3). Central to this 'creative ethos' is a notion of creativity as the embodiment of individual self-definition and identity creation. Recent romantic comedies such as *Her, (500) Days of Summer* and *Frances Ha* (Noah Baumbach, 2014) not only situate their protagonists firmly within this creative class milieu and the gentrified neighbourhoods that Florida champions, but also work through tensions and anxieties about this ethos of creative work as 'authentic' self-expression. These issues are frequently explored through a second narrative line about work and creative fulfilment that meshes together with the primary romantic plot. In *Her*, Theodore and his close friends, Charles and Amy, are linked firmly within the creative class paradigm through their occupations (copywriter, filmmaker) and lifestyle ('You've got to eat your fruits and juice your vegetables').

In this respect, it is not coincidental that the aforementioned romantic comedies are all located somewhere on the 'indie' spectrum. *Her* was financed and produced by Megan Ellison's boutique production house Annapurna Pictures and distributed by Warner Bros., placing it firmly within the quasi-independent zone between the major studios and smaller companies.[6] Such films tend to establish a degree of difference that is central to their position in the market, their search for prestige through critical recognition and awards, and their production of distinction and cultural capital. As Brendan Kredell has argued, independent cinema in the 1990s and 2000s has been closely bound up with 'the taste culture of gentrification' (2012: 83). This has operated both at the level of exhibition, with the expansion of boutique cinemas in gentrifying neighbourhoods, and at the level of representation. For Kredell, filmmakers such as Wes Anderson have created abstracted and aestheticised screen cities that do symbolic violence to the lived experience and history of urban communities (2012: 84). Yet, as *Her* suggests, these films operate within a double bind, whereby they frequently invest in notions of authenticity as a perceived resistance to exactly this kind of homogenisation. As Sharon Zukin (2009) argues, the accelerated gentrification and upscaling of urban centres has led to a perceived crisis of authenticity, a widespread cultural response to the homogeneity and soullessness of generic redevelopment projects and an associated loss of urban diversity and cultural vitality. Though we need to be circumspect about such ideas of 'authenticity', which is at best a discursive construction, it nevertheless provides a useful framework unpacking some of the film's underlying concerns. Alongside a number of recent films, *Her* projects such an anxiety, but its relationship to the city is conflicted and contradictory. The aesthetic beauty of its production design and cinematography appear to celebrate the *mise-en-scène* of the generic city, while at the same time, it is steeped in a sense of melancholy and loss for an 'authentic' urban experience, which is figured through the film's retro sensibility, and in its central concerns about love in the digital city.

The film's retro aesthetics and its oscillation between irony and sincerity has also led critics to link it, its audience and its moustachioed protagonist Theodore Twombly to the figure of the hipster. Peter Debruge in *Variety* noted its 'benign hipster aesthetic' (2014: np), and *Hollywood Reporter* suggested the fashions were influenced by 'the hipster programmers of Brooklyn's Dumbo neighbourhood' (Patches 2013: np); one blogger even dubbed it 'the hipster answer to *Blade Runner*' (Ruscoe 2014). Though the hipster remains an amorphous concept that vaguely links a particular set of tendencies and fashions to the broader culture of gentrification, it nevertheless has colloquial currency. The hipster is an ambivalent figure, sometimes construed as part of a resistant subculture (for example, promoting local businesses in opposition to Starbucks and other paragons of what Zukin calls 'hegemonic global urbanism' (2009: 544)), or alternatively, as an active agent of accelerated gentrification (or at the very least, an unwitting catalyst of it). Perhaps the most cogent analyses locate the hipster at the conjunction of these alternatives: as *New York* magazine put it in its somewhat premature obituary of the type, the hipster 'in fact aligns himself [sic] both with rebel subculture and with the dominant class, and thus opens up a poisonous conduit between the two' (Greif 2010: np). *Her* is too mainstream to be a genuine hipster artefact, though it clearly draws from the same well in its aestheticisation of both the future city and artefacts of the past, and in its equivocation between irony and sincerity.

Her is therefore structured by an anxious discourse about authenticity, which is manifested in its representation of human interactions and emotional bonds, the nature of work, and city space itself. This is established in the opening scene, which provides a view of the future workplace and the kind of labour that it might involve. Theodore sits at a computer terminal, where he uses software to compose faux-handwritten letters for customers. This job, a humorous *reductio ad absurdum* of outsourcing, is 'affective labour' in the sense defined by Michael Hardt – 'production defined by a combination of cybernetics and affect' (1999: 97) – in that it relies on his ability to channel empathy and emotional intensity that can be captured and commodified. The office space, which evokes a contemporary design studio or advertising agency, is tasteful and pleasant with pastel shades and hints of mid-twentieth century modernism. Though Theodore's letters are bespoke, it is nevertheless routine and relatively standardised work, and there are subtle suggestions (not least his designation 'Letter writer 612' – a trace of the bureaucratic organisation) that we might question the process by which the intimate sphere has been enveloped into this highly aestheticised corporate world. But what is the status of these letters – are they to be seen as less than 'real', even if they express the feelings of the writer and evoke emotions in the receiver, because they have been written by a third party? This question, first invoked at the level of work, becomes the film's defining question about the authenticity of Theodore and Samantha's relationship.

At a narrative level, Theodore's issues with authenticity in love and work are resolved in differing ways. At work, he redeems the inauthenticity of his writing by publishing it in the outmoded (or residual) media form of the printed book, which appears to persist as a specialist, boutique product. By doing so, he claims ownership and authorial control over the products of his alienated affective labour, and transforms emotional work into an aesthetic object. The analogue object stands in as a guarantor of authenticity, while the publication validates his creative potential beyond the confines of the corporation. The film concludes with Theodore composing a real handwritten letter to his ex-wife, in contrast to the fake letter that began the film. This rediscovery of authentic human connection is mirrored in the implicit coupling of Theodore and Amy at the end of the film. New possibilities of digital romance and post-human subjectivity are implicitly rejected by the ending, which also reunites the couple with a traditional view of urban (rather than virtual) space, a panoramic skyline that echoes a whole tradition of city films.

These themes are also figured via the film's production design. Unlike comparable LA romcoms such as *(500) Days of Summer* and *In Search of a Midnight Kiss*, both of which capitalise on the historic legacy of downtown and its architectural heritage, *Her* shows downtown's past as irrecoverably lost. In its functional yet homogenous smoothness, it recalls Rem Koolhaas's notion of the 'generic city' and his contention that the (perceived) homogenisation of global cities has been an active process of stripping away local identity. For Koolhaas, the generic city also offers a distinctive aesthetic and emotional experience:

> It is a place of weak and distended sensations, few and far between emotions, discreet and mysterious like a large space lit by a bed lamp [...] Instead of concentration – simultaneous presence – in the Generic City individual 'moments' are spaced far apart to create a trance of almost unnoticeable aesthetic experiences: the color variations in the fluorescent lighting of an office building just before sunset, the subtleties of the slightly different whites of an illuminated sign at night. (1998: 1250)

This description resonates with the aesthetic created by Jonze, production designer Barrett and cinematographer Hoyte van Hoytema. *Her* creates a space defined by smoothness and modulation rather than the shock and fragmentation of the modernist city. As Barrett puts it, the future city of *Her* was designed to appear 'convenient, comfortable, and bespoke' (in Curbed Staff 2013). Inspired by the photography of Rinko Kawauchi, they wanted 'a future that was soft and intimate' (Geffner 2014: np). Coloured Plexiglas and warm toned gels were used to create the mood of interior spaces. Without apparent irony, Jonze also mentions the chain Jamba Juice as an inspiration for the film's production design. As Jonze put it, 'Design is a big part of the world in a way it wasn't 20 years ago. There's great food everywhere and even McDonald's uses nice wood now… We tried to make a more comfortable L.A. that's easy and warm' (in Brooks 2013: np). To create this world, Jonze took guidance from Elizabeth Diller, of Diller, Scofidio and Renfro, architects of New York's emblematic redevelopment project the High Line, a link that implies a strong correlation between the film's imagination of the urban future and the objective conditions of the urban present.[7]

However, while this generic city is predicated on its erasure of the past, this loss of the historic city is counterbalanced in the film – and, we might add, in urban culture more generally – by an almost obsessive desire to recreate former styles and objects, an impulse to return to the material culture of the earlier city. This is enacted in *Her* through its persistent interest in the retro and the analogue, which is visible at the level of décor, costume and visual style. The office design is influenced by mid-twentieth century modernism, and high-tech objects such as computer displays are lined with a wood finish. The costume feels contemporary – as if Gap or Uniqlo designs from the present had been subtly inflected with fashions from the 1920s. This retro sensibility also extends beyond the *mise-en-scène* to the film's visual style, which was achieved using a combination of digital and analogue technology. The

Fig. 5 Advertising aesthetics in *Her*.

film was shot using ARRI Alexa digital cameras, creating a clean and modern look that is subtly retrofitted by using 1970s Canon lenses (reportedly used on one of Ingmar Bergman's films) to give it a vintage patina (see Geffner 2014). Jonze has worked extensively in commercials, notably for IKEA and Gap, and van Hoytema's corporate film for Ericsson (2010) develops a similar visual style to that used in *Her*. As Peter Bradshaw noted in the *Guardian*, the film creates 'a place where a contented, diverse population mills happily around, rather like a TV spot for Apple computers' (2014: np). *Her* also displays a number of stylistic strategies that contribute to this admixture of the digital and the vintage. Van Hoytema frequently uses shallow depth of field, overexposure and lens flare to create signifiers of analogue warmth and an 'organic' rather than high-tech feel to the image. As van Hoytema has explained, he intentionally removed the colour blue from the film's palette in order to avoid its associations with science fiction and technology. This was intended to create, in van Hoytema's words, 'a world that was tactile and pleasant: the very opposite of a dystopian future' (in Geffner 2014).

SCIENCE FICTION LEGACIES: REMEDIATING THE CINEMATIC CITY

In this sense, *Her*'s romantic comedy tendencies and retro discourse are also in tension with the other side of its genre identity, science fiction. The film therefore displays a complex temporality as a retro-futurist film that simultaneously mobilises ideas of the near future and the recent past. Critics connected *Her*'s concern with artificial intelligence to a wide variety of textual precursors and influences from *Pygmalion* and *Pinocchio* to classic science fiction films including *Westworld* (Michael Crichton, 1973) and *2001: A Space Odyssey* (Stanley Kubrick, 1968), and explorations of emergent digital culture such as *Electric Dreams* (Steve Barron, 1984). Science fiction has, of course, been a key genre for the projection of future cities, though they have been persistently read as offering commentary on contemporary urban issues (Kuhn 1999). Here, I focus less on the genre's predictive possibilities than on its capacity, as Fredric Jameson has put it, 'to defamiliarise and restructure our experience of our own present' (1982: 151). This section draws on the critical legacy of two of the film's intertexts, *Metropolis* and *Blade Runner*, arguing that *Her* draws on this science fiction lineage to navigate questions of gender and technology in the digital city.

As a pivotal film of European modernity, *Metropolis* may seem like an unlikely precursor for *Her*. However, Jonze's film and its articulation of gender and technology draws on a lineage cemented by Lang's work. As films such as *Weird Science* (John Hughes, 1985), *S1m0ne* (Andrew Niccol, 2002) and *Ex Machina* (Alex Garland, 2015) suggest, that Samantha is female is not incidental. Indeed, the female gendering of artificial intelligence is a trope that can be traced back to the late eighteenth century, when the figure of the robot became closely bound up with anxieties about female sexuality, otherness, and loss of male authority (see Huyssen 1986).

Thereafter, women and technology became interlinked in a complex process of cultural displacement. This is mobilised in *Metropolis* through the figure of Maria, whose split identity (in human and robot versions) is called on to play a crucial mediating role. As Andreas Huyssen shows, the film not only seeks to perform a reconciliation of capital and labour, but also works through opposing views of technology in Weimar culture. While the human version of Maria is depicted as increasingly passive and virginal, the machine-vamp Maria becomes threateningly sexualised and out of control, inciting the workers to revolution. Unbridled female sexuality is mapped directly onto the image of technology's destructive potential (ibid.)

Yet, as Thomas Elsaesser notes, Huyssen's critique has since become somewhat complicated by Maria's re-evaluation by contemporary audiences as a 'post-human, post-gender figure of ambiguous, but ultimately positive appeal' (2000: 57). This suggests, for Elsaesser, that technology is now so deeply imbricated in our daily lives that it has ceased to create such anxious responses. Nevertheless, it is clear that recent films such as *Ex Machina* and *Her* are rooted in what Huyssen calls 'male mystifications of female sexuality as technology-out-of-control' (1986: 78), though they operate in a context where digital technologies and portable media have become profoundly intertwined with the personal and the intimate. Like *Metropolis*, *Her* projects the virgin/vamp dichotomy onto technology, which is viewed as alternately obedient (Samantha as personal assistant and sexual partner) and dangerously non-compliant (Samantha's 641 virtual partners is a comic rendering of male fears of female promiscuity).

The female OS in *Her* is therefore called on to mediate between cultural oppositions and anxieties in a similar fashion to *Metropolis*. In the first instance, the film works through contemporary ambivalences about technology and the impact of the digital on everyday life. On the one hand, the possibility of love with an OS, which the film enacts quite earnestly, aligns with a Silicon Valley techno-utopianism of the kind associated with *Wired* magazine. To simplify somewhat, this tendency sees technology as imbued with liberating potential, fulfilling the individualist freedoms offered by the free market and post-1960s social liberalism. This notion of technology and personal freedom is quite openly set out in the middle section of *Her*, when Theodore first explores his relationship with Samantha. In this section, there are also strong metaphorical suggestions of non-normative sexuality in their relationship, which Theodore fears might lead to him being socially stigmatised (James Franco suggested in his piece for *Vice* that Samantha's ethereality 'provides an opening for a queer reading of the film' (2014: np)). The utopian aspects of technology are also figured through the film's production design, which as Stefano Baschiera and Elena Caoduro note, recalls the 'graphic design of contemporary virtual environments offered in operative systems and smartphone applications' (2015: np).

Alternately, the film can easily be read as a parable about the corrosive and alienating effects of technology on our social capacities – a milder form of the techno-dystopianism perhaps best encapsulated by fears about the so-called 'singularity' and the rise of the machines that have fuelled countless science fiction films from *2001: A Space Odyssey* to *The Terminator* (Jams Cameron, 1984). These anxieties are clearly present in *Blade Runner*, which not only reworked the modernist city of *Metropolis* but also updated the female robot in the central figure of Rachel, the replicant with whom Deckard falls in love. A direct link between *Her* and *Blade Runner* is also suggested by the screenplay: when Theodore first boots up OS1, he is asked a series of questions, including 'How would you describe your relationship with your mother?', a strong echo of the Voight-Kampff test in the earlier film.

Aside from the female replicants, the clearest link between *Her* and *Blade Runner* is the use of an East Asian city to create the *mise-en-scène* of a hybrid metropolis. Whereas *Blade Runner* referenced Tokyo, *Her* cross-pollinates Los Angeles, for many theorists the emblematic city of the late twentieth century, with Shanghai, one of the acknowledged global hubs of the twenty-first.[8] From one perspective, the shift from Tokyo to Shanghai indicates a wider shift from Japan to China as the USA's principal economic competitor. From an industrial standpoint, *Her*'s use of the Chinese city must also be understood within the context of a broader recalibration of Hollywood's strategic relationship to global markets. The rapid expansion of East Asia's global box office share has created a new interest in location filming in China, in part as a potential route into its highly regulated exhibition sector. Films such as *Mission: Impossible III* (J. J. Abrams, 2006), *Transformers: Revenge of the Fallen* (Michael Bay, 2009), *Looper* (Rian Johnson, 2012), *Skyfall* (Sam Mendes, 2012) and *Transformers 4: Age of Extinction* (Michael Bay, 2014) have made extensive use of Chinese cities as shooting location and narrative setting.

However, while Annapurna's decision to shoot in Shanghai was undoubtedly shaped by this economic and industrial backdrop, a relatively small-scale film such as *Her* has little chance of penetrating the Chinese market. In this case, the filmmakers' use of Shanghai was also motivated by creative concerns, and its choice both attests to the industrial relationship between Hollywood and China and the significance of East Asian cities in our current urban imaginary.[9] If in the 1980s, the Los Angeles School saw the urban conditions of Southern California writ large across the globe, the notion of LA as global paradigm has since been supplanted by the rapid urbanisation of China. Playing on Benjamin's famous proclamation that Paris was the capital of the nineteenth century, Michael Keith questions whether Shanghai might now be seen as the capital of the twenty-first, noting that 'in a growing stream of serious journalism and academic description, Chinese urbanism in general and the experience of Shanghai in particular, are held up to represent the future of the city' (2011: 398).

The composite city has a long history in the visual arts that extends at least as far back as the *capricci* or architectural fantasies of the seventeenth and eighteenth centuries, Canaletto's views of Venice being among the most famous examples. In this tradition, the composite compresses monuments and perspectives to produce a view of the ideal city. In recent years, in the context of globalisation and accelerated 'time-space compression', such composite cityscapes have become a recurring feature of the global city imaginary, especially in advertising and marketing. This trend is perhaps best exemplified by the 2007 promotional campaign for the *Financial Times* (tagline: 'We Live in Financial Times'), which playfully combined iconic buildings from world financial districts into a compressed skyline, from the Oriental Pearl Tower and the Petronas Towers to London's 'Gherkin' and the Grande Arche at La Défense. While the *FT* campaign invoked positive associations of global markets, international travel and frictionless information exchange – almost utopian in its interpellation of the reader as world citizen – other contemporary uses of the composite city have had more critical applications.[10] Michael Winterbottom's *Code 46* (2003), pieces together elements of London, Shanghai, Dubai and Kuala Lumpur to create a generic city that melds tier one global cities with the landscapes of the global South. More recently, Pacific Rim fusion and technological dynamism is also visible in Disney's animated feature *Big Hero 6* (Don Hall and Chris Williams, 2014), set in the self-evidently hybrid surroundings of 'Sanfransokyo'.

As Jane Chi Hyun Park has shown, Hollywood films have repeatedly aligned East Asia with technology and modernity to produce what Park calls 'a collective fantasy of the futuristic, high-tech Orient' (2010: viii) While *Her* certainly draws on this coding of the East Asian city as futuristic, the specificity of Pudong is also worth some consideration. Situated across the Huangpu River from the historic centre of Shanghai, Pudong was transformed into Shanghai's financial nerve centre by a state-funded building boom in the 1990s and 2000s which urbanised twice the surface area of Manhattan in a decade and a half (see Areddy 2011: C8). Its function was explicitly symbolic as well as economic, a marker of China's rising importance in the global economy and the ambition of the Deng government. As Thomas Campanella puts it, 'Pudong is not only the signature skyline of China's spectacular urban revolution; it is also a symbol of the urban revolution gripping nearly all the East. It is Asian ambition made visible, a steel and glass bar-graph of surging global power' (2010: 63). Pudong's skyline, which includes world-famous buildings as the Oriental Pearl Tower, the Jin Mao Tower and the Shanghai World Financial Centre, was part of a strategic effort to project Shanghai into the global city imaginary. In a symbiotic process, the futuristic nature of this cityscape has been provided a location for Western films – including *Code 46*, *Transformers: Revenge of the Fallen* and *Looper* – which in turn have helped to reinforce its image.

However, unlike these other films, *Her*'s use of Pudong as LA generally avoids its iconic buildings, allowing it to provide textures rather than recognisable places. As Barrett puts it, the locations were 'curated' from Shanghai: 'It's Los Angeles; we just borrowed some buildings and planted them where they're not' (in Zeitchik 2013: np). It is neither spectacular nor overtly disjunctive, though it does have a defamiliarising effect. While *Her*'s hybrid city symbolically enacts the decentring of the Los Angeles School vision, its invocation of Pudong also speaks to the film's broader investment in notions of authenticity. For Jeroen de Kloet and Lena Scheen,

Pudong occupies a unique position within the global city imaginary; reformulating Rem Koolhaas's notion of the generic city and Abbas's notion of the fake, they adapt the Chinese term *shanzai*, a widespread vernacular term that primarily refers to imitation consumer goods. Rather than see Pudong as simply 'fake', with its strong implication of a (Western) original, they suggest that reading it as a *shanzai* global city helps to accentuate the ways in which the city is at once a 'copy' of other global cities, yet 'not quite' (2013: 3). Thus the city imagined by *Her* invokes Pudong as a *shanzai* global city – that is to say, its specifically Chinese character is of minimal interest to the filmmakers compared to its status as a troublingly generic landscape, which is almost uncanny its combination of the familiar and the unfamiliar.

Beyond its conflation of Los Angeles and Tokyo, *Blade Runner* has also been widely discussed in relation to the state of the American city. In Giuliana Bruno's (1987) and David Harvey's (1989) influential analyses of *Blade Runner*, the interest of its production design lay not in its unfamiliarity but rather its exaggeration of the already existing post-industrial decline of many American cities in the early 1980s. The film invites audiences to take pleasure in what Bruno terms an 'aesthetic of decay' through its *mise-en-scène* of ruins, garbage and abandoned buildings which, like J. F. Sebastian, are subject to an 'accelerated decrepitude' (1987: 63). While Bruno and Harvey view the city of *Blade Runner* as an allegorical extrapolation of the urban present, Mike Davis critiqued the film for having failed to engage with the realities of Los Angeles. Arguing against claims for its diagnostic power, Davis points out that the film in fact relied on much the same modernist architectural projection as *Metropolis* – 'another edition of the core modernist fantasy of the future metropolis – alternately utopia or dystopia, ville radieuse or Gotham City – as monster Manhattan' (1999: 361). Taking a characteristically realist position, Davis argued that the film and the commentary it generated had missed the ways in which the actual Los Angeles was *already* dystopian in its de facto racial segregation, gated communities, securitised zones and semi-militarised law enforcement. *Her* attempts to reposition the image of the city away from both of these alternatives. But in moving away from the darkness of dystopian nightmare, plugging science fiction into romance rather than *noir*, *Her* not only sidesteps the clichés of *Blade Runner* but also elides the class and race divides that Davis rightly invokes. Placing *Blade Runner* in its historical context, we can see how it drew on an existing public image of the American city in ruins, evoking suburban fears of urban decline and cultural heterogeneity. In contrast, *Her*'s outwardly positive take on the future city meshes with the downtown revival and the gentrification of urban cores.

In this respect, the absences and elisions of *Her* are telling. What is missing from *Her*'s image of the future city is clear enough in comparison to both *Metropolis* and *Blade Runner*. However the political stance of Lang's film is to be interpreted, the defining feature of its cinematic city was division and hierarchy – a city ordered by class antagonisms and the division of labour. For David Harvey, these issues of class, labour and power are no less visible in *Blade Runner*. As simulacra of human beings designed specifically for short-term, flexible labour, the replicants are for Harvey emblematic figures for the precarious worker of post-Fordist capitalism. The stratified, segregated city of corporate control, off-shore labour colonies and sweatshops is the backdrop for the replicants' revolt, which Harvey sees as an allegory for class struggle (1989: 310). In the film's initial version, at least, the escapist ending and the perceived lack of class solidarity between Deckard and the replicants mutes the political potential of the film. Yet like *Metropolis*, the ending cannot fully recuperate the force of the images it has generated.

While *Her* revisits many of the themes of these two earlier films, it repurposes them into what we might describe as a post-class scenario, where the recurring issues of identity and authenticity are posed as individual rather than collective concerns. *Her* elides issues of class and power, and the spatial opposition between high and low that drives both of the earlier films has been flattened out into a smooth and undifferentiated space where class relations are less obviously visible or tangible. The relationship between the individual and the corporation, which is the central antagonism of *Blade Runner* (the replicants vs. Tyrell), is also essentially absent. At Theodore's workplace, there is no visible hierarchy or power structure – we never see a line manager and we might speculate that management itself has become automated. Element Software, the manufacturer of OS1, is barely fleshed out, mentioned only in an extended advert that first introduces us, and Theodore, to the idea of an artificially intelligent operating system. Our successful emotional investment in Samantha as a personified OS encourages us to forget that she is a product and, most likely, a conduit for mining all possible kinds of data, from Theodore's personal emails to the most intimate details of his private life and sexual preferences. Thus, whereas *Blade Runner* is driven by concerns about the Tyrell corporation and the potentially simulacral nature of our memories and desires, *Her* draws back from any serious appraisal of corporate over-reach into the private sphere. Yet, in the final instance, the film evades political critique through its tone and audience address, which is split between whimsical humour and aestheticised melancholy. In this sense, the central problem of the narrative – the issue of authenticity and emotional resonance in the digital era – is one duplicated by the film itself and its ambivalent tonal oscillation between irony and sincerity.[11]

CONCLUSION

The city of *Her* is neither utopia nor dystopia in any straightforward way. As such, it manages to transcend the 'sunshine or noir' dialectic that has long characterised cultural representations of Los Angeles (see Davis 1992). The film vacillates between celebratory and sceptical positions on technology, and the smooth, safe functionality of the future city in *Her* is counterbalanced by a sense of melancholy and loss. Having persuasively drawn the audience into believing in the possibility of love with an operating system, it intentionally draws back and undermines it. The ending of the film is ambiguous, though it strongly hints at the possibility of romance between Theodore and Amy. From this perspective, it is their love – not that of Theodore and Samantha – that provides the traditional arc and resolution of the romantic comedy. Having worked through ultimately unfeasible alternatives – in this case, digital romance – the pair find themselves drawn to each other. Thus, the ending implies, the possibility of authentic love and human connection comes from interactions in physical city space rather than virtual media space. While this is easily construed as a conservative ending, it does allow Theodore to move on from Samantha (in some senses, a fantasy projection) in favour of 'real' experience and human bonds. In the final shot, the romcom returns home again – the material space of the city – and its ideology of romance overcoming obstacles is gently reaffirmed. Yet, despite the partial closure of this ending, we are left not only with the film's melancholy mood but also the sincere evocation of a post-human romance that cannot completely be erased by the narrative conclusion.

Working through the complexities of *Her* as a contemporary urban text demonstrates the collision of existing cinematic traditions of genre and urban representation with new imaginaries of the digital city, with its new forms of connection and disconnection, proximity and distance, and of the global city, with its tendencies towards homogenisation and hybridisation. *Her* is a product as well as an exploration of this digital media city, yet it relies on the traditions of the cinematic city. In mapping out the creative city as urban future, the film repurposes existing tropes of the city and technology, proximity and distance, romance and alienation. This suggests that our narrative and aesthetic forms fall back, with nostalgia or via a retro sensibility, on older ideas of the city. In this sense, films such as *Her* demonstrate how the digital media city frequently relies on the genres and tropes of the cinematic city to represent and figure it: the digital city and the cinematic city interact in a complex relationship of recombination and remediation.

NOTES

1   From an audience perspective, one impact of the digital turn has been a massive expansion in the critical, promotional and viewer-created content that circulates online, or what we might define as a proliferation of paratexts and paratextuality. Critical discussions of the film's representation of the city, and cartographic paratexts such as the *Los Angeles Times* map are therefore not merely appendages to the film but an integral part of the audience's engagement with it. In many cases, this 'discursive surround' precedes the consumption of the film itself, priming the audience and framing their understanding of the text. As Jason Mittell has argued with respect to complex television, such digital paratexts make media works not just spreadable but 'drillable': they significantly extend and deepen

audience engagement and participation, encouraging us to 'drill' down beneath the surface of the text (2015). Though we might conceptualise such intensified online activity as drawing audiences away from the physical space of city and cinema into the 'virtual' space of the web, such oppositions are unwieldy and do not do justice to the complex imbrication of material and immaterial in the contemporary media city. Rather, we need to recognise the ways that paratexts might reconfigure the viewer's relationship to screens and spaces.

2 Brian Henderson also notes that 'the romantic comedy has always been urban and urban-oriented, aggressively, smugly assuming the superiority of city over country' (1978: 19)

3 Significant exceptions include *Pretty Woman* (Garry Marshall, 1990) and *L.A. Story* (Mick Jackson, 1991).

4 My use of the term 'shoe leather time' is adapted from Richard Combs's (2002) analysis of *Dirty Harry* (Don Siegel, 1971).

5 Throughout the 2000s, local development policies were deeply influenced by interpretations of Florida's work, in particular the alluring notion that generating 'buzz' and a 'hip' urban culture to attract a particular group of creative professionals might provide a shortcut to regeneration and economic growth. Yet, as Jamie Peck has persuasively argued, this 'urban development script' neatly meshed with existing neoliberal agendas, including 'interurban competition, gentrification, middle-class consumption, and place marketing' (2005: 740).

6 While technically an independent, Annapurna is well capitalised (its founder, Megan Ellison, is daughter of tech billionaire Larry Ellison), frequently works in collaboration with the major studios, and its mid-budget productions, such as *Zero Dark Thirty* (Kathryn Bigelow, 2012) and *American Hustle* (David O. Russell, 2013), have gained substantial commercial and critical success.

7 In his recent monograph, Dimendberg notes that Diller, Scofidio and Renfro are 'creators of moving images as much as architects', adding that Diller 'has sometimes quipped that her ideal second career would involve relocating to Hollywood and working in the movie business' (2013: 4)

8 The notion of Los Angeles as paradigmatic was central to the discourse of the Los Angeles School theorists. See Soja and Scott (1986).

9 The choice of Shanghai to invoke a sustainable city future is ironic, given the intense pollution problems experienced by Chinese cities, and the importance of the car to Chinese urbanism more generally.

10 Of course, the cinematic city is frequently heterogenous in its construction, in the sense that material shot on location in different cities can be combined, along with studio-based (and now CGI-assisted) footage to establish a relatively seamless experience for the viewer. Such routine acts of 'creative geography' may reconstruct a real city for the audience, combining second unit footage with studio work and a cheaper location standing in more-or-less convincingly for its setting. In other cases, such as *The Dark Knight* (Christopher Nolan, 2008),

a fictional city (Gotham) may be created from multiple shooting locations to render a city that is both familiar and unfamiliar.

11 This tendency, which Peter Bradshaw called the 'Frankensteinian sewing together of two tonal imperatives' (2013: np) is part of a wider pattern in independent cinema, in which the irony of the 'smart film' is counterbalanced by the earnestness of the 'New Sincerity'.

BIBLIOGRAPHY

Areddy, James T. (2011) 'Shanghai's Pudong, Once Soulless, Rises Up', *Wall Street Journal*, 21 December, C8.

Baschiera, Stefano, and Elena Caoduro (2015) 'Retro, faux-vintage and anachronism: when cinema looks back'. *NECSUS: European Journal of Media Studies*; http://www.necsus-ejms.org/retro-faux-vintage-and-anachronism-when-cinema-looks-back/

Bradshaw, Peter (2014) '*Her* – Review', *The Guardian*, 13 February; http://www.theguardian.com/film/2014/feb/13/her-review

Brooks, Brian (2013) 'Spike Jonze on Femininity and His Vision of the Future', Catalogue for New York Film Festival, *Film Society of Lincoln Center*, 8 August; http://www.filmlinc.org/nyff2013/blog/interview-spike-jonze-her-joaquin-phoenix-scarlett-johansson-nyff.html

Bruno, Giuliana (1987) 'Ramble City: Postmodernism and *Blade Runner*', *October*, 41, 61–74.

Bull, Michael (2007) *Sound Moves: iPod Culture and Urbam Experience*. London and New York: Routledge.

Campanella, Thomas J. (2010) 'China: As We Once Were', *Journal of Architectural Education*, 63, 2, 63–4.

Combs, Richard (2002) '8 Degrees of Separation', *Film Comment*, Jul/Aug., 50–3.

Curbed Staff (2013) 'How the Her Filmmakers Created a Utopian Los Angeles of the Not-Too-Distant Future', *Curbed Los Angeles*, 18 December; http://la.curbed.com/tag/kk-barrett

Dargis, Manohla (2013) 'Disembodied, but Oh, What a Voice', *New York Times*, 17 December; http://nyti.ms/Jyldgh

Davis, Mike (1992) *City of Quartz: Excavating the Future in Los Angeles*. London: Verso.

____ (1999) *Ecology of Fear: Los Angeles and the Imagination of Disaster*. London: Picador.

Debruge, Peter (2014) 'Is Your Computer a "Him" or "Her"? – and Other Questions Raised by Spike Jonze's Speculative Romance', *Variety*, January 7.

De Kloet, Jeroen and Lena Scheen (2013) 'Pudong: The *Shanzai* Global City', *European Journal of Cultural Studies*, 16, 6, 692–709.

Dimendberg, Edward (2010) 'Cinema and the Making of a Modern City', in William Deverell and Greg Hise (eds) *A Companion to Los Angeles*. Chichester: Wiley-Blackwell, 346–64.

Dimendberg, Edward (2013) *Diller, Scofidio + Renfro: Architecture After Images*. Chicago: University of Chicago Press.

Elsaesser, Thomas (2012) *Metropolis*. London: British Film Institute.

Florida, Richard (2004) *The Rise of the Creative Class and How it's Transforming Work, Leisure, Community and Everyday Life*. New York: Basic Books.

Foundas, Scott (2013) 'Film Review: *Her*', *Variety*, 15 October; http://variety.com/2013/film/reviews/film-review-her-1200710608/

Franco, James (2014) 'Who is "Her"?' *Vice*, 2 January; https://www.vice.com/en_uk/read/who-is-her

Geffner, David (2014) 'The Way She Haunts My Dreams', *International Cinematographer's Guild Magazine*, 2 January; http://www.icgmagazine.com/web/the-way-she-hunts-my-dreams/

Greif, Mark (2010) 'What Was the Hipster?', *New York* magazine, 24 October; http://nymag.com/news/features/69129/

Hardt, Michael (1999) 'Affective Labor', *boundary 2*, 26, 2, 89–100.

Harvey, David (1989) *The Condition of Postmodernity: An Enquiry into the Origins of Cultural Change*. Oxford: Blackwell.

Hawthorne, Christopher (2014) 'Spike Jonze's "Her" a Refreshingly Original Take on a Future L.A.', *Los Angeles Times*, January 18.

Henderson, Brian (1978) 'Romantic Comedy Today: Semi-Tough or Impossible?', *Film Quarterly*, 31, 4, 11–23.

Huyssen, Andreas (1986) *After the Great Divide: Modernism, Mass Culture, Postmodernism*. Bloomington: Indiana University Press.

Jameson, Fredric (1982) 'Progress versus Utopia: Or, Can We Imagine the Future?', *Science Fiction Studies*, 9, 2, 147–58.

Jermyn, Deborah (2009) 'I [heart] NY: the Rom-Com's Love Affair with New York City', in Stacey Abbott and Deborah Jermyn (eds) *Falling in Love Again: Romantic Comedy in Contemporary Cinema*. London: I.B. Tauris, 9–24.

Keith, Michael (2011) 'City-zenship in Contemporary China: Shanghai, Capital of the Twenty-First Century?', in Gary Bridge and Sophie Watson (eds) *The New Blackwell Companion to the City*. Chichester: Blackwell, 398–406.

Koolhaas, Rem and Bruce Mau (1998) *S, M, L, XL*. New York: Monacelli Press.

Kredell, Brendan (2012) 'Wes Anderson and the City Spaces of Indie Cinema', *New Review of Film and Television Studies*, 10, 1, 83–96.

Krutnik, Frank (2002) 'Conforming Passions?: Contemporary Romantic Comedy', in Steve Neale (ed.) *Genre and Contemporary Hollywood*. London: British Film Institute, 130–47.

Kuhn, Annette (ed.) (1999) *Alien Zone II: The Spaces of Science Fiction Cinema*. London and New York: Verso.

Mittell, Jason (2015) *Complex TV: The Poetics of Contemporary Television Storytelling*. New York: New York University Press.

Park, Jane Chi Hyun (2010) *Yellow Future: Oriental Style in Hollywood Cinema*. Minneapolis: University of Minnesota Press.

Patches, Matt (2013) '10 Visions of the Future from Spike Jonze's "Her"', *Hollywood Reporter*, 15 October; http://www.hollywoodreporter.com/news/10-visions-future-spike-jonzes-648768

Peck, Jamie (2005) "Struggling with the Creative Class", *International Journal of Urban and Regional Research*, 29, 4, 740–70.

Renninger, Bryce J. (2013) 'Spike Jonze, Why Are There No Brown People in Your Future Los Angeles?' *Indiewire.com*, 14 October; http://www.indiewire.com/article/spike-jonze-why-are-there-no-brown-people-in-your-future-los-angeles

Rosen, Christine (2014) 'What Do you See Here?' *Slate*, 9 January; http://www.slate.com/articles/technology/technology/2014/01/spike_jonze_s_her_is_a_rorschach_test_for_your_feelings_about_technology.html

Rosen, Christopher (2013) '7 Things to Know About Spike Jonze's "Her"', *Huffington Post*, 10 December.

Ruscoe, Emilie (2014) 'The Hipster Answer to *Blade Runner*', *Mediander Blog*, 22 January; http://blog.mediander.com/the-hipster-answer-to-blade-runner/

Scheible, Jeff (2014) 'Longing to Connect: Cinema's Year of OS Romance', *Film Quarterly*, 68, 1, 22–31.

Schneider, Susan (2014) 'The Philosophy of "Her"', *New York Times*, 2 March; http://opinionator.blogs.nytimes.com/2014/03/02/the-philosophy-of-her/

Shatkin, Elina (2014) 'Her and Us: How Spike Jonze's New Movie Gives L.A. the Future Blade Runner Couldn't', *Los Angeles Magazine*, 15 January; http://www.lamag.com/culturefiles/her-and-us-how-spike-jonzes-new-movie-gives-la-the-future-blade-runner-couldnt/

Shiel, Mark (2012) *Hollywood Cinema and the Real Los Angeles*. London: Reaktion.

Soja, Edward W. and Allen J. Scott (1986) 'Los Angeles: Capital of the Late Twentieth Century', *Environment and Planning D: Society and Space*, 4, 249–54.

Steffen, Alex (2015) 'Designing the Future of *Her*', *Medium.com*; https://medium.com/@AlexSteffen/designing-the-future-of-her-b865347a8895#.b0tnsysre

Stevens, Dana (2013) 'Her', *Slate*, 19 December; http://www.slate.com/articles/arts/movies/2013/12/spike_jonze_s_her_reviewed.html

THR Staff (2014) '"Her": What the Critics are Saying'. *Hollywood Reporter*, 10 December; http://www.hollywoodreporter.com/news/her-what-critics-are-saying-669998

Turkle, Sherry (2011) *Alone Together: Why We Expect More from Technology and Less from Each Other*. New York: Basic Books.

Varnelis, Kazys (2003) 'The City Beyond Maps: From Bonaventure to One Wilshire', *Pasajes de Arquitectura y Critica*, September; http://varnelis.net/articles/the_city_beyond_maps

Zeitchik, Steven (2013) 'Five Days of "Her": How to Shoot the Future', *Los Angeles Times*, December 26.

Zukin, Sharon (2009) 'Changing Landscapes of Power: Opulence and the Urge for Authenticity' *International Journal of Urban and Regional Research*, 33, 2, 543–53.

CINEPHILIA AND THE CITY: THE POLITICS OF PLACE IN CONTEMPORARY BENGALI CINEMA

MALINI GUHA

> In its countless alveoli space contains compressed time. That is what space is for.
> (Bachelard 1994: 8)

A recent Bengali film titled *Bhooter Bhabishyat* (*The Future of the Past*, Anik Dutta, 2012) features an opening credit sequence that establishes its satirical intensions: the eyes and voices of a series of ghosts launch a stringent critique of recent development practices in the city of Kolkata that have crafted a newly minted topography of high-rises, multiplex cinemas and shopping malls. These are the markers of global city architecture at its finest, alluding to the fact that Kolkata is in the midst of its reinvention as such. Through the use of song, these ghosts lament the razing of colonial mansions required to make way for Kolkata as generic city. The future of Kolkata's ghosts is in jeopardy and as they tell us, organised resistance to these expansive topographical changes is non-existent. The homage to Satyajit Ray's *The Adventures of Goopy and Bagha/Goopy Gyne Bagha Byne* (1955) is unmistakable as the music in this sequence recalls that which accompanies the celebrated 'ghost sequence' in Ray's film. The actual music from *The Adventures of Goopy and Bagha* serves as a ring tone for one of the central characters, who happens to be a film director. Near the end of this sequence, the ghosts situate the film as a form of protest against these development practices. This is a defence of the *topos* mounted through the cinema and one where the increasingly spectral nature of the urban past is literalised as the city's ghosts engage in a battle of wits against the 'law' of the urban developer.

In their introduction to a recent dossier on the topic of cinephilia, Jonathan Buschbaum and Elena Gorfinkel pose the question of 'what is being fought for by today's cinephilia(s)?' (2009: 176), an inquiry framed by the desire to unearth the social, political and historical conditions that animate contemporary outpourings of love for the cinema. If we ask this question of *The Future of the Past*, it is the city itself that is at stake; Kolkata is threatened with the incremental loss of its material history on an accelerated scale, a condition allegorised through the conventions of the ghost story that tell a second narrative of the city as vanishing *topos*. If we extend this question to address a larger number of films that comprise a recent trend in Bengali cinema dubbed by its practitioners as 'middle of the road' cinema, then what becomes clear is that the myriad gestures towards cinephilia located across these films are often imbricated with topophilia, or love of the city. *The Future of the Past* is a case in point as the evocation of Ray's film implicates the cinematic past in its plea to preserve the city's history in built form.

Films such as *Autograph* (Srijit Mukerjee, 2010), *Hawa Bodol* (Parambrata Chattopadhay, 2013), *Maach, Mishti and More* (Mainak Bhaumik, 2013) and, of course, *The Future of the Past* pay homage to an earlier wave of Kolkata-based films made by 'Parallel Cinema' directors Satyajit Ray, Mrinal Sen and Ritwik Ghatak.[1] These references raise the spectre, sometimes literally, of the urban past through representational means that find points of convergence with a topophilic sensibility. However, these films simultaneously differentiate themselves from their cinematic predecessors in ways that coincide with the often-stated intention of their directors to create a distinctly popular cinema tailored to the contemporary conditions of the city.[2]

As cultural geographers such as Doreen Massey have long claimed, yearnings for the specificity of place are never quite obliterated in the age of globalisation, even in the face of the overwhelming spread of generic architecture and spatial construction across cities the world over (1994: 147). From within a film studies context, Elena Gorfinkel and John David Rhodes claim in their introduction to *Taking Place: Location and the Moving Image* that a prevalent thesis regarding the 'death of place' has been prematurely established and in fact, the cinema is instrumental in contributing to the circumvention of the homogenising tendencies of globalisation (2011: xii).

Following on from Gorfinkel and Rhodes's assertion, we can make the claim that longings for the distinctiveness of place are often amplified at this historical crossroads, foregrounding the tensions as well as contradictions that the global city in particular presents. The tensions activated in these films between nostalgic longings for the past coupled with aspirations for the present are transposed onto both a city and a film industry in a period of transition, careening towards a future that is increasingly and ambivalently global in its guise. This chapter will address the complex reasons as to why both cinema and city seem to assume such significance at this historical juncture and precisely, for whom.

CINEPHILIA ONE AND TWO

The existing scholarship on cinephilia emphasises its enduring relationship to what

Thomas Elsaesser has deemed 'retroactive temporalities', encompassing journeys into the past that are inclusive of the timelines of the eventual and continual discovery of past films as well as the desire to remember cinema's past (2005: 27). The further potential to generate nostalgic longings *for* that past is evinced by Susan Sontag's (1996) well-known polemic concerning contemporary cinema's deficiency in stimulating the fervent cinephilia that she, among others, heavily associates with the post-war period. Privileging cinephilia's penchant for the past returns us to the historical moment of its origin in the film cultures of post-war France, as Hollywood's European distribution circuits became operational once again. This first generation of cinephilia was invested in the places within which its activities blossomed, including the space of the theatre, extending outward to encompass the cinephile capitals of the West such as Paris and New York (see Elsaesser 2005: 30; Hilderbrand 2009: 215).

Elsaesser concludes that the experience of cinephilia does not simply denote a 'love of cinema' but is riven with desire, anxiety, loss, remembrance and nostalgia, among other kinds of affective impulses (2005: 30). Similarly, topophilia exceeds its primary definition as 'love of place' to encompass complex emotional responses linked to remembrance and nostalgia. Topophilia, as articulated by French philosopher Gaston Bachelard in *The Poetics of Space*, is the name given to the emotional residues borne from the activity of topoanalysis (1994: 12). Topoanalysis is a type of memory work where intimate spaces, located primarily within the locus of the home, operate as compressed repositories of 'time past'; as Bachelard states, 'that is what space is for' (1994: 8). He observes that time does not achieve the status of duration within these spaces but acquires an abstract quality, shorn of what he refers to as its 'thickness' as time becomes ensconced within space (1994: 9). Topophilia then, speaks to the yearning for time to come to a standstill, however briefly, through the spatialisation of memory. Yi-Fu Tuan provides an expanded usage of the term that moves us beyond the confines of the home when he defines topophilia as 'the affective bond between people and place or setting' (1990: 4).

Topophilia and cinephilia merge in various accounts of post-war cinephilia, including Elsaesser's analysis of 'cinephilia, take one', where place and cinema are intertwined in this early generation's account of the cinephiliac experience. But the historical narrative he sketches is largely Western in its orientation, made clear in the lack of direct reference to 'cinephilia one' as experienced outside of Europe or the US. An expanded view of Elsaesser's historical framework takes us to numerous cities, including Calcutta, as it was previously known, and to the city's flourishing ciné-club movement that was modelled upon its French counterparts (2005: 38). In the 1950s and 1960s, the Calcutta Film Society was comprised of many of the leading figures of the Parallel Cinema movement, including Ray, Ghatak and Sen. As Rochona Majumdar explains, the film society movement fostered two ideals of cinema. In its early phase, 'good cinema' constituted a taste building initiative that was intended to develop an alternative viewing culture for global art cinema, running the gamut from Eisenstein to Bergman, in place of popular Indian cinema (2012: 743). In its second phase, the notion of 'good cinema' took a politicised turn in favour of leftist oriented film practices, by Indian filmmakers and those across the globe driven by the increasingly turbulent brand of politics experienced within Indian cities in the 1960s and 1970s (2012: 735).[3]

This example, which attributes the shifting desire for viewing certain kinds of films to the changing circumstances of the city within which they are screened, is a complex illustration of the mingling of cinephilia and topophilia. Cinephilia in this instance becomes entangled with the politics of place, so that 'love' of either place or cinema is fraught with ambivalence stemming from the conditions of urban decline. An account of 'cinephilia take one' in the Indian context can lead us to an examination of some of the films of this period in terms of their figurations of place. A number of Parallel Cinema directors involved within the ciné-club movement, including Ghatak, Ray and Sen, lean towards conflicted expressions of topophilia in their varying engagements with the post-colonial city as it pertains to the problems of unemployment, overcrowding and the arrival of the Naxalite movement to the city. These events constitute the underside of the celebratory aspects of the nation's entry into the domain of post-colonial modernity, characterised more positively in terms of achievements in science and technology and the establishment of independent India as a democratic, secular state (see Sarkar 2015: 462).

Some of the Parallel Cinema films referenced by contemporary Kolkata-based cinema foreground the post-colonial city as a site of conflict.[4] While these films do not engage in an overt celebration of place, their investment in representing the plight of the city both narratively and through moments of formal experimentation constitutes an act of topophilia that is about love as much as anxiety and loss. If we make the claim that a parallel period of transition and change is being experienced by the city in the present, it seems that an earlier preoccupation with the city is invoked by contemporary filmmakers equally in thrall to the city of their times through implicit or even direct reference to the work of the Parallel Cinema movement.

Elsaesser distinguishes the topographically laced cinephilia of 'cinephilia one', from its contemporary counterpart, 'cinephilia take two', which splits into two variations: the first continues the tradition of large screen, auteur-driven viewing while the second moves further into virtual terrain, where place matters less than accessibility and the potential for new filmic discoveries via digital channels (2005: 36). The distinctions that separate 'cinephilia one' from 'two' can be grafted onto debates regarding the demise of place in the era of globalisation as the classic *topoi* of postwar cinephilia take on an increasingly diminished role within cinephilia, the next generation. But it is essential to note, as Elsaesser does, that there isn't a complete rupture between cinephilia one and two, as the desire for large screen viewing, coupled with the continued valorisation of the auteur is indicative of the persistence of cinephilia one.

Given the predominance of 'cinephilia take two' in its digital variation, the question of precisely how topophilia and cinephilia converge in the contemporary moment leads us back to the claim that the specificity of place continues to matter, and that it does so precisely in response to the threats of eradication that haunt any articulation of a 'sense of place' (Massey 1994: 146). The gestures that numerous 'middle of the road' films make towards a previous cinephile culture in conjunction with an explicit engagement with the present day city is a second way of gauging the continued presence of 'cinephilia one' as intertext. While Elsaesser's framework of cinephilia addresses shifting conditions of viewing, this chapter engages with an expanded understanding of 'cinephilia one' in terms of how films that are the objects of this early generation of cine-love are addressed through the cinephiliac overtures of these contemporary 'middle of the road' films. Beyond this, I want to explore how the complex and conflict driven expressions of love of place and the cinema, both of which are often theorised in accordance with their predilection toward the past, might also assume significance in relationship to the time of present and future in this case study of Kolkata-based cinema.

FOR THE LOVE OF THE TOPOS

Topophilia is a term that resonates with two competing discourses concerning recent transformations of the topographical landscape of Kolkata. Yet it must be acknowledged at the outset that topophilia denotes an experience that is not immediately associated with a city like Kolkata, especially since phrases such as 'urban failure', 'black hole' or 'the city of dreadful night' come more readily to mind.[5] This discursive history is at best ambivalent, but at worst, upholds a disparaging view of a city that often obscures its more 'positive identities' as model colonial city, for instance. It is against the backdrop of a popular, decidedly topophobic discourse concerning the city's perpetual poverty, chaotic layout, and dense population that we can situate recent topophilic tendencies invested in lauding or defending Kolkata rather than participating in the long history of its denigration.

A strand of journalistic discourse has proclaimed that Kolkata has entered a period of renewal as the city has finally divested itself of its imperial and communist past. The latter was heralded by the election of Chief Minister Mamata Banerjee in 2011, spelling the end of 34 years of communist governance. This discourse celebrates what I term as 'Kolkata take two', as a welcome change from 'Kolkata one', a post-colonial city in a state of perpetual decline. The rapid transformation of the city in recent years signifies the apex of an economic shift that began in 1991, when India first opened its doors to neoliberal economic reforms (in Bose 2007: 120).

In this narrative, Kolkata aspires to the visual appearance of London, in accordance with Banerjee's stated desire to transform the city into the spitting image of the former imperial capital of the British Empire (see Bose 2011). A number of these plans are in the development stage, including the revamping of the waterfront where London's South Bank is held up as a model, and the building of the 'Kolkata eye' (see

Patel 2014; Niyogi 2015). Some of these initiatives have already been implemented, such as the installation of Victorian style trident lamps and the proliferation of high-rise apartments and condos in the suburban reaches of the city. A cogent example is New Town, one of numerous satellite townships that have cropped up across the subcontinent, built on mostly agricultural land. New Town is comprised of high-rise residential buildings and IT offices, cut across by a spacious highway called the Eastern Metropolis Bypass. New Town and other townships of its kind operate as global cities in microcosm, home to financial and service sectors encased in high-rise buildings that meet the demands of a vertical aesthetic belonging to *the* global city, writ large.[6]

The evocation of 'London' in this discourse signifies as an ambition, one that involves Kolkata's impending metamorphosis from city of decline into a modern, global city replete with the kinds of architectural features generally found in such cities (see Bose 2007: 113). As Bishnupriya Ghosh argues in her recent work on 'high-rise horror' in Mumbai cinema, the proliferation of luxury flats in cities such as Mumbai and Kolkata assumes the patina of the aspirational, a marker of global cities that are 'yet to come' in all of their fullness (2014: 7). These new urban developments are not simply targeted towards what Pablo S. Bose terms as 'an emerging and global middle class', but one that is inclusive of the Indian diaspora abroad (2007: 113). Bose provocatively claims that it does not matter whether diasporic populations actually live in these flats; it is the *idea* of them that counts, one that signifies middle class ambitions for a cosmopolitan, global Kolkata (2007: 126).

A second discourse unveils a certain apprehensiveness that has arisen as a result of these dramatic topographical changes. Author Amit Chaudhuri (2015), for example, mourns the destruction of colonial homes. A collectively authored plea helmed by Chaudhuri argues that Kolkata should take steps to ensure that such areas of the city are declared as heritage sites. Chaudhuri speaks to a larger cultural anxiety regarding the gradual transformation of Kolkata into a non-space, typical of the state of global cities worldwide that are overrun with nondescript forms of architecture. There is the further question of the exact cost of these development practices and who is being displaced to make way for 'global Kolkata'. In particular, there has been controversy regarding the dislocation of farmers and the forced acquisition of land required for the development of 'New Town', laying bare the gentrifying aims that underscore Kolkata's development plans; there are also concerns of an environmental nature as the condo developments on the Eastern edges of the city threaten the fragile ecosystem of the East Kolkata wetlands made up of fisheries and farms (see Bose 2014: 4).

The two narratives of the city outlined above offer competing illustrations of topophilia. The story of urban renewal celebrates the future of the Kolkata as global city so that the narrative arc of 'Kolkata rising' is readily superimposed onto that of 'India rising'.[7] In this instance, topophilia is translated into a matter of urban pride and by extension, national pride where Kolkata is deemed to be narrowing the gap between itself and its global city counterparts. The second narrative, in laying claim to the city that once was, assumes an air of defensiveness and nostalgic longing precisely because a very specific and generic iteration of modernisation is lauded as the city's only way forward.

Since 2009, a series of commercial Bengali films later dubbed 'middle of the road' cinema has embraced the city as their primary shooting location.[8] The late Bengali filmmaker Rituparno Ghosh remarked in 2011 that he had little use for the category of 'Bengali film' but rather, wanted to focus specifically on Kolkata-based cinema as marking new ground, both aesthetically and thematically. This comment alludes to the ascendance of the category of 'Kolkata-based cinema' in a manner that correlates with the narrative arc of 'Kolkata rising'. A recent journalistic piece in *The Times of India* also suggests that it is hardly a coincidence that a renewed interest in Kolkata as shooting location has become discernable in this period as the 'Banerjee' era of governance heralds a new face for the former 'city of decline'. As the article details, Banerjee sent actor Arindam Sil as part of the government's official delegation to the 2015 Cannes Film Festival in order to induce international production houses to choose Kolkata as their shooting location, an offer accompanied by financial incentives including cost-free shooting locations and nominal fees for security (see Dasgupta 2015). While the article details the way in which Banerjee is intent on selling the city as international shooting destination, 'middle of the road' cinema has already paved the way for a newfound significance for urban locations that provides specifically cinematic recalibrations of both variations of topophilia.

These films have been self-proclaimed as 'middle of the road' because they walk the line between commercial cinema and art cinema. We can describe them as an increasingly commercial version of a longer tradition of 'Middle Cinema', which combined the more serious themes of Parallel Cinema with 'popular cinematic devices' (Chaudhuri 2005: 146), as exemplified in the films of Rituparno Ghosh and Aparna Sen. While 'middle of the road' films avoid the kind of spectacle one associates with popular Hindi films, they are not examples of rigorous art cinema. Some of these films are genre films, and more specifically, urban thrillers, comedies and melodramas. They typically involve a revolving cast of actors, including Parambrata Chattopadhay, Raima Sen, Neha Panda and Prosenjit Chatterjee, some of whom also direct these films, which is true of Chattopadhay who helmed *Hawa Bodol*. Recurring figures can also be traced across these films including the contemporary musician, actor, film director and the 'modern' woman, defined as such through her defiance of tradition.

But even when not directly about the city, directors and other personnel involved in the making of these films situate them as a distinctly urban form of cinema, designed to draw urban middle class audiences away from their television screens back to theatres to watch Bengali films (see Mazoomdar 2014). The ample use of urban locations in these films must be viewed, in part, through an industrial lens as they emerge in a transitional phase of the Bengali film industry geared towards recouping a Kolkata-based film viewing audience.

KOLKATA 'OLD' AND 'NEW'

In her relatively recent work on the subject, Giuliana Bruno characterises topophilia as a form of amorous mapping, where landscape and subjectivity are intertwined as representations of the former are driven by the 'philic' drives of the latter (2002: 355). Like Bachelard, she privileges examples whereby topophilia is constituted through vestiges of the past that are subject to various instantiations of mapping in order to convey 'the story of the landscape' (ibid.). Bruno argues that the entanglement between landscape and psyche in most examples of topophilia guarantees that landscape must meet the demands of 'the psychic process' so that depictions of place are ultimately tailored to the emotionally driven claims placed upon them (2002: 356).

Building on the work of Bruno, I want to propose that cinematic depictions of place that transpire in the wake of a topophilic encounter between a particular location and a specific set of directorial subjectivities can emerge through recurring configurations of landscape. These configurations are inclusive of monuments, popular landmarks as well as city-specific events that become discernable and most importantly, *familiar*, across a body of films. I include such a broad array of place-making overtures because place in cinema is construed not only through iconography but also through modes of narrative that contribute to the distinctiveness of location. To borrow Bruno's phrasing, a 'story of the landscape' is illuminated through the fact of repetition, shot through, of course, with variation (2002: 355).

The cinematic city of films such as *Autograph*, *Hawa Bodol* and *Maach Mishti and More* is remarkably consistent both visually and narratively, even though the films vary with respect to their generic status; *Maach Mishti and More* and *Hawa Bodol* are comedies while *Autograph* is a dramatic feature. The version of Kolkata generated within these films is a hybrid city, oscillating with relative ease between 'old' and 'new', in accordance with facets of the two contemporary discourses of the city in transition. More to the point, the urban settings of these films are comprised of images that romanticise their historical connotations, situated alongside of a contemporary series of images that conjure the cosmopolitan, global aspirations of the city.

The city of old is elicited through repeated clusters of imagery inclusive of tram rides devoid of crowds and rides on boats that glide across the largely deserted expanse of the Hooghly River, of rain drenched streets, and sequences that chronicle aspects of 'Durga Puja', the Hindu festival that has made the city famous. Occasionally, the colonial past makes an appearance through the presence of monuments such as Victoria Memorial. There are various forms of idealisation at work in the presentation of these images, already suggested by the diminished character of 'the crowd', a marker of Kolkata's megacity status. While nearly all of the films discussed in this chapter feature a 'monsoon in the city' sequence, it is only in *Hawa Bodol* that characters walk with deliberation into torrential downpours, set specifically to the music of Rabindranath Tagore. This is a sequence where little of consequence happens but it serves as an implicit reminder of location via the cultural prestige of Tagore. A sequence where a central character in *Autograph* is in a state of deep contemplation by the riverside is not a wasted opportunity for the city, as it depicts the statue of the goddess Durga's final descent into the depths of the Hooghly.

These examples are instances of 'implied topophilia', where a certain love of the city that rests upon the romanticisation of its longstanding, popular associations is made palpable but not narrativised. Explicit examples of a similar phenomenon can be located in *Maach, Mishti and More*. There are two touristic sequences that operate as urban centrepieces in this film, one of which involves an actual tour of the city while a second depicts characters embarking on this activity to renew their affection for the urban. These sequences feature rides on rickshaws, trams and boats, in both sunshine and rain. They also include walks and motorcycle trips that transpire within iconic Kolkata areas, such as College Street lined with its bookstalls, the New Market area and the Red Road. The lyrics of the music utilised in the latter of these sequences proclaim that one can see the city through new eyes, adding a touch of reflexivity to a narrative event that is cemented by the film's closing dedication to the city of Kolkata.

The city's past acquires a 'snapshot' effect in these films, rendered through the logic of citation that resonates with the compressed and abstract nature of the past that Bachelard delineates as an intrinsic component of the topophilic experience. The city of old is not historically specific, though the tram images do implicitly recall an earlier period of modernisation as previously delineated. Rather, these images exude a sense of timelessness that idealises the past as eternal and unchanging. The snapshot version of Kolkata's past is fused in particular ways with the iconographic sites of Kolkata as burgeoning global city that are similarly abstracted. These films often demonstrate their alliance with the vertical imaginary of the city, the most obvious and grandiose marker of Kolkata's 'global turn'. In *Autograph*, there are numerous sequences where one of the central characters, actor Arun Chatterjee, walks out onto his balcony, a seemingly innocuous narrative event that doubles as a way of highlighting views of New Town from above. *Hawa Bodol* features a central character, Jeet, who elicits verticality in all of its diffuseness; not only does he work in a high rise office space, but the interiors of this space are luxurious, sleek and minimalist in their decoration, an appropriate setting for a job at an international design firm. All of these details situate Jeet within the city's sphere of global finance. Other recurring sequences in these films include boat rides along the Hooghly that showcase the splendour of the Vidyasagar Setu Bridge, also known as the Second Hooghly Bridge. The Bridge partakes of the aesthetic of the global that constitutes both the material and representational repertoire of Kolkata's global aspirations in its minimalism and grandeur, as it is considered to be one of the longest cable bridges in Asia.

What seems to be at stake in these films is the question of what it means to be 'modern' in a city that is rapidly globalising. Ben Highmore offers a useful definition of modernity, broadly conceived, as being enveloped within and often over taken by, a series of dramatic changes (2005: 12). In the case of these films, substantial topographical transformations are showcased or even narrativised, but crucially, either through a resolution or sidestepping of the friction between old and new that Highmore deems as essentially constitutive of the modern. But this question of how the broader phenomenon of urban modernisation is mitigated in these films returns us to their cinephiliac references towards the cinema of the past as well as their occasional reflexivity regarding their status as 'middle of the road' films. What is unique about this particular corpus of films is the manner in which topophilia is often configured through cinephilia and vice-versa.

An explicit example of the merging of 'Kolkata one' and 'two' is found in the credit sequence of *Maach, Mishti and More*. The sequence begins with a series of hand drawn, black and white images of the Kolkata cityscape accompanied by voice-over narration. The narrator says, 'It's time to get up, Rip Van Winkle. Witness the beauty of our city with your own eyes. If you had been awake these past 30 years, you would have been able to see your Kolkata.' The voice-over narration addresses an implied spectator who has not borne witness to changes that have transformed the city over a thirty-year period. The voice-over details altered street names, the building of flyovers and changes taking hold of the inhabitants of the city including women donning Western clothes and sporting their 'boy cuts'. This sequence features an urban landscape that evokes past and present, including images of the Second Hooghly Bridge, trams, trident street lamps, high rise buildings under construction, the Oberoi Grand Hotel as well as Victoria Memorial. But the hand-drawn images visually signify the gaze of the past upon the present, corresponding to the voice-over narration that aligns itself with an older generation of Kolkata inhabitant.

This example offers an overt instance of topophilia, where the city moves from background to foreground through voice, image and even the lyrics of a song that situates the city as a long lost love to be encountered once again. The sentiment of nostalgia mixed in with the acceptance of transition pervades the opening sequence through numerous registers, laying the foundation for the film's management of tensions between old and new. The voice-over narrator confesses to this returning inhabitant of the city that it is better that he/she did not bear witness to these dramatic changes through he himself approves of them. This is the first of many insinuations scattered throughout the film that it is, in large part, addressed to a diasporic spectator, one that returns to visit and perhaps even live. Two of the central characters, a married couple named Rahul and Reena, leave their jobs in New York to return to Kolkata to open a restaurant after a seven-year absence. As Rahul states, this establishment must cater for the middle classes, chiming more broadly with a city positioning itself toward its middle class population while maintaining 'old world' charm. Part of the film's overtures towards the global involves the inclusion of the Indian diaspora as a marker of the city's truly international and cosmopolitan status; the implication is that Kolkata is nearly on par with its global city counterparts.[9]

Maach Mishti and More summons the spirit of Ray in its casting of Soumitra Chatterjee as patriarch of the family. Crucially, he remains unnamed so that his presence in the film is largely defined through his star persona as leading male actor in a previous era of Bengali art cinema. Chatterjee was, as Sharmistha Gooptu puts it, a 'Ray find' as he was a theatre actor essentially discovered by Ray who went on to star in fourteen of his films (2010: 237). It is fitting that the voice of the city in the opening sequence belongs to none other than Chatterjee, so that the hand drawn images of the city signify the past not only in relationship to the city itself but also to a earlier era of Kolkata-based cinema.

What is 'old' both in terms of the city and the cinema in this film, rendered as complex in the opening sequence, is rather easily passed over in favour of new sites and new narratives as the film draws to a close. The film draws a rather disturbing link between Kolkata of the past and Chatterjee upon his death in the film. The lyrics of the soundtrack heard over a montage sequence of mourning announces a dazzling day in the city of Kolkata, where tram lines and asphalt smile once again as it is time for old stories to fade and new ones to take their place. At the narrative level, the death of the character signifies a loss for the family but implicitly, 'Kolkata one' and its various associations, including a cinematic one, are rendered ripe for replacement. Recent cinematic trends affiliated with the local film industry are also referenced, which are valorised, alongside the film's eventual alliance with 'Kolkata take two'. The character of Raj has one foot in the local film industry, with dreams to pursue a career in Mumbai that leads to an audition for a Yash Chopra film. In the end, he chooses to remain within the local film industry, while also articulating the film's overall alignment with a vision of Kolkata as cosmopolitan city by declaring it to be such. If the film gradually does away with both the old city and its cinematic emissary, in the form of Soumitra Chatterjee, by the time we reach its end, both a new film industry and a new vision of Kolkata are explicitly situated in its place.

In *Hawa Bodol*, a key plot event that returns Jeet and Raj to their rightful bodies is attributed to an electrical current running through several close-ups of a tramline. This image recalls the opening sequence of *Mahanagar/The Big City* (1963), which begins with a long take of close-up of a tramline. The tramline is an iconic image closely affiliated with 'Kolkata one', evoked in a film that deliberately blurs the lines between the city's past and its projected future. *Hawa Bodol* has virtually nothing in common with Ray's film in relationship to plot, style or genre. However, a relationship of affinity can be established. *Mahanagar* serves as an ode to the Kolkata as divided city in 1960s and *Hawa Bodol* similarly offers its own take on the current state of the city as experienced through contrasting registers. Implied topophilia meets implied cinephilia through a very subtle reference to Ray's film.

The city in *Hawa Bodol* is split into two, in accordance with the two central characters, Jeet and Raj. As is the case with *Mahanagar*, this division is based on social class, but unlike Ray's film, it is rendered through comic rather than dramatic means. Their contrasting career paths, the former a corporate executive and the latter, a singer-songwriter, are set in seemingly two different versions of the city. As described previously, Jeet's city falls in line with its global inclinations. Raj's city, however, resurrects the Kolkata of old, conveyed through images of his decaying and chaotic apartment interior, his intimate knowledge of the city's cramped alleyways that lead to clandestine storages of alcohol as well as a visit to his parent's house that showcases the typical structure of a traditional North Kolkata home.

As the film continues, the 'two cities' coalesce into a hybrid of old and new. When Jeet and Raj spend a late evening on the town reminiscing, they both agree that the life of the other seems more appealing. In a comedic twist that doubles as a form of wish fulfilment, while the pair drunkenly urinate in front of the Oberoi Grand Hotel in a tic-tac-toe formation, they both wake up the following day in each other's bodies. While the 'switch' takes place in previously colonial section of the city, afterward they frequently have meetings on the edge of the empty expanse of the Hooghly River, with the Second Hooghly Bridge appearing in the background of the images. Further moments of explicit hybridisation concern the modern rendition of a Tagore song by Raj's love interest Inca as well as Raj's (while trapped in Jeet's body) recommendation to international clients to create hotel bathrooms that make ample use of terracotta, a material associated very specifically with Bengali art. Though these latter examples do not directly address the city in its material structure, they imply that the inhabitants of Kolkata do not have to choose between a select evocation of the city's past and its impending future. This is where the film definitively parts ways with *Mahanagar*, as Ray is more intent on depicting the divisive and corrupt undercurrents of modernisation in ways that resist offering easy solutions to urban poverty.

Autograph interweaves references to both the cinema of the 1960s and that of the present even more deliberately, as the film concerns a young director named Shubho who remakes Satyajit Ray's *Nayak/The Hero* (1963) into *Today's Hero*, starring an actor named Arun Chatterjee. Ray's *Nayak* is a star vehicle, where Bengali icon Uttam Kumar essentially plays himself in the guise of a famous Bengali actor named Arindam Mukerjee who travels by train to Delhi to receive an acting award. The film is comprised of his encounters with several passengers, including Aditi, who coaxes Arindam to tell her private details about his life that she initially intends to publish in her magazine, though later she chooses to tear her notes to shreds.

Autograph's very title is derived from *Nayak*; Aditi's first encounter with Arindam involves asking him for an autograph for her friend. *Autograph* declares its status as 'middle of the road' film through a discernable self-consciousness directed towards the act of filmmaking in its similarities and differences from *Nayak*. The most noticeable shift between the two films concerns their treatment of what constitutes 'the modern' vis-à-vis the cinematic. The narrative action in *Nayak* takes place on a train, a backdrop conducive to the film's projection of modernisation, extending from flashback sequences that depict Arindam's rejection of a theatrical acting style of the past, to Aditi's magazine dedicated to the needs of the modern Bengali woman. In

Autograph, the train as signifier of urban modernity is replaced by the entire city as setting alongside a quasi declaration of a new modality of filmmaking that is indebted to the past while also breaking from it. In an early sequence in *Autograph*, a discussion occurs between Arun and his team about a producer who claims in a television interview that he is responsible for making a film starring Arun famous and in effect, diminishes the actor's box office appeal in his own right. In this sequence Arun decides to make a feature film with Shubho, in part, because he is a first time director.

When viewed in conjunction with details sprinkled throughout the film, this sequence recounts a typical story of the 'middle of the road' filmmaker. More recently, some of these films have been directed by first time filmmakers, often armed with previous experience in advertising or acting, but not in feature film production.[10] These are directors who have been given their first break from risk-courting producers. This particular narrative concerning the origins of 'middle of the road' cinema exudes the patina of 'newness', of a novel approach towards commercial filmmaking for a contemporary era of cinema-goers and one that these filmmakers explicitly link to the contemporary cityscape. *Autograph* complements these narratives through its own narrativisation of the making of such a film.

In this context, *Nayak* functions as 'source material', a cinematic past to which the contemporary independent filmmaker pays tribute but remakes as his own, which is inclusive of the cinematic Kolkata that stars in this film. The film situates Arun within a Kolkata context as this opening sequence comes to a close. As he walks onto his balcony, declaring his intentions of making *Today's Hero*, the camera tracks upwards to reveal the cityscape below. The vertical imaginary of the city is privileged in the same breath as Arun insists on making an independent film with a director that seems to operate as a stand-in for Srijit Mukerjee himself. The cinematic as well as spatial modernity of *Nayak* is updated in *Autograph* to privilege a reflexive version of a 'middle of the road' film set within a contemporary Kolkata cityscape.

THE PERSISTENCE OF PLACE: A CITY IN EMERGENCE

The contemporary middle-of-the road films provide certain pleasures of recognition, veering towards the nostalgic and the eternal in their referencing of Kolkata's past, both in relationship to urban images and to the cinema of the past, while simultaneously offering visions of the city under development that evade conflict or anxiety. In accordance with scholarly remonstrations regarding the 'death of place' in the era of globalisation. The question that is immediately raised is: why does this particular image of Kolkata as frictionless, hybrid city loom large in a number of these films and why alongside a discernable meditation on Bengali cinema of the past and the present?

Even while nestled within their various generic formulations, these films assume a reflective stance upon both the city and cinema that is seemingly generated by the transitional status that is in the air. A closer look at this tendency might unveil more concrete reasons for its recurrence within this particular body of work. We can begin to make the claim that affective expressions of place as portrayed in these films fall under the categorical imperatives of emergence, of representations of landscape that herald the modernisation of the Kolkata as a definitive sign of its entry into the privileged ranks of the global city.

Returning to Highmore's observations concerning the tensions between old and new as an intrinsic component of the modernising experience, the lack thereof in these films suggest that they themselves are embroiled within the tensions that arise between the homogenising and differentiating tendencies of globalisation. The sameness of the city across these films inexorably points towards its specificity as a largely uniform middle class imaginary of the city. As previously noted, this is the class that has steadily climbed to great heights alongside India's economy. The narrative of Kolkata's global emergence falls in step with that of 'India rising' in the present day, particularly in the wake of alternative alliances that India has forged with other nations similarly on the rise, such as the BRICS nations. While the complexities and contradictions of BRICS cannot be addressed in this chapter, the formation certainly presents itself as an emerging entity, forging a multi-national economic and political alliance that offers a series of challenges to Western nations.[11] We can situate the 'story of the landscape' told in these films against a larger socio-political backdrop of emergence, but in microcosm, as Kolkata in a state of global becoming acquires an unmistakable middle class sheen that sidesteps politicised friction related to caste, religion, gender or regionalism. This is a case study that is demonstrative of the continued significance of place to certain facets of globalisation whereby the process of global emergence takes on an ambience of pride, celebration and even defiance. In the case of Kolkata, an implied sense of defiance can be gleaned when this particular narrative of the city is situated within a larger discursive history of Kolkata marked by the stigma of decay and nearly unrelenting decline. Gorfinkel and Rhodes argue that the desire for the specificity of place might just serve as a form of resistance to the circumstances that threaten the uniqueness and political scope of both cinema and place (2011: xii). But in this instance, the cinematic proclamation of place constitutes yet another facet of the globalising process rather than being resistant to it; the specificity of place in these films ultimately succumbs to sameness rather than difference, in line with the flattening tendencies of globalisation.

The cinephiliac tendencies of these films are a constitutive component of the overall sensibility of emergence enveloping cinematic Kolkata. As noted previously, cinephilia in these films is anchored within the recesses of the Bengali version of 'cinephilia take one' as intertext. The recurring presence of Ray in these films signifies in more than one direction. Certainly Ray, considered to be the foremost practitioner of art cinema in a Bengali context, is part of a longer lineage of prestige cinema that is a staple of the Bengali film industry. As Gooptu argues, despite the fact that Ray's films were not products of the commercial Bengali film industry and though many of his cinematic influences were indeed international in their orientation, his work still bears the distinctiveness of 'Bengal' made manifest through language and place, among other markers (2010: 227). Kolkata in particular assumes prominence in Ray's films and as Gooptu speculates, this is perhaps due to the rapid transformations that overtook the city in the post-colonial era as a result of Partition (2010: 227–8).

But even more to the point, Gooptu argues that significance of Ray and his international acclaim soars to the level of the nation; as she puts it, the Bengali public, including its film-going public, had aspirations of an international or global orientation in the immediate post-colonial period that were being fulfilled in a variety of registers, including through the cinema (2010: 245). A similar aspiration marks this current period of both cinema and the city that I have labelled as a time of emergence. In returning to Ray, in the form of tribute or homage, these contemporary films ground their own cinematic practice within a filmic genealogy that is drastically different from the present moment and yet runs on parallel tracks in relationship to both the city and the film industry caught up in period of flux and global ambition. As such, the films, in their reflexivity concerning 'middle of the road cinema', are enveloped within an aura of becoming that is produced within the filmic text *itself* against the backdrop of the cinema of the past.

The lack of friction that characterises the representation of the city is similarly a feature of the references to a previous era of Bengali cinema; Ray's *Nayak* is simply remade into a 'middle of the road film' and a key image from Ray's *Mahanagar* is evoked in a film that is unlike its predecessor in nearly every way. These contemporary films situate themselves within the Bengali cinephiliac lineage of 'good cinema', though the fit is hardly exact. There is next to no acknowledgement in these films that there are distinct aesthetic, thematic and contextual differences between the work of directors such as Ray and the commercial bent of 'middle of the road' cinema. Most notably, the 'middle of the road' films surveyed thus far in this chapter do not allude to the underside of Kolkata's post-colonial modernising phase. The intertextual references to Ray's films neatly sidestep the circumstances of the Kolkata that stars in a number of his films and even more explicitly so, in the films of Sen and of Ghatak, among others. Instead, the images of the past are largely ahistorical in their orientation, evoking a timeless, mythical city in its place. In effect, the presence of 'Ray' signifies largely in the vein of 'Bengali cinematic pride', in tandem with the aura of urban pride that envelops their presentation of the contemporary cityscape. The nostalgic longing for the past in these films is ostensibly for an idealised cityscape, cleansed of its social problems. This gesture can be understood as a form of intervention within the topophobic discourse haunting Kolkata for much of its recent history but it is one that is achieved through apolitical means, marginalising histories of displacement, protest and loss. Similarly, there is a 'Ray' that these films chose not to remember, a figure whose city films became increasingly politicised in line with the declining circumstances of the city. This particular brand of nostalgia can also be viewed as a response to Kolkata's impending status as global city; if such cities, the world over, are typically thought to give rise to a fragmented, often illegible and ephemeral experience of the urban, these films mitigate this experience by offering legible and communal visions of Kolkata in their place.[12] 'Middle of the road films' enact careful balancing acts between an urban and a cinematic past and present, blending both into nearly seamless depictions of a city and a cinema where the future can only ever appear as a natural extension of the past.

DISLOCATION AND DISPLACEMENT: AN ALTERNATIVE VIEW OF 'KOLKATA TAKE TWO'

While the 'middle of the road' films examined thus far virtually obliterate potential friction between past and present, there are alternative examples. One such film is *The Future of the Past*; while the film adopts the formula of 'middle of the road' cinema to a certain extent, it nonetheless demonstrates the possibility of this form of filmmaking to yield another set of insights concerning the relationship between Kolkata's past and present as configured through instances of homage to Parallel Cinema directors. Like *Autograph*, the film makes implicit pronouncements regarding the 'middle of the road' film. The film's star, Parambrata Chatterjee, plays Ayun, a first time film director whose previous experience is in advertising. Ayun arrives at an old mansion known as Choudhury House to shoot an advertisement and soon after, meets Biplob, who tells him a story about the house, which he eventually decides to transform into his first feature film. We later learn that Biplob can be none other than a Choudhury House ghost. But this ghost story doubles as a narrative of the city articulated by way of the interior of the home so that Bachelard's stricter definition of topophilia and cinephilia intersect.

What differentiates the reflexive stance adopted by *The Future of the Past* from the films analysed thus far is that Ayun tells Biplob that he would like to make a feature titled 'Badly Bengali', a film focused upon a young Bengali musician in a band, who cannot relate to his parent's ambition for his future career and whose romantic prospects are in limbo as his girlfriend's parents want her to marry someone on a conventional career path. The plot that he outlines sounds suspiciously like a typical middle of the road film, its resemblance extending to elements of the films discussed above. Again, with *The Future of the Past*, we have a 'middle of the road' film that performs a meditation upon itself, but one that takes a critical position in relationship to these films as Ayun, upon hearing elements of Biplob's story, as rendered through flashback narration, gradually comes to the conclusion that Biplob's ghost story is more suitable for the making of a first feature.

The film's deviation from the standard 'middle of the road' formula extends toward the cityscape itself. In returning to the opening scene with which this chapter began, it is evident that a marked discord between the past and the present lies at the very heart of its central conflict, and one that evokes Ray in a politicised rather than nostalgic portrait of the contemporary city. This story of Kolkata, conveyed through the use of flashback narration, is one of perpetual displacement, taking us from the colonial period, to Partition, the Kargil War and finally to the present. These ghosts, all gathered together within Choudhury House, are fighting against dislocation once again, as their home is threatened with demolition by an urban developer, who wants to raze the mansion in order to build a five-story mall that will resemble those found in Singapore. The horizontal plane of the city is again deemed less desirable than its new found verticality.

Despite the unified stance the ghosts eventually take against the developer, friction between the ghosts is on display in the film in numerous registers, suggesting that disputes between past and present are not easily reconcilable. The ghosts of the Choudhury Home are described by Ayun as an 'ensemble cast', a phrase that brings the cinema and the city into close proximity. This statement finds fruition within the fiction as one of the ghosts is a famous Bengali actress from the 1940s who implicitly recalls some of the iconic actresses of the period such as Kanan Devi. This 'ensemble cast' is made to convey the conflicts between different historical pasts as well as those that pit the ghosts against present day urban developments in true parodic fashion. For example, the guardians of the home, *zamindar*/landowner Darpo and colonial officer Ramsay Sahib, initially seem to follow a 'master/slave' relation, slyly indicating that history remains on course even within the spectral realm. Two ghosts, Atmaran the rickshaw driver and Bhootnath, a refugee from the Partition era, complain of being forced from their ghostly abodes as the sidewalks and trees they have been inhabiting have been torn down in order to build flyovers and bypasses, two markers of the 'new' Kolkata. Issues related to caste difference are raised as Darpo rallies against allowing Atmaran upstairs, while Pablo the musician sings about the need to do away with caste prejudice. While these differences are made humorous and quickly set aside in order to mount an organised, ghost-driven resistance against the urban developer, the seams between past and present still remain visible. These conflicts can be tied to the film's overall intention to foreground the story of the landscape as one of strife, loss and disappearance so that in fact, this film reconfigures the vision of 'Calcutta as divided city' found in a number of Parallel Cinema films through comedic means.

The identity of the 'ghost in chief' also differentiates this film from the others as it aptly raises the spectre of politics. Biplob describes himself to Ayun as a cinephile, proudly bearing the mantle of 'cinephilia take one' as former ciné-club member. Mrinal Sen receives special mention as Biplob's own story is one of politicised resistance; Biplob's demise references the tumultuous history of the Naxalite movement as he is imprisoned and later gunned down by the police for his political beliefs. The style in which Biplob's death is filmed resembles the aesthetic parameters of Mrinal Sen's *Calcutta 71* (1971), a suggestion confirmed by Ayun who says that he will shoot this aspect of his film in the style of Sen's film. The second, politicised ideal of 'good cinema' as articulated during the era of 'cinephilia take one', is privileged, in keeping with an urban story that is sharply and satirically politicised and one that finds ways to bring together references to both Sen and Ray. Biplob operates as the historical epicentre of the film, as his Marxist worldview coincides with the projection of the ghosts as figures that reside on the fringes of the neoliberal ethos overtaking the city. As is articulated in the prologue, ghosts are not consumers, nor are they voters or viewers and thus, the loss of their abode does not constitute a problem. The film launches an appeal for the preservation of history that it delineates as lying outside of market demands. But as Ghosh claims in her work on high-rise horror, the conditions of speculative capitalism are haunted by the spectral traces of 'dematerialised capital…that apprehends the concrete' (2014: 66). Following Ghosh, we can argue that the spectral realm, in the case of this film, apprehends the material, time-bound histories of place that are decimated in the name of global aspiration, which operates on a speculative plane. And yet this suggestion is mired in a utopian gesture, in line with the film's comedic sensibility, which sees the ghosts declare victory in scaring the urban developer into giving up the property.

Though *The Future of the Past* is a typical of the 'middle of the road' film, it parts ways with its established parameters in foregrounding the elimination of the city's material history as an unacceptable consequence of the neoliberal order of the city. The film additionally mounts the thesis that the urban past cannot be incorporated into the already 'exclusionary visions of the future' with any sense of ease, though the film does affirm that the cinema itself is a medium conducive to the preservation of the past; the film ends just as Ayun begins to shoot his ghost story in Choudhury House (see Bose 2007: 121). Although the film's politics do not directly probe leftist ideals of addressing and dismantling various instances of social difference, it does proffer an alternate path for the 'middle of the road' film in its handling of the imbrication between contemporary Kolkata-based cinema and the cityscape.

The Future of the Past demonstrates that an attachment to place fostered within the confines of globalisation need not succumb to the sentiment of nostalgia nor celebration and that the cinema itself can be drawn upon to facilitate an engagement with place in historical and political terms. History and conflict go hand and hand and as such, this film presents the city and the cinema as sites of difference and displacement, even if only fleetingly and limited largely by the confines of a 'middle of the road cinema' that marginalises the political in favour of the commercial. The film offers yet another facet of exactly what is at stake in this case study: meditations on the nature of Kolkata's identity as emerging global entity and that of *her* cinema. Though both cinephilia and topophilia are often linked in scholarly discourse to a love of what is past, this case study illustrates the potential for topophilia and cinephilia to also be oriented towards the future. To return to Bachelard, if the true calling of space is to contain time in compressed form, then the spatial politics of the earlier group of 'middle of the road' films encapsulates the time of global becoming but largely devoid of any of the 'thickness' that might account for its contradictions.

NOTES

1. The term 'Parallel Cinema', originating in the mid-1950s, denotes what these directors envisioned as their opposition to the norms of Indian popular cinema. See Chaudhuri (2005).
2. In a series of quotations from film industry personnel in *The Telegraph* (2011), directors affiliated with 'middle of the road' cinema connect their films to contemporary urban audiences. For example, Anjan Dutt remarks that 'urban Bengali cinema has found its strength', a declaration he makes on the basis of a trend beginning in the early 2000s of directors catering themselves once again to an urban audience, shored up in recent years by the inclusion of new talent.
3. Calcutta was hit by waves of unemployment and the arrival of the Naxalite movement, a series of armed struggles against class exploitation that took root in the Naxalbari region in 1967
4. Examples include Ray's *Mahanagar/ The Big City*, which establishes a portrait of post-colonial Calcutta as falling into a state of corruption. Mrinal Sen's Calcutta films of this period are characterised by formal experimentation, coupled with an overtly leftist approach to the social politics and strife of the period.
5. For a fuller account of this discursive history, see Chakravorty (2000), Bose (2007) and Gupta (2014).
6. For further reading on the vertical aesthetic of global cities, see Sassen (1991). For contemporary material on satellite townships across the Indian continent, see Ghosh (2014).
7. This is a term, along with others such as 'New India', and 'India shining', have increasingly been put to use in describing India's economic rise since the 1990s. For an overview of the foundations of this terminology, particularly as it relates to a literary context, see Varughese (2013).
8. Bengali actor Rahul Bose is lauded in the popular press as having launched this term, likening 'middle of the road' cinema to a rebirth of the Bengali film industry (see Sharma 2012).
9. It is telling that Rahul and Reena move back to New York to open a restaurant called 'Maach, Mishti and More'. This narrative event constitutes a moment of slippage in a film that otherwise valorises the 'new' city, where the couple's visit to Kolkata is transformative but only in terms of their return to life in the diaspora.
10. For example, Aniruddha Roy Chowdhury, director of a 'middle of the road' film *Antaheen* (2009) began his career in advertising. Some 'middle of the road' filmmakers are actors turned directors, as is true of Parambrata Chowdhury.
11. As Kaarle Nordenstrengh and Daya Kishan Thussu have noted, BRICS summits in 2009 and 2011 have delved into the domain of global politics in their critique of Western policies towards Libya, Syria and Iran (2015: 5). For further reading on this topic, as it pertains to media in particular, see Nordenstrengh and Thussu (2015).

12 This is a well-known thesis concerning global cities, advanced by Saskia Sassen in her pioneering work on the subject (1991).

BIBLIOGRAPHY

Anon (2011) 'New Wave: Tollywood comes of age'. Online. Available at: http://www.telegraphindia.com/1111223/jsp/entertainment/story_14915902.jsp#.Vb7S5lw0Ng1

Bachelard, Gaston (1994) *The Poetics of Space: The Classic Look at How We Experience Intimate Places*, trans. Maria Jolas. Boston: Beacon Press.

Bose, Pablo S. (2007) 'Dreaming of Diasporas: Urban Developments and Transnational Identities in Contemporary Kolkata', *Topia*, 17, 110–30.

Bose, Raktima (2011) 'Mamata Wants to Turn Kolkata into London'; http://www.thehindu.com/news/national/mamata-wants-to-turn-kolkata-into-london/article2317137.ece

Bruno, Giuliana (2002) *Atlas of Emotion: Journeys into Art, Architecture and Film*. New York: Verso.

Buchsbaum, Jonathan and Elena Gorfinkel (2009) 'Introduction to Dossier Cinephilia: What is Being Fought for by Today's Cinephilia(s)?', *Framework: The Journal of Cinema and Media*, 50, 1/2, 176–80.

Chakravorty, Sanjoy (2000) 'From Colonial City to Globalizing City? The Far-from complete Spatial Transformation of Calcutta', in Peter Marcuse and Ronald van Kempen (eds) *Globalizing Cities: A New Spatial Order?* Oxford: Blackwell.

Chaudhuri, Ami (2015) http://scroll.in/article/726310/calcutta-must-take-urgent-steps-to-save-its-historic-neighbourhoods-from-real-estate-developers

Chaudhuri, Shohini (2005) *Contemporary World Cinema: Europe, Middle East, East Asia, South Asia*. Edinburgh: Edinburgh University Press.

Dasgupta, Priyanka (2015) http://timesofindia.indiatimes.com/city/kolkata/CM-Mamata-Banerjee-puts-Bengal-in-Cannes-spotlight/articleshow/47378912.cms

Elsaesser, Thomas (2005) 'Cinephilia or the Uses of Disenchantment', in Marijke de Valck and Malte Hagener (eds) *Cinephilia: Movies, Love and Memory*. Amsterdam: Amsterdam University Press, 27–44.

Ghosh, Bishnupriya (2014) 'The Security Aesthetic in Bollywood's High-Rise Horror', *Representations*, 26, 1, 58–84.

Gooptu, Sharmistha (2010) *Bengali Cinema: An Other Nation*. New Delhi: Roli Books.

Gorfinkel, Elena and John David Rhodes (eds) (2011) *Taking Place: Location and the Moving Image*. Minneapolis: University of Minnesota Press.

Gupta, Nilanjana (ed.) (2014) *Strangely Beloved: Writings on Calcutta*. New Delhi: Rainlight by Rupa Publications.

Highmore, Ben (2005) *Cityscapes: Cultural Readings in the Material and Symbolic City*. Basingstoke: Palgrave Macmillan.

Hilderbrand, Lucas (2009) 'Cinematic Promiscuity: Cinephilia after Videophilia', *Framework: The Journal of Cinema and Media*, 50, 1/2, 214–17.

Majumdar, Rochana (2012) 'Debating Radical Cinema: A History of the Film Society Movement in India', *Modern Asian Studies*, 26, 3, 731–67.

Massey, Doreen (1994) *Space, Place and Gender*. Minneapolis: University of Minnesota Press.

Mazoomdar, Jay (2014) 'What you didn't know about Bengali Cinema's Resurgence'; https://in.lifestyle.yahoo.com/what-you-didn-t-know-about-bengali-cinema-s-resurgence-070741111.html

Niyogi, Subhro (2015) 'Kolkata can wait, here comes "Big Ben"'; http://timesofindia.indiatimes.com/city/kolkata/Kolkata-Eye-can-wait-here-comes-Big-Ben/articleshow/45783673.cms

Nordenstreng, Kaarle and Daya Kishan Thussu (eds) (2015) *Mapping BRICS Media*. London and New York: Routledge.

Patel, Heenali (2014) 'The riverside story: a tale of two cities'; http://www.telegraphindia.com/1140907/jsp/calcutta/story_18805119.jsp#.Vb7Rclw0Ng1

Sarkar, Bhaskar (2015) 'Plasticity and the Global', *Framework: The Journal of Cinema and Media*, 56, 2, 451–71.

Sassen, Saskia (1991) *The Global City: New York, London, Tokyo*. Princeton: Princeton University Press.

Sharma, Test (2012) 'Bengali cinema has got a new rebirth: Rahul Bose'; http://m.ibnlive.com/news/india/bengali-cinema-has-got-new-birth-rahul-bose-445391.html

Sontag, Susan (1996) 'The Decay of Cinema', *New York Times*, 25 February.

Tuan, Yi-Fu (1990) *Topophilia: A Study of Environmental Perceptions, Attitudes and Values*. New York: Columbia University Press.

Varughese, Dawson E. (2013) *Reading New India: Post-Millennial Indian Fiction in English*. London: Bloomsbury.

PUBLIC SCREENS AND NEW MEDIA LANDSCAPES

SCREEN CULTURES AND THE 'GENERIC CITY': PUBLIC SCREENS IN CAIRO AND SHANGHAI

CHRIS BERRY

INTRODUCTION

The post-industrial city is also, in a sense, post-cinematic. If you believe that cinema requires celluloid, in many global cities today you will struggle to find a cinema projecting a celluloid print of a film. If you associate moving images with the gaze at the movie screen, as theorised by Laura Mulvey (1975), or even at the television receiver in your living room, that experience has become the exception rather than the norm. Not only have multiple windows open all at once on computer screens and tablets become our primary objects of attention, moving images have also moved out of the movie theatre and the living room, proliferating across screens of all kinds in public spaces. As Francesco Casetti (2013) has argued, the cinematic culture of the gaze has been superseded by the post-cinematic screen culture of the glance. What is the relationship of this new post-cinematic screen culture of the glance to the contemporary global city?

To begin to answer this question, this essay draws on research about public screens some colleagues and I have conducted in Shanghai and Cairo.[1] First, I consider the common assumption that under conditions of globalisation, media become ubiquitous and participate in a process of homogenising the city. Instead, I argue that, in the case of public screens at least, the evidence indicates that they are concentrated at particular locations and far from ubiquitous. Furthermore, the most common uses of moving image screens in public spaces that we were able to identify indicate a considerable degree of localisation. In Cairo, this is the use of the screen as a television receiver, often in the form of a cathode ray set, in small retail stores, *ahwa* cafés and coffee shops. In Shanghai, localisation takes the form of the proliferation of two types of screen at entrances to office and residential compounds, shops, and even public transport vehicles. These are slide-show style screens and tickertape-style screens. The latter are known in Chinese as *zouzi* or 'walking word' screens.

Second, I argue that the global city is also the city of neoliberalism. I go on to engage with debates on the nature of neoliberalism. Some scholars, such as Francis Fukuyama (1992), have celebrated the neoliberal culture of globalisation and others, such as Guy Debord (1998), have lamented it, but both tend to see it as a total and eternal regime with no outside, marking the point where politics and history end. In line with my argument on localisation, I argue that although the everyday uses of public screens in Shanghai and Cairo are most often part of neoliberal culture, they also demonstrate that neoliberal cultures are plural and not homogenous. This diversity in itself indicates that contestation and change may not be over yet. Furthermore, I argue that unexpected everyday uses of public screens in Cairo and Shanghai's retail and recreation sites of consumerism, along with exceptional uses of the space, also indicate that neoliberalism may be more fragile than is often thought.

GLOBALISATION, UBIQUITY, AND THE 'GENERIC CITY'

In his essay on contemporary screen cultures, Francesco Casetti not only argues that we glance rather than gaze at many screens, but also notes that digitised images are in the air, everywhere, in their invisible electronic form. We live among them, they pass through us, and the screens act like lightning rods that draw the images out of the air and make them visible to us (2013: 13). This very striking imagery echoes some contemporary theorisations of media and the city. First there is the idea – and sometimes ideal – of 'ubiquitous media' (see Featherstone 2009); for example, instead of the phone anchored to the landline, our mobile phones draw audio out of the air and into our ears almost anywhere we like. Second, this ubiquity is a characteristic of the rise of what Harvard professor and star architect of signature buildings like the China Central Television headquarters in Beijing, Rem Koolhaas, calls the 'generic city' (1995). Here, one city looks much the same as another, and cities no longer have distinctive sectors but are becoming a generalised sprawl of offices, factories and apartment buildings. Koolhaas's insights are heavily based on his own observation of the Pearl River Delta, where he has done a lot of work.

However, our data on public screens in Shanghai and Cairo contests both ubiquity and the idea of the generic city. This became clear in the beginning stages of our project. Our method involved three steps in each city. First, we had an exploratory stage based on random walking and inspired by the *dérive* associated with Situationism (see Debord 1981). Second, we carried out an 'audit' of screens in selected sites. We selected three types of site: retail and recreation centres; public exhibition sites like museums; and transport hubs like train stations. Third, we also pursued close observation of selected individual screens at our sites. All this work has been taking place over a number of years, and has been supplemented with some interviews, as has been detailed elsewhere (see Berry and Harbord 2015).

In the initial walking stages of the project, we soon discovered that although the images may be everywhere in the air, the lighting rod-like screens that make them visible certainly are not. For example, in Cairo on 3 March 2010, I embarked on a random walk by taking the metro to a station I had never alighted from before – El Khalafawi on line number two – and then walked around the neighbourhood for a couple of hours. This was a residential area, and on the basis of the cries of 'Welcome to Egypt!' from various young men, I got the impression foreigners were not a common sight. Throughout the walk, I saw no large screens on the sides of buildings or screens being used to offer information, only the screens of television receivers inside stores and cafés. In Shanghai, on 6 November 2008, I set out east from Fudan University in the northeast part of the city, and, after walking a short distance to the Wujiaochang intersection, where there were numerous stores, cinemas, restaurants, and so on, turned south and walked all the way down Siping Road until I got to Tongji University. While there were many screens of all kinds at the Wujiaochang intersection, I did not encounter another screen until I arrived at the entrance of Tongji University, where a large screen inside the entrance proclaimed it to be a 'world-famous university' and also aired other information.

Indeed, it was the rapid realisation that screens were *not* ubiquitous that led us to select the three types of site for audits in the second stage of our data collection, because these places are where screens congregate. Installing a public screen of any size is not cost-free, and the large screens installed on the sides of some buildings are expensive. In these circumstances, it is not surprising that screens tend to be found in areas that large numbers of people pass through. In the case of these two walks, the example would be the Wujiaochang intersection, the retail and recreation hub for the Yangpu District of Shanghai. Two large and highly luminescent screens topped department stores facing each other across the intersection, creating focal points in a riotous lightscape composed of traffic lights, neon, and numerous smaller screens.

However, it is also clear that numbers of people alone are not enough to merit the installation of LED public screens. During my walk through the El Khalafawi neighbourhood, I passed through a busy street market, which was at least as thronged as the Wujiaochang intersection. Yet, screens were confined to television receivers inside some shops along the street. Neither the Yangpu District nor the El Khalafawi neighbourhoods are rich, so what accounts for this difference? Perhaps ordinary people in Shanghai do have more disposable income than their Cairo counterparts. But it is also significant that Wujiaochang has been designated a 'sub-centre' of Shanghai (Zhong 2009: 113), intended to drive the regeneration of a neighbourhood marked by relatively high unemployment following the closure of the textile factories that used to dominate the neighbourhood (see Zhang 2009). In other words, Wujiaochang is aspirational, its redevelopment is designed to make it attractive to upscale residents and service their needs, and investment in LED screens is one way of signifying that aspiration.

The clustering of public screens in areas of high traffic and potential high yield to advertisers is also confirmed by the practices of the NASDAQ-listed company, Focus Media, which pioneered installing public screens for advertising purposes in Shanghai beginning in 2002. They aimed initially at the white collar end of the market, in the belief that this is the most lucrative segment but also the most difficult to reach, because, according to CEO Jason Jiang, 'High income earners are very busy, they don't have much time to read newspapers or watch TV at home' (in Madden 2006). Therefore, Focus did not try to put their screens everywhere, but instead installed them strategically, next to the elevator doors in office buildings, as well as golf clubs, beauty salons and so forth (see Massy 2005).

If public screens are not ubiquitous, perhaps the emphasis on advertising in the above paragraphs might suggest that they are used in pretty much the same way no matter where they are, making them part of the generic city. However, again, our data indicates a more complex situation. In this regard, the deployment of public screens can be seen as part of the debates about the nature of globalisation. During the era of territorial empire, innovations and inventions originated in the metropolis, and then were gradually rolled out to the peripheries. But today, the same technology is available almost simultaneously anywhere around the world. Is this also part of the trend towards the generic city? Arjun Appadurai (1990) writes of globalisation as characterised by transborder flows, but he also argues that as the flows encounter the local, the result is not homogenisation or the production of the generic, but heterogenisation. Similarly, Roland Robertson (1995) coined the English term 'glocalisation' to characterise this process, identified originally by Japanese researchers.

Examples to support the idea of local specificity in screen culture are numerous, and two types of localisation can be noted. The first invokes singularity, the very opposite of the generic. This is the concept of site specificity, argued for by Anna McCarthy (2001) in her pioneering work on cathode ray television sets in public spaces in the United States. McCarthy observed that to understand what was on each cathode ray television set, how it was being used, where it was positioned, and so forth required close attention to the specific site it was located in. In other words, one doctor's office was *not* pretty much like any other. The same is true of each contemporary LED public screen. They come in different shapes and sizes, carry different content, and are positioned according to the specificities of the local topography and demography.

Nevertheless, from a perspective that wishes to emphasise the generic, it might be possible to argue that the distinctions of local topography are minor variations within a generic sea of advertising featuring global brands and styles. However, our data demonstrates that, patterns of screen usage are also part of ever-changing and diverse but specific local cultures. To illustrate this second argument about local specificity, we can turn to the most common types and uses of public screens in Cairo and Shanghai, which are quite distinct. Although this would have to be checked with further research, these patterns may well be found in other cities in each region.

First, in Cairo, although large public screens are relatively rare, small screens being used as television receivers in the manner studied in the United States by McCarthy are very common. They appear most frequently in three types of publicly accessible site: shops, *ahwa* cafés and coffee shops. These are sometimes small flat screen televisions, and sometimes cathode ray sets. Their presence is a product of the everyday retail and recreation environment in Cairo. First, the retail sector is dominated by small shops, with seventy per cent of grocery stores in independent hands as of 2013. The self-service culture of supermarkets is not common yet. In these circumstances, shopping is a social interaction. There is no self-checkout option with machines barking strange phrases like 'unexpected item in bagging area', as encountered in London, where I live. Instead, a purchase entails at least a minimal conversation with the shopkeeper, who may well also be a neighbour. The television gives the customer something to watch while waiting for the shopkeeper to get the requested goods, or something to talk about if he has an assistant who does the fetching. And, of course, it also gives the shopkeeper something to watch during the slow periods. It is relatively affordable, and it can be set to whatever channel the shopkeeper chooses.

Small screens, usually functioning as television receivers, are also found in *ahwa* cafés and coffee shops. In a culture where few people consume alcohol, especially in public, these carry some of the same social functions as the American bar or British pub. Every neighbourhood has many *ahwa*, and these are usually establishments where only men gather. More recently, they have been supplemented by a middle class culture of international-style coffee shops, where both men and women gather (see Peterson 2009; de Koning 2011). Ratiba Hadj-Moussa (2010) has written about how, before the arrival of the satellite dish in Algeria, domestic space was female and men were expected to spend most of their time outside the home, returning to eat and sleep. Although satellite dishes are also common in Egypt, it seems a similar gendered pattern still applies. In a city where there is a great deal of both underemployment and unemployment, the *ahwa* is a place where men can pass time at relatively little cost. The television set is a relatively low-cost investment that gives customers something to talk about and something to watch when they do not want to talk or if they are alone. Special television events, like football matches, also draw customers to the *ahwa*, much as they do in bars and pubs elsewhere.

In contrast to Cairo, television receivers in shops are less common in Shanghai. The most common use of the public screen that we found there, even in places where no other kind of public screen was situated, is to mark entrances to shops, public buildings, residential compounds, and so on. The screen at the entrance to Tongji University mentioned above, which functioned like a slide show, is one example. To give another, on 29 March 2010, local research assistant Wu Dan and I set off on another exploratory walk, to Songjiang New Town Station at the end of subway line nine. We started out at the commercial heart of Songjiang, but there were no advertising pillars with screens embedded in them lining the sidewalks, as we saw in downtown Shanghai, nor were there screens on the sides of the buildings. But walking north from the station, we came across a 'walking word' (*zouzi*) screen featuring red characters, moving tickertape-style on a black background, over the entrance to a building supplies and decoration store, and another one over the entrance to a branch of China Construction Bank. Both advertised current offers. A bit further on, we discovered similar walking word screens at a spa and a restaurant. Apart from the eye-catching quality of movement and light, another advantage of this form of advertising is local control and the ability to change the message at will. Later informal enquiries indicated that the prices of these screens had dropped rapidly in recent years and they were considered to be affordable for most small business owners now.

Similar screens are found all over Shanghai, and all other Chinese cities that I have visited. They are the latest variant in a long history of Chinese writing in public spaces. Climb a mountain in China, and if someone else has got to the top before you, you are likely to find Chinese characters inscribed into the rock at the summit. These are called *moya*, and they have been around for at least 2,000 years. As Robert Harrist points out, they 'are traces of the mind … imposing cultural order on the accidents of geology' (2000: 39). At lunar New Year, it is customary to stick good luck couplets written on paper on either side of the doorway to your home. This habit is believed to date back more than a thousand years, although it was only in the fourteenth century that the use of red paper by ordinary citizens became a standardised and formalised practice (see Hsieh and Chou 1981: 125). More recently, after the founding of the People's Republic, a 'blackboard newspaper' (*heibanbao*) culture developed. This medium was seen as an effective way to generate and circulate local news and to reach ordinary people who might not buy or attend to newspapers. Guidebooks on how to produce effective news blackboards have been published since the 1950s, often profusely illustrated (see Zhou 1952). These blackboards were (and sometimes still are) located at the entrances to residential areas and workplaces.

This history of writing in public can be understood with reference to Louis Althusser's (1971) concept of ideology as interpellation, or a hailing effect on the subject to whom the ideology is directed. From this perspective, the prevalence of writing in public spaces in China suggests a public culture where spaces are clearly divided and differentiated according to the roles, activities, and values expected of people in those places, which the writing communicates. The historical changes in the medium of writing, from inscription to blackboard to 'walking word' screen can also be understood through Jay David Bolter and Richard Grusin's (2000) concept of remediation of earlier media forms. However, it is important to point out that they are not simply a case of old wine in new bottles. Rather, these remediations are better understood as a genealogy, in Michel Foucault's (1977) sense that emphasises contingency and disjuncture rather than linear historical development. And implied in the case of the transition from the blackboard to the walking word screen is the shift from socialist prioritisation of production to today's neoliberal exhortation to consumption. The second part of this essay extends the questions of the first part of this essay to neoliberal culture.

NEOLIBERALISM, THE END OF HISTORY, AND THE INTEGRATED SPECTACLE

Koolhaas's generic city is not only the city of globalisation but also the city of neoliberalism. He observes that the simultaneous arrival of cyberspace and generic sprawl means that whatever is left of public culture is on the net, and the physical spaces of the city are only for work and consumption (1995: 1250). Here, the idea of the global city as homogenised is conjoined with the idea of neoliberal culture, which is also characterised by an ideology that claims politics are over, morality is privatised, and public life is devoted to accelerated cycles of production and consumption in the pursuit of accumulation of wealth.

Neoliberalism is much debated. One of the most quoted texts on the topic is David Harvey's *A Brief History of Neoliberalism* (2005). In it he emphasises a political economic analysis of the rollback of the state and emphasis on the market as a strategy for re-entrenching global elites. A point of controversy in the book has been the inclusion of a chapter on China (2005: 121–51). Donald M. Nonini (2008) argues against the idea of China as neoliberal, on the grounds that although China has engaged with the market economy and global capitalism, the state continues to be the dominant player in the economy. Indeed, if neoliberalism is understood solely as an economic phenomenon, this argument has value.

However, if neoliberalism is also understood as a culture, then a more complex picture emerges. In *Desiring China* (2007), Lisa Rofel analyses contemporary Chinese culture as not only shaped by neoliberal practices such as the command economy giving way to a market economy and the state moving housing, healthcare, and increasingly education over to the market, but also by the adoption of an ethos that encourages people to see themselves as individuals engaged in lifelong projects of self-making, for which they are responsible, and which are to be realised through consumption. These she calls 'experiments in neoliberalism'. Once we understand neoliberalism as both economic and cultural, we can see how China has developed its own neoliberalism, and we can also acknowledge that perhaps the change from the command economy to Chinese neoliberalism has been far greater than the changes experienced in Western liberal democracies, even if the state continues to play a dominant economic role in China. Much the same can be said of Egypt, which also transitioned from a state-controlled command economy and culture inherited from Nasser to its own neoliberal economy and culture under Mubarak (see Osman 2010).

Not only is this neoliberal culture one where as much as possible is given over to market-based practices of production and consumption, but also it is also understood, by both its critics and its proponents, as a culture where there is no more political contestation. This is the argument of Francis Fukuyama's famous 'end of history' thesis (1992), where he celebrates the idea that since the fall of the Berlin wall in 1989, liberal democracy has emerged as a global winner. (This was, of course, written before 9/11, the Iraq War, the rise of Islamic State, and so on.) This vision echoes Koolhaas's vision of the generic city as one where public culture (including political contestation) has departed the public spaces of the city, and shopping is the primary public activity.

Whereas Fukuyama celebrates neoliberalism as the end of politics, others see it as a dystopia. An example is Guy Debord's idea of the 'integrated spectacle'. Debord previously described the concentrated and diffuse spectacle in an essay originally published in 1967 (see Debord 1994). The former referred to totalitarian modernity, where attention was focused on a dictatorial personality such as Stalin, Mao or Hitler, whereas the latter designated consumerist modernity characterised by advertising. Insofar as the subject might look away from the object of the gaze, there was always the possibility of disruption. However, in an essay originally published in 1992, shortly before his suicide, he argued that the victory of the diffuse spectacle had ushered in a third form, the integrated spectacle, which fuses both previous types and is global and all-encompassing (see Debord 1998). In a remark that echoes Jameson's (1991) comments on lack of critical distance in late capitalism or Baudrillard's (1983) idea of the postmodern simulacrum, Debord concludes, 'When the spectacle was concentrated, the greater part of surrounding society escaped it; when diffuse, a small part; today, no part. The spectacle has spread itself to the point where it now permeates all reality' (1998: 9).

Debord's integrated spectacle takes us back to Casetti's post-cinematic screen culture, where we live amongst images rather than gaze at them. And, indeed, the dominant deployment of public screens to promote consumption would seem to place the post-cinematic screen culture of the global city securely in the service of the neoliberal project of colonising public space for consumption. Yet, even here, our data indicates some complications. First, even the way in which screens are deployed in consumer cultures is also site-specific and culturally specific, suggesting a multiplicity of competing neoliberal cultures rather than a static and generic world were history has come to an end. And, second, perhaps today's screen culture also indicates that neoliberalism may be less monolithic than either Fukuyama or Debord believes.

To deal with local specificity first, screens are found at sites of high-end or wannabe high-end consumption in both Cairo and Shanghai, but the characteristics of these sites are quite different. In Shanghai, Wujiaochang typifies a pattern where department stories, cinemas, hotels, and so on all cluster at major intersections, and the potential consumers gather and swarm on the streets.

In Cairo, in contrast, upper middle class consumption occurs in box malls. Our chosen research site was the City Stars Heliopolis mall. Located a short drive from the airport where the middle class suburbs of Nasr City and Heliopolis meet, it is 'certainly inspired by a pharaonic temple' (Abaza 2006: 31). City Stars sits here like a UFO that has just landed – it has little if any apparent connection to the surrounding neighbourhood. A forbidding and windowless fortress-like development, it is most easily accessed by the car-owning minority of Cairo's population, who can drive and enter from 'indoor parking facilities for over 6,000 vehicles' (Anon. 2012) underneath the building. For those who dare to approach from the street, it has a small number of well-guarded entrances, where all who enter are security checked. Nominally, it is open to all shoppers, but we never saw anyone walking in from the apartment blocks in the neighbourhood.

City Stars is not only segregated but also aspires to be somewhere else entirely. Whereas the Shanghai intersection of Wujiaochang aspires to lead the redevelopment of the entire Yangpu District of Shanghai, the Cairo box mall implies the impossibility of or lack of interest in broader social change. Like the Tardis time machine in the British television series *Doctor Who*, stepping into City Stars Heliopolis provides, for the class that can access it, the uncanny experience of being transported into an elsewhere of global brand culture with a few local touches, and without actually leaving Cairo at all. Whereas Wujiaochang is open and indeed integrated into the surrounding streets, attempting to draw the neighbourhood with it, City Stars and the other new indoor malls of Cairo are part of a logic of what Mona Abaza calls 'walling off' (2006: 26) the lives of the upper middle classes and the elite from scenes and experiences like the teeming shoppers of the market near El Khalafawi metro station.

This 'not El Khalafawi' quality of the City Stars experience extends also to its screen culture. The mall is traversed by 'boulevards', where there are many LED screens – as opposed to the cathode ray television receivers that predominate around El Khalafawi. Furthermore, these LED screens are arranged as pairs placed back-to-back in four-screen pods hanging from the ceiling. Each one of these screens featured the same mall video loop, mostly advertising the stores, facilities, and upcoming events of the mall itself, as well as some public service messages about children's healthcare and the activities of a charity. If the everyday street market is congested, the 'boulevards' of City Stars are spacious and, as the appropriation of the French word might imply, made for promenading. If the street market is hot, City Stars is air-conditioned and cool. If the street market is local and dominated by piles of produce, City Stars is cosmopolitan, almost all its wares well packaged and bearing regional and international brand names. Whereas the street spaces of the market are screen-free, but each independent shop has its own cathode ray television set, with a different programme blaring out, in City Stars there are relatively few screens inside shops, but almost the entire environment is populated by the pods of four Samsung flat screens playing the City Stars loop. Why this redundancy? Again, it contrasts with the market areas outside and is part of the overall effort to communicate City Stars Heliopolis mall as the opposite of the apparently chaotic, hot, disordered and

Fig. 1 The four-screen pods inside City Stars, Cairo, 2010.

overcrowded streets of Cairo; instead, City Stars is excessively and redundantly ordered, cool, and busy but uncongested. Doubling the screens emphasises order and control at the same time as it excludes options.

The screen culture of Wujiaochang is as devoted to aspirational consumption as that of the City Stars Heliopolis mall. But the arrangement of its screens and their signification is quite different. Not only is Wujiaochang an open space, designed to connect with and lead the Yangpu neighbourhood, but also the screens are varied in size and content. They range from the massive screens on the sides of the two department stores, with the newer one advertising global brands, to 'walking word' screens at the entrance of stores like a jewellers as well as banks and restaurants, and to pillars lining some of the streets and carrying yet more advertising on their LED screens. These screens merge with regular advertising lightboxes, streetlights, and even a network of pulsating neon over the 'egg' that encloses a road overpass arching through the space of the intersection. The result is a vibrant and diverse lightscape full of the '*renao*' (literally 'hot noise') character that Chinese people find attractive (see Warden and Chen 2009) but is so different from the cool order of the screens in City Stars.

The diversity of consumption screen cultures illustrated by the differences between Wujiaochang and City Stars indicates a diversity in neoliberal cultures that challenges the idea of neoliberal culture as monolithic. However, diversity in itself does not suggest an 'outside' to neoliberal culture. Yet, here, too, there are signs that the spectacle culture of the glance at the LED screen may not be quite as integrated and all-encompassing as Debord feared. First of all, although City Stars may strive to make those inside it forget about the rest of Cairo, the majority of the city's citizens have very limited access to a culture of self-making through consumption.

In Shanghai, too, the many older, retired and unemployed in the areas around Wujiaochang come to the intersection in the evening, not to shop, but to dance. They bring their own boomboxes and, as the stores close, take over the areas outside to line dance and ballroom dance. The huge screens on the sides of the buildings are their spotlights, the pulsating neon patterns on the 'egg' their disco ball. These are not activities devoted to accelerating the cycles of production and consumption.

But while the dancers at Wujiaochang and the ordinary citizens beyond City Stars might be in some sense beyond the integrated spectacle, we must acknowledge there is no evidence that they are resisting or challenging it. For that, we need to look elsewhere. First, there is the very redundancy of the screens and their contents. The sheer effort to get people to even glance at them let alone retain what is on them suggests that perhaps we are not so eager to participate in self-making through consumption as the advertisements and public service messages might suggest. Add to this the security cameras – surely there as many as there are screens? – and the suggestion is that the post-cinematic screen culture does not trust its subjects and fears they would just as happily steal as pay for the goods, or possibly vandalise them.

Finally, let us not forget Tahrir Square in Cairo, the Maidan in Kiev, Taksim Square in Istanbul, the Umbrella Movement in Hong Kong, the Sunflower Movement in Taipei, the London riots, and all the other events that have demonstrated the public

Fig. 2 The lightscape on the streets of Wujiaochang, Shanghai, 2009.

is far from being as politically disengaged as both the critics of neoliberalism fear and its proponents hope. While the post-cinematic screen culture of the streets and squares of the global city has indeed been colonised for the mundane promotion of consumption and neoliberal values, perhaps the very excessive nature of the effort is also a mark of its fragility.

NOTE

1   I acknowledge with gratitude the funding of this project by the Leverhulme Trust as part of the activities of the Goldsmiths Media Research Centre, and also the work of my colleagues Janet Harbord, Rachel Moore, and Amal Khalaf. The larger project also included London, which there is no space to consider here.

BIBLIOGRAPHY

Abaza, Mona (2006) *The Changing Consumer Cultures of Modern Egypt: Cairo's Urban Reshaping*. Cairo: American University in Cairo Press.

Althusser, Louis (1971) 'Ideology and Ideological State Apparatuses', trans. Ben Brewster, *Lenin and Philosophy and other Essays*. New York: Monthly Review Press, 121–76.

Anon. (2012) http://www.citystars.com.eg/citystars/index.asp

Appadurai, Arjun (1990) 'Disjuncture and Difference in the Global Cultural Economy', *Theory, Culture & Society*, 7, 2, 295–310.

Baudrillard, Jean (1983) *Simulations*. New York: Semiotext(e).

Berry, Chris and Janet Harbord (2015) 'Tracking the Screen in Public Spaces: Everyday Dis/Enchantment', in Helen Grace (ed.) *Technovisuality: Cultural Re-enchantment and the Experience of Technology*. London: I.B. Tauris, 179–207.

Bolter, Jay David and Richard Grusin (2000) *Remediation: Understanding New Media*. Cambridge: MIT Press.

Casetti, Francesco (2013) 'What Is a Screen Nowadays?', Chris Berry, Janet Harbord and Rachel Moore (eds) *Public Space, Media Space*. London: Palgrave Macmillan, 16–40.

Debord, Guy (1981) 'Theory of the Dérive', ed. and trans. Ken Knabb, *Situationist International Anthology*. Berkeley: Bureau of Public Secrets, 50–4.

_____ (1994) *The Society of the Spectacle*, trans. Donald Nicholson-Smith, New York: Zone Books.

_____ (1998) *Comments on the Society of the Spectacle*, trans. Malcolm Imrie. London: Verso.

De Koning, Anouk (2009) 'Class and Cosmopolitanism Belonging in Cairo's Coffee Shops', in *Global Dreams: Class, Gender, and Public Space in Cosmopolitan Cairo*.

Cairo: American University Press, 97–130.
Featherstone, Mike (2009) 'Ubiquitous Media: An Introduction', *Theory, Culture & Society*, 26, 2/3, 1–22.
Foucault, Michel (1977) 'Nietzsche, Geneaology, History', in *Language, Counter-Memory, Practice: Selected Essays and Interviews*. Ithaca: Cornell University Press, 139–64.
Fukuyama, Francis (1992) *The End of History and the Last Man*. New York: Free Press.
Hadj-Moussa, Ratiba (2010) 'The Undecidable and the Irreversible: Satellite Television in the Algerian Public Space', in Chris Berry, Soyoung Kim and Lynn Spigel (eds) *Electronic Elsewheres: Media, Technology and the Experience of Social Space*. Minneapolis: University of Minnesota Press, 117–36.
Harrist, Robert E. Jr. (2000) 'Reading Chinese Mountains: Landscape and Calligraphy in China', *Orientations*, 31, 10, 64–9.
Harvey, David (2005) *A Brief History of Neoliberalism*. Oxford: Oxford University Press.
Hsieh, Jiann and Ying-Hsiung Chou (1981) 'Public Aspirations in the New Year Couplets: A Comparative Study between the People's Republic and Taiwan', *Asian Folklore Studies*, 40, 2, 125–49.
Jameson, Frederic (1991) *Postmodernism, or, The Logic of Late Capitalism*. London: Verso.
Koolhaas, Rem (1995) 'The Generic City', in Rem Koolhaas, Bruce Mau, Jennifer Sigler and Hans Werlemann (eds) *S, M, L, XL*. New York: Monacelli, 1248–64.
Madden. Normandy (2006) 'With Urban China Focus, Jiang Elevator Ads Have Nowhere to Go but up', *Advertising Age*, 27 March; http://adage.com/article/people-players/urban-china-focus-jian-elevator-ads/108239/
Massy, Kevin (2005) 'In Focus: A Closer Look at the Sector's Chinese Poster Child', AKA TV, 7 November; http://media.corporate-ir.net/media_files/irol/19/190067/press/AKA.pdf
McCarthy, Anna (2001) *Ambient Television: Visual Culture and Public Space*. Durham: Duke University Press.
Mulvey, Laura (1975) 'Visual Pleasure and Narrative Cinema', *Screen*, 16, 3, 6–18.
Nonini, Donald M. (2008) 'Is China Becoming Neoliberal?', *Critique of Anthropology*, 28, 2, 145–76.
Osman, Tarek (2010) *Egypt on the Brink: From Nasser to Mubarak*. New Haven: Yale University Press.
Peterson, Mark Allen (2011) 'Coffee Shops and Gender in Translocal Spaces', in *Connected in Cairo: Growing up Cosmopolitan in the Modern Middle East*. Bloomington: Indiana University Press, 138–69.
Rofel, Lisa (2007) *Desiring China: Experiments in Neoliberalism, Sexuality, and Public Culture*. Durham: Duke University Press.
Robertson, Roland (1995) 'Glocalization: Time-Space and Homogeneity-Hetero

geneity', in Mike Featherstone, Scott Lash and Roland Robertson (eds) *Global Modernities*. Thousand Oaks: Sage, 25–44.

Warden, Clyde A. and Judy F. Chen (2009) 'When Hot and Noisy Is Good: Chinese Values of *Renao* and Consumption Metaphors', *Asia Pacific Journal of Marketing and Logistics*, 21, 2, 216–231.

Zhang, Tingwei (2009) 'Striving to Be a Global City from Below: The Restructuring of Shanghai's Urban Districts', in Xiangming Chen (ed.) *Shanghai Rising: State Power and Local Transformations in a Global Megacity*. Minneapolis: University of Minnesota Press, 176–86.

Zhong, Song (2009) '上海五角场环岛下沉式广场景观设计' ('Landscape Design for the Pentagon Plaza, Shanghai'), 风景园林 *Landscape Design*, 3: 113–15.

Zhou, Wuji (1952) 怎样办好黑板报 ('How to Produce a Successful Blackboard Newspaper'). 上海: 北新书局 Shanghai: Beixin Press.

THE CITY AS FOUND FOOTAGE: THE REASSEMBLAGE OF CHINESE URBAN SPACE

YOMI BRAESTER

The urban environment of the twenty-first century is to a large extent defined by two forms of the moving image: surveillance videos and found footage. By virtue of their presence, security cameras identify public space as subject to regulation. These cameras, often forming large networks, capture the city's temporal flow and trace the movement of citizens through space. The ubiquity of surveillance videos is an exponent of the increased data gathering and production of information. Found footage is also a symptom of a shift of a larger scale, toward a comprehensive sharing of content produced by individual citizens. In its broader sense, found footage includes any images made for occasions other than the ones in which it is used. Now the majority of these images are generated by private devices – most prominently smartphones – and subsequently disseminated and circulated on the Internet, especially through peer-to-peer platforms and social media.[1]

At first glance, surveillance videos and found footage seem to stand on opposite ends of the spectrum that marks our relation as visual subjects to the spaces we inhabit. Surveillance videos are an extreme manifestation of spatial control, in which sites function as theatrical sets for a spectacle regimented by security cameras. Built environment is reduced to scaffolding for events that are primarily visual. The contemporary city in particular is immersed in a system of images that renders everything visible, practically everywhere and always. Found footage, on the other hand, is the outcome of loss of control. Whatever intent may have lied behind its initial production, found footage is at the mercy of its finder. The images are appropriated and reinterpreted. Even insofar as found footage retains its reference to the time and place of recording, its indexical value is attenuated, compromised by its new use.

Taken out of the spatial and temporal context of its production, found footage does not uphold the primacy of vision. It denotes the arbitrary repurposing of images, the discarded gaze, the relinquishing of visual agency.

Yet surveillance videos and found footage complement each other, creating a new urban media ecology. On the one hand, surveillance videos are less controlling than they might first seem. Surveillance studies stress how interconnected cameras compromise citizens' privacy, yet I argue that such systemic analysis replicates the imagined viewpoint of network controllers and ignores the true effect of surveillance videos.[2] In practice, even though we may imagine ourselves watched by concealed cameras and hovering aircraft, very few have direct access to the resulting images. The popular imagination is based on those clips leaked to the press and uploaded to sites such as YouTube. Notwithstanding the real threat to human rights posed by security cameras (as well as the benefit to public safety), surveillance videos enter public circulation in a form already removed from their initial intended use. At the phenomenological level, surveillance videos are no different from found footage.

On the other hand, found footage accrues added intentionality once it is appropriated and reinterpreted. Indeed, my use of 'found footage' is meant as a nod toward a number of practices associated with the term, which suggest an auteurial agency behind the use of readymade images. As a form of avant-garde cinema, found footage films (also known as collage or compilation films) resuscitate the authority of the image by offering 'a radical disassociation of content and form that becomes reconstructed, reconfigured' (Verrone 2012: 168). The collage alludes to the vulnerability of the image and at the same time invokes the possibility of recovery through the artist's actions. Moreover, the reuse of found footage accentuates the value of fragments as the source of alternative narratives.

Reprocessing media fragments is arguably a sign of our times, due to the ease of digital reproduction, resampling and redistribution. The large amount of clips available on sites such as YouTube brings to an extreme the ability to reassemble found footage. For Andreas Treske, online video is 'reassembled in new contexts, levels, affordances, customizations and personalisations' (2014: 22). Yet whereas Treske thinks of video reassemblage in terms of reshuffling and material modification, the reassemblage to which I refer here consists mostly (at least in the hands of lay netizens) of recycling the same images in other media and new urban ecologies. (Furthermore, although I place reassemblage in the context of social critique and affective virality, I use the term in a rather narrow sense, skirting the implications of Deleuzian assemblage theory.)

As the repurposing of found footage, reassemblage often amounts to a rearrangement of perceived reality. The logic of reassemblage renders the profilmic irrelevant and redefines indexicality as reference to the chain of recycled images. This emphasis on the medium does not, however, amount to doing away with the signified, as in the semantics of the simulacrum. Rather, reassemblage shifts the economy of signification from the material to the visual medium as the subject of discourse. Jaimie

Baron (2014) notes the historiographical crisis at the foundation of reusing documentary film fragments, which requires a recognition that our use of found footage partakes in creating the event at hand. Found footage amounts to a fluid archive; its incorporation into other films, as the case of *Forrest Gump* (Robert Zemeckis, 1994) demonstrates, both lends credibility to the new images and adds a playful tone. By dint of referring both to its time of production and to the occasion of its reuse, found footage points to the multilayered significance of the image.

The reconfiguration of visual representation is in turn followed by a shift of auteurial agency and a modification in the role of the citizen in reimagining public space – both material (architectural) and figurative (social). The confluence of surveillance videos and found footage blurs the boundaries between the individual and public spheres, between spontaneous and designed images, and between material and virtual spaces. As a result, built environment becomes a visual ecosystem that produces, trashes and recycles images. The city, in turn, functions both as a watching eye and as a visual *objet trouvé*, at the same time.

In this chapter I examine the contemporary urban ecology of the image in the People's Republic of China through specific cases that lie on the borderline between surveillance video and found footage. They include self-made videos and selfies in Beijing's business district of Sanlitun, the video of the death of Wang Yue, Tan Tan's video art 'Shui de yanjing' (Whose Eyes, 2011), Li Juchuan's video art 'Sharen guocheng jin qi miaozhong' (Murdering six people in seven seconds, 2008), and Ai Weiwei's 'WeiweiCam' (2012). These cases vary widely: from a sex scandal to incidents of brutality and crime, from clips circulating widely on the Internet to video art viewed by few. Yet together they outline a discourse on the use of screens and cameras in public space.

The resulting practices give the lie to the dichotomy that assumes citizens to be either subjected to surveillance or masters of their visual representation. Citizens are both end-users and consumers of visual media, and they cannot be described or identified as standing either before or behind the camera, either in front of or on the screen. Contemporary citizens have often been depicted as viewers: framing, recording, storing and sharing at will the views at their disposal. At the same time, citizens are constantly imaged: photographed by passersby, captured by security cameras, scanned and collected in image databases. Yet urban dwellers are not limited to the roles of either the subjects of spectacle or the objects of surveillance. Rather, their interaction with screens and cameras is mutually constitutive.

I have argued in *Painting the City Red* that the built environment should not be regarded as a given, described after the fact by film. Continuing this line of thought, I contend here that the urban visual ecology does not simply mediate and enforce a preexisting power structure. Rather, citizens define the use of cameras and screens and are at the same time defined by that act. The citizen is integrated into the social structures and technological networks that constitute the urban at large. The networked interface of cameras and screens reconstitutes public space as the site of a particular economy, in which images are reused, reappropriated and reassembled. Insofar as urban space is produced by these images, it also functions as found footage.

A MEDIATISED SEX SCANDAL

One of the newer forms of images intended for their producers' use but susceptible to being intercepted and reused as found footage is the selfie. The significance of the selfie often relies on showing the subject at a specific location and marking a particular occasion. Such images are not new; in fact, they hark back to painterly conventions, and photography has been central to the formation of modern individuality (see Gunning 1995). But the advent of the selfie as a readily identifiable genre (and lexical term, celebrated as the Oxford Dictionaries Word of the Year 2013) has introduced a new economy of the image. The selfie derives its meaning from being nestled within practices that include posting it on Facebook or Instagram, tweeting and retweeting it, 'liking' and commenting on it, and pinning it onto a map using the embedded GPS coordinates. The technology of social media plays a crucial and visible role in creating the selfie experience. From ownership of the Facebook account to using a selfie stick, the subject takes pride in reassembling a digital record of the event and the site of its occurrence. Such practices redefine the concept of visual agency, as the Uniqlo incident demonstrates.

On 14 July 2015, a 71-second homemade video, probably shot in April of that year, was released through WeChat and Weibo links, which showed a young man using a mobile phone to record himself and his woman partner having sex in a fitting room, located at the Uniqlo store in Sanlitun, Beijing. The video went viral. It attracted the attention of urban youth, legal authorities, the media and scholars, who commented on the semi-public, semi-illegal, graphic sex. Less attention was given to the use of cameras and screens during the event and in the following netizens' tributes. I will argue that the Uniqlo incident demonstrates how citizens refashion public space through user-generated images, and through selfies in particular. Rather than subjecting citizens to a regime of control and surveillance, the new imaging practices establish netizens as agents of the new visual economy.

The official response to the sex video focused on the need to regulate sex in public space. Tadashi Yanai, the founder of the Uniqlo chain store, commented that 'Just hearing it makes me sick', and the company issued a statement distancing itself from the incident (in Porter 2015). The Chinese police arrested the two participants – Beijing college students – and three people involved in distributing the video, for violating the country's 'core socialist values'. The police also harshly reprimanded the two social media venues through which the video spread at first (Anon. 2015a). Popular opinion picked up the same discourse, if only to disapprove of the authorities. In one case, fans of a soccer team playing against the Public Security Bureau (PSB) team held up signs stating, 'PSB, caonima! Papapa in the Uniqlo fitting room'

(Anon. 2015b). The term *caonima*, literally 'grass mud horse' and a homonym for 'fuck your mother', referred to popular discontent with policing obscenity through the caonima meme in early 2009; *papapa*, an onomatopoeic reference to the sexual act, was another direct affront to PSB regulations on public speech. The knee-jerk reaction of the authorities, which immediately tagged the video as an affront to the government, was mirrored by Western media, which seized the opportunity to discuss the sexual mores of urban Chinese youth and portray the video and subsequent popular response – with the help of the prominent sex sociologist Li Yinhe – as a comment on the Chinese government's sexual repression (see Lu and Chan 2015).

The incident may indeed reflect a growing gap between official and popular conceptions of morality, use of public space, and Internet freedom. Yet the majority of responses to the incident were not overtly political; instead, they addressed citizens' concerns as consumers of social media. Many netizens reposted the video and commented on it. Youth gathered at the Uniqlo store and took photos and selfies. (Although the photographs may be attributed to a general penchant among Chinese youth, the wide reporting on media sites about photo-taking at Uniqlo suggests an exceptional phenomenon.) T-shirts were sold, bearing uncensored screen grabs from the video; others etched unredacted tattoos commemorating the incident. Spoofing images followed suit as well, such as a rearrangement of the Uniqlo logo in the form of two people having sex, or a meme saying, 'let's go to uniqlo: If you know what I mean' (see Anon. 2015c; McComic 2015; Nelson 2015). Such reactions fit into the Chinese media environment, which teems with textual appropriations (such as slash fiction), memes and video spoofs. More specifically, the responses imitate the visual practices and trace the same spatial routines as the couple in the video. The respondents identify to a large extent with the couple, even transferring images from the video onto the body, on clothes and tattoos. Judging by photos and social media usage habits, the couple and the respondents share a similar age group and socio-economic background. In commenting on the incident, the respondents also refer to their own condition, as youth operating within a specific media ecology. They condone the use of public space and screen technologies involved in producing and distributing the video.

In fact, as a sex scandal the Uniqlo sex video was in many ways a non-issue. Since around 2008, shooting sex videos of oneself became commonplace in the PRC. As Katrien Jacobs notes, netizens have been eager to upload and distribute sex videos despite the legal risks; in particular, documenting sex in public locations such as classrooms, computer labs and city parks is common (2012: 31). The genre of homemade sex videos is referred to as *zipai*, literally 'self-shot', which is also the term for selfies. It does not seem that the public sees a need to mark the semantic difference between prurient content and other forms of recording oneself. The Uniqlo video and subsequent selfies, which cover both definitions of *zipai*, participated without special provocation in a widespread culture of image-making. What made the Uniqlo incident more noticeable was probably the fact that the link was listed by bloggers with large followings, under the names Guda baihua and Ma Boyong, and circulated through Yunpan, a Chinese equivalent to Snapchat (Anon. 2015d). The sex video was highly visible on social media and easy to download without trace; moreover, the media through which it was distributed distinguished it from straightforward sexual content on pornography sites.

THE ECONOMY OF REASSEMBLAGE

Rather than as a sex scandal, Uniqlo video may be understood in terms of a media event. Taking selfies to emulate the couple's act of shooting themselves (sometimes alluding to the posture assumed by the couple), choosing Uniqlo as the location for the selfies, and sharing the new images on the Internet – all these suggest identification not only with the mentality of the couple in the sex video but also with their use of the smartphone as camera and social media interface. Smiling at the camera, the youth who pay tribute to the sex video comment also on the medium in use. Photography is seen as a vehicle of carnivalesque participation, a vicarious sharing in the couple's carefree pleasure (arguably more visual than sexual), a performance that both symbolises and enacts the photographed subject's indulgence in contemporary urban lifestyle.

Insofar as the selfies at Uniqlo resist the regulation of spatial use and public expression, the images are effective precisely because they are not created by conscientious dissidents but rather by enthusiastic participants in consumer culture. The selfie-takers may challenge accepted decency, but even then they are careful not to cross the red lines set by the authorities. The political dimension is secondary at best. What is at stake is the citizens' and netizens' ability to take into their hands the graphic representation and symbolic use of public space.

Selfies function in the Uniqlo incident as a form of mimicry, exposing the shortcomings of the authoritative discourse by reappropriating its representational modes. The images gain their significance through a dynamics of repurposing – first by the couple, who availed themselves of the fitting room for an unintended use; then by their friends and other netizens, who spread the video; later by the visitors to Uniqlo, who posed by substituting themselves for the couple; and finally by the media that reported on the event and its aftermath. At all these stages, mobile screens and social media were involved, but each time they served in different capacities and for different ends.

The selfies at Sanlitun may be seen as a form of *détournement*, resistance to the consumerist spectacle by creating new spatial practices (see Debord 1956). Even so, inquiry into the Uniqlo incident must include an understanding of how it feeds into a discourse of media reassemblage. A closer look shows that the chain of reappropriation in the Uniqlo case is longer and of wider implications than it appears at first. The immediate responses to the Uniqlo video incident placed the incident in the context of media literacy. A photo essay explaining how to best take a selfie asked: 'Are you still "re-experiencing" the image of the woman facing the mirror in the Uniqlo incident? Actually the Uniqlo incident tells you that taking a selfie is also a science' (Yoka 2015: np). The essay ignores the sexual content of the video; instead, it invokes the incident to harp on the netizen's anxiety about social media. The teaser seems to blame the woman not for appearing in the sex video but for technical pedestrianism. Addressing female netizens, who seem to constitute the majority of selfie-takers (and are sometimes denigrated as *zipai biao*, or 'selfie bitches'), the photo essay suggests that any selfie is at its core a version of the sex video, and that selfie-takers (of any hue of *zipai*) should be assessed first and foremost for their media savvy.

The discussion of the Uniqlo incident has also ignored Uniqlo's active involvement in the selfie culture. In late 2014, the chain store launched an international 'Selfless Selfie Project'. People were encouraged to take pictures of themselves and pledge an act of good will or money for charity. The photo would be posted to one's 'favorite social network' with the wording: 'I give my #3DSelfie to _____' and the additional hashtag #UNIQLOCity. Selfie posters chosen by Uniqlo would be invited to make 3D images of themselves, to be exhibited in the chain's stores (see Thimmesh 2014). The campaign took place in the US and Europe, but was reported also in China (Anon. 2014). This promotion scheme associated Uniqlo specifically with netizens who were eager to take selfies, use social media to spread them, and link their posts to hashtags identifying them with the chain store. No wonder a rumor claimed that Uniqlo was behind the sex video, as an advertisement ploy.[3]

The sex video and following selfies at Sanlitun may be seen as an unintended offshoot from the Uniqlo campaign. Whereas the advertising campaign fashioned taking selfies as a form of social consciousness and responsibility, the Beijing selfies showed that in independent-minded hands the same technology was likely to be used to dissociate netizens from the altruistic image used to promote Uniqlo's commercial interests. Contrary to the ad's rhetoric, selfies are neither selfish nor selfless. Rather, they are a form of performative self-assertion. Uniqlo, which stands for 'unique clothing' in Japanese-style abbreviation, encouraged consumers to participate in the 3D campaign with the words, 'Make it unique, interesting and not just about you.' Only that netizens took the idea of focusing on oneself too far for the taste of the chain store's owners.

The Uniqlo incident shows how selfies and homemade videos feed into a culture of reappropriation that renders them immediately into found footage, used well beyond the scope of the initial intention. In fact, netizens are likely to provide such content with the awareness if not desire that it should be reused as found footage. The eagerness on the part of selfie-takers to place themselves in public view and at the centre of social media celebrates the culture of reassemblage.

The selfie has often been seen as a symptom of generational malaise and narcissism, yet this interpretation ignores the self-consciousness and active role of the photographers. Uniqlo's 'selfless selfie' campaign also exploits the widespread assumption that selfies represent a self-absorbed youth, focused on getting attention and promoting themselves as media celebrities. Yet the sociologist Peter Kaufman (2014) claims that this common perception ignores the selfie's function within the netizens' social environment. Kaufman notes that selfies are used to control one's public image, as a form of what Erving Goffman has called 'impression management' (see 1990: 203–30). Like other forms of social interaction, taking selfies includes a performative aspect, designed to show the subject's action in a certain light and elicit specific responses. Staging one's image in selfies, and placing selfies on social media, offer occasions for subjects to project their desired image and see it reflected back. Through the process that David Snow and Leon Anderson call 'identity work' (1987: 1348), selfies bridge one's image of oneself and social perceptions – creating, maintaining and modifying one's identity within the collective. Selfies present individuals with an opportunity to influence how others presumably see and judge them (see Kaufman 2014). In other words, selfies are not an indulgent leisure activity, a vain dallying with superficial media, but rather a vital social interaction, a defence against the collective usage of visual and social images, usage that can be invasive and even violent. Selfies are a form of social self-empowerment, a performative act; their social function is intrinsically linked to their role facilitating participation in, and implicitly commenting on, the media environment. The Uniqlo incident illustrates how citizens and netizens create through selfies identities embedded in the culture of reassemblage.

Citizens become *bricoleurs*, enterprising craftspersons who piece together in new ways the haphazard media resources at their availability. Whereas some sociologists regard the privatization of media production as outsourcing surveillance – Zygmunt Bauman (see Bauman and Lyon 2012: 52–75) calls this condition 'post-panopticism' – citizens' ability to produce and disseminate images suggests a repossession of agency. Netizens often identify themselves as smartphone photographers (*paike*) in the service of the public, proud of producing original content (*yuanchuang*). The novelty stems, however, not only from generating never-seen-before photos and videos but also from reassembling them, thereby redefining the public sphere and the urban environment.

REASSEMBLING THE URBAN ARCHIVE

The dislocation of the self-made image and its appropriation as found footage modify also the function of urban space. In the Uniqlo incident, the selfies notably place the subjects back in the setting that gave rise to the original video. The Sanlitun Uniqlo became a site of pilgrimage, as the visitors found it significant to return to the place where the video was taken. Even though many Uniqlo branches have opened throughout Beijing and dozens of other Chinese cities, the selfie-takers gathered at the Sanlitun store. (In some photos, the visitors are carrying small suitcases, which suggests that they have traveled to the spot from outside town.) Only a few have taken photos inside the fitting rooms, staying instead outside the store entrance (for a counterexample, see Heping 2015). The sex video took advantage of the absence of security cameras in the fitting room, creating a private space within public space. In so doing, it underlined how the line between public and private is often blurred – a column in the Chinese-language website of Radio Nederland compared shooting the sex video to gay cruising (see Zeng 2015). The later selfies take up this strand of appropriating public space by recording performances for all to see. The selfies shift the event back to public space and more specifically to Sanlitun's urban chic.

As I have discussed elsewhere (Braester 2016), user-generated photography in China's cities follows the pattern dubbed by Helen Grace as 'horizontal monuments', eye-level records of the everyday. Grace notes how mobile screens create aggregate cityscapes, 'an archive of the present' (2007: 470). The selfies at Uniqlo form such a horizontal monument, commemorating the present while also preserving traces of the earlier video image at that site. The figure of the archive invoked by using found footage finds a patently spatial expression. The images create a visual history of Sanlitun, establishing the sex video as the foundational moment and all subsequent selfies as either a return to the primal scene or at least an involuntary retracing, inevitably complicit with the Uniqlo incident. In the aftermath of the incident, selfies have produced an urban palimpsest. Elsewhere I have expressed caution at using the term, since the concept of the palimpsest has been abused to justify fake façades and Dineyfied gentrification projects (see Braester 2016). In the Uniqlo case, however, the consciousness of layered space has little to do with reconstructing a material site. Rather, the palimpsest-like nature of the site relies here on the inherent inadequacy of the visual archive: Sanlitun invokes the figure of memory rather than offering access to the past.[4]

Indeed, in the context of the Uniqlo incident, urban space may be better fashioned as an interface to collective memory rather than as the surface covering multiple layers to be excavated. (In a different context, Martijn de Waal (2014) has pointed to 'the city as interface'.) Alexander Galloway suggests that treating the interface as a palimpsest places excessive weight on deep interpretation (2012: 45). Instead, as part of a networked interface, built environment can only be comprehended when it interacts with cameras and screens. This interaction is a new, powerful mode of spatial production. It is not that urban space is relocated to the virtual realm. Rather, the reassemblage of images establishes the temporal dimension of the city as a continuation of the history of the visual medium.

The images taken by smartphones and spread through social media present a new form of social documentation. Like exponents of the Chinese independent New Documentary Movement, the cumulative oeuvre of the Uniqlo selfies captures the current atmosphere in an urban milieu at the grassroots level, with a hint of youthful rebellion. Just as the documentaries of the Yuanmingyuan and Beijing East Village in the 1980s and 1990s were intrinsically linked to the resident artists' performance art, so are the selfies at Uniqlo performative acts of allegiance to a netizen community.[5] The Uniqlo selfies and other mobile screen practices are part of consumer culture and hardly share the avant-garde spirit of the New Documentary Movement. Yet the transformative potential of the selfies should not be underestimated. Unlike documentary filmmakers, selfie-takers can produce and spread their images with relative immunity, since the content of social media is privatised, decentralised, produced en masse, and reused as found footage. In so doing, selfie-takers reinvent the city – not as a profilmic space to be recorded but rather as readymade media to be ceaselessly reassembled.

FOUND FOOTAGE AS REALITY TV

The Uniqlo incident revolved around a sex scandal and generated found footage produced by smartphone owners. Another form of found footage originates from surveillance cameras and typically features images of violence and murder. The glaring differences notwithstanding, the two kinds of found footage complement each other and shape together the mediascape of contemporary Chinese public space.

Selfies and surveillance videos – together with the devices that produce them, smartphones and security cameras – have been associated with repressive control, yet they also point to the potential for renewed individual agency through media reassemblage. In addition to Bauman's aforementioned view that smartphones are part of a post-panopticist regime of public scrutiny and control, the willingness of selfie-takers may confirm the perverse pleasure that we derive, according to Slavoj Žižek (2002), from being observed always and everywhere. Such is, purportedly, the work of dominant ideology. Nevertheless, selfies also suggest the ambivalent role of contemporary media. In *Loving Big Brother*, John McGrath argues that the excess of contemporary surveillance provides opportunities beyond the limitations of the Foucauldian spectacle (2004: 8). Revenge videos aside, even sex videos may be seen not as a sign of the deterioration of control over one's image and space, but rather as exponents of a transparency to which all social media aspire. Insofar as the radical upsurge in visibility poses a danger, it is because the recycled images are consumed much like reality TV.

One of the best-known recent cases of repurposed surveillance videos is the one capturing Wang Yue's death. On 13 October 2011, the two-year-old from the Guangdong city of Foshan wandered away from her mother and was injured in a hit-and-run. She lay in the street for about seven minutes, during which eighteen passersby did not tend to her and another car drove over her. She was eventually picked up by a trash collector and died in hospital from her wounds. The 'Incident of Little Yueyue' (*Xiao Yueyue shijian*), as the media called it, raised anger across the country and even abroad.

The incident provided an occasion for introspection about society's ills.

Hit-and-run accidents, and even cases in which the perpetrators repeatedly ran over the victims to ensure their death and avoid higher compensation fees, were becoming commonplace (see Sant 2015). Reporters and netizens alike asked, was the callous reaction of passersby the sign of deteriorating social cohesion? Was the incident due to the fact that Wang Yue's neighborhood was temporary home to labuor migrants, with no sense of community? Was citizens' caution against getting involved in other people's affairs a legacy of the Cultural Revolution? (see Zhang 2011).

Although the popular outrage was instigated by security camera footage, little attention was given to the role of the imagery in the incident.[6] The accident and subsequent lack of response by passersby were recorded in full, broadcast on TV, and distributed on major Internet domains such as Youku, where it was watched and commented on by millions.[7] It was the powerful images that mobilised public opinion, and the visual information made it possible to identify the drivers and bring them to justice. Yet when scholars discussed the incident as a media event, they focused on the role of netizens, turned 'citizen journalists' (*gongmin jizhe*), in spreading the video (see Wang 2012; Zhang 2014). Despite the graphic nature of the incident, few reports and comments referred to the video itself: its origin, the identity of those who made it public, or how it was further distributed.

The narrow focus on the content of the surveillance video, at the expense of the visual apparatus, missed also part of the human story. As Singapore's *Lianhe zaobao* reports, it was Wang Yue's mother who noticed that an adjacent store had installed a security camera and requested to check for images from the time of the accident. The store owner complied, and the mother collapsed on the floor after watching the footage. It was Wang's mother, then, who first saw the video. On 14 October, a day after the accident, the girl's parents gave the material to the local TV station, TVS (Nanfang dianshitai), which broadcast it on its daily news for 15 October. Other media followed suit the next day, and netizens distributed the footage, captured from TV, on social media (see Zeng 2011). The image gained power precisely because social media used the video as found footage and adapted it to new agendas.

To a large extent, the disregard of the video's materiality could be expected in an age when the presence of security cameras is practically guaranteed, media venues appeal regularly to users to sell newsworthy clips, law enforcement agencies publicise such images to facilitate their work, and citizens keep security camera recordings for legal purposes. Twenty years after the Rodney King trial, the existence of third-party images, their public impact, and their legal and social manipulation can all be taken for granted. Yet in seeing right through the visual and social media, commentators on Wang Yue's death ignored the dynamics of reassemblage.

Although many viewers were doubtless truly scandalised, the video of Wang Yue's death was consumed much like infotainment. By using the video of Wang Yue's death as found footage to be shown as anyone in possession of the video saw fit, the media reduced screen users to passive viewers. The extensive reassemblage involved in the incident (from security camera to TV and to Internet) and the appropriation of the video (by the mother, media, legal authorities and netizens) unmoored the images from the material circumstances of their production and brought the entire event close to the realm of reality TV (a genre popular in China since 2004). The media used emotive tagging ('Little Yueyue') and showed the video – in essence, a snuff movie – without inhibition. The incident demonstrates the obsolescence of the paradigm, advanced for example by Lev Manovich (1996), that networked imaging is always a form of regulatory surveillance; at the same time, the incident points to the danger in assuming that netizens, by dint of producing and consuming media, are necessarily empowered.

For the purposes of this study, the reassemblage in the Incident of Little Yueyue raises a more important line of inquiry, about how the new visibility reconfigures public space. Beyond the proof – if any is still necessary – of the ubiquity of security cameras in built environment, the seamless repurposing of the surveillance video demonstrates how any site can become the setting for a spectacle defined not by regulators but by citizens and netizens; at the same time, the reassemblage of the spectacle falls short of taking control over the material space or its visual representation.

THE REALITY THAT IS NOT ONE

The issues around mediatisation of public space are made explicit in Tan Tan's video art 'Whose Eyes' of 2011. The 15-minutes-and-30-seconds-long artwork combines images from security cameras – some found footage, some staged by the artist. They present violent events and the callous reaction of bystanders. Like the discourse around the Incident of Little Yueyue, 'Whose Eyes' focuses on the deterioration of collective moral standards. Yet as a video artwork, Tan Tan's piece foregrounds more explicitly the visual properties of surveillance videos and their effect on perceptions of public space. The direct referential value of the moving image gives way to a mediatised temporal and spatial indexicality that challenges the ethical efficacy of reassemblage.

The video artwork consists of images all of which seem to originate from security cameras. Often the 4:3 aspect ratio screen is split into four black-and-white video channels, much like feed from cameras sending their real-time signal to a control center.[8] The incidents featured in 'Whose Eyes' are four cases that drew public attention after appearing on the Internet. The first took place in Guizhou, where a man entered a bank, mugged a woman, shot her and left the place unhindered. She was left for seven minutes and bled to death while witnesses stood by. The second incident happened in Taizhou, where an old woman was run over by a car. As in similar cases, the driver would not risk the liability of taking care of hospital bills. He therefore reversed the car twice, rolling over the body four more times and thereby confirming the victim's death. After the car left, passersby did not stop to tend to the woman. The third incident involved a bus driver in Wuhan, who instructed a passenger to add a coin for the bus fare. In response, the passenger hit the driver repeatedly. The twenty-eight bus passengers did nothing to stop the violence; instead, they demanded to be let off the bus. The fourth incident occurred in the province of Guangdong, as two men robbed a grocery store owner. A knife scuffle ensued, during which the owner was stabbed and sank to the ground. Two customers entered the store separately, but each left without helping the dying man (Anon. nd). The four incidents cited in 'Whose Eyes' represent the pervasive violence and unconcern in contemporary society.

The video artwork is a piece of social criticism. Tan Tan introduces it as follows:

The film combines videos of real events and shots of similar life scenes, producing four 'fake surveillance video recordings'. Interweaving reality and reality has created a contiguity of false images of life. Is our life truly normal? Are we truly normal? The four real cases took place in public space, but no one intervened, as if no one saw the scene of crime. [In the video artwork] one can only hear, in disorderly and intermittent fashion, the sounds of news commentary on the incidents. It is as if we understand the facts, but we can only perceive them in retrospect while living in darkness. Is it really that no one's eyes can see? (2011a: np)

The artist protests the absence of collective ethics, manifested in the purported 'normalcy' of violent incidents and the public's lack of response. In referring to 'us', possibly conflating society at large and the audience of her artwork, Tan Tan questions whether the viewers of 'Whose Eyes' fare any better – even though the viewers may be scandalised, they remain passive onlookers. Netizens watching clips such as that documenting Wang Yue's death believe themselves to be responsible citizens, yet 'Whose Eyes' shows such self-congratulatory attitude toward the consumption of found footage to be groundless.

Tan Tan also draws attention to the role of the video clips in conveying the incidents in 'disorderly and intermittent' media snippets, which imitate our partial understanding of social conditions. We fail to see reality, because we are unequipped to deal with visual evidence. Tan Tan does not denounce mediatised images as less real. Rather, the task for the viewer of 'Whose Eyes' is to learn to distinguish between the interwoven 'reality and reality', two kinds of images both of which have equal indexical value.[9] As a comment on the condition of visuality in the twenty-first century, and in particular the relation between the media consumer and the moving image, 'Whose Eyes' shows our inability as viewers to differentiate between staged and found footage is the result of a moral handicap as much as a visual incapacity. At the mimetic level, found and staged footage are indistinguishable from each other, yet found footage carries a different ethical value.

The found footage in the Uniqlo incident and the Incident of Little Yueyue may be said to always find its addressee: it is reassembled time and again, each transformation bringing it to new audiences and making additional impact. By contrast, the found footage in 'Whose Eyes' – even when restored into context by Tan Tan – seems to be never truly found out and enter the viewer's consciousness. 'Whose Eyes' exposes social insensitivity – not by separating mediatised images from the profilmic, but by showing such distinction to be untenable. By creating 'a contiguity of false images of life', the artist enhances the confusion between various mediatised forms. Reassemblage does not rescue the image but rather accentuates the inherent indexical crisis in found footage.

Tan Tan is well aware of her intervention in the mediascape. She places her work in the context of other video art – from Stan Brakhage and Maya Deren to her Chinese contemporaries – and further elaborates:

> The narrative in my 'Whose Eyes' reconstructs the result of recording … what happens in each shot has truly taken place, each has its temporal flow and plot. But the interweaving of reality and reality creates a contiguity of false images of life. […] One may say that experimental films that contain narrative elements often don't aim at telling any story, only at producing 'illusion'. (2011b: np)

In other words, Tan Tan takes narrative incoherence, a defining characteristic of experimental film, and turns it into a reflection of the citizens' visual and social dysfunction. The narratively muddled images in 'Whose Eyes', in which the 'reality' of the found footage and the 'reality' of the staged videos become indistinguishable from each other, becomes a metaphor for the challenges posed by a mediatised environment.

'Whose Eyes' creates a disruption in the media ecology that otherwise takes for granted the reassemblage of found footage. Where the Uniqlo selfies and Incident of Little Yueyue rely on bandying the image around without change, Tan Tan introduces subtle but significant modifications. She uses low-resolution images, delays the sound track, and displays simultaneously multiple Time Code Reading signals. Tan Tan's artwork reveals the perceptual dissociation that lies at the foundation of reassemblage. In presenting even her staged scenes as found footage, Tan Tan shows the need for critical viewing. 'Whose Eyes' stresses the danger in confounding found footage and the profilmic, a confusion that might result in viewing it the same way that one watches reality TV.

UNFOUND FOOTAGE

'Whose Eyes' uses staged scenes as a complement to the found footage, thereby relying on the ability of readymade images to represent public space. Reassemblage is taken a step further in two works that re-create settings that are likely to have been captured on video but access to which has been denied to the general public. In different ways, both Li Juchuan and Ai Weiwei imagine what the unavailable images might look like. Their artwork consists of producing what may be called unfound footage.

Li Juchuan's video art restages a well-known incident that took place on 1 July 2008, in which a disgruntled young man, Yang Jia, stabbed a guard and nine Shanghai police officers, wounding mortally six of them. Public opinion largely sided with Yang and doubted the veracity of the official account.[10] Yang's legal battles against the police, leading to the murder incident and during the trial that ended with his execution, were seen as emblematic of the authorities' indifference to citizens' plight. (Yang's story was portrayed also in Ying Liang's *Wo hai you hua yao shuo / When Night Falls*, 2012.) In particular, two details seemed suspicious: how could Yang have stabbed so many people in a short time, reported as seven seconds altogether? And how did he do that while climbing up to the twenty-first floor? Li Juchuan responded with two pieces. 'The Killing Only Took Seven Seconds' shows a man darting into a room and confronting four police. The scene is seven seconds long (followed by nineteen seconds of credits) and barely leaves time for the man to engage with more than one officer. 'Ershiyi lou you duo gao?' (How high is the 21st floor?) is a single point-of-view shot of the artist climbing up twenty-one floors, a process that took five minutes and forty seconds and left Ju breathless. As imaginary forensic evidence, the videos discredit the news reports.

'The Killing Only Took Seven Seconds' is shot as if from a security camera installed in the ceiling. In an interview, Li Juchuan makes it clear that imitating the viewpoint of a security camera is essential to his vision: it would have been of no interest to use conventional cinematic techniques. Li – an architect by profession – identifies security cameras as an essential aspect of contemporary environment. For Li, security cameras have taken over the function of urban planning and have 'redistributed space' (Ni 2014: np). In choosing the viewpoint of a security camera, 'The Killing Only Took Seven Seconds' demonstrates how the gaze at the foundation of spatial access must now pass through security cameras. There is no vision outside that of surveillance videos, real or imagined.

Li's artwork protests the inaccessibility of the original images. The incident was captured on video and was used by police during the investigation. Yet the images were not released to the public, further fueling outrage at the authorities' lack of transparency. The video art replaces the images taken by the security camera, both drawing attention to the original's absence and making the original redundant. Reassemblage, if only in the form of fake footage, retrieves total visibility.

A similar logic lies behind Ai Weiwei's 'WeiweiCam' of 2012. As a vocal critic of the Chinese government, Ai's movements were regularly monitored, especially after he started investigating into the 2008 Wenchuan earthquake, culminating in his detention for 81 days beginning in April 2011. Ai has constantly challenged his surveillance, accosting the plain-clothes police following him and hanging festive lanterns on the security cameras around his residence. In this context, two artworks stand out. In 'WeiweiCam', Ai went a step further and created his own counter-images to the videos assumably streamed to the Public Security Bureau from the cameras around his house. Ai set up four cameras inside his house, including one directly over his bed. The images were streamed live on the Internet around the clock beginning 3 April 2012, exactly one year after his detention. Forty-six hours after the feed went live, the authorities ordered 'WeiweiCam' to be shut down. During this period, the site received some 5.2 million views. Much shorter edited versions were later shown in art galleries and posted on sites such as YouTube.

As in the case of Li Juchuan's 'The Killing Only Took Seven Seconds', Ai responds to images inaccessible to him by creating his own images. 'WeiweiCam' creates an uncomfortable symmetry between the exterior and interior of Ai's house, between surveillance and art, and between invisible and visible images. Like Tan Tan's 'Whose Eyes', both forms are equally real, recording different aspects of Ai's life. Ai's act of reassemblage, in the form of presenting alternative images rather than reusing found footage, comports with his highly original and manipulative use of readymade objects – most famously, Chinese antiques. Having been directly influenced by Marcel Duchamp and his artwork made of *objets trouvés*, Ai radically retools any object that comes under his hands. Just as Ai takes apart and assembles found objects, he redefines the very idea of found footage. 'WeiweiCam' reconfigures the discourse around surveillance video; he reconceptualises visual control in a way that undermines the monopoly of the authorities, and even the exclusive agency of any one in possession of a security camera.

'WeiweiCam' continues in the vein of Ai's earlier work, 'Surveillance Cameras' of 2010. Ai made fourteen marble sculptures, the life-size look-alikes of the security cameras placed by the authorities outside his house. The everyday object is transformed to an art piece associated with monumentality, craftsmanship and high art. It is turned into a commodity exhibited and possibly sold in art galleries. The device for real-time recording is frozen in time. Little remains of the *objet trouvé*; it is both sublimated and ridiculed. Likewise, 'WeiweiCam' shifts the discourse around found footage to include the imaginary unfound. Ultimately, what matters is not the visual images but rather the public space that their repurposing creates.

Ai's art brings to the extreme tendencies present also in the cases discussed earlier in this chapter. I have argued that the reassemblage of found footage does not amount to critique of surveillance. And yet there is a clear counter-authoritarian streak in media events such as the Uniqlo incident. The selfies at Sanlitun likely would not have the same edge were it not for the strict control over Chinese social media. Indeed, Uniqlo's 'selfless selfie' campaign does not seem to have sprouted any alternative practices in other countries. I have also argued that the cases cited above show that netizens do not recoil from placing themselves at the centre of public spectacle; Ai's concern for privacy highlights, however, that in China public gatherings carry an especially strong connotation of collective callousness. Indeed, modern Chinese literature and film – from Lu Xun's '*Nahan* zixu' (Preface to *Outcry*, 1923) to Jia Zhangke's *Xiao Wu* (1997) – has a long tradition of commenting on crowds numbed by spectacles.

From the pretty innocuous youthful rebellion at Uniqlo to the overt political dissent of Ai Weiwei, the cases I have examined outline a new media ecology that redefines the relation between the netizen and public space. Li Juchuan's remark about his lack of interest in conventional cinema and his need to visualise space through a security camera points to a fundamental shift, not only in what is seen and in whose eyes (as Tan Tan asks), but also in how one sees.

Networked imaging has destabilised the meaning of urban environment, which can be reclaimed through cameras and screens and reassembled as found footage. Netizens no longer seem to fashion themselves as film viewers to whom the city reveals itself as if on a large screen. Walking in the contemporary city is not akin to a cinematic experience, whereby the citizen attempts to approximate the profilmic image. Rather, the fluid manipulation of the urban image produces the city's meaning and the citizen's identity.

NOTES

1   I have benefited from feedback given when presenting earlier versions of this essay at the University of London School of Oriental and African Studies, Oxford University and Haifa University. I am especially grateful to the participants of my graduate seminar at the University of Washington and in particular Belinda Qian He.
2   For a representative argumentation that stresses the infringement on privacy by surveillance cameras, see Lyon (2003: 104–5).
3   As the report on the provenance of the sex video notes, it is highly unlikely that the 'VIP users' could have been employed by Uniqlo (Anon. 2015d).
4   The impact of the Uniqlo incident on the memories associated with the Sanlitun location became apparent a month later, when a married couple, a Frenchman and a local woman, were stabbed near the store. Reports mentioned the earlier Uniqlo incident, despite the lack of any apparent connection (see for example Sonmez 2015).
5   On the New Documentary Movement, see Berry and Rofel (2010).
6   The role of media in conjunction with the Incident of Little Yueyue is explored in Milcho Manchevski's short 'Thursday,' included in the omnibus *Venice 70: Omnibus Reloaded* (2013). In Manchevski's film, a woman is shocked when watching the video on her smartphone while walking in a New York street. The short addresses the issue of relating to one's immediate surroundings, somewhat different from the concerned raised in China by the Incident of Little Yueyue.
7   See the Wikipedia entry "Death of Wang Yue" and the comments to the video, for example at http://v.youku.com/v_show/id_XMzE3NDc1NzYw.html; http://v.youku.com/v_show/id_XMzE0MjM2Nzg0.html; http://v.youku.com/v_show/

id_XMzEzMDY4OTcy.html.
8   The video was circulated in this form online, on YouTube and Vimeo. The artwork was also shown in art galleries on four separate screens.
9   The translations of Tan Tan's words are mine. Other English versions have rendered the phrase 'real' and real' as 'reality with irreality', thereby changing the meaning (Anon. 2015e).
10 See the Wikipedia entry on Yang Jia.

BIBLIOGRAPHY

Anon. (nd) 'Details – *Shui de yanjing*'; http://www.reelport.com/index.php?id=300&movie_id=50263

_____ (2014). 'Shizhuang pinpai Youyiku tuichu 3D dayin paizhao' (Clothing brand Uniqlo rolls out 3D selfie), 5 October; http://www.51shape.com/?p=977

_____ (2015a) 'Shiyijian shipin shijian buzhi 5 ren bei daizou she chuanbo yinhui wupin' (More than five people arrested for distributing prurient material in the Uniqlo fitting room incident), Fazhi wanbao, 19 July; http://news.sina.com.cn/c/2015-07-19/161832123941.shtml

_____ (2015b) 'Shenhua qiumi yinyong "Youyiku buya" ruma guoan qiuyuan' (Shenhua fans use the 'Uniqlo indecency' to insult the PSB team), 15 July; http://news.163.com/15/0715/20/AUJH39DO00014AED.html

_____ (2015c) 'Sanlitun Youyiku cheng xin jingdian! Shimin zhadui paizhao' (Sanlitun Uniqlo becomes a new destination! Citizens are crowding to take pictures), 16 July; http://travel.163.com/15/0716/10/AUL0UFJU00063KE8.html

_____ (2015d) 'Ruhe kandai Youyiku shiyijian shipin shijian?' (How to look at the Uniqlo changing room video incident?), 15 July; http://www.duanzhihu.com/answer/17466433

_____ (2015e) 'Whose Eyes'; http://eximacau.blogspot.co.il/2011/12/whose-eyes.html

Baron, Jaimie (2014) *The Archive Effect: Found Footage and the Audiovisual Experience of History*. New York: Routledge.

Bauman, Zygmunt and David Lyon (2012) *Liquid Surveillance: A Conversation*. Cambridge: Polity Press.

Berry, Chris and Lisa Rofel (2010) 'Alternative Archive: China's Independent Documentary Culture,' in Chris Berry, Lu Xinyu and Lisa Rofel (eds) *The New Chinese Documentary Film Movement: For the Public Record*. Hong Kong: Hong Kong University Press, 135–54.

Braester, Yomi (2016) 'Traces of the Future: Beijing's Politics of Emergence', in Carlos Rojas and Ralph Litzinger (eds) *Ghost Protocol: Development and Displacement in Global China*. Durham: Duke University Press.

Debord, Guy-Ernest (1956) 'Mode d'emploi du détournement', Les Lèvres Nues, 8;

http://sami.is.free.fr/Oeuvres/debord_wolman_mode_emploi_detournement.html

Galloway, Alexander (2012) *The Interface Effect*. Cambridge: Polity Press.

Goffman, Erving (1990) *The Presentation of Self in Everyday Life*. London: Penguin.

Grace, Helen (2007) 'Monuments and the Face of Time: Distortions of Scale and Asynchrony in Postcolonial Hong Kong', *Postcolonial Studies*, 10, 4, 467–83.

Gunning, Tom (1995) 'Tracing the Individual Body: Photography, Detectives, and Early Cinema', in Leo Charney and Vanessa Schwartz (eds) *Cinema and the Invention of Modern Life*. Los Angeles: University of California Press, 15–45.

Heping (2015) 'Youyiku shiyanshi – wuyin liangpin, zara, HM, Gap shiyijian zipai na jia qiang' (The Uniqlo fitting room: Muji, Zara, H&M, and Gap AP no-logo – which one has the best fitting room selfies?), 22 July; https://www.youtube.com/watch?v=l6A7ASlEYHA

Jacobs, Katrien (2012) *People's Pornography: Sex and Surveillance on the Chinese Internet*. Bristol: Intellect.

Kaufman, Peter (2014) 'A Sociological Snapshot of Selfies', 13 January; http://www.everydaysociologyblog.com/2014/01/a-sociological-snapshot-of-selfies.html

Lu, Shen and Wilfred Chan (2015) 'Could the Uniqlo Sex Video Be China's Sexual "Rebound"?', 24 July; http://www.cnn.com/2015/07/23/asia/china-uniqlo-sex-video-aftermath

Lyon, David (2003) *Surveillance after September 11*. Cambridge: Polity Press.

McComic, Cristina (2015) '5 Scandals Demonstrating China's Moral Decay', 22 July; http://socialbrandwatch.com/5-scandals-demonstrating-chinas-moral-decay

McGrath, John E. (2004) *Loving Big Brother: Performance, Privacy, and Surveillance Space*. London and New York: Routledge.

Manovich, Lev (1996) 'On Totalitarian Interactivity (notes from the enemy of the people)'; http://manovich.net/content/04-projects/017-on-totalitarian-interactivity/14_article_1996.pdf

Nelson, Katie (2015) 'Uniqlo denies that it's behind fitting room sex tape as web users revel in scandal', 16 July; http://shanghaiist.com/2015/07/16/uniqlo-denies-that-its-behind-fitting-room-sex-tape.php

Ni Kun (2014) 'Zai women dangdai de huanjing zhong zaici kashi jianzhu – Ni Kun yu Li Juchuan duihua (Starting to build again in our contemporary environment: A dialog between Ni Kun and Li Juchuan), 27 January; http://site.douban.com/organhaus/widget/notes/1476198/note/328529725

Porter, Tom (2015) 'Uniqlo founder describes Beijing store sex tape as "disgusting"', *International Business Times*, 3 August; http://www.ibtimes.co.uk/uniqlo-founder-describes-beijing-store-sex-tape-disgusting-1513867

Sant, Geoffrey (2015) 'Driven to Kill: Why drivers in China Intentionally Kill the Pedestrians They Hit', 4 September; http://www.slate.com/articles/news_and_politics/foreigners/2015/09/why_drivers_in_china_intentionally_kill_the_pedestrians_they_hit_china_s.html

Snow, David A. and Leon Anderson (1987) 'Identity Work Among the Homeless: The Verbal Construction and Avowal of Personal Identities', *American Journal of Sociology*, 92, 6, 1336–71.

Sonmez, Felicia (2015). 'Woman Stabbed Dead by Man with Sword Outside Beijing Uniqlo', 13 August; http://blogs.wsj.com/chinarealtime/2015/08/13/woman-stabbed-dead-by-man-with-sword-outside-beijing-uniqlo

Tan Tan (2011a) 'Whose Eyes', 25 October; http://site.douban.com/129499/widget/photos/5467621/photo/1270598727

—— (2011b). '"Zhuoying" yu "zaoxiang" – guanyu shiyan dianying, luxiang yishu ji CIFF8 "shiyan duanpian jiqing zhan"' ('Video capture' and 'making idols': on experimental film, video art, and the CIFF8 'experimental shorts guest exhibition'), 26 October; http://site.douban.com/129499/widget/notes/5246566/note/180339239

Thimmesch, Debra (2014) 'Trendy Japanese Clothing Retailer Uniqlo Introduces the "Selfless Selfie" via 3D Printing', 4 October; http://3dprint.com/16667/uniqlo-3d-print-selfie

Treske, Andreas (2014) *Video Theory: Online Video Aesthetics or the Afterlife of Video*. Bielefeld: Transcript.

Verrone, William E. B. (2012) *The Avant-Garde Feature Film: A Critical History*. Jefferson: MacFarland.

de Waal, Martijn (2014) *The City as Interface: How New Media Are Changing the City*. Rotterdam: nai010.

Wang Chunyan (2012) 'Shenshi yu fanxi: dui "Xiao Yueyue shijia" de duo shijiao pouxi' (Examination and self-reflection: An analysis from multiple angles of the Incident of Little Yueyue), *Sheke zongheng*, 1, 66–7.

Yoka (2015) 'Qu Youyiku qian xian xuehui zipai – Yang Mi, Liu Wen qinshen shifan shiyijian zhao laixi' (Before going to Uniqlo, learn how to take a selfie: Yang Mi and Liu Wen demonstrate the fitting room photo tsunami), 25 July; http://www.icaijing.com/eladies/article4922971

Zeng Shi (2011) 'Xiao Yueyue shijian yige yue Foshan Wujincheng huifu wangri renao' (One month after the Incident of Little Yueyue, Wujincheng in Foshan returns to its previous liveliness), Lianhe zaobao, 14 November; http://www.zaobao.com.sg/special/report/politic/cnpol/story20111114-139489

Zeng Xiaoliang (2015). 'Youyiku shipin men: "ci gonggong kongjian" li de gongsiquan zhi zheng' (The Uniqlo video scandal: the battle for the right to privacy in 'secondary public spaces'), 17 July; http://helanonline.cn/article/13291

Zhang Lei (2014) 'Posui yu liuli: cong redian shijian chuanbo kan "gongmin jizhe" dui xinwen lunli de yingxiang' (Fragmentation and alienation: the influence of 'citizen journalists' on news theory, based on the coverage of hot items), *Xiandai chuanbo*, 4, 50–4.

Zhang Yajun (2011) 'Shocking Foshan incident reveals an unspoken illness at China's core', *The Guardian*, 19 October; http://www.theguardian.com/

commentisfree/2011/oct/19/foshan-incident-unspoken-illness-china

Žižek, Slavoj (2002) 'Big Brother, or the triumph of the gaze over the eye', in Thomas Y. Levin, Ursula Frohne and Peter Weibel (eds) *CTRL [SPACE]: Rhetorics of Surveillance from Bentham to Big Brother*, 224–7. Cambridge: MIT Press.

REMEDIATING THE 'OTHER HALF': PLANET SLUM AS TRANSMEDIA PROJECT[1]

IGOR KRSTIĆ

INTRODUCTION

Jonas Bendiksen's photo book *The Places We Live* (2008) consists of pictures of slum-dwellers and their homes. More precisely, it provides a combination of written text and photographic imagery in the form of panoramic folding images of slum exteriors and interiors in four of the most rapidly expanding megacities of the world: Mumbai (India), Caracas (Venezuela), Nairobi (Kenya) and Jakarta (Indonesia). *The Places We Live* thus promises a quasi-global perspective on what the urban sociologist Mike Davis has called a 'planet of slums'; that is, a planet in which by now a vast number of people, approximately one billion, call slums their home. In fact, *The Places We Live* was published in the exact same year in which, according to many sociologists, mankind encountered a pivotal turning point: since 2008, for the first time in history, more people live in cities than in the countryside. According to Bendiksen, his project is an artistic response to these staggering figures and the historical watershed it involves. It was also conceived as a media experiment that sought to challenge our stereotypes about the urban poor, rather than as a survey-like global 'documentation' of slums: 'I was trying to think of other ways that we could really bring out the enormous diversity, the incredible variety, of personal stories in the slum' (RFI 2009: np). Hence, Bendiksen's main goal was to challenge our expectations, to provide counter-images and -stories, precisely through emphasising the 'enormous diversity' of our planet of slums. Accordingly, his photographs do not, or not exclusively, focus on supposedly 'spectacular' scenes of urban squalor and despair – on images of poverty, garbage, hunger, illness or domestic and public violence – but mostly on positive aspects that illustrate the slum-dwellers' incredible creativity, entrepreneurship and inventiveness, or their sense of hospitality, neighbourly help and communal solidarity.

Bendiksen not only published his images in a photo book; they have also been used for an interactive web documentary (theplaceswelive.com) as well as for a touring exhibition installation, in both of which slum-dwellers tell their personal stories via recorded (but dubbed) interviews directly to their audience. In fact, the Magnum photographer envisioned the project from the very beginning as such a cross-media experience: 'It was very much conceived as a project where I wanted to use the same device put into all these different incarnations' (RFI 2009: np). He also claims that with this transmedia framework in mind his standard approach to photographic practice has been challenged, since it forced him to establish more personal relations with his photographic subjects, akin to the way some social documentary filmmakers (rather than photographers) work:[2] 'It was really about sitting down with people, getting to know them ... I think it made people really interested and really want to positively be part of the project much more than if I was just running through the streets snapping away' (RFI 2009: np).[3] This aspect of Bendiksen's work has also been highlighted by the American journalist Philip Gourevitch. In his foreword to the photo book, Gourevitch praises not only Bendiksen's physical or social 'immersion in the slums', his interactive or participatory approach to social documentary photography, but also the artistry of his images, which, according to Gourevitch, creates a 'complete sensory immersion' for its observers (Bendiksen 2008: np). The notion of 'immersion' is, of course, even more accentuated in both the website and the touring installation exhibition: whereas the former invites its users on a non-linear, interactive journey through our 'planet slum', the latter creates not merely a quasi-cinematic experience for its visitors – a 'window on the world' of squatters – but literally immerses them as 'experiencers' of a 'windowed world' of virtual (slum) realities through the use of life-size images on life-size screens.

Accordingly, this chapter will argue via new media theories (see Bolter and Grusin 2000; Manovich 2001; Grau 2004; Jenkins 2006), that it is in this case not so much the 'artistry' of the photographer that lends a new sensory (or immersive) experience to the spectator, but rather the new possibilities of digital media technologies. It will thus provide a reading of *The Places We Live* which emphasises it less as artistic innovation, and more as what Jay David Bolter and Richard Grusin called a *remediation*. I consider remediation in a double sense: firstly, in the sense of 'reform', because Bendiksen's project promises to reform 'our' mediated encounter with the (urban) Other; and secondly, in the sense of 'refashioning', since it attempts to refashion older ways of mediating the urban poor, while still also containing or referencing them. In the conclusion I will then critically scrutinise whether Bendiksen's benevolent media-reformist attempt really achieves its goal of challenging stereotypical notions of life in the slums, or whether it merely provides a more sophisticated (or hypermediated) experience of 'slum tourism'. However, before doing so, I will first try to bring urban studies into a dialogue with (new) media studies by introducing a critical and historical framework with regard to the notion of a 'planet of slums' and its representation on screen, which will allow for a more layered reading of Bendiksen's transmedia project.[4]

'PLANET SLUM': A CRITICAL PERSPECTIVE

A photo essay titled 'Planet Slum' – which Bendiksen published together with journalist Christina Larson in the US news magazine *Foreign Policy* – makes the link between Mike Davis's notion of a 'planet of slums' and Bendiksen's project quite evident. The Norwegian photographer explains here that when he became a father he started thinking: 'What will the world look like when my son becomes my age ... Then I came across those statistics about urban slum-dwellers being the fastest growing segment of the global population. That really struck me' (in Larson and Bendiksen 2009: np). The statistics to which Bendiksen refers – that by the end of the twentieth century 32 per cent of the world's urban population called slums their home – have thus obviously triggered his photographic journeys to the slums of Mumbai, Caracas, Nairobi, and Jakarta.[5] These numbers were first published in 2003 in a 'global report' commissioned by the United Nations Human Settlements Programme, titled *The Challenge of Slums: Global Report on Human Settlements*. This report has since been widely discussed in the media, as well as by social scientists, since it consists of a vast quantity of empirical data that has been gathered by sociologists from around the world. Apart from its pioneering global approach, the report also provides a novel (global) definition of 'slums'. According to the report, no matter where they are located, slums share five key characteristics: inadequate access to safe water, inadequate access to sanitation and other infrastructure, the poor structural quality of housing, overcrowding, and an insecure residential status for its inhabitants (UN 2003: 12). Thus, even though the 'planet slum' is immensely diverse, they all share the same inadequate conditions with regard to housing, safety and infrastructure.

Mike Davis has described *The Challenge of Slums* as a 'historic report', in that it provides 'the first truly global audit of urban poverty' (2004: 11). Davis also insists in his *New Left Review* article 'Planet of Slums' (2004) – the precursor to his 2007 book with the same title – that the report is also 'unusual in its intellectual honesty' (ibid.). For the first time, he argues, an official body (the UN) acknowledges that the increase of urban poverty is not simply an issue of 'bad governance'. Instead, Davis applauds the UN's straightforward indictment of economic globalisation, and more precisely, the imposition of a neoliberal capitalist system in the developing world. Even though the sheer number of slums and the multitude of terms that label them illustrates that one can indeed speak of a 'planet of slums', for Mike Davis the rise of slums is not merely a supposedly 'natural' outcome of demographic changes, the 'population explosion' in the global South; rather, it has political dimensions beyond demographic as well as beyond local, municipal or national decision-making processes ('bad governance'). Written in response, or rather as an extension to UN's survey, Davis's book outlines the macro-political and macro-economic reasons for the exponential rise of slums. Unlike the authors of the UN report, Davis is far less concerned with using empirical data to support his arguments; he also does not believe that there are any 'slums of hope' as the UN would have us believe (UN 2003: 9). Instead, he provides a much gloomier picture – one might even call it a dystopic future vision of an urban 'planet in despair'. For Davis, slums are in the first instance urban spaces of social exclusion populated by the planet's surplus population – redundant people who are relegated to a life without any hope and opportunity. Much more so than the UN report, Davis blames the gradual abandonment of the welfare state and the orchestrated enforcement of a neoliberal capitalist system for the exponential rise of this surplus population.[6] More specifically, he blames the Structural Adjustment Programmes (SAPs) that have been imposed on developing countries by the World Bank and the International Monetary Fund since the 1970s.[7] Davis explains the reasons for the 'mass production of slums' thus: '[R]apid urban growth in the context of structural adjustment, currency devaluation, and state retrenchment has been an inevitable recipe for the mass production of slums ... Since 1970, slum growth everywhere in the South has outpaced urbanization *per se*' (2007: 17).

Some reviewers have praised Davis for confronting a complacent Left in the global North with a lurking, but widely ignored humanitarian disaster in the global South. Others have applauded his essayistic, non-academic style of writing, which has unsurprisingly reached a more general readership beyond the academic world. Many critics, however, attacked Davis, for instance for excavating the word 'slum' and the history of pejorative meanings and stereotypical images that it evokes.[8] Others were outright annoyed with his dramatic, or, as some claim, literary rhetorical style, as well as with the book's methodological flaws.[9] With regard to the latter, *Planet of Slums* has particularly been criticised for its reductionist perspective on the causes of urban poverty; that is, Davis's indictment of institutions like the IMF or, more generally, the Western world's imposition of a neoliberal economic system in what used to be called the 'Third World'. Urban sociologist Tom Angotti has furthermore remarked that Davis generalises and thus oversimplifies the complex processes of urbanisation and globalisation by providing rather simplistic rich/poor and urban/rural dualisms. As a result, Davis's 'apocalyptic rhetoric' (Sansom 2006) only feeds into long-standing anti-urban anxieties about working people in the cities. His implicit 'anti-urban' bias thus only serves conservative political agendas, which, as Angotti argues, Davis himself opposes. Instead of providing a genuine Marxist analysis of the rise of urban poverty in the twentieth century, Davis rather obscures the true economic asymmetries and social inequalities in today's world. Even more problematic is his political pessimism, since in Davis's 'dismal description of urban poverty, there are no people or social forces capable of challenging the social order'

(Angotti 2006: 961), which, according to Angotti, is a slap in the face to all engaged activists and slum-dwellers that work to improve slum conditions on a daily basis.

Another response to Davis's political pessimism and apocalyptic view is provided by Slavoj Žižek, who argues that slum-dwellers are far from global capitalism's disposable 'human waste'. Although he describes slum-dwellers as the 'living dead' of global capitalism, dwelling 'in the twilight zone of slums' (2008: 425), Žižek believes that new forms of social awareness could emerge from the global shantytowns, not unlike the Marxist notion of a proletarian class-consciousness. For Žižek, slum-dwellers are, in this sense, potentially a new revolutionary 'counter-class to the other newly emerging class, the so-called "symbolic class" (managers, journalists and PR people, academics, artists, and so on)' (ibid.). He argues further that while 'slum-dwellers are literally a collection of those who are "part of no-part", the "supernumerary" element of a society, excluded from the benefits of citizenship; the uprooted and the dispossessed, those who, in effect, "have nothing to lose but their chains"', he also believes that slum-dwellers are 'freed from all substantial ties; dwelling in a free space, outside state police regulation ... they are "thrown" into a situation where they have to invent some mode of being-together, and simultaneously deprived of any support in traditional ways of life' (2008: 424–5). In other words, slums are for Žižek anarchic or 'free spaces' – freed from all (historical, ideological/capitalist or bureaucratic) ties. According to this (post)Marxist view, slum-dwellers are thus for the twenty-first century what the proletariat was for the nineteenth: a new revolutionary class.

BACK TO RIIS: A HISTORICAL PERSPECTIVE

It is obvious that Jonas Bendiksen does not share Davis's apocalyptic view of our 'planet slum', and neither is his transmedia project particularly political in that it portrays slum inhabitants as a potential revolutionary class, ready to overthrow the capitalist establishment. Despite its use of new digital media technologies, however, Bendiksen's project has links to earlier ways of representing the urban poor, which then nevertheless connects it to one of Davis's major theses. In a chapter which is tellingly entitled 'Back to Dickens', Davis argues that the contemporary 'dynamics of Third World urbanization both recapitulate and confound the precedents of nineteenth and early twentieth-century Europe and North America' (2007: 11).[10] Davis thus states that there is less development and progress, but some sort of iteration, a 'return of the slum' in contemporary urban landscapes. The same can be said about the (return of) slum *representations* in the media, as well as their representation in various different media, both on and off screen.[11] Even though *The Places We Live* seems from a contemporary perspective quite the typical product of today's convergent media environment – or of what Henry Jenkins famously described as 'the flow of content across multiple media platforms' (2006: 2) – the flow of content across (new and old) media is not a unique hallmark of our digital age. *The Places We Live* has, in this sense, a very concrete historical predecessor in Jacob Riis's *How The Other Half Lives* (1890). This was a photo book that contained images of slum-dwellers and their homes in the Lower East Side of Manhattan, but it was also a magic lantern show, in which Riis – a Danish immigrant who became one of America's most famous social reformers in the Progressive Era – lectured about the dreadful housing conditions in New York's slums via the help of life-size images projected on screen.[12]

Around 1900 the slum became a cultural commonplace in the Western world, multiply depicted in various competing, complementing or even merging media. Magic lantern 'slum shows' not only projected (graphic or photographic) images of slums, but they also referenced popular fiction and non-fiction stories from the 'urban underworld' – journalistic sketches, essayistic travelogues, theatrical plays or naturalistic novels about life, crime or social misery in the slums, which by this time had already become well-established genres, thoroughly enjoyed by their middle-class audience and readership.[13] Metropolitan citizens, however, not only read spectacular stories of misdemeanour and vice emanating from the slums, but also increasingly found pleasure in gazing at the spectacular sights that slums seemed to have offered. Many photographers, writers or journalists implicitly or explicitly responded to these new spectatorial desires. Keith Gandal has emphasised exactly that aspect, namely what he calls the 'spectacularization of turn-of-the-century slums' by popular culture. He argues that turn-of-the-century journalistic and literary discourses as well as graphic or photographic images of slums, circulating in magazines, newspapers and novels, not only reflected the decline of previous representational conventions of the urban poor – sentimentalist, picturesque and moralistic depictions of 'poverty types' – but also the rise of a modern aesthetics of excitement and spectacle: 'In the course of the 1890s, the slum emerged as a spectacle in the popular arts of representation: the urban poor were discovered as fresh topic by police reporters, novelists, photographers, true-crime writers, muckrakers, and social reformers' (Gandal 1997: 8). Turn-of-the-century metropolitan visual culture was, in fact, saturated with photorealistic or documentary – and for this reason, at least in the eye of the nineteenth-century middle class spectator, also sensational – images of impoverished immigrants and working class families living under appalling conditions in big city slums.

The parallels between the popular culture of today and that of the fin-de-siècle are even more striking if one takes into account how by the end of the nineteenth century the enthusiasm to produce photorealistic pictures of urban slums coincided with a growing spectatorial appetite for visual attractions of 'the Real'. In other words, then, as today, slums provided vital sources for stories and images of a popular (and consumer) culture for which reality itself has become a spectacle. For Vanessa Schwartz the notion of reality as spectacle – an emerging 'public taste for reality', as she calls it – lies at the origins of modern, popular mass culture, which ultimately also explains the rise of cinema as the most popular entertainment medium around 1900. In her *Spectacular Realities: Early Mass Culture in Fin-de-Siècle Paris* (1998)

Schwartz shows how this 'public taste for reality' emerged first and foremost as a *touristic* phenomenon in turn-of-the-century metropolises such as Paris. This 'public taste for reality' was facilitated by the growing spectacularisation of newspaper reporting (for example, the emergence of the boulevard press) and the exhibition of what Schwartz describes as 'realist attractions'.[14] It therefore comes as no surprise that 'slumming' emerged as a popular tourist activity for middle class urbanites in turn-of-the-century metropolises, satisfying this emerging 'desire for the real as spectacle', transforming the slum into such a 'realist attraction' as, for example, two monographs by Seth Koven (2004) and Chad Heap (2009) illustrate with regard to New York and London. And unsurprisingly, today we encounter a similar 'public taste for reality' in the form of slum tourism, but it now has global dimensions: the recent rise of township tourism in South Africa, *favela* tourism in Rio de Janeiro or slum tourism in Mumbai have truly created a 'new global slumming phenomenon', as the editors of a recently published volume, Fabian Frenzel and Ko Koens (2014), call it.

Slumming, slum tourism, 'poorism', social voyeurism – these are some of the most common terms that describe a phenomenon that not only occurs when the social worlds of the rich and poor continuously diverge and then spatially collide (whether on a local or a global scale), but also when visual and other cultural representations provide fertile ground on which such phenomena can flourish. This is even more true today, considering the sheer amount of recent reality television shows such as *The Big Switch* (UTV Bindass 2009), global media coverage from the world's 'Other Half' on channels like CNN, and, of course, the numerous television features, reports or documentaries about slums, from Al Jazeera's six-part series on Manila's infamous neighbourhood Tondo, *The Slum* (2014), to the BBC's three-part series *Welcome to Lagos* (2010).[15] Some of these shows have been criticised for their social voyeurism, but the most vehement objects of this kind of criticism were

Fig. 1 Manila's infamous Tondo neighborhood is the topic of Al Jazeera's six-part documentary series *The Slum* (2014).

two extraordinarily popular films that have been viewed by millions: the eight-time Academy Award-winner *Slumdog Millionaire* (Danny Boyle, 2008), infamously criticised for being a form of 'poverty porn', and the Brazilian cult film *City of God* (Fernando Meirelles, 2002), accused for its 'cosmetics of hunger' (see Bentes 2005).

However, the problematic ethics of representing poverty via visual media has long been a subject of critical debate. For example, in the 1970s Susan Sontag attacked the far less popular genre of social documentary photography in her essay collection *On Photography*:

> Social misery has inspired the comfortably-off with the urge to take pictures, the gentlest of predations, in order to document a hidden reality, that is, a reality hidden from them ... Gazing on other people's reality with curiosity, with detachment, with professionalism, the ubiquitous photographer operates as if that activity transcends class interests as if its perspective is universal ... Photography conceived as social documentation was an instrument of the essentially middle-class attitude, both zealous and merely tolerant, both curious and indifferent, called humanism – which found slums the most enthralling of decors. (1977: 55–6)

For Sontag, the supposedly humanist documentation of social misery through the distanced gaze of the camera, what she calls 'the gentlest of predations', equals 'slumming'. She assumes that an outsider, a non-slum-dweller with a middle class background, necessarily has a touristic (or voyeuristic) attitude towards the supposed spectacle of social misery. Additionally, she contends that the photographer is always unavoidably detached and distanced and thus not empathically involved with the subject he or she depicts, because of his/her higher social background. Yet, Sontag's critique not only attacks the photography's 'customary users', but also implicitly the medium itself. Her critique questions whether photography is the appropriate medium through which to convey issues such as urban poverty. For her, it seems, visual media ultimately turn slums into nothing more than 'enthralling decors'.

From today's perspective, Sontag's critique may sound obsolete, considering that cameras are, even for those living in slums, far from unaffordable luxury goods. However, the critical debates about slumming and the media are, it seems, more topical than ever. Referring to examples such as *The Places We Live*, but also to controversial films like *Slumdog Millionaire* or *City of God*, architecture scholar David D. Fortin has expressed his mixed feelings about these recent (new) media representations of slums in a quite representative way. Even though, he says, we 'must assume, or perhaps hope, that such efforts and accompanying representations are intended to raise awareness towards improving the living conditions in slums', we must also 'be mindful of the tendency for these representations to turn into spectacles, consumed from the safety of more comfortable places' (Fortin 2010: np). Interestingly, Fortin thus expresses not only his fears that these examples may exploit slums for commercial

Fig. 2 New York's slum-dwellers caught 'off guard' while sleeping in Jacob Riis's 'Five Cents a Spot' (1890).

means, but he also hopes that such (new) media representations may, in fact, help the urban poor, that they may contribute to improving slum conditions through raising awareness of them; a hope that was, of course, also shared by social reformers such as Jacob Riis in the nineteenth century. We thus find here another historical continuity, since, not unlike Bendiksen, Boyle or Meirelles, Riis's primary aim was not to document, but rather to shock, challenge or emotionally engage his audience by showing the bodies of immigrants – the 'Other Half' – caught 'off guard'.[16] As Christopher Carter fittingly puts it, with his magic lantern shows that 'Riis lent sensory immediacy to the tenement problem' (2008: 118).[17] It is in this sense, I argue, that we can regard Bendiksen's transmedia project *The Places We Live* as a form of 'remediation'.

REMEDIATING THE 'OTHER HALF': *THE PLACES WE LIVE*

According to Bolter and Grusin's definition of remediation, older media are always preserved as well as refashioned in new ones. Consequently, whenever a new medium is introduced, users (in our case, social documentary photographers) expect that it will improve (or reform) the flaws of an older medium and will deliver representations that are more transparent or immediate. As 'remediation' etymologically means 'reform', it is interesting to observe that the slum has not only been the subject of the reforming impulses of users of new media technologies (from daguerreotypes to magic lantern shows and the cinema), but also of the rhetoric of social reform.[18] And so, with regard to nineteenth-century slum mediations, the 'logic of remediation' has a double meaning: social reformers not only pleaded for the improvement of sanitary, housing and moral conditions in the slums, but they also continuously reformed their use of (old and new) media technologies. They aimed to present images to a middle class public that desired ever more immediate (or sensational, in the sense of 'sensually stimulating') viewing experiences. That the actual attraction lies in the technological *how* of the (re-)presentation rather than in its content – hence, that the 'medium is the message', as Marshall McLuhan would have put it (2013: 19) – is an important insight into the actual function and logic of remediation processes. In other words, remediation describes a process in which new media do not necessarily appear to provide novel sights or stories, but rather novel ways of experiencing (often already familiar) sights or stories. In this respect we can view Riis's magic lantern shows from a different perspective: they generated not only morally enraged responses, but also a sense of astonishment at how screen or media technologies could be used to generate new forms of 'sensory immediacy to the tenement problem' (Carter 2008: 118). We can observe a similar logic at work in Bendiksen's digital transmedia project, which can be illustrated by comparing it to Riis's work.

THE PHOTO BOOK: FROM VICTIMS TO BRICOLEURS

Like *How The Other Half Lives*, Bendiksen's photo-book *The Places We Live* provides a combination of written text and imagery, but unlike Riis's visual conception of Five Points as a dark, 'urban underworld', in Bendiksen's mind it may have been the concept of 'diversity' which he conceived to be crucial while selecting the photographs for the book. This notion also corresponds with the way the Magnum photographer experienced these places onsite: 'Kibera', Bendiksen says, 'is controlled by mob rule', whereas in 'Indonesia, I was constantly looking under bridges to find people … in Caracas, you can't wander around the barrios [because] they are strictly divided between the gangs' (in Fouché 2009). The way Bendiksen presents the four slums in visual terms varies accordingly. Topographically, we see Dharavi (Mumbai) and Kibera (Nairobi) as more or less self-enclosed places; the *kampungs* (translated as 'village') of Jakarta, on the other hand, spread between the formal infrastructures of the city's official grid. Architecturally, the *barrios* of Caracas look more familiar to the Western eye, since they mostly consist of multi-storey apartment blocks made of concrete, similar to those we would encounter in the *banlieues* of Paris, or in any other European *Problembezirk* (German for urban 'problem district'). In contrast, the rather spectacular (perspective-of-God) images of Dharavi show an uninterrupted row of one- or two-storey shacks, built out of tin, plastic and concrete, strung together in what look like incredibly dense spaces.

Unlike Riis's black and white photographs, which naturally emphasise the play of light and shadow, Bendiksen's are printed in high quality as colourful panoramic folding images.[19] One of these images, titled 'When I grow up', has been used as the book's cover; it shows an almost dream-like scene, in which we see a girl

Fig. 3 A Jonas Bendiksen photograph of the facade of an apartment building in Barrio 23 de Enero in Caracas, Venezuela.

in a red dress seemingly juggling coloured lights that were hung across a narrow alley for a wedding in Mumbai's Dharavi. Narrow alleys also feature prominently in Riis's *How The Other Half Lives*, but contrast strongly with Bendiksen's depiction of alleys. In Riis's images, they are dark, dirty and unwelcoming places, inhabited by similarly shadowy characters, as in one of Riis's most famous photographs, 'Bandit's Roost'. Similarly antithetical are Riis's and Bendiksen's depictions of the mostly overcrowded homes. Bendiksen emphasises the creativity of slum-dwellers as urban *bricoleurs*, as inventive creators of liveable shelters, despite often miserable, sometimes incredibly bizarre circumstances. For instance, 'Family Portrait' shows the modern-day Dickensian reality of a family of five in Jakarta's *kampungs*, occupying a space so menial that one can barely sit upright. However, the place is so perfectly tidy and lovingly decorated with wallpaper and framed family pictures that it nevertheless appears to be cosy, spacious and welcoming. In contrast, the comparable 'Five Cents a Spot' in *How The Other Half Lives* shows a much larger space, occupied by six anonymous people sleeping in beds and exposed to the intruder's photographic flashlight. The space appears to be stuffed with people, things, suitcases or clothes, so much so that it seems unbearably small.

Above all, Riis gives us the impression that these people are victims of circumstance (lack of space, hygiene and so on), in order to emphasise his environmental determinist argument that the crime and vice emanating from the slums is largely due to those terrible living conditions.[20] In contrast, Bendiksen is far less concerned with the causes of social problems and neither does he want to provide visual evidence of appalling living conditions. In *The Places We Live* we get the impression of wide spaciousness (in contrast to overcrowded narrowness, one of UN's five characteristics of slums), which is further enhanced by the book's inventive panoramic design, since twenty double gatefold images unfold to build up the four walls of each individual's home. In short, unlike Riis, Bendiksen emphasises diversity, the positive and the unexpected, thus attempting to 'remediate' (or reform) the very image of the slum itself: while the 'old' image of the slum as a dystopic place of misery and despair (Mike Davis's and Jacob Riis's visions) is present as a frame of reference, the 'new' image of the modern, inventive slum-dweller as *bricoleur* is created via the use of equally inventive print designs and a fresh approach to 'social documentary photography'.

THE WEB DOCUMENTARY: FROM PERSPECTIVE-OF-GOD TO POLYPERSPECTIVITY

Web documentaries are usually defined as transmedia productions that use the internet's unique possibilities to employ several different media – including photography, infographics, hyperlinks, database archives, video and animation – to create a non-linear documentary depiction of a subject, which allows the users to choose their own (narrative) paths.[21] Hence, one can say that a web-documentary 'remediates' the traditional film or television documentary: it contains the older form, but it significantly alters and expands it as well. The traditional documentary film features are emphasised from the very beginning in theplaceswelive.com: when we enter the page it provides us with expository, or sociological 'perspective-of-God' information on statistics of population numbers, geographical locations or topographic shapes of slums, gathered from such authoritative sources as UN's global report *The Challenge of Slums*. Through a point-and-click interface we then advance to a world map where we can navigate to the respective cities and enter their slums. A set of 'establishing shots' of slum exteriors, with additional, now local instead of global, information, introduces us to specific areas such as Kibera in Nairobi. Now we can choose from four households and virtually enter the private interiors of various slum houses, shacks and tenements that in some cases resemble Riis's images.

Not unlike Riis, Bendiksen intrudes with his camera into the often cramped and improvised sleeping and/or living rooms of slum-dwellers. Yet, contrary to Riis, who lectured and narrated as a 'voice-of-God' in front of his audience, here we are entering a testimonial interview situation. We are invited to listen to the (English-dubbed) slum-dwellers speaking about their families, biographies, financial situations, or, indeed, about 'the places they live' in. For instance, we can listen to the insurance agent Amit Singh, who lives in Asia's largest slum: 'Dharavi is heaven for me. Even if I am asked to leave, I won't be able to because of my memories. The years I have spent – my school life, my college life, it's all here.' Needless to say, not all slum-dwellers are as content with their neighbourhoods as Amit Singh, but it is in this sense that we can conceive of theplaceswelive.com as an instance of interactive (documentary) story-telling, since we, as 'users', may choose to ignore the positive (or, respectively, the negative) aspects of slum life. Together with Bendiksen, as producer, and the slum-dwellers, as storytellers, we are the joint constructors of many different possible 'diegetic slum worlds'. In other words, the website offers the possibility to interweave several life-/plot-lines in a multiple perspective 'network narrative' on global slum-dwelling, so to speak.

So, users may navigate the website to uncover the diversity of personal life stories in the slums, but it can also take us, much more so than the photo-book, on

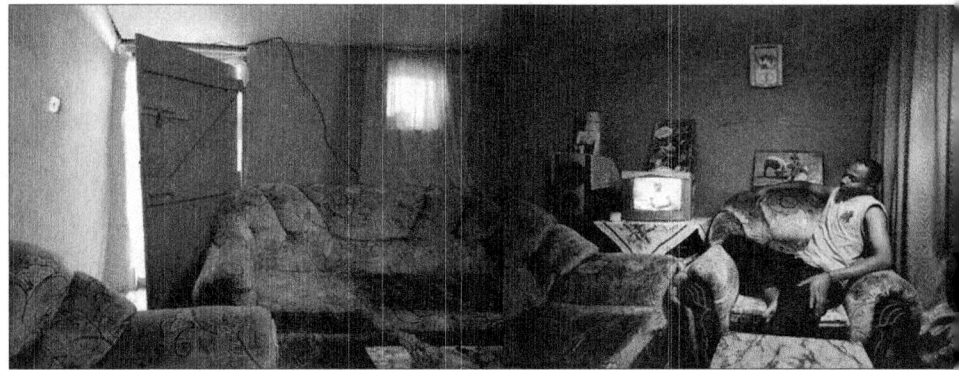

Fig. 4 A panoramic view of Andrew Dirango's home in Kibera, Nairobi on theplaceswelive.com

a visually stunning world trip through our planet slum (since we may, of course, also choose to ignore the speaking slum-dwellers altogether). Unlike both documentary filmmakers and photographers, who usually carefully frame their motifs – which ultimately provokes the observer to ask what remains outside the frame – this web-documentary additionally invites its users to play with the possibilities of panoramic photography and web design. While we may, or may not, choose to listen to the slum-dwellers' life-stories, we can explore their entire shacks with mouse-clicks, as the digital panoramas present these interiors as apparently 'frameless surroundings' in the most literal sense: they are navigable in a 360° circle. A final significant aspect that suggests that theplaceswelive.com is a 'remediation' or 'refashioning' of the (indexical claims of the) documentary form are the digitally reworked pictures themselves, since they truly aestheticise the shack environments, transforming their décors into picturesque panoramas – which simultaneously illustrates Lev Manovich's thesis that digital imagery is a 'sub-genre of painting', rather than an 'indexical media technology' (2001: 295). This aesthetic perception of slum shacks corresponds, however, also with what Bendiksen believes to be the self-perception of, at least, some of its inhabitants, for instance of Kibeira inhabitant Andrew Dirango: 'When I asked [Andrew Dirango] to describe his life, he started talking about interior decoration, how the place looked nice after he'd painted the walls blue' (in Fouché 2009).

THE EXHIBITION INSTALLATION: FROM WALLS TO SCREENS

The installation *The Places We Live* was exhibited in numerous museums and galleries across Europe, Asia and the US, but unlike Riis's lectures and touring magic lantern slum shows, Bendiksen's exhibition creates an immersive, or physically engaging virtual reality slum show. It is thus, once again, a remediation of the social documentary genre, but, unlike the website, it is a spatialised kind of documentary which apparently blurs the distinctions between the real and the virtual; that is, the

observer/experiencer enters the image of the slum shack physically, rather than looking at it from a safe distance on screen. Bendiksen described how he wanted to blur the boundaries between lived space (or, in German, *Lebensraum*) and image-space (*Bildraum*) as follows: '[I]n the exhibition installation there are actually four rooms. Each room represents one city and you actually step into the room and the room all round you, 360°, comes alive. And you stand inside the photograph while you're hearing the stories spoken over a loudspeaker' (RFI 2009).

What exactly is 'remediated' in Bendiksen's installation exhibition of documentary images that blur the boundaries between lived and image-spaces? To begin with, immersive panorama exhibitions are no news to art and media historians. According to Oliver Grau, they are a phenomenon that can be traced as far back as to wall paintings in ancient Rome.[22] In his *Virtual Art: From Illusion to Immersion* (2004), Grau argues that the 'most effective examples of these frescoes use motifs that address the observer from all sides in a unity of time and place, enclosing him or her hermetically. This creates an illusion of *being in the picture*, inside an image space and its illusionary events' (2004: 25). Bendiksen's exhibition installation, in which the observer is given the illusion of *being in the photograph*, is thus, from a media and art historical perspective, a remediation of a long-existing art practice, which not only sought to immerse the observer into image-spaces through its depicted subjects, but also through its panoramic technique. However, these ancient panoramas spatialised mythical stories featuring gods, rather than those of real people. And unlike nineteenth-century panorama exhibitions of exotic landscapes and cityscapes, in Bendiksen's exhibition the visitors virtually enter the private spaces of the urban poor.

Unlike historical panorama exhibitions, therefore, the screens/homes of *The Places We Live* ought to be literally 'inhabited' by the exhibition's visitors, since it invites them to 'forget reality' (the exhibition framework) and slip for a moment into the shacks (and lives) of slum-dwellers. As Bendiksen himself has put it, he 'wanted to create more of an experience, an illusion of standing in one of these (slum) houses, rather than just looking at prints on the wall' (in CPN Canon 2008). Hence, the exhibition installation aims to generate a form of telepresence – a feeling of 'being there' – and thus to create a new 'sensory immediacy to the tenement problem' (Carter 2008: 117), since it is now the whole body of the observer that becomes 'participatory'. These kinds of physically, cognitively and emotionally interactive new media environments are often described as 'immersive'. As mentioned above, the journalist Philip Gourevitch has praised Bendiksen's 'immersion in the slums', since, according to him, Bendiksen creates 'a new way to make a camera take us through our eyes to an experience of complete sensory immersion, so that we can experience a photograph, not only as a picture, but also as something we can hear and smell and taste' (in Bendiksen 2008: np). However, much more so than the artistic quality of the photos themselves, the exhibition installation creates an immersive experience through its use of digital screens as walls – which ultimately illustrates another of Manovich's theses, namely that we today live in 'the society of the screen' (2001: 94).

CONCLUSION

As the fastest growing human habitat on the planet, the slum is increasingly connected to a number of highly topical socio-*political* issues: from inequality, global capitalism and the north-south divide to rural-urban migration and local urban policies. Yet, we should also start to consider the slum as an increasingly crucial socio-*cultural* site in today's globalising world. It is therefore all the more relevant to look closely at examples like *The Places We Live*, a media project that is, perhaps to a larger extent than many others, situated at the crossroads of a variety of interrelated phenomena. In this sense, we should consider contemporary installation art and humanitarian activism alongside global slum tourism, social documentary photography and the slum imagery of reality television and world cinema. As for activism, there are, of course, numerous NGOs that deal with issues of slum improvement or 'slum remediation', as it is sometimes called when urban planners envision eco-friendly, sustainable slum communities. Many of them are participatory but practically minded grassroots movements that have lost their faith in governmental solutions to improve slum conditions. But there are also a number of humanitarian initiatives that are best described as art and media projects. Some of these initiatives aim at empowering slum-dwellers. For instance, *Slum-TV* in Nairobi's Mathare provides technologies (DV cameras, laptops) and services (film schooling, workshops) to enable slum-dwellers to become filmmakers or citizen journalists.[23] On the other hand, there are humanitarian projects that rather fit the category of 'slum tourism', for instance the 'Living in Poverty' area of the 'Global Village & Discovery Center' in Americus (USA).[24] The Center could be described as a 'poverty housing theme park', since it consists of full-scale replica of shacks into which visitors can freely enter in order to empathise with those who live in cramped, unsafe conditions without immediate access to basic services.

Related, but nevertheless also opposed to this idea, is a relative novelty in the world of art galleries and exhibitions, namely installations that explicitly focus on slum houses, hutments or shacks. The work of the Slovenian artist Marjetica Potrč is probably the most accomplished of its kind. Just like Bendiksen, Potrč suggests with her installations (such as *Caracas: Growing House*) that slum-dwelling is a precarious, but also highly creative (or *bricoleur*) form of living.[25] Unlike Bendiksen, however, Potrč has also developed an onsite project in the slums in collaboration with the inhabitants of the La Vega *barrio* of Caracas. Apart from being an art object, her installation, titled *Dry Toilet*, is also a case of participatory urban planning and design, because it is a useful, eco-friendly utility: a waterless toilet that was installed in a community that has no access to the official water grid. It is exactly in comparison to projects like *Slum-TV* or *Dry Toilet* – rather than in comparison to historical examples (Jacob Riis), reality television or contemporary world cinema – that Bendiksen's transmedia project becomes morally problematic. Even though Bendiksen's counter-stereotypical images, the website's polyperspectivity and interactive design, as well as the exhibition's promise of a more personal or intimate encounter with the urban poor, are decidedly innovative in the context of 'social documentary photography', obviously *The Places We Live* does not really provide any empowering agency to slum-dwellers, nor does it offer any practical solutions to pressing everyday problems in the slums. One might, of course, object that this is not the primary task of photography or art, but Bendiksen's benevolent (media-) reformist intentions, and especially the exhibition's promise of an apparently personal '3-D encounter' between slum-dweller and gallery visitor, remains intrinsically a one-dimensional affair, in which the exhibition's visitors become virtual, rather than actual slum tourists. The problem is that *The Places We Live* ultimately suggests that the only places 'we' may inhabit and share together in today's digitally interconnected, but socially divided world are, indeed, those 'slums on screen'.

NOTES

1. The following chapter draws on some ideas presented at more length in my monograph *Slums on Screen: World Cinema and the Planet of Slums* (Edinburgh University Press, 2016).
2. This strategy could be defined using Bill Nichols's (2001) terminology as a 'participatory' or 'interactive' approach and thus as a standard filmic, rather than photographic mode of production.
3. *The Places We Live* was a three-year project. It began in 2005 when Bendiksen moved into a shack in Nairobi's Kibera slum in order to get accustomed to the neighbourhood's daily life and to understand the hazard such a life involves. Over the next three years, he visited the households of families living in the slums of Caracas, Mumbai and Jakarta. Bendiksen has repeatedly emphasised that he was

4   I use the term 'transmedia' in the sense that projects such as *The Places We Live* are constructed across various platforms, in this case across both traditional and new media.

5   The UN estimates that today's one billion slum-dwellers live in around 200,000 slums, most of them located in African, South American and Asian urban areas – a 2,500 per cent increase from the estimated thirty-five million slum-dwellers in 1957. This global expansion of slums can also be illustrated with a variety of terms used in different languages and in a range of world regions, countries and cities to describe overcrowded squatter settlements: from *bidonvilles*, *taudis* or *quartiers irréguliers* in French, *barraca*, *barrio marginal*, *villa miseria* or *colonias populares* in the Spanish speaking world, to *trushchobi* in Russian, *umjondolo* in Zulu, *mudun safi* in Arabic and *gecekondu* in Turkey (UN 2003: 9–10).

6   The notion that slum-dwellers are today's 'surplus population' was also outlined by Zygmunt Bauman in his *Wasted Lives: Modernity and Its Outcasts* (2004), where he claims that not only 'global capitalism', but modernity itself is to blame, that is, the tendency of modern, bureaucratised societies to create zones of exclusion, since they are based on the instrumental rationality of ordering strategies (on sorting and culling, including and excluding), hence constantly organising who is deemed 'useful' and who is not.

7   SAPs are economic policies introduced by the World Bank and the International Monetary Fund in which receiving loans or obtaining lower interest rates on already existing loans is only granted under certain conditions (sometimes also called the 'Washington Consensus'). Only if the respective country implements free market policies, for instance through the reduction of trade barriers and the deregulation of its economy, is it allowed to receive loans. In line with Davis's critique, this policy has been criticised not only by neo-Marxist or Keynesian economists but also by Hernando de Soto and Joseph Stiglitz.

8   This criticism could have been directed towards the authors of the UN report as well, who have, however, argued for its use despite the term's problematic history. They contend that 'polite' terms such as 'community', even though politically more correct, often remained mere euphemisms and 'served to maintain rather than counteract the negative prejudices against slum-dwellers' (UN 2003: 9). The major reason for excavating the word 'slum' by the UN is thus, in the first instance, to counter such euphemisms and to challenge policy makers (thus, the report's title, *The* Challenge *of Slums*).

9   See Ian Sansom's review for *The Guardian*, titled 'Shantytown apocalypse' (2006), in which he claims that Davis's rhetorical style is reminiscent of Dickens or Conrad.

10 Similar analogies between the Victorian slums of the nineteenth century and the shantytowns of the twenty-first century have not only been drawn by

sociologists, but also by artists, filmmakers, or writers. Danny Boyle has, for instance, compared Mumbai to Charles Dickens's Victorian London and the American journalist George Packer has argued in his essay 'Dickens in Lagos' that 'Dickens' real heirs are less likely to have grown up in London than Bombay' (2010: np).

11 A good starting point to explore the parallels and continuities of such transmedia flows in the nineteenth, twentieth and twenty-first century is provided by the volume *Multimedia Histories: From the Magic Lantern to the Internet* (Lyons and Plunkett 2007).

12 Before *How The Other Half Lives* was published as a book, Riis had already toured with a magic lantern show through the United States, presenting stereopticon pictures of New York's slum life. *The Battle with the Slum: Illustrated by scores of original Stereopticon pictures of New York City life* was the title of one of Riis's magic lantern shows. Another magic lantern 'slum show' was *Slum Life in Our Great Cities* (1892), which was produced and marketed by the Riley Brothers of Bradford. It contained 52 hand-coloured slides of photographs that were all made in the streets of Liverpool.

13 Some of the most prominent examples of turn-of-the-century books that address slum life as a fictional or non-fictional topic are Arthur Morrison's novel *A Child of the Jago* (1896), Stephen Crane's novel *Maggie: A Girl of the Streets* (1893) and Jack London's social reportage *The People of the Abyss* (1903). For an astute analysis of turn-of-the-century journalistic sketches on slums, see Entin (2001). More recently, Westgate (2014) has analysed the theatricalising of urban poverty in Progressive-Era American theatre.

14 One of Schwartz's most captivating examples for this emerging 'desire for the real as spectacle' is how the exhibition of dead bodies in the Paris Morgue became an immensely popular tourist attraction for urban strollers. Schwartz's other examples include dioramas, panoramas and wax museums.

15 *The Big Switch* is an Indian survivor show for Indian D-list celebrities, who were teamed together with Mumbai slum-dwellers in a simulated slum. The British reality television show *Famous, Rich and in the Slums* (BBC, 2011) has a similar concept. For a critical discussion of these reality shows, see Mehta 2012.

16 Riis went into the slums often during the night, since, as he writes in his autobiography *The Making of an American*, 'I liked to walk, for I saw the slum when off its guard' (Riis 2007: 95). Some of Riis's most arresting photographs indeed appear to frame slum-dwellers caught 'off guard', for instance while sleeping.

17 Joseph B. Entin makes a similar argument, proposing that turn -of-the-century popular visual culture generated 'sensational' viewing experiences (in the sense of an 'exciting experience' or a 'sensory stimulation'), often by displaying 'low', 'exotic', and 'alien' figures (immigrants and slum dwellers, criminals and cabaret dancers), or in other words, the abject 'bodies of the dispossessed' (2007: 3).

18 The Latin term *remediatio* describes the process of curing or healing, but it can

also be used to describe a process of reform, that is, as 'remedying or correcting something' ('remediation,' def. 1, *Oxford English Dictionary*).
19 Originally, Riis's book contained mostly reprinted engravings as illustrations and only seventeen photographs reproduced in halftone. However, it was especially because of its vivid, photographic illustrations, as well as because of Riis's captivating rhetoric that the book became an instant success.
20 The 'environmental determinist' argument that better housing/living conditions would produce better people was crucial for Riis and indeed influenced American policy making on the issue of social housing in the decades to come, leading to slum clearance campaigns and the establishment of public or social housing projects.
21 Web documentaries are also referred to as webdoc, interactive documentary, multimedia documentary or docuweb.
22 Grau discusses the Great Frieze of Room 5 in the Villa die Misteri in Pompeii as the earliest surviving example for an immersive type of panoramic virtual art. The frieze was created circa 60 BC and consists of 29 highly realistic, life-size figures, painted across the entire walls of the room and so immerses the observer in a virtual image space that depicts the interaction between these figures across the room (2004: 25–9).
23 *Slum-TV* was launched in 2006 by two Austrian and one Kenyan artist, as well as by two local residents of Mathare. The organisation also organises the annual *Slum Film Festival*. For more information visit: http://www.slumfilmfestival.net/
24 The Global Village & Discovery Center was built by the international Christian NGO *Habitat for Humanity*, which is specifically devoted to improving the housing conditions of the poor.
25 The architectural historian Patricio del Real argues that most of these artists perceive the slum-dweller not simply as an 'informal' citizen of 'irregular' squatter settlements, or as a passive victim of global capitalism, but rather as an active '*bricoleur*, and his or her way of being in the world as bricolage' (2008: 85). Real primarily discusses the work of Marjetica Potrč and Jesús Palomino, but he also mentions other art exhibitions that have addressed slum life in a similar way, e.g. those by Carlos Garaicoa (Cuba), Grupo Grafito (Colombia), Franklin Cassar (Brazil), Meyer Vaisman (Venezuela) and Felix Schramm (Germany).

BIBLIOGRAPHY

Angotti, Tom (2006) 'Apocalyptic Anti-Urbanism: Mike Davis and his planet of slums', *International Journal of Urban and Regional Research*, 30, 4, 961–7.

Bauman, Zygmunt (2004) *Wasted Lives: Modernity and Its Outcasts*. Cambridge: Polity Press.

Bendiksen, Jonas (2008) *The Places We Live*. London: Thames & Hudson.

Bentes, Ivana (2005) 'The Aesthetics of Violence in Brazilian Film', in Else R. P. Vieira (ed.) *City of God in Several Voices: Brazilian Social Cinema as Action*. Nottingham: Critical, Cultural and Communication Press, 82–92.

Bolter, Jay David and Richard Grusin (2000) *Remediation: Understanding New Media*. Cambridge: MIT Press.

CPN Canon (2008) 'Magnum's Jonas Bendiksen projects life in the urban slums', *Canon Professional Network;* http://cpn.canon-europe.com/content/news/jonas_bendiksen.do

Carter, Christopher (2008) 'Writing with Light: Jacob Riis's Ambivalent Exposures', *College English*, 71, 2, 117–41.

Cities Alliance (2009) 'The Places We Live: Sights and Sounds from the Slums', *Cities Alliance: Cities without Slums*; http://www.citiesalliance.org/spotlight-theplaceswelive

Davis, Mike (2004) 'Planet of Slums', *New Left Review*, 26, 5–36.

____ (2007) *Planet of Slums*. New York: Verso.

Entin, Joseph B. (2007) *Sensational Modernism: Experimental Fiction and Photography in Thirties America*. Chapel Hill: University of North Carolina Press.

Fortin, David D. (2010) 'Slum Fictions: De-delimiting Place in Nairobi', unpublished conference paper presented at the 2010 *International Conference of Architecture Research*; http:/info.aia.org/arc/program.program.html

Fouché, Gwladys (2009) 'The photographer capturing the reality of life in the slums', *The Guardian*; http://www.theguardian.com/artanddesign/2009/jan/14/jonas-bendiksen-photograph-slums

Frenzel, Fabian and Ko Koens (2015) *Tourism and Geographies of Inequality: The New Global Slumming Phenomenon*. London and New York: Routledge.

Gandal, Keith (1997) *The Virtues of the Vicious: Jacob Riis, Stephen Crane and the Spectacle of the Slum*. Oxford: Oxford University Press.

Grau, Oliver (2004) *Virtual Art: From Illusion to Immersion*. Boston: MIT Press.

Heap, Chad (2009) *Slumming: Sexual and Racial Encounters in American Nightlife, 1885–1940*. Chicago: University of Chicago Press.

Jenkins, Henry (2006) *Convergence Culture: Where Old and New Media Collide*. New York: New York University Press.

Koven, Seth (2004) *Slumming: Sexual and Social Politics in Victorian London*. Princeton: Princeton University Press.

Krstić, Igor (2016) *Slums on Screen: World Cinema and the Planet of Slums*. Edinburgh: Edinburgh University Press.

Larson, Christina and Jonas Bendiksen (2009) 'Planet Slum', *Foreign Policy*; http://foreignpolicy.com/slideshow/planet-slum/

Lyons, James and John Plunkett (eds) (2007) *Multimedia Histories: From the Magic Lantern to the Internet*. Chicago: Chicago University Press.

Manovich, Lev (2001) *The Language of New Media*. Cambridge: MIT Press.

McLuhan, Marshall (2013) *Understanding Media: The Extensions of Man*. Berkeley:

Ginko Press.

Mehta, Rijuta (2012) 'Living for the other half: Slum specials on reality TV', *Studies in South Asian Film & Media*, 4, 1, 39–59.

Nichols, Bill (2001) *Introduction to Documentary*. Bloomington: Indiana University Press.

Packer, George (2010) 'Dickens in Lagos', *Lapham's Quarterly*; http://www.lqbeta.org/essays/dickens-in-lagos.php?page=all

Real, Patricio del (2008) 'Slums do Stink: Artists, Bricolage, and Our Need for Doses of "Real Life"', *Art Journal*, 67,1, 82–99.

RFI (2009) 'Shortlisted webdocumentary: The place we live', *Radio France Internationale*; http://www1.rfi.fr/actuen/ articles/116 /article_4821.asp

Riis, Jacob August ([1890] 1971) *How The Other Half Lives. Studies among the Tenements of New York*. New York: Dover Publications.

_____ ([1901] 2007) *The Making of an American*. Middlesex: The Echo Library.

Sansom, Ian (2006) 'Shantytown apocalypse', *The Guardian*; http://www.theguardian.com/books/2006/aug/19/shopping.society

Schwartz, Vanessa R. (1998) *Spectacular Realities: Early Mass Culture in Fin-de-Siècle Paris*. Berkley: University of California Press.

Sontag, Susan (1977) *On Photography*. London: Penguin.

UN (2003) *The Challenge of Slums*. London: Earthscan.

Westgate, J. Chris (2014) *Staging the Slums, Slumming the Stage: Class, Poverty, Ethnicity, and Sexuality in American Theatre, 1890–1916*. Basingstoke: Palgrave Macmillan.

Žižek, Slavoj (2008) *In Defense of Lost Causes*. London: Verso.

NEW NARRATIVE TOPOGRAPHIES

INTERSTITIAL CITYSPACE AND THE IMMIGRANT EXPERIENCE IN CONTEMPORARY FRENCH CINEMA

WILL HIGBEE

Since the 1970s and 1980s, when filmmakers of Maghrebi origin gained a degree of visibility in French cinema, there have been, broadly speaking, two representational approaches employed to portray the experience of immigrant minorities and their French-born descendants, as well as the spaces they inhabit, on French screens. The first directs its attention to the 'real' localised spaces of neighborhoods of specific French cities in which immigrant communities have traditionally lived and worked. The second is predicated on an encounter between the immigrant protagonist and host nation that deliberately moves away from the real spaces that the immigrant is presumed to inhabit on screen.

The first approach outlined above is, arguably, inspired by a predisposition in contemporary European cinema towards social realism as a means of depicting the immigrant experience. Whilst the way that the spaces associated with the first approach are represented on screen may vary – from the documentary realism of militant immigrant cinema of the 1970s, to the more conventional narrative and aesthetic approach of the *policier* (French crime film) of the 1980s, where the North African immigrant population tended to be depicted as belonging exclusively to a criminal underworld – the geographical locations themselves remain fairly constant. Unsurprisingly, the districts of Paris that have traditionally been home to a large proportion of post-colonial immigrant minorities, such as Barbès, La Goutte d'Or and Belleville, feature prominently in these films.[1] More recently, first in *beur* cinema of the 1980s and then the *banlieue* films of the mid-1990s, the run-down housing estates of the Parisian urban periphery have played an equally prominent role in French cinema as an emblematic space of social exclusion occupied predominantly by non-European immigrants and their French-born descendants.[2] Though the comedy genre has always been prominent in immigrant narratives (see for example *Le Thé à la menthe* (Abdelkrim Bahloul, 1984), *Salut cousin!* (Merzak Allouache, 1997)), in the 2000s, a range of more mainstream genre films have emerged, especially comedies and romantic comedies, that have foregrounded the experiences of immigrant communities and their French descendants: *Mauvaise foi* (Roschdy Zem, 2006), *Tout ce qui brille* (Hervé Mimran and Géraldine Nakache, 2010), *Beur sur la ville* (Djamel Bensalah, 2011), *Samba* (Olivier Nakache and Eric Toledano, 2014). While these films draw on both working class and middle class immigrant protagonists, the districts and neighbourhoods employed tend to remain those typically associated with immigrant minorities in the French capital.

The centrality of Paris to representations of immigrant minorities in French cinema can be explained most directly by the fact that it is both the nation's capital and the hub of film production in France, as well as being a multi-ethnic city with a high immigrant population. This central position is, moreover, also an inevitable consequence of its status as a 'world city'; a cosmopolitan centre of economic migration and transnational hub of cultural and economic exchange (see Hannerz 1996: 128). Marseilles, France's second city and a multicultural port that has been built on successive waves of immigration, is, after Paris, the most prominent location for narratives about immigrant minorities in French cinema (see for example *Bye-bye* (Karim Dridi, 1995), *Comme un aimant* (Akhenaton and Kamel Saleh, 2000), *Samia* (Philippe Faucon, 2000) and, to varying degrees, almost all the films of Robert Guédiguian that focus on the working class district of L'Estaque). Speaking to *Cahiers du cinéma* of the decision to locate his second feature, *Bye-bye* (a drama about inter-generational conflict in an extended Maghrebi immigrant family) in the Le Panier district of Marseilles, Franco-Tunisian director Karim Dridi stated:

> Setting my film over there [in Marseilles] allowed me to look at Africa from the other side. Just as I am half Arab and half French, so Marseilles is a city at the intersection, a very hybrid city. (In Jousse and Lalanne 1995: 39)[3]

As the above quote from Dridi suggests, the decision to locate *Bye-bye* in Marseilles, with its geographic location on the southern Mediterranean coast and historical positioning as the gateway to the colonies of French North Africa, also indicates how the cine-spatial representation of the immigrant experience in contemporary cinema is also bound up in what Sharon Zukin describes as the 'symbolic economy' (1997: 8) of the city, whereby the 'narrative' associated with specific places reflects not only how these spaces are experienced in every day social encounters but also the way that they are produced, imagined and represented in culture and the arts. Interestingly, Lyon, France's third city and home to a significant immigrant population from the Maghreb, hardly features as a clearly identified location in French films focusing on immigrant protagonists, adding further weight to Zukin's notion of the symbolic economy of the city (in this case Paris and Marseilles) coded as emblematic spaces of immigrant experience in France that move beyond sheer weight of numbers in terms of population or an extended historical presence of immigrant minorities within a given city.[4]

If the first cine-spatial approach to representing the immigrant experience outlined above is centripetal, directing its attention to the 'real', localised spaces of neighborhoods of specific French cities in which immigrant communities have traditionally lived and worked, the second, which can be seen as an almost inevitable corollary of the first, is centrifugal: propelling the immigrant protagonists away from these more 'familiar' locations into (supposedly) alien socio-economic, geographical and cultural environments, where the narrative is characterised by an encounter between the immigrant other and host nation. When immigrant protagonists (and their French born descendants) appear in cine-spatial locations beyond Paris in French cinema of the 1990s and early 2000s, they tend to be marked as outsiders, transient voyagers or temporary guests. Given the emphasis on movement and border crossing in these films (the arrivals and departures that generate the encounter between immigrant and host nation), ports feature heavily in these films, such as *Welcome* (Philippe Lioret, 2009) and *Le Havre* (Aki Kaurismäki, 2011). The road movie is often also the genre of choice: think, for example, of the Russian immigrant and the Spanish salesman travelling through the backwaters of Brittany in Poirier's road movie without a car, *Western* (Manuel Poirier, 1997) or *Drôle de Félix* (Olivier Ducastel and Jacques Martineau, 2000), where the eponymous Félix, the French-born son of Maghrebi immigrants, embarks on a symbolic road trip from Dieppe to Marseilles in an attempt to reconnect with his estranged father. Before his departure, Félix establishes a series of 'rules' for his journey. Firstly, he must avoid major cities in order to journey through *la France profonde* and, secondly, he will not pass through any town where the far-right Front National is in charge. Though he never finds his father, the road trip (in line with the conventions of the road movie more generally) becomes a journey of (self-)discovery whereby Félix connects with other French citizens who are symbolically qualified in the narrative as his alternative 'family'. *Drôle de Félix* highlights one other important point about the way that such 'immigrant' narratives are perceived in contemporary French cinema. Félix is, in fact, French of immigrant origin, indicating how the 'immigrant' protagonist is often conflated in French cinema to include the French-born descendants of immigrants; especially those of non-European origin, whose ethnic or religious difference is seen to mark them out as Other or outsider in relation to the contemporary cultural and socio-political landscape in France.

The principal aim of this chapter, then, is to examine three French films from the 2000s that, in quite different ways, extend the two approaches outlined above by employing new and distinctive features in terms of the type of urban space, and, more particularly, the type of city foregrounded in the narrative. The three films selected for analysis, *La Graine et le mulet* (Abdellatif Kechiche, 2007), *Dernier maquis* (Rabah Ameur-Zaïmeche, 2008) and *De rouille et d'os* (Jacques Audiard, 2012) are located in spaces 'between' the world cities of Paris and Marseilles and the French provinces. Two of these films – *La Graine et le mulet* and *De rouille et d'os* – take place in smaller, coastal cities. The third, *Dernier maquis*, maintains the previous focus on the urban periphery found in the *banlieue* film since the mid-1990s but replaces the marginalised space of the *cité* with a pallet yard on an industrial estate that, as well as being qualified as a locus of labour and production is also a space inscribed with what the director describes as a neglected history of Islam in France (Ameur-Zaïmeche cited in Widemann 2008).

The neologism 'interstitial cityspace' will be employed to describe the different kind of urban spaces that emerge in *Dernier maquis*, *La Graine et le mulet* and *De Rouille et d'os*. The term develops Hamid Naficy's description of accented or diasporic filmmaking as an 'interstitial' mode of production, whereby the accented filmmaker operates both 'within and astride the cracks of the system … at the intersection of the global and the local' in a context that is 'produced in the articulation of differences' (2001: 46). The interstitial cityspace is thus different from the binary representation of the immigrant space that one typically finds in French cinema of the 1980s and 1990s (and most obviously in the *banlieue* film), whereby the marginalised immigrant protagonists are isolated in the urban periphery or immigrant *quartier* at a safe distance from the rest of the city and its inhabitants. In contrast, interstitial cityspace refers to the representation of urban space found increasingly in French cinema since the early 2000s, where the immigrant protagonist has a greater mobility within the city, and where the question of identity, place and belonging is far more ambiguous (to the extent that the immigrant protagonist oscillates between inclusion and exclusion as well as an association with the immigrant or diasporic community at the same time as being identified as belonging to a community or group by virtue of other types of markers such as class, gender or sexuality). When considered in this way, the representation of the immigrant in this interstitial cityscape appears drawn to a cine-spatial geography in which zones of affluence, influence, production and consumption overlap with those of poverty, inactivity and exclusion. Indeed, the location is palimpsestic in the sense that immigrant characters inhabit these urban spaces in relation to multiple points of identification – such as ethnic origins, class and gender – as well as co-habiting alongside members of the host nation, sometimes together and, at other times, in totally separate ways. The interstitial cityspace in these three films is therefore distinct from either the immigrant quartier or *cité* found in earlier immigrant narratives in French cinema, which tended to be defined by their isolation from the rest of the city. However, as the analysis of the case study films will show, this does not mean that the immigrant protagonists who live, function and are represented in these interstitial cityspaces are necessarily or unproblematically included within the polis or host nation.

Moving now to look in more detail at the three case study films, the principal concern will be to analyse how and why these films place an immigrant protagonist, family or community in these interstitial spaces within the city and what effect this has on the way that these diasporic protagonists are represented. What happens to the immigrant narrative and the symbolic economy of the urban space represented on screen when the immigrant Other is located away from the 'global' or 'world' city such as Paris or Marseilles, on the one hand and the local, marginalised spaces of the *cité* or the immigrant quartier, on the other? How is a sense of community and belonging constructed in these interstitial spaces that are neither clearly identifiable as belonging to the provinces nor the global city? What are the markers of difference and are they exclusively confined to ethnicity? Do these films indicate a greater sense of polycentrism in the way that immigrants and their relationship to the host nation are articulated on screen, or are they simply replicating the same binary models of socio-spatial exclusion that have traditionally functioned in earlier French films dealing with immigrant communities? And, finally, is the immigrant's status as Other transformed as a result of the new, in-between spaces that they navigate in these films?

DERNIER MAQUIS

Rabah Ameur-Zaïmeche is one of the truly original voices to have emerged within the auteur-led independent sector of French cinema over the past decade. His politically engaged filmmaking has garnered critical acclaim from festival organisers, highbrow critics and a niche cinephile audience in France.[5] Ameur-Zaïmeche's working methods (a low-budget, auteurist approach that sees the filmmaker act as writer, director and lead actor in his films) closely relates to Naficy's description of the interstitial mode of production in accented cinema (2001: 48). *Dernier maquis*, the director's third feature, forms the final part of a self-styled trilogy of films addressing contemporary socio-political issues facing immigrant minorities in France. In the first instance, the decision to locate the film at the very extremities of the city (*Dernier maquis* was shot on the outskirts of Paris, though we are never given this information in the film itself) appears to align Ameur-Zaïmeche's film in cine-spatial terms with the *cinéma de banlieue* of 1990s and 2000s. However this association is only partially correct, since *Dernier maquis* employs the location of the urban periphery to explore the issue of religion in the (immigrant) workplace in ways that are quite distinct from the *banlieue* film's typical focus on the experience of an alienated youth underclass, characterised most frequently by their exclusion from the world of work. The dual function of the pallet yard as a site of both immigrant labour and religious community further emphasises the palimpsestic nature of the interstitial cityspace, as well as Naficy's sense of the interstitial in accented cinema producing an articulation of (cultural) difference (2001: 46).

The episodic narrative of *Dernier maquis* is relatively simple and revolves around events that unfold in a pallet-repair business owned by Mao (Rabah Ameur-Zaïmeche), a French Muslim. The decision to give the Muslim boss who wishes to appear as a benevolent leader but in fact intends to exploit his workers the name Mao, invites a curious association with the Communist dictator Mao Tse-tung: one that is further suggested by the predominance of the colour red in the pallet yard. Mao's employees are divided into two distinct groups: recently arrived immigrants from Sub-Saharan Africa, and workers of Maghrebi-origin, some of whom are first-generation immigrants and others who appear to be the French descendants of North African immigrants. Reflecting this distinction between newly-arrived immigrant and more established members of an immigrant diaspora, a hierarchy exists within the workplace: the Sub-Saharan immigrants undertake unskilled, manual labour in the yard, while the workers of Maghrebi-origin tend to occupy more skilled positions as mechanics. Any sense of working class, religious or migrant solidarity within the workplace is thus compromised by ethnic origin; a point that Mao uses to his advantage as the narrative unfolds to drive a wedge between different groups of workers in an attempt to better control them. This division between the migrant workers points to another difference between *Dernier maquis* and the *banlieue* film, whereby the multi-ethnic *banlieue* youth in films such as *Ma 6-T va crack-er* (Jean-François Richet, 1997) and *La Haine* (Matthieu Kassovitz, 1995) are united by a shared sense of socio-economic exclusion more than ethnic origins.

Located on a remote industrial site on the outskirts of a large, unnamed city, bordered by a canal and directly beneath an airport flight path, the workshop and yard of the pallet business of *Dernier maquis* is the arena in which a dispute between the workers and their boss (as well as between the different groups of immigrant workers themselves) will unfold. The spatial continuity of this location, combined with the shifting industrial landscape created by the distinctive red pallets that dominate the *mise-en-scène* and are constantly being moved around the yard by the workers, lends the film an anti-realist, theatrical quality. Tension arises in the narrative when Mao constructs a small mosque for his (mostly) Muslim workforce and makes the mistake of appointing an Imam without first consulting his employees. The subsequent disagreement between Mao, and the more militant members of his workforce (in particular the garage mechanics), extends the confrontation from the politics of religious protocol to the realm of class struggle. Mao informs the mechanics that he is going to shut down the garage, citing economic reasons as the basis for his decision, though, in reality, his actions appear to be a punishment for the mechanics' collective dissent over the choice of imam. In a desperate attempt to save their jobs, four of the Maghrebi-French mechanics mobilise to occupy the yard. A violent confrontation ensues, as the workers first attack Mao and then barricade themselves in the workplace by using the ubiquitous red pallets – at which point the film comes to an abrupt end.

With its focus on tension between bosses and workers played out in an industrial environment, *Dernier maquis* appears to draw on the dramaturgy of class struggle found in French political cinema of the 1970s. However, as Martin O'Shaughnessy notes, in ideological terms, the film itself could also be viewed as interstitial:

> Like any clear-sighted political film at the current time, *Dernier maquis* is condemned, of necessity, to ambiguity, having to exist in the space between the defeat of the twentieth century left and emergent or residual possibilities. (2015: 125)

Thus in *Dernier maquis*, while class struggle persists, the workers are not unionised to fight the bosses. Some do not even have the correct papers to work in France, highlighting a different kind of precariousness and threat of social violence (expulsion and exploitation as clandestine migrants) that hangs over many workers. Similarly, the final blockade of the yard that foregrounds the possibility of resistance to the often unseen violence inflicted by neo-liberalism on both the working-class but also (documented and undocumented) immigrant workers only serves to underline the rift between, one side, the mechanics of Maghrebi origin, who form part of the settled North African diaspora and, on the other, the Sub-Saharan African labourers, who are identified as recently arrived immigrants and thus outsiders.

Ameur-Zaïmeche does not suggest that class attitudes may run deeper than ethnic difference or religious affiliation. Instead, *Dernier maquis* explores a social dynamic and industrial environment in which these two elements are, to all intents and purposes, inseparable. Rather than confining the film's representation of Islam to the private sphere (the home, immigrant foyer or mosque, for example) Ameur-Zaïmeche instead uses *Dernier maquis'* industrial location as the backdrop for exploring and representing the daily rites, rituals and protocol of the Islamic faith. The complications that arise in the workplace between religion and the principles of *laïcité* are illustrated by the extent to which the influence of Islam is embedded into the very fabric of the workplace via the *mise-en-scène* itself. In response to the imposition of Mao's mosque, the garage mechanics construct their own alternative prayer room in the workplace from that the pallets stacked across the yard, with a hose typically used for washing down the pallets serving as the source of water for the worshippers to perform their ritual ablutions in advance of prayers. In one of the film's most memorable images, the *muezzin* stands atop of the walls of the pallet mosque, incanting a call to prayer, that mixes with the sounds of the industrial environment, as a plane flies overhead. This sense of embedding the private rituals and practices of *salat* into the semi-public, material spaces of the workplace, mirrors the approach taken by the filmmakers when shooting on location in an industrial estate for *Dernier maquis*. Ameur-Zaïmeche has commented that filming *Dernier maquis* on location forced the crew were to forced to adapt (artistically speaking) to the pre-existing industrial landscape they encountered.[6] The most obvious example of this is the way that the stylised use of red in the yard and the way that the pallets are employed as a staging device to transform the industrial landscape in which the narrative unfolds. (Just as the alternative mosque is constructed from the material objects found in the workplace – the pallets upon which Mao's business functions and generates capital – so religion is almost never a private matter in the film.)

In another sense, though, the workplace has to incorporate the religious and social characteristics of the various immigrant groups, since the pallet yard is the only location to appear in the film. *Dernier maquis*' immigrant, male workforce is removed from any social, political or cultural interaction with the outside world. This isolation is further evoked by the pallet yard's geographical location on the very extremity of the city, bordered by a canal and tucked away at the end of a road on an industrial estate that leads nowhere.[7] In a similar way to the *cité* in the *banlieue* films of the 1990s, Mao's business is thus qualified as a space at once geographically, culturally and socially excluded from the rest of society; ghettoising the film's (Muslim) immigrant protagonists, rather than, as one contemporary French reviewer saw it, transcending religious difference to produce a democratic working-class space at the very site of cultural and economic exclusion (see Neyrat 2008: 21). For all the radical potential of its politicised aesthetic and the director's claims concerning the film's potential to present a long history of Islam in France – even one that might offer the potential for the debate around the access of Muslim minorities in France to a greater sense of dignity and inclusion (see Ameur-Zaïmeche cited in Widemann 2008) – *Dernier maquis* reaches an impasse in its cine-spatial representation of the immigrant experience, condemning the immigrant workers in the film to a kind of social marginalisation and invisibility to the outside world that has been all to familiar in previous representations of the immigrant in French cinema.

LA GRAINE ET LE MULET

A greater sense of community and connection appears to exist in Abdellatif Kechiche's *La Graine et le mulet*, released the year before *Dernier maquis*. The film tells the story of Slimane, a first generation immigrant from Tunisia, who, having been made redundant from his job as a shipyard worker, attempts to transform a dilapidated barge into a floating couscous restaurant. Although it was his third feature as a director, *La Graine et le mulet* had in fact been conceived before any of his other films and was an intensely personal project for the Franco-Tunisian writer-director. Kechiche had intended to cast his father in the lead role of this immigrant narrative and shoot in the areas of Nice where he grew up. However, the death of his father in 2004 not only caused the film to remain on hold for a number of years, but also led Kechiche to decide to shoot in the neighbouring Mediterranean port of Sète, as a means of providing some emotional distance for the director from the project (see Delorme and Frodon 2007: 15). *La Graine et le mulet* revolves around the relationships within an extended Tunisian immigrant family who are very much part of their local working class community. The film was a critical and commercial success in France; winning a series of awards at the Césars (the French equivalent of the Oscars) and attracting over a million spectators. Whilst not the first film by a French director of immigrant origin to achieve such success, *La Graine et le mulet* is, however, notable for the critical discourse that surrounded its release. Rather than framing Kechiche's work in the context of *beur* filmmaking, in a way that places him simultaneously within and outside of French national cinema, most French reviewers made a point of identifying the Frenchness of Kechiche's particular brand of social cinema, as the latest in a line of great 'humanist' *auteurs* (see Delorme 2007: 11; Kaganski 2007). Jean-Michel Frodon, former editor of *Cahiers du cinéma* and one of France's most influential cinema critics, typified this inclusive response, describing *La Graine et le mulet* as: 'not a *beur* film, nor a film about immigrants but a film about France today' (Delorme and Frodon 2007: 10).

This sense of inclusion and the interstitial positioning of the film's immigrant protagonists within *and* between the diasporic community and host nation is mirrored in the film's urban location. *La Graine et le mulet* is, first of all, defined by its setting in the port of Sète. The film's geographical location, on the Mediterranean coast, facing out towards North Africa, offers the possibility of the port functioning as a cross-cultural contact zone between France and the Maghreb. However, unlike the larger, more industrial southern port of Marseilles that features in films such as *Bye-bye* (see the quote from director Karim Dridi at the start of this chapter), Sète is not considered a symbolic point of arrival and departure, nor is it depicted as a historical point of cultural intersection, between France and the Maghreb. Indeed, in cinematic terms, prior to the release of *La Graine et le mulet* Sète was most famous for having been the location for Agnès Varda's *La Pointe courte* (1954), a film (considered by many historians of French cinemas as one of the precursors to the *nouvelle vague*) that juxtaposes the narrative of a failing relationship between a young married couple visiting from Paris against the modernisation of the fishing industry in Sète.

Of equal significance for locating *La Graine et le mulet* in Sète is the fact that, while the port remains a commercial fishing centre, the city is in the process of de-industrialisation with an economy that is increasingly dependent on tourism. From the opening sequence, Sète is introduced as a port city that is rapidly losing links to its industrial past; the working class community of fishermen and shipyards being reduced to little more than a sideshow for the pleasure cruises that pass by. As the boat tour of the port led by Slim's son, Majid (Sami Zitouni), navigates the interior canals leading to the harbor at the start of the film, he draws the tourists' attention to the piles of scrap metal destined for Turkey, lamenting the fact that 'France used to make ovens, now it seems we've run out of matches'. As O'Shaughnessy perceptively notes, Kechiche's film 'self-consciously sets out to bring the normally invisible immigrant experience within the larger story of working-class decline' (2015: 121). This observation is crucial, since unlike earlier films from the 1970s, 1980s and 1990s in which immigrant minorities appeared to be defined solely by their origins, ethnic and religious difference – a community apart – in *La Graine et le mulet*, Slimane and his extended family – made up of Tunisian, Portuguese and Russian immigrants – are identified as members of a working class community who simply happen to be of immigrant origin. Indeed, the fact that Slimane has spent so many years working and living in France means that, to the other members of the working class community in Sète, he *is* effectively French. When he breaks the news of his redundancy to his eldest daughter and her husband, José, his son-in-law's response epitomises this sense of inclusion: 'It's simple', notes José, 'They no longer want French workers' (a category in which Slimane is clearly included).

Unlike in other films focusing on protagonists of Maghrebi-descent situated on the south Mediterranean coast, the port location of Sète does not appear to evoke the ambivalent pull between host and homeland for the diasporic subject. Whereas in *Bye-bye*, Ismael is repeatedly framed staring out across the Mediterranean at the boats carrying passengers between France and the Maghreb, the view from the window of Slimane's lodgings opens onto the internal waterways of Sète, not out to sea. This is not to say, though, that Slimane denies or obscures his Tunisian immigrant origins. His place within both the working class community of Sète and its Maghrebi diaspora is highlighted by the evocatively named Hotel de l'Orient, where Slimane lodges with other first generation male immigrant workers from Algeria, Tunisia and Morocco.

Various social spaces, public and domestic, are therefore represented in *La Graine et le mulet*: the port as a site of both work and leisure; the bank where Rym (Hafsia Herzi) and Slimane apply for their loan and offices at the town hall where they request the relevant permissions to open their business; the shipyard and quayside where Slim renovates the boat; the modest working class apartment of Slim's estranged wife. The port, family home and Hotel de l'Orient are the principal geographical locations of the film. It is, however, the boat that Slimane renovates and transforms into a floating couscous restaurant which functions as a point of convergence for all of the protagonists in the final third of *La Graine et le mulet*.

The boat itself is, again, representative of the transformation of Sète from an industrial port to a city whose economy is increasingly dependent on the service industries of the restaurant trade and tourism. Significantly, Slimane begins his renovation of the boat in an area of the port that now appears as a wasteland, devoid of any industrial activity but one with the potential for activity and transformation. Indeed, this cine-spatial location perfectly illustrates the architect and urban theorist Rubió Ignasi Solà-Morales' notion of *terrain vague*, evoking the seemingly abandoned, marginal and un-productive spaces within the modern city that, while appearing to be in 'suspended redevelopment' nonetheless remain in a constant state of flux and house potential for rejuvenation (1995: 119–20). In a scene laden with visual symbolism, when Slim appears with Rym on his moped to inspect the boat for the first time, the camera track the couple's arrival against a backdrop of idle cranes surrounded by scrap metal on an empty quayside; reinforcing Majid's earlier comments about the decline of manufacturing and industry in Sète. When his renovation of the boat is complete, Slimane plans to transport the vessel from the vestiges of the industrial port to the (symbolically named) *Quai de la République*, a quayside dominated by leisure boats and restaurants that epitomises the new tourist economy upon which local politicians and businesses are staking the city's future.

Locating *La Graine et le mulet* in Sète, Kechiche continues the trend established earlier in the 2000s by certain Maghrebi-French filmmakers of moving away from the Parisian urban periphery, and more specifically the run-down housing estates on the fringes of Paris as the near-exclusive setting for *beur* protagonists (see Tarr 2005; Higbee 2007). However, unlike other films released since 2000 in which the Maghrebi-immigrant protagonists actively journey beyond the *banlieue* into new and unfamiliar spaces of *la France profonde*, or else attempt to reconnect with their Maghrebi-roots through a return to the bled (for example: *Ten'ja* (Hassan Legzouli, 2005); *Exils* (Tony Gatlif, 2004); *Bled Number One* (Rabah Ameur-Zaïmeche, 2006)), the spaces occupied by the protagonists of *La Graine et le mulet* are, precisely, settled and familiar. Kechiche thus emphasises the sedentary nature of the North African diaspora in France rather than its displacement, or a continuing search for place that dominates the narratives of so much Maghrebi-French and North African émigré filmmaking. Slimane's redundancy may well cause uncertainty for his extended family but Sète is their home and even the first generation of immigrants have no intention of leaving. Slimane thus politely entertains his sons' suggestions that he return to the *bled* (family home in the Maghreb) with his redundancy payment, though his actual response is to set up his own business (the couscous restaurant-boat moored in Sète), building a legacy for his children in France. In *La Graine et le mulet*, Slimane is thus offered far greater mobility than in earlier immigrant narratives in French cinema. He is able to move between the diasporic space of the Hotel de l'Orient, the multi-ethnic extended family home and the working class community within Sète, where he is clearly accepted as an insider. The film promotes a mobility and inclusion for the immigrant protagonist that is clearly lacking from *Dernier maquis*, though one that, as the suspicion and latent hostility of local restaurateurs to his couscous barge suggests, is not as unproblematic or idyllic as it might first appear.

DE ROUILLE ET D'OS

At first glance, the inclusion in this chapter of the Franco-Belgian production *De rouille et d'os*, co-written and directed by celebrated French filmmaker Jacques Audiard might strike the reader as something of an anomaly, given that the other two features are directed by French filmmakers who are themselves of (Maghrebi) immigrant origin and place an extended community of immigrants at the centre of their narrative. In contrast, *De rouille et d'os*, a loose adaptation/amalgamation of two stories found in a collection by the Canadian writer Craig Davidson (2005), is constructed around an unlikely and at times brutal love story that develops between Stéphanie (Marion Cotillard), a former orca trainer, who loses her legs in a freak accident at the aquarium and Ali (Matthias Schoenaerts), a selfish and unstable former boxer, who has drifted to the Antibes with his young son, Sam, in tow. The pair meet by chance while Ali (whose name, whether intentionally or not, cannot help but evoke that of the African-American boxer Muhammad Ali) is working in a nightclub as a bouncer. They then reconnect a short time later as Stéphanie struggles to come to terms with the psychological, physical and material consequences of orca attack in which she lost both her legs. In order to make ends meet, Ali is drawn into the shadowy world of bare-knuckle fighting (that takes place in the *terrain vague* on the outskirts of Antibes), while also working for an acquaintance who, as well as running the betting on his fights, installs clandestine surveillance equipment in supermarkets and outlet stores at the behest of the store managers. The equipment allows management to illegally spy on their workers, an activity that will lead Ali to be unwittingly responsible for his sister losing her job – fired on the spurious charge of 'stealing' out-of-date produce from the supermarket where she works as a cashier.

In spite of these clear differences in tone, focus and genre to the other two films analysed in this chapter, *De rouille at d'os* could nonetheless be classed in part as an immigrant narrative. Ali is Belgian, not French, and arrives in France to stay with his sister, Anna, who emigrated from the Low Countries some years earlier, eventually settling in Antibes. Little reference is made, however, to the fact that Ali is a Belgian immigrant. The observant viewer might notice a majority of Belgian number-plates on cars in the opening sequence of the film as Ali and Sam attempt to hitch a lift, and Ali mentions having won 'regional championships in Belgium' in an interview for a job as a security guard just over ten minutes into the film. The casting of Schoenaerts, a rising star of Belgian cinema, as Ali, further cements the link of his character to the Low Countries. However, none of the other characters refer to him specifically as an immigrant (nor does Ali define himself in this way) and he does not encounter the usual hostility or prejudice experienced by non-European immigrants. Similarly, there is no attempt in the film to construct a space of diasporic or immigrant community in the narrative (such as the Hotel de l'Orient in *La Graine et le mulet*). Moreover, as a white, European immigrant who speaks fluent French, Ali possesses characteristics that would normally qualify him in the French context as a quasi-insider and 'the right kind of migrant'. And yet, in other ways, Ali is clearly identified in the narrative as an outsider: an economic marginal and social misfit, involved in activities that are barely legal and whose behavior at times borders on the sociopathic. Ali is therefore poorly integrated into the 'host' society of the Antibes, occupying a position of alterity and deviance that, until the 1990s at least, was routinely assigned in French cinema to non-European or post-colonial immigrant protagonists.[8] In this context, it is telling that Audiard begins *De rouille et d'os* with an expository montage of Ali's journey from Belgium to the Antibes with Sam, showing father and son walking along the roadside, boarding a train, scavenging food left by other passengers on the long journey to the south of France and killing time near the beach in Antibes before finally being picked up and driven to Anna's modest home by her partner Richard (Jean-Michel Correia) – emphasising the significance of this journey for the incoming migrant.

In cine-spatial terms, the film shares some similarities with *La Graine et le mulet* in that its narrative takes place on the southern Mediterranean coast, in Antibes, an affluent city that, like Sète, relies as much on tourism and the service economy for its future as it does on industrial activity. When interviewed at the time of the film's release, Audiard suggested that the choice of location was a practical not artistic one – Antibes is the only French city with an aquarium housing killer whales – and that the film was not intended as 'an assault on the plushness of the Côte d'Azur' (Pulver 2012: np). *De rouille et d'os* nonetheless subverts the audience's preconceptions of the French Riviera as a site of glamour and affluence by highlighting the rundown apartments, ramshackle workshops and desolate waste-ground where Ali participates in bare-knuckle fights. This is not the Antibes of wealthy tourists, jetsetters and prosperous residents who live comfortably from the money that the service and leisure industries bring to the small city. Rather, the narrative of *De rouille et d'os* explores a parallel world that exists alongside the chic allure of the Riviera of poorly paid supermarket workers, edgy nightclubs where the threat of aggression and confrontation simmers beneath the surface, not to mention the excessive violence and criminality of the illegal fight network that Ali and (later) Stéphanie immerse themselves into. Certain elements of this world remain hidden from view: the bare-knuckle bouts are held at secret locations, while Ali and Martial (Bouli Lanners) visit stores in the dead of night to install clandestine surveillance equipment used to spy on workers. However, unlike in *Dernier maquis*, where the immigrant narrative unfolds in the exclusive location of the pallet yard, at other times in *De rouille et d'os* these two worlds come into deliberate and direct contact. A clear example of this encounter can be found in the scene where Ali encourages Stéphanie to swim in the sea for the first time since losing her legs. Ali takes Stéphanie to the beach where lines of sun loungers and parasols wait to pamper affluent tourists; a privileged leisure space that is quite different to the more modest surroundings of the beach where he meets his sister Anna later in the film to discuss regaining access to his son. Refusing to be intimidated by an environment that he would normally be excluded from due to his limited financial means, Ali slumps on one of the sun loungers after his swim, presumably without paying. As both economic marginal and immigrant Other, Ali (surprisingly) occupies this space of tourism, leisure and affluence without fear or prohibition. The beach in this scene functions less a point of contact between the visiting tourists and affluent residents of Antibes and the poor immigrant, and more a palimpsestic space in which the two groups co-exist without necessarily making any extended or meaningful contact. Like Slim in *La Graine et le mulet,* Ali is, moreover, a highly mobile character, able to navigate between the murky underworld of the illegal fight circuit and the more glamorous beachfront of Antibes. Again, this mobility is quite different from that found in other French films that deal with postcolonial or immigrant minorities, most obviously *banlieue* films of the 1990s, whose narrative are structured around exclusion or a lack of access to spaces beyond the deprived urban periphery. For example, both *La Haine* and *Raï* (key banlieue films from the mid-1990s) use prohibition or ejection from spaces of culture, capital or leisure (such as the art gallery or nightclub) as symbolic moments in the narrative that emphasise their youthful protagonists' status as victims of social exclusion (see Reader 1995: 13).

Whilst a film such as *La Graine et le mulet* uses its location to 'self-consciously … bring the normally invisible immigrant experience within the larger story of working class decline' (O'Shaughnessy 2015: 121), *De rouille et d'os* does little to promote either the sense of an immigrant narrative or a broader feeling of working class solidarity between the immigrant and host nation. Instead, Antibes is depicted as a soulless city inhabited for the most part by an atomised society of self-absorbed individuals. Ali repays the generosity and hospitality of his sister and her partner by working as a hired muscle for the illegal surveillance operation that will ultimately be used by the bosses to exploit and dispose of workers who are on already precarious employment contracts. Following her accident, Stéphanie spirals into depression and is quickly forgotten by her co-workers and fellow trainers at Marine Land (except for one reunion that she herself instigates) and is effectively left to rot in her sparse apartment until the arrival of Ali.

Indeed this is the very dramatic premise upon which the relationship between Stéphanie (a trainer at the aquarium but essentially little more than a cog in the leisure industry that drives the city's economy) and Ali, the immigrant outsider, is built. Following her accident, Stéphanie's status as a social and economic marginal is largely determined in the narrative by her disability – and ironically it is only by being drawn into the shady world of the illegal fighting syndicate, ultimately taking the place of Martial as Ali's manager and promoter when Martial is forced to flee Antibes following the discovery of his illegal surveillance racket, that she is able to reassert a sense of her own self-worth.

This idea of social fracture amongst the working-class in Antibes is further suggested by the techniques involved in much of the editing and cinematography in *De rouille et d'os*. Locations are rarely presented to us in their entirety but rather as fragmented spaces; the city is often viewed from the inside of vehicles or at night, with very few establishing shots to give any sense of location, place or community within the urban environment. Indeed, in the final analysis, it is only by 'escaping' from Antibes at the end of the film that, in the wake of Sam's near-fatal accident, Stéphanie, Ali and Sam can find some semblance of normality as a family unit as Ali attempts to resume his boxing career.

CONCLUSION

The aim of this chapter has been to consider how French cinema has explored new cinematic spaces in order to re-imagine the immigrant experience on French screens in the 2000s within what has been termed an interstitial cityspace. The three examples that have been selected as case studies offer distinct but connected approaches, suggesting that a more polycentric model is emerging, as immigrant protagonists are permitted to occupy a greater diversity of lived social spaces on screen. If *Dernier maquis* and *La Graine et le mulet* share a common aim to 'correct the neglect of the role of migration in the industrial history of modern France' (O'Shaughnessy 2015: 123), the representation of the spaces that the immigrant protagonists in these respective films inhabit arguably achieves markedly different results. The stylised and in some ways anti-realist isolation of the pallet yard in *Dernier maquis* seems to condemn the immigrant workers to a place that sits outside of any sense of belonging to a shared history of modern France, potentially negating the more productive exploration of class and religious difference found in the film. In contrast, *La Graine et le mulet* allows its immigrant protagonists (and their French-born descendants) to exist as fully integrated members of an extended working class community in Sète, while not denying or eliding ethnic, generation or gender difference, or, indeed, the pressures of neoliberalism and the deindustrialisation of Sète that threatens the continued existence of the very same working class community. In part, the greater integration of the immigrant protagonists in *La Graine et le mulet* is permitted, precisely, by the ability of Slimane to move between the different spaces (industrial, familial and diasporic) within the city. In *De rouille et d'os*, Ali, a far less 'visible' immigrant presence, is afforded a similar degree of mobility within the city of Antibes. Though in his case, rather than unifying the working class inhabitants, this movement is a potentially destructive force, exposing the extent of social fracture, even on the French Riviera. Finally, the significance of *La Graine et le mulet* and *De Rouille et d'os* is that they offer a new, more interstitial space between the 'world city' of Paris, or the 'symbolic economy' of the port of Marseilles as point of arrival and departure for successive waves of immigrants to France, and the provincial locations of films such as *Western* and *Drôle de Félix* where an unusual or unlikely location is employed to engineer a narrative space for the encounter between host nation and the immigrant protagonist.

NOTES

1   See, for example, *Les Ambassadeurs* (Naceur Ktari, 1976), *La Balance* (Bob Swaim, 1982), *Tchao pantin* (Claude Berri, 1983) and *Le Thé à la menthe* (Abdelkrim Bahloul, 1984).
2   Key examples of the 1990s *cinéma de banlieue* are: *Hexagone* (Malik Chibane, 1994), *La Haine* (Matthieu Kassovitz, 1995), *Raï* (Thomas Gilou, 1995) and *Ma 6-T va crack-er* (Jean-François Richet, 1997).
3   'Situer mon film là-bas me permettait de tendre vers l'autre rive, de regarder l'Afrique de l'autre côté. Marseille c'est une ville à l'intersection, comme moi qui suis à moitié arabe et à moitié français. C'est une ville très métissée.'
4   In contrast to Marseilles and Paris as prominent locations for immigrant

narratives, the economically depressed north (Nord-pas-de Calais) appears to emerge in films such as *La Vie de Jésus* (Bruno Dumont, 1997) and *La Vie rêvée des anges* (Erick Zonca, 1998) as a new space primarily for marginalised *white*, French youth. The exception in this region is the port of Calais, which, for obvious reasons has featured in both narrative and documentary feature film making focusing on immigrants and the politics of immigration in France (for an example of a narrative feature, see *Welcome* (Philippe Lioret, 2009), for a more recent example of this trend in French documentary, see the work of Sylvain George, *L'Impossible: pages arrachées* (2009) and *Qu'ils repose en révolte* (2010)). This location has emerged both due to the the acute socio-economic disadvantage within the region – Nord-pas-de-Calais has suffered consistent industrial decline as a result of the collapse of manufacturing industries, such as textiles, shortly after the second world war – as well as the increasing regional funding for film production that was made available in the 1990s and early 2000s In this way, both *La Vie de Jésus* and *La Vie rêvée des anges* received funding from the Nord-Pas-de-Calais region (Dumont was awarded a grant of 900,000 francs towards a total shooting budget of eight million francs). Although the combined budget offered by regional authorities for cinema production in the 1990s remained relatively small in relation to the total cost of film production in France (approximately two per cent) the significance of its input for first-time filmmakers, working on low budgets and with no bankable box-office reputation, cannot be discounted.

5   *Wesh-wesh* (2001) 63,997 spectators, France; *Bled number one* (2006) 68,010 spectators, France; *Dernier maquis* (2009) 29,021 spectators, France; *Les Chants de Mandrin* (2012), 12,601 spectators, France.

6   Comments made by Ameur-Zaïmeche in an interview contained on the French DVD release of *Dernier maquis*.

7   The proximity of the industrial estate to the outlying countryside and its location beneath a flight-path on the very extremities of the city, evoke the locations in iconic *banlieue* films such as *Hexagone* and, indeed Ameur-Zaïmeche's own debut feature *Wesh-wesh qu'est-ce qui se passe?* (2001).

8   For more on the representation of post-colonial minorities in French cinema of the 1980s and 1990s see Tarr (1997); for an updated survey of developments in the 2000s see Higbee (2015).

BIBLIOGRAPHY

Delorme, Stéphane (2007) 'Bateau ivre', *Cahiers du cinéma*, 629, 11–13.

Delorme, Stéphane and Jean-Michel Frodon (2007) 'Entretien avec Abdellatif Kechiche', *Cahiers du cinéma*, 629, 15–19.

Hannerz, Ulf (1996) *Transnational Connections: Culture, People, Places*, London and New York: Routledge.

Higbee, Will (2007) 'Re-Presenting the Urban Periphery: Maghrebi-French Filmmaking and the "Banlieue" Film', *Cineaste*, 33, 1, 38–43.

____ (2013) *Post-beur Cinema: North African Émigré and Maghrebi-French Filmmaking in France since 2000*. Edinburgh: Edinburgh University Press.

Jousse, Thierry and Jean-Marc Lalanne (1995) 'Bye-Bye. Propos de Karim Dridi', *Cahiers du cinéma*, 494, 39–41.

Kaganski, Serge (2007) '*Couscous*' [Review], *Les Inrockuptibles*, 12 December; http://www.lesinrocks.com/cinema/films-a-l-affiche/la-graine-et-le-mulet/

Naficy, Hamid (2001) *An Accented Cinema: Exilic and Diasporic Filmmaking*. Princeton: Princeton University Press.

Neyrat, Cyril (2008) 'Rabah, le patron', *Cahiers du cinéma*, 638, 20–2.

O'Shaughnessy, Martin (2015) 'Contemporary Political Cinema', in Alistair Fox, Michel Marie, Raphaëlle Moine and Hilary Radner (eds) *A Companion to Contemporary French Cinema*. Cambridge: Wiley-Blackwell, 117–33.

Pulver, Andrew (2012) 'Jacques Audiard: my work is like rolling thunder', *The Guardian*, 24 October; http://www.theguardian.com/film/2012/oct/24/jacques-audiard-interview-rust-bone

Reader, Keith (1995) 'After the Riot', *Sight and Sound*, 5, 11, 12–14.

Solà-Morales, Rubió Ignasi (1995) 'Terrain Vague', in Cynthia C. Davidson (ed.) *Anyplace*. Cambridge: MIT Press, 118–23.

Tarr, Carrie (1997) 'French cinema and post-colonial minorities', in Alec G. Hargreaves and Mark McKinney (eds) *Post-colonial cultures in France*. London: Routledge, 59–83.

____ (2005) *Reframing Difference: Beur and Banlieue Filmmaking in France*. Manchester: Manchester University Press.

Widemann, Dominique (2008) 'Rabah AmeurZaïmèche "Où se trouve mon dernier maquis?"', *L'Humanité*, 22 October; http://www.humanite.fr/node/38952

Zukin, Sharon (1997) *The Cultures of Cities*. Cambridge: Wiley-Blackwell.

SEOUL, BUSAN AND SOMEWHERE NEAR: KOREAN GANGSTER NOIR AND SOCIAL IMMOBILITY

JINHEE CHOI

In the late 1990s and 2000s, South Korean cinema emerged as one of the most commercially viable film industries in East Asia; domestically produced blockbusters such as *Gongdong gyeongbiguyeok* (*JSA*, Chan-wook Park, 1999), *Swiri* (*Shiri*, Je-gyu Kang, 2000), *Taegukgi hwinallimyeo* (*Taegukgi: The Brotherhood of War*, Je-gyu Kang, 2004) and *Gwoemul* (*The Host*, Joon-ho Bong, 2006) out-earned most Hollywood blockbusters competing for the same South Korean market share.[1] Gangster cinema was, and still is, one of the principal beneficiaries of this industry boom and has in turn helped to sustain it. It belongs to a broader hybrid category of *kkangpae* (gangster), *jopok* (organised criminal gang members) cinema – a discursive term that refers to films in which gangsters appear across a wide range of genres, including crime films, comedy, youth films and melodrama.

Although *Janggunui adeul* (*The General's Son*, Kwon-taek Im, 1990), set in colonial Seoul, reignited the trope of gangster patriotism that was popular in Korean *hwalgeuk* (action films) of the 1970s, it was *Geimui beopchik* (*Rules of the Game*, Hyeon-su Jang, 1994) that signalled the beginning of gangster cinema set in contemporary Seoul, followed by a film cycle that appeared in 1997: gangster/youth film *Biteu* (*Beat*, Sung-su Kim, 1997), gangster/comedy *Neombeo sseuri* (*No. 3*, Neunghwan Song, 1997) and gangster/crime film *Chorok mulgogi* (*Green Fish*, Chang-dong Lee, 1997). The popularity of *kkangpae, jopok* cinema peaked with the then-highest grossing film *Chingu* (*Friend*, Kyung-taek Kwak, 2001). Based on the director Kwak's semi-autobiographical story, *Friend* is set in Busan, his hometown. For the older generation, the film evoked a sense of nostalgia through its setting, fashion and music (see Shin 2005: 122), while for the younger generation it boasted 'cool' gangster iconography, codes of conduct and humour. Elsewhere, I have examined the industrial context – both local and regional – for the rising popularity of contemporary South Korean gangster cinema; that is, how local film producers in South Korea filled a market that was left open with the waning popularity of Hong Kong cinema and its reduced number of imports (see Choi 2010).

The Korean film industry has seen a resurgence of gangster and crime cinema since *Friend*: a noir cycle in 2005–6 including *Dalkomhan insaeng* (*A Bittersweet Life*, Jee-woon Kim, 2005), *Biyeolhan geori* (*A Dirty Carnival*, Ha Yoo [also spelled as Ha Yu] 2006), and *Sasaeng gyeoldan* (*Bloody Tie*, Ho Choi, 2006), which gave way to new crime action films in the 2010s such as *Ajeossi* (*The Man from Nowhere*, Jeong-beom Lee, 2010), *Hwanghae* (*The Yellow Sea*, Hong-jin Na, 2010), *Mujeokja* (*A Better Tomorrow*, Hae-seong Song, 2010), *Sinsegye* (*New World*, Hoon-jung Park, 2013) and *Yonguija* (*The Suspect*, Shin-yeon Won, 2013), which increasingly employ the ethnic other – Korean-Chinese and North Korean – in transnational spaces. In this chapter I will examine gangsters in urban and transnational spaces, focusing on the spatiality of two South Korean metropolises, Seoul and Busan. I will discuss how centripetal and centrifugal space operates simultaneously in these cities, arguing that the films offer a site to deal with the loss of individual agency and identity within the late capitalist system. In this regard, this chapter builds on Edward Dimendberg's approach in *Film Noir and the Spaces of Modernity* (2004), which discloses the centripetal and centrifugal dynamic through which characters are displaced in, and alienated from, urban space – specifically New York and Los Angeles, two prominent post-war Hollywood noir cities. Centripetal and centrifugal space, according to Dimendberg, could be characterised in terms of Henri Lefebvre's typology: spatial practices, spaces of representation, and representations of space (2004: 108). If centripetal urban space is conceived in terms of its density and visibility and is manifested through skyscrapers, monuments, landmarks and inner-city neighbourhoods, centrifugal space foregrounds the city's immateriality, invisibility and speed (2004: 177). The verticality of the urban core in centripetal space is replaced by the horizontal sprawl of suburbs in centrifugal space (2004: 176). If in the former the protagonist escapes through the invisibility provided by an urban crowd, in the latter one must have recourse to both transportation and communication technology that yield mastery of space and superior knowledge (2004: 178).

Dimendberg considers the film noir cycle animated by centripetal space, 'a compensatory response to the *actual* disappearance of older urban forms' (2004: 108; emphasis added). That is, the Hollywood noir cycle between 1939 and 1959 addresses as well as remedies the anxiety and discomfort that result from transformations in the metropolis by articulating fantasies about public space and engaging with problems of spatial orientation (2004: 114). One may make parallel observations on the relationship between the transformation of urban spaces in South Korea and the gangster/crime cycles that have emerged since the 2000s. During this period, Seoul underwent major reconstruction and renovation of the old city centre: the

Seoul Train Station, which was originally built in 1925, was renovated into a modern space in 2004 (see Song 2009: 26); in 2003–5, Cheonggyecheon, a stream that runs through the city and was covered and elevated into roads in the 1960s and '70s, was renovated to restore its original form under then Seoul Mayor Myung-bak Lee (see Lee *et al.* 2014); and the new city hall was completed in 2012, which arches over the original city hall (founded in 1926) from the colonial era (1910–45). Such physical transformation of urban space and spatial disorientation are important concerns for contemporary South Korean films. The second half of the art film *Kape neuwareu* (*Café Noir*, Sung-il Jung, 2009), for instance, unfolds against the newly renovated Cheonggye stream in downtown Seoul, registering the loss of lived experience of the stream (see Choi 2015). Nonetheless, my approach in this chapter departs from that of Dimendberg. Instead of postulating a causal connection between the emergence of the Korean noir cycle and the transformation of urban space – that is, the latter being a trigger of the former – I argue that the spatial configurations of Seoul and Busan employed in the Korean noir cycle is a response to social immobility – a major theme of South Korean gangster and noir films (see Choi 2010: 69) – rather than a reaction to the spatial anxiety caused by the urban development and transformation recently seen.

The protagonists in the Korean noir cycle are caught in complex layers of temporality and spatiality – the traditional and the modern, the past and the future, and the local and the transnational. Seoul and Busan typify the lifestyle of late modernity in these films, which become increasingly decentralised with characters constantly moving in and out of the city. Dimendberg's conceptual typology of centripetal and centrifugal space helps one to discern and locate the textual strategies that underscore the lack of agency in such relations. This chapter will delineate the spatial trajectories manifest in contemporary gangster and crime cinema, underlining conflicting forces – inward and outward as well as upward and downward – that govern characters' desires and wishes to trespass the social boundaries and yet constantly thwart and inhibit the satisfaction of such desires.

POST-WAR SEOUL, URBAN DEVELOPMENT AND CHEOLGEOCHON

Urbanity is a longstanding salient element of South Korean gangster cinema, and Seoul remains a primary locale. Myeongdong, an urban centre in the northern part of Seoul comparable to Shinjuku in Tokyo and Tsim Sha Tsui in Hong Kong, has provided an iconic space for numerous cycles of Korean gangster and action films of the 1960s and 1970s: *Myeongdong 44 beonji* (*44 Myeondong*, Yong-nam Go, 1965), *Myeongdong chulsin* (*A Native of Myeongdong*, Hyo-cheon Kim, 1969) *Myeongdong nosinsa* (*Old Gentleman in Myeongdong*, Hyo-cheon Kim, 1970), *Myeongdong bureuseu* (*Myeongdong Blues*, Ki-duk Kim, 1970) and the omnibus film *Myeongdong janhoksa* (*Cruel History of Myeongdong*, Byeon, Choe and Im, 1972). In contrast, the patriotic acts of Du-han Kim (1918–72), a real-life gangster-turned-politician, have been associated with Jongno, a district in Seoul where both Japanese and Korean merchants congregated during the colonial era (see J. Kim 2011: 70), as seen in *Silrok Kim Du-han* (*A True Story of Kim Du-han*, Hyo-cheon Kim, 1974) and *The General's Son* series (Im Kwon-taek, 1990–2). In contemporary Korean gangster cinema, Seoul provides a site that conditions and curtails gangsters' social aspirations. Gangsters are often represented as coming from the working class and/or from the provinces outside of Seoul, which is underscored by their provincial accents and dialects. The iconic working class home in South Korean cinema is epitomised by *cheolgeochon* – an area designated to be demolished for urban redevelopment, which attracts investors and corporations for quick turn-around in profit. Urban redevelopment is a principal trope in contemporary South Korean gangster cinema that either sets up narrative conflict or leads to the climax in such films as *Beat*, *Ddong gae* (*Mutt Boy*, Kyung-taek Kwak, 2003) and *Ddongpari* (*Breathless*, Ik-jun Yang, 2008).

In the 1960s and 1970s, the country witnessed the modernisation and expansion of living spaces in the capital city. The Korean War (1950–3) swept through Seoul, with over seventy per cent of houses being completely destroyed in the central city, especially in the Jung-gu and Yongsan-gu areas (see Jeon *et al.* 2009: 157). Although the government attempted to rebuild the city shortly after the war, primarily relying on foreign subsidies and resources provided by the Civil Relief in Korea and the United Nations Korean Reconstruction Agency, it was during the First Five-year Economic Development Plan (1962–6) that the so-called 'modern' housing, epitomised by the apartment complex built in Mapo area, began to emerge (2009: 189, 192). But the rapid construction of apartments also brought about unwelcome consequences, such as the collapse of an apartment building in the Wau complex in 1970, with 33 people killed and many more injured (2009: 207). The 1970s marked the era of suburbanisation of Seoul, during which large-sized 'luxury' high-rises were built in the areas below the Han river, and the middle class was lured to move to Gangnam (literally meaning south of the river) with government led efforts to provide the infrastructure necessary for the creation of new habitats; bridges were built that would ease travel from central Seoul to the newly developing areas in Gangnam, and prestigious junior high and high schools were relocated to the south of the river (2009: 212). In 1976–9, the Hyundai Development Company constructed over three thousand apartments in Apgucheong, and Hyundai remains a brand identified with the high-end apartment complexes in Gangnam (2009: 223–4).

Gangnam 1970 (*Gangnam Blues*, Ha Yoo, 2015) the final instalment of Yoo's 'street' trilogy, along with *Maljukgeori janhoksa* (*Once Upon a Time in High School*, 2004) and *A Dirty Carnival* (2006), revisits the history of, and the politics behind, the expansion of the Gangnam area in the 1970s. An establishing aerial view of Gangnam prior to its development as an affluent urban centre of Seoul – when it was merely an undeveloped greenfield without any architecture or buildings – is followed by a shot of secret service agent Kim and civil servant Mun, who contemplate the space as the next 'capital'. The aerial view, although that of Gangnam prior to its development into an urban centre, signals both the 'disciplinary society' that would 'order in time' and 'distribute in space' (Deleuze 1992: 2; cited in Dimendberg 2004: 83) and the transposition of the spectator from the government authorities' 'delimited synoptic view' to the gangsters in the 'dark street corners, alleyways, and other relatively inaccessible interior spaces' (Dimendberg 2004: 69). As the film unfolds, it heavily relies on and conforms to the spectator's foreknowledge of the geography and future significance of the now well-known areas in Gangnam: Apgujeong, Yeoksam and Jamsil. The spatiality of Seoul is replaced by a representation of Seoul – a map of the city – which is used for a briefing about a development plan and provides a backdrop for the characters' conversation. Two orphans, Jong-dae and Yong-gi, who grew up together, are separated when they become accidently involved in a gang hired to disrupt a political rally held in Seoul; both subsequently become involved in the criminal underworld. Jong-dae facilitates the illegal acquisition of land for the development of real estate in Gangnam for various parties including Madam Min and a politician, Seo, while Yong-gi does the dirty work for other politicians, and in return is placed in charge of a nightclub in Myeongdong. Behind the backs of their respective bosses, the two collaborate to eliminate a rival gang, led by Jang. In their secret rendezvous in Gangnam, Yong-gi shouts '*ddang* (land) Jong-dae, *don* (money) Yong-gi', which neatly sums up their shared desire to escape their childhood poverty and accumulate wealth but through different means (see Park 2016).

The given reason for Jong-dae and Yong-gi becoming involved in the illegal gang activity had to do with their loss of an illegal wooden shanty house, emphasising the cyclical nature of violence – that is, the violence inflicted on their innocent selves and subsequent recourse to violence in order to either disrupt or reinforce the existing hierarchy. The film casts a sceptical outlook on the authoritarian hierarchy, materialism and pseudo-familism that had formed a 'developmentalist mentalité' (see Kang 2011) in the dictatorship era and still governs contemporary Korean society. Myungkoo Kang notes that the hierarchical structure of both South Korean governmental and gang organisations not only demands complete compliance and obedience from their subordinates, but also requires exclusivity; no one from outside could intervene in the action or stop the violence – if possible, one can do so only momentarily. Kang further pays attention to the fact that class-consciousness in the second half of the twentieth century developed along the idea of 'rank' in terms of material wealth accumulated (2011: 181). As a result, Kang continues, individualism in South Korea manifests itself in a 'strong self-defensive' propensity; thus 'instead of rational and self-reliant individuals, excessive, rugged individualism prevails' (2011: 182). Yong-gi decides to disobey his boss, Yang, and betray his friendship with Jong-dae in the name of self-preservation, yet his actions have more to do with his desire for So-jeong, the boss's girlfriend. The gangster narrative in contemporary Korean cinema does not allow such a transgression, and characters driven by egoistic desire are punished by death, either intended or accidental. Such an individual character provides a sharp contrast to the patriotic collectivism associated with the gangster-protagonist working against the colonial authority in such a film as *The General's Son*.

Constant urban (re)development, both below and above the Han river, and the emergence of several satellite cities around Seoul in the 1990s and Pangyo in the 2010s, have kept the city of Seoul in a constant state of demolition and construction, yet with chances for upward social mobility forestalled due to increasing economic insecurity and youth underemployment during the economic crisis (see Song 2009: 17–19). In the 1990s, Ilsan was developed along with four other satellite cities (Bundang, Pyeongchon, Sanbon and Jungdong) to alleviate soaring housing prices in the capital (see Jeon *et al.* 2009: 283). *Green Fish* (1997) touches upon the displacement of the male protagonist Mak-dong in a newly developed suburb of Seoul. After having been discharged from his military duty, Mak-dong witnesses the disappearance of the familiar landscape of his hometown, Ilsan, which now serves as a satellite city located to the north of Seoul, and further experiences the disintegration of his family as a result.

In the 'noir' cycle of 2005–6 – *A Bittersweet Life* (2005), *A Dirty Carnival* (2006) and *Bloody Tie* (2006) – urban space becomes more pronounced as the filmmakers are more conscious of its specificity as well as its construction. In the remainder of this chapter, I will examine how the theme of social immobility is manifest in this cycle, with a focus on the spatiality of Seoul and Busan. 'Noir' is certainly an illusive term, yet the films that will be discussed are classified both as noir and crime films in both critical and academic discourses in South Korea. *A Bittersweet Life* and *Bloody Tie* were advertised as 'hard-boiled noir' in the Korean film industry (see Choi 2010: 75–6) as well as discussed as 'noir' in academic discourse (see Lee 2014); whereas *A Dirty Carnival* along with *Green Fish* are examined as 'crime' films, despite the fact that, as Yong-kwon Chung claims, both share the conventions of the Korean gangster 'noir' of the 1990s: organised crime, urban space (Seoul in particular), gangster iconography (night clubs, outfits, sunglasses) and noir-esque visual aesthetics (2008: 355–6). The term 'noir' is used in this chapter to further underline the continuity between Korean gangster cinema and Hollywood noir in their spatial configurations.

GANGSTER, URBAN SPACE AND SOCIAL IMMOBILITY

Set in contemporary Seoul, *A Dirty Carnival* features a complex and ultimately tragic web of relationships among four characters: local hoodlum Byeong-du, his boss Mr. Hwang, his childhood friend-turned-screenwriter Min-ho and the object of his infatuation Hyeon-ju. The underprivileged status of the protagonists, who are usually uneducated and/or transposed from a rural to an urban space, is signalled through their dialect and living environments. Both Byeong-du's mother and Byeong-du speak with an accent, hinting at their provincial background. Byeong-du's speech, however, oscillates between Jeonla dialect and *pyojunmal* (standard Korean), depending upon whom he interacts with. When he gives commands, his accent is more pronounced. Further, Byeong-du's family is about to be evicted from home, as it is designated as part of a redevelopment area.

The film begins with Byeong-du bailing out his adolescent younger brother. The absence of his father, along with his sick mother and younger adolescent siblings, situates Byeong-du as a surrogate father to his family. His responsibility to be the breadwinner for his 'family' – both his kin and gangster family – brings forward Byeong-du's conflicting loyalties. The paradoxical nature of gangster violence is easily detected when violence is directed not only toward the privileged upper class within the system – i.e. Byeong-du's murder of corrupted lawyer Bak – but also toward the lower classes like himself, who must abandon his home for the sake of corporate profits. The 'sponsor' (or patron) figure that gangsters are in desperate need of in order to run their business further demarcates the relationship between the two as parasitic. Byeong-du serves to maintain and reinstate the social hierarchy that is already in place, into which he painstakingly hopes to fit but will never be fully accepted in given his social and educational background. As Byeong-du promises to collect the contracts that will grant his boss Hwang the right to build high rises from the current tenants in the *cheolgeochon* area, we see a shot of the two standing on the hill looking over the lot that is soon to be bulldozed. The site is a reminder of the poverty from which Byeong-du and his family have just recently escaped. The cramped spaces in *cheolgeochon* will soon disappear, replaced by another form of urban density, a generic cityscape of homogeneous high-rise buildings. The contemplation of Hwang and Byeong-du on the prospect of this site occupies a moment between 'the modern as "yet-to-come" and the urban past as "yet-to-be-destroyed"' (Dimendberg 2004: 91).

Despite corporate dependence on criminality to execute redevelopment plans, violence is pushed either to the city's edge – dark tunnels, back streets and *cheolgeochon* – or outside the city – a nameless mountain or an isolated hut in a desolate field. In metropolitan Seoul – nightclubs, arcades and karaoke bars – gangsters are endlessly consumed and replaced, but have no place to belong or hide. During a melodramatic moment when Byeong-du is about to propose to Hyeon-ju, he is chased by police in front of Yeongpung mungo, a mega-bookstore located in Jongro. Instead of running outward to the streets in order to lose the police, Byeong-du escapes 'into' the bookstore, running through its aisles. The bookstore becomes a microcosm of the city, where bookshelves partition the space like the narrow alleys of the city. This chase ironically underscores the changed status of gangsters and their position in the city, given the fact that Jongro used to be the urban core that 'belonged' to, and was protected by, Korean gangsters as in *The General's Son*. In *A Dirty Carnival*, Byeong-du, who is betrayed by his own boss, is herded into the urban core – a space of the past.

Byeong-du's plan to eliminate his friend Min-ho, who incorporated in his film the story of Byeong-du's murdering the lawyer Bak, fails, as Byeong-du is attacked by a rival gang as well as betrayed by his own henchmen in a parking lot. Beaten and stabbed, Byeong-du crawls along the creek with his back to the cityscape that is glimpsed yet slowly disappearing in the background. A high angle shot of Byeong-du's body collapsing in front of his subordinates inversely mirrors a low angle shot of Byeong-du looking up toward the high-rise apartment building earlier in the film. Byeong-du tries to embarrass a debtor businessman, by shouting his name and flat number from outside, before he literally invades his private space to threaten him and his family and collect his debt; a sign of Byeong-du's determination and wish to go up the social ladder. Byeong-du's body is buried on a small hill in the snow, with his identity and credit cards, as well as the photos tossed into burning flames; his desire to protect his family and yearning for the beginning of a new family with Hyeon-ju vanishing with his death.

Although some scenes in *A Dirty Carnival* are filmed in Seoul, including the arcade in Cheonho-dong and the Yeongpung bookstore (mostly the interior), the spaces in the film are abstract in the sense that they are generically identified rather than conveying the specificity or texture of each space: *cheolgeochon*, the modern luxury home of president Hwang, Min-ho's unidentifiable flat, Byeong-du's generic office in the city and the unnamed parking lot where Byeong-du faces death.[2] *A Bittersweet Life* shows more sensitivity towards the spaces of Seoul, and was indeed shot during the period when the downtown of Seoul was undergoing a major change – the renovation of Cheonggye stream. Yet as the film progresses, the city slowly disappears to the background and becomes generic, as the protagonist, Seon-u, increasingly loses his agency.

Seon-u receives an order from his boss, Kang, to spy on his young mistress Hui-su while he is away for a business trip in Shanghai. As Seon-u tails her, we see the landmarks of Seoul – the streets and architecture around the Kwanghwamun area, including the Sejong Centre for the Performing Arts. Exterior spaces are sombre and empty, and the night of the city is less than vibrant, perhaps reflecting the economic downturn at the time as well as defamiliarising the cityscape. Susie Jie Young Kim characterises this cityscape as a space of passage despite its landmarks; 'it is meant to be passed by – and driven by', devoid of any human presence (2010: 125). As Dimendberg notes, 'the most striking feature of centrifugal space remains its frequently *nonarchitectural* character', in which landmarks may exist within centrifugal space, but only as 'remnants of an older spatiality [that] do not capture its specific identity' (2004: 178).

Seon-u constantly moves within and between these spaces, either on foot or in a moving vehicle. His mobility, be it vertical or horizontal, does not guarantee his freedom or agency. After he impressively fights against local hoodlums in an underground club, we see Seon-u swiftly returning to La Dolce Vita, the sky lounge and bar on the top floor of the same hotel. He reports to his boss that they will close the place for the night. Seon-u finishes his espresso and stands by the glass window checking himself out via his reflection in the window, which is overlayed onto the beautiful cityscape by night. However, his mastery of space and vertical movement from the bottom floor to the top is illusory – perhaps even an apparition – as there is a cut to show Seon-u in this space the very moment after the climatic gun battle in La Dolce Vita. The film concludes by prolonging this earlier shot of Seon-u – when he appreciates a moment of tranquillity after drinking a shot of espresso – but this time showing him shadowboxing in front of the glass window. Traces of individuality slowly disappear into the dark mechanism of criminality and are absorbed into and by the city, as the lights of the buildings outside are turned off one by one as the end credits roll.

We never learn the background of Seon-u, but his loss of agency is further tied to his spatial displacement in addition to his unconscious rebellion against his boss via an infatuation with Hui-su. After listening to Hui-su's performance at a recording studio, which marks a psychological turning point for Seon-u, he offers her a ride but she refuses. Seon-u returns to Hui-su at the studio after paying a visit to the sky lounge in order to confront Mr. Baek and Mun-seok. He walks to her direction with the camera first leading and then following him, but quickly retreats at the sight of Hui-su's secret boyfriend approaching her. The continuous horizontal movement toward and away from her nicely embodies both his desire toward her and her unavailability as the object of his desire. Such horizontal figure movement rhymes with that of Seon-u after his return to Seoul after he has been tortured in someplace near. He meets up with his subordinate Min-gi in a construction site near the hotel. Seon-u, with a close-up view of his feet or with a full shot of his entire body, is seen to walk from screen left to right towards Min-gi. As the two face each other, Seon-u expresses his determination to 'go all the way down' for his revenge. A subsequent mobile shot links the entrance of the hotel to the nearby construction site from which Seon-u looks down, then arcs around Seon-u to show him against the abstract grids of the hotel building in the background and construction skeletons in the middle. First the vertical, then followed by the horizontal camera movement in the shot underscores the two dominant spatial vectors of centripetal and centrifugal space, and here Seon-u's view connotes less visual mastery than his spatial displacement, removed from a place where he once worked and belonged, and his place within the rigid social hierarchy.

Seon-u's apparent agency and mobility in the first third of the film is, then, confined to the roles allotted by his boss within the rigid strata of their gangster organisation. Seon-u's small apartment, with its minimalistic and monochromatic interior, is in sharp contrast with his workplace – the sky lounge with its high contrast and vibrant red accenting. The familiar space becomes uncanny, as Seon-u's flat is suddenly occupied by South Asian workers, whom Seon-u had spotted in a convenience store, attacking him. Seon-u is ultimately transposed from a fish market storehouse, to a warehouse and finally to an archaic office, for torture, punishment and an illegal arms deal – taken further and further away from the urban centre. The apparent specificity of Seoul is counterbalanced by these enigmatic 'timeless' spaces

Fig. 1 Seon-u against abstract grids of urban space (*A Bittersweet Life*, Jee-woon Kim, 2005).

(Kim 2010: 130), and Seon-u's revenge sets him on a return journey back to Seoul, rendering the urban space both centrifugal then centripetal.

If the Hollywood noir cycle of the 1940s and 1950s depicted the decline of urban core and addressed anxieties about suburbanisation and decentralisation, in both *A Dirty Carnival* and *A Bittersweet Life* the transformation of Seoul is registered but, more importantly, functions to underscore a character's desire for social upward mobility, that is, a character's very social identity and marginality are substantiated and signalled by his connection to and/or disconnection from the city (Kim 2010: 128). It may be true that compared to *A Dirty Carnival*, *A Bittersweet Life* is more self-reflexive in its use of city space, while *A Dirty Carnival* self-consciously reveals the paradoxical relationships existing between the romanticised gangster prototype and the Korean film industry, which is suggested through Byeong-du's relationship with screenwriter Min-ho, who exploits Byeong-du's personal story, shared with Min-ho in confidence, for the purpose of achieving his own individual fame and financial gain. Nonetheless, in both films the city is very much tied to class stratification and social immobility and violence is used to stir up the order (although momentarily).

Since the box office success of *Friend* in 2001, Busan has emerged as another or even more prominent locale than Seoul in contemporary gangster cinema. Busan offers an emotional setting for the films directed by Kwak, a native of the city. Kwak's *Friend* and *Sarang* (*A Love*, 2007) feature the city, with its protagonists conversing in the local dialect. Due to its proximity to the sea and neighbouring Japan, Busan further adds verisimilitude to drug trafficking activities. Busan underscores the negative consequences of late modernity in films such as *Bloody Tie* and *A Better Tomorrow* (Song Hae-sung, 2010). In *A Better Tomorrow*, which is a Korean remake of *Ying hung boon sik* (*A Better Tomorrow*, John Woo, 1986), two brother escapees from North Korea are relocated to Busan. Whether the protagonists wish to lead a 'normal' life or ascend the social ladder, in gangster cinema Busan connotes the distance, both physical and metaphorical, from where they hope to be or belong. In *Friend*, Sang-taek, who Jun-seok envies, moves to Seoul to attend university. In *A Love*, when

In-ho is invited by a corporate president to work for him, the licence plate protrudes in the foreground, informing the viewer of In-ho's next destination: Seoul. In Seoul, In-ho and Mi-ju enjoy momentary freedom, succumbing to their mutual attraction and driving through the orange Dong-ho Bridge that links Apgujeong and Oksu. While looking over the cityscape, the couple reminisce about their adolescent hardships in Busan.

The spatial shift from Seoul to Busan as a salient film location is further facilitated by the local government's effort to lure and host filmmaking to the city. With the establishment of local governance in 1995 and the inauguration of the Busan International Film Festival in 1996, over 260 feature films were shot in Busan in the 2000s (see Anon. 2010). Founded in 1999, the Busan Film Commission has been awarding a support fund since 2001, first loaning out production equipment and now even providing post-production facilities via the AZworks post-production company, a co-venture by the commission and the Seoul-based company HFR. The historical significance of Busan, however, has been two-fold: geographical and industrial (see Ahn 2012: 35–6). As a port city, Busan faces Japan across the Korea Strait, and thanks to its geographical advantage it had been in demand for trade by Japan for many centuries, prior to its annexation in 1910. During the Yusin period (1972–9), when the Constitution was amended to provide then-president Chung-hee Park with complete control over parliament, an industrial belt was formed that extended to the north and west of Busan. During the Third Five-Year Economic Development Plan (1972–76), the six target industries – heavy machinery at Changwon, steel at Pohang, shipbuilding at Okpo, electronics at Kumi, petrochemicals at Yeoncheon, and nonferrous metals at Onsan (H. Kim 2011: 28) – were promoted, yet only one of the six went to the southwest, Yeoncheon, favouring then president Park's home region, Gyeongsang over Jeonla (also spelled as Jolla) province, which yielded an uneven industrial development between the south-western and south-eastern parts of the country (see Cumings 1997: 326). And the political tension between the two provinces escalated even further with the Gwangju uprising on 18 May 1980 that demanded not only the freedom of their political leader Dae-jung Kim but also the fair share of economic growth (cited in Lie 1998: 121). When Chun's military regime suppressed the demonstration by killing hundreds of civilians along with students and activists; it was reported that by the third day of the demonstration on 21 May, five hundred hundred people had already died and over nine hundred were missing (Cumings 1997: 377). The cultural significance of Busan, as the hub of the international film festival and production, came about only in the last two decades.

Busan not only provides the setting or locale for gangster films but also for films across genres, and filming locations have become tourist attractions advertised along with the film festival. The disaster film *Haeundae* (*The Tidal Wave*, Je-kyun Yoon (also known as JK Youn), 2009) shows the city of Busan being washed away by a tsunami. A national epic, *Gukjesijang* (*Ode to My Father*, Je-kyun Yoon, 2014) depicts a family who fled from North Korea during the Korean War and settled in Busan.

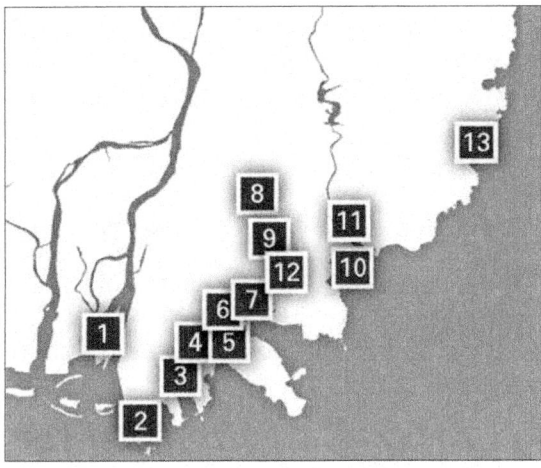

Fig. 2 **1: Uelsuk Island** – *Yeopgijeokin Geunyeo* (*My Sassy Girl*, 2001), *Maeumi* (*Hearty Paws*, 2006); **2: Dadaepo Beach** – *Taepung* (*Typhoon*, 2005), *Yeuieopneun geotdeul* (*No Mercy for the Rude*, 2006); **3: Gamcheon Port** – *Bloody Tie* (2006), *Beutipul sseondei* (*Beautiful Sunday*, 2007), *Nimeun meongote* (*Sunny*, 2008), *The Yellow Sea* (2010). **4: Gamcheon-2-dong** – *Hieoro* (*Hero*, 2007), *Mai nyu pateuneo* (*My New Partner*, 2008), *Nebeoending seutori* (*Never Ending Story*, 2011). **5: Jungang-dong Munhwa-kwangwang Tema (Theme) Street** – *Fun Movie* (2002), *Haryu insaeng* (*Low Life*, 2004), *Jeonuchi* (*Woochi*, 2009). **6: Choryang-dong Sanghae Street**: *Oldeuboi* (*Oldboy*, 2003). **7: Beomil-5-dong**: *Friend* (2001), *Gangjeok* (*Les formidables*, 2006), *The Man from Nowhere* (2010). **8: Sajik Baseball Stadium**: The Tidal Wave (2009). **9: Jeonpo-2-dong**: *Bakjwi* (*Thirst*, 2009). **10: Kwangan Bridge**: *Radio seuta* (*Radio Star*, 2006), *Insadong seucandeul* (*Insadong Scandal*, 2009), *The Tidal Wave* (2009). **11: Centeom City**: *Ulhakgyo iti* (*Our School ET*, 2008), *Mubangbi dosi* (*Open City*, 2008), *Gut moning peurejideonteu* (*Good Morning President*, 2009), *Budang georae* (*The Unjust*, 2010). **12: Munhyeon-dong Andongne**: *1 beongaui gijeok* (*Miracle on 1st Street*, 2007), *Madeo* (*Mother*, 2009), *Pureun sogeum* (*Hindsight*, 2011). **13: Gijang Daebyeonhang**: *Friend* (2001), *Bokmyeon dalho* (*Highway Star*, 2007), *Aeja* (*Goodbye Mom*, 2009) (Yu 2011).

However, the spaces of Busan in some of these films, including *My Sassy Girl*, *Thirst* and *The Man from Nowhere*, function as no more than filmed locations with their specificities erased. In contrast, *Bloody Tie* foregrounds the spatiality of Busan. A rapid montage sequence of news headlines presents Busan as a contradictory site that, following the 1997 economic crisis, has become a place where residents suffer from, as well as foster, illicit activities. Following the opening sequence, the voice-over narration of the low-life drug dealer Sang-do introduces Yeonsan-dong – a district of Busan with hundreds of saloons, nightclubs and arcades – where he works as a middleman delivering narcotics to customers with divergent backgrounds. The aerial shot of darkly lit Busan is followed by the credit sequence. Mostly shot on location, except for a few built sets for the police station and the office of drug lord Jang, the film fully takes advantage of the spatiality of Busan.

The film unfolds against landmarks across Busan – Busan Bridge, Yongdusan Park, Choryang Texas, Daedongsumun, Gamcheon Port – and features local performers and extras who command the 'correct' accent, as if the film asserts the local identity of Busan over the generic settings that the city provided for so many recent films shot in the region. Unlike Seoul, Busan has sprawled more laterally. Seoul has two major 'centres' – one above and the other below the Han river (Jung-gu and Gangnam-gu, respectively) – with its suburbs and satellite cities sprawling concentrically (see Nelson 2000: 40), while districts in Busan have developed along the seashore. However, the film successfully creates a sense of entrapment, by alternating

Fig. 3 A Tati-esque shot of the roundabout (*Bloody Tie*, Choi, 2006).

a few main sites between Namjeon-dong *daldongne* (shanty town), Yeonsan-dong and the port. Detective Do is eager to catch the drug lord, Jang, who is responsible for the death of Do's partner. Detective Do describes his relationship with Jang as a carousel, from which neither party can descend until the music ends. A Tati-esque shot of a roundabout, in which the vehicle of Do and Sang-do circles around in order to trail Jang's henchman Yong-nam, nicely captures both the entrapment and the vicious circle established among the characters.

The South Sea may provide an easy way in for illegal substances and migrant workers, but for the protagonists there is no easy way out. The open sea does not offer the possibility of escape but instead functions as an impasse; the new community is trapped by the ocean while the old Busan was serviced by it. Early in the film, when Sang-do refuses to cooperate, Detective Do and his assistant threaten to push Sang-do off Busan Bridge and into the sea. Indeed, the 'accidental' death of Sang-do takes place at Gamcheon port along the sea. The two anti-heroes – Sang-do and Detective Do – are visually trapped against the sea, as they are shot through the iron grids that demarcate the port from the street. The apocalyptic imagery – the explosion of a van, the fences and the menacing look of the ships in the background – signals an unwelcome ending. Sang-do hides on a ship when being chased by Detective Do. Despite Do's effort to prevent Sang-do from escaping and save his life, Sang-do is shot by another detective from a far. As Sang-do's dead body falls into the sea then floats to the surface, the camera plunges into the water, circles around the corpse, and glides out over the sea on which the dim city lights in the far background leave their trace reflections.

With the emergence of 'noir' as both a cycle and a marketing strategy (see Choi 2010: 75–6), urban space in South Korean noir films is pronounced and 'promoted' for its specificity. The effort results in a growing awareness of space as an actant in the Barthesian sense and fosters a mode of filmmaking that 'reveals practices of representing and inhabiting space' (Dimendberg 2004: 11). As Dimendberg insightfully notes, such filmmaking can be both 'a symptom and a catalyst of spatial transformation' by constructing and creating 'common spatial fantasies and anxieties' (2004: 12). Subsequent gangster and crime films set in Busan, such as *Beomjoewaui jeonjaeng* (*Nameless Gangster: Rules of the Game*, Jong-bin Yun, 2012) and *New World* (2013) further explore such a perception of Busan, albeit less attention is given to its spatiality.

CODA – WHERE IS THE YELLOW SEA?

During the 2010s, gangster and noir cinema were followed and/or replaced by a cycle of crime films that evoke the transnational imaginary and spatiality: *The Yellow Sea* (Hong-jin Na, 2010), *Bereullin* (*The Berlin File*, Seung-wan Ryu, 2013) and *The Suspect* (2013), all of which feature either ethnic Korean or North Korean characters as protagonists. *The Yellow Sea*, a 2010 sophomore feature directed by Na, signals this trend and expands the space across the Yellow Sea for its crime action. Addicted to gambling and feeling bitter about his now-estranged wife who left him for work in South Korea, Gu-nam, a *joseonjok* (ethnic Korean-Chinese), takes up an offer from local mobster Myeon-ga to kill a man named Seung-hyeon in Seoul. In exchange, Gu-nam will be excused of his outstanding debts. Seung-hyeon, however, is killed in front of Gu-nam's eyes, and Gu-nam is then chased by multiple parties including the police; Tae-won, who is responsible for the death of Seung-hyeon; and Myeon-ga, who betrays Gu-nam and helps Tae-won to track him down. The film takes multiple routes and turns in terms of both its narrative and tone, as Gu-nam travels from Yeonbyeon in China, arrives in Ulsan, travels to Seoul, hides in Hwacheon and Busan, and then flees to Incheon, during which he chases his estranged wife, the brokers that tricked him and the person who originally ordered Myeon-ga to murder Seung-hyeon.

The entire nation becomes the site for the clashes between the rural, the urban and the transnational, as well as those between varying ethnicities and conflicting individual desires. The spectator is as disoriented as the characters, whose sole means of survival is to kill before being killed. Gu-nam's unwavering goal of finding his estranged wife further complicates his spatial trajectory. Despite the spatial disorientation, disparate spaces are connected through technology, especially television broadcasting. Dimendberg makes a similar observation on the use of technology in his analysis of *Plunder Road* (Hubert Cornfield, 1957). That is, the simultaneity of centrifugal space in the film is thematised through the use of communication technology – the radio broadcasts that accompany the criminals during their escape (2004: 228). In a similar manner, it is on the television news that Gu-nam discovers that his wife, as he has suspected, has been having an affair with, and was murdered by, a South Korean fish merchant.

If in *The Yellow Sea*, the country becomes the proving ground for endless chases, forming a centrifugal space, *The Suspect* effectively utilises the spaces of Seoul, such as Yongsan Electronics Market and a residential area in Oksu-dong, to create a centripetal space despite the protagonist Dong-cheol's transnational background of having served as a North Korean secret agent. Betrayed by his own government, Dong-cheol defected to the South and has worked as a chauffeur for corporate head Bak, who is murdered in the beginning of the film. Repeated alternations between the bird-eye views of the city and the shots of Dong-cheol's gliding through the urban space via either driving or running throughout the film, emphasise the sense of surveillance as he is wrongly accused of Bak's murder and chased by the South Korean agents. Yet, ironically Dong-cheol outwits them in major chase sequences, thanks to his experience as the chauffeur for Bak and *dari unjeon* (driver-for-hire) for drunken customers who wish to go home in their own vehicles after heavy drinking.

In these two films, Seoul (or the entire nation-state) is rendered as a transnational space, which may allude to the fact that South Korea has become a globalised country due to its transnational investments and the resulting economic inter-dependence among nation-states; and that the number of foreign nationals living and working in South Korea has more than tripled in the last decade since 2006, accounting for 3.4 percentage of the registered population in 2015 (see Eom 2015). Yet its cinematic rendering runs the risk of othering ethnic minorities. Kim notes, albeit in a different context, 'the renewed interest in identifying China or North Korea as South Korea's ethnic Other helps to shore up national identity in the South rather than diminishing it' (K. H. Kim 2011: 121).

The typology proposed here – gangsters in urban and transnational spaces – nicely captures both the shifts in salient settings and filming locations and the changing status of gangster heroes and anti-heroes within these spaces. However, I do not wish to suggest an 'evolution' of gangster cycles that corresponds to a teleological trajectory of postcolonial modernity and transnational capitalism. Rather, I have examined how gangster and crime cycles quickly respond to both public perception and industry need in their habituation and incorporation of changing spatiality within the conventions of the genre. The spatial trajectory in the films discussed, in fact, is tightly associated with social immobility rather than apparent physical mobility and individual agency, however limited.

NOTES

1 In this chapter, for the romanisation of Korean character names, film titles and locations I follow the Revised Romanisation of Korean issued by Ministry of Culture and Tourism in 2000. In the case of proper names, such as directors, are retained more commonly and widely circulated forms; for instance Chan-wook Park, instead of Chan-uk Bak.
2 In the commentary that accompanies the DVD release of the film, director Yoo states that the *cheolgeochon* scene was shot in In-cheon, a sea port city east of Seoul, Hwang's house in Bundang, a suburb of Seoul and the parking lot in Namyangju.

BIBLIOGRAPHY

Ahn, Soo Jeong (2012) *The Pusan International Film Festival, South Korean Cinema and Globalization*. Hong Kong: Hong Kong University Press.

Anon. (2010) 'Small land, Big Biz: Film Commissions from Seoul to Busan Nurtured Production and Post', *Variety*, 31 October, 10, 4: A4.

Choi, Jinhee (2010) *The South Korean Film Renaissance: Local Hitmakers, Global Provocateurs*. Middletown: Wesleyan University Press.

____ (2015) 'Seoul Flâneur: *Breathless* and *Café Noir*', *The Journal of Japanese and Korean Cinema*, 7, 1, 57–72.

Chung, Yong-kwon (2008) 'Hanguk beomjoeyeonghwaeseo dosi, kajok, gyegeupui munje – Chorok mulgogiwa Biyeolhan georireul jungsimeuro' (Family, Urban Space and the Problem of Family in Korean Crime Films – Focusing on *Green Fish* and *A Dirty Carnival*), *Yeonghwa yeongu* [*Film Studies*], 38, 391–420.

Cumings, Bruce (1997) *Korea's Place in the Sun: A Modern History*. New York: W.W. Norton.

Deleuze, Gilles (1992) 'Postscript on the Societies of Control', *October*, 59, 3–7.

Dimendberg, Edward (2004) *Film Noir and the Spaces of Modernity*. Cambridge: Harvard University Press.

Eom, Sung-won (2015) 'Number of Foreign Residents in S. Korea Triples over 10 Years', *Hankyoreh*, 6 July; http://english.hani.co.kr/arti/english_edition/e_international/699034.html

Han, Sunhee (2009) 'Pusan's Fresh Post', *Daily Variety*, 18 February: 6.

Jeon, Nam-il, Son Se-kwan, Yang Se-hwa and Hong Hyeong-ok (2009). *Hanguk Jugeoui Sahoesa* (A Social History of Korean Living). Seoul: Dolbaege.

Kang, Myungkoo (2011) 'Compressed Modernization and the Formation of a Developmentalist Mentalité', in Hyung-a Kim and Clark W. Sorensen (eds) *Reassessing The Park Chung Hee Era, 1961–1979: Development, Political Thought, Democracy, and Cultural Influence*. Seattle: University of Washington Press, 166–86.

Kim, Jong-guen (2011) 'Sikmindosi gyeongseongui ijungdosirone daehan bipanjeok gochal' (A Critical Inquiry on Colonial City, Gyeongseong and its Dual Status), in Dongguk daehakgyo munhwahaksulwon (ed.) *Munhwajiriwa dosigongganui pyosang* (Cultural Geography and Representation of Urban Space). Seoul: Dongguk daehakgyo chulpanbu, 49–81.

Kim, Hyung-a (2011) 'Heavy and Chemical Industrialization, 1973–9: South Korea's Homeland Security Measures', in Hyung-a Kim and Clark W. Sorensen (eds) *Reassessing The Park Chung Hee Era, 1961–1979: Development, Political Thought, Democracy, and Cultural Influence*. Seattle: University of Washington Press, 19–42.

Kim, Kyung Hyun (2011). *Virtual Hallyu: Korean Cinema of the Global Era*. Durham and London: Duke University Press.

Kim, Susie Jie Young (2010) 'Noir Looks and the Flash of Transgression', in Yomi Braester and James Tweedie (eds) *Cinema at the City's Edge*. Hong Kong: Hong Kong University Press, 119–36.

Lee, Hyeon-jung (2014) 'Filreum Neuwareuui jangreu byeonhwareul tonghae bon jangreujeok kwanseupkwa hyangyu kwajeongui yeonkwanseong – <L.A. Keonpidensyeol> <Mugando> <Dalkomhan Insaeng>eul jungsimeuro' (A Study on the Connection between Genre Convention and Enjoyment through Genre Changes of Film Noir – *L.A. Confidential, Infernal Affairs, A Bittersweet Life*). *Yeonghwa yeongu* [*Film Studies*], 62, 227–52.

Lee, Yong-ki, Choong-Ki Lee, Joowon Choi, Seol-min Yoon, and Robert John Hart (2014) 'Tourism's Role in Urban Regeneration: Examining the Impact of Environment Cues on Emotion, Satisfaction, Loyalty, and Support for Seoul's Revitalized Cheonggyecheon Stream District', *Journal of Sustainable Tourism*, 22, 5, 726–49.

Lefebvre, Henri ([1974] 1991) *The Production of Space*, trans. Donald Nicholson-Smith. Oxford: Blackwell.

Lie, John (1998) *Han Unbound: The Political Economy of South Korea*. Stanford: Stanford University Press.

Nelson, Laura C. (2000) *Measured Excess: Status, Gender and Consumer Nationalism in South Korea*. New York: Columbia University Press.

Park, Hyun Seon (2016) 'Wasteland and Theater: Spatial Affects in Yu Ha's *Gangnam 1970*'. Affects of Korea's Soft Power (Workshop). Los Angeles: University of Southern California, 5 February.

Shin, Chi-yun (2005) 'Two of a Kind: Gender and Friendship in *Friend* and *Take Care of My Cat*', in Julian Stringer and Chi-yun Shin (eds) *New Korean Cinema*. Edinburgh: Edinburgh University Press, 117–31.

Song, Jesook (2009) *South Koreans in the Debt Crisis: The Creation of a Neoliberal Welfare Society*. Durham: Duke University Press.

Yu, Sang-ho (2011) *Hanguk Ilbo*, 5 October.; http://news.hankooki.com/lpage/health/201110/h2011100522015484510.htm

CHASE SEQUENCES AND TRANSPORT INFRASTRUCTURE IN GLOBAL HOLLYWOOD SPY FILMS

CHRISTIAN B. LONG

James Bond gets around. In the seven films released between 1995 and 2012, the Bond series featured major European-north Atlantic locations such as Bregenz, Austria; Prague, Czech Republic; the French Pyrenees; Hamburg, Germany; Iceland; Lake Como, Venice and Siena, Italy; Monte Carlo; Montenegro; Arkhangelsk, Kazan and Saint Petersburg, Russia; Scotland; Bilbao, Spain; Ticino, Switzerland; Miami, USA; and, of course, London. The series' non-Western locations include Baku, Azerbaijan; the Bahamas; La Paz, Bolivia; the Caspian Sea; the Atacama Desert, Chile; Beijing, Shanghai and Hong Kong, China; Havana and the Cuban jungle; Port au Prince, Haiti; Kazakhstan; the Khyber Pass; the Korean DMZ; Macau; Madagascar; North Korea; Lahore, Pakistan; the South China Sea; Bangkok and Phuket, Thailand; Istanbul, Turkey; Mbale, Uganda; and Ho Chi Minh City, Vietnam.

Bond films may well be British imperial fantasies, but outside of seeing MI6 as the omnipresent force in the world, rather than the CIA or NSA or the Men in Black, the Bond films from the 1990s and on are nearly indistinguishable from generic Hollywood spy thrillers. They are formula filmmaking, and I want to take the generic formula of spy thrillers like the Bond and Jason Bourne movies seriously as an as-yet unexamined explanation for narrative location, with the rapidly-growing cities in Asia and, to a lesser extent, Africa, as key destinations made desirable by their transportation infrastructure. The large city – a city of one to five million people – and the megacity – an urban agglomeration of ten million of more people – serve a key generic function in spy thrillers: they offer a multi-level, multi-modal transportation infrastructure in which to stage chase sequences. The generic requirement of staging exciting and novel film chases necessitates – and will continue to necessitate

– locating action thrillers, particularly in franchises like Bond and the Bourne series, in the growing cities outside of Europe and North America, the places most likely to provide the chaotic multi-level, multi-modal transportation infrastructure conducive to an entertaining chase sequence.

DOMESTIC AND INTERNATIONAL BOX OFFICE

At the box office, *GoldenEye* (Martin Campbell, 1995) was the least successful Bond film in the US and Canada since 1990 – it made $106 million. However, that was only 30 per cent of its total box office take – it made $246 million outside of the US and Canada. This tilt toward non-US and Canada box office (domestic box office) is consistent throughout the series: *Skyfall* (Sam Mendes, 2012) and *Casino Royale* (Martin Campbell, 2006) made 72 per cent of their box office internationally. *Quantum of Solace* (Marc Forster, 2008) 71 per cent, *The World Is Not Enough* (Michael Apted, 1999) 65 per cent, and *Die Another Day* (Lee Tamahori, 2002) and *Tomorrow Never Dies* (Roger Spottiswoode, 1997) 62 per cent. Hollywood spy action-thriller franchises, and Hollywood films in general, have seen the importance of international box office increase since the 1980s.[1] In the *Mission: Impossible* series, the first two are 40 per cent domestic 60 per cent international, the third 34–66 and the latest has a 30/70 split. The *Bourne* series progresses similarly: *The Bourne Identity* (Doug Liman, 2002) and *The Bourne Supremacy* (Paul Greengrass, 2004) took in 60 per cent of their total box office from the US and Canada. *The Bourne Ultimatum* (Paul Greengrass, 2007) saw its box office split 50/50; most recently, *The Bourne Legacy* (Tony Gilroy, 2012) took in 60 per cent of its box office outside the US and Canada.

As generic narratives, spy thrillers tell similar stories over and over; Bond and Bourne stay the same, the novelty comes from their villains and their settings. Box office performance presents one instrumental explanation for the internationalisation of film settings; the increased presence of non-US locations in Hollywood films acknowledges the importance of the international market, which has increased its relative share of the box office markedly since the late 1990s, as the Motion Picture Association's Worldwide Market Research report, *U.S. Theatrical Market: 2005 Statistics* makes clear. To a degree this explanation is true. The Bond films show the importance of the Chinese market. With a quota on the number of foreign films released in China, the partially-Shanghai-set *Skyfall* made its inclusion as one of the imported films more likely, and it opened on more than 8,000 screens en route to $60 million in Chinese box office (see Stewart 2013).

Another explanation for location choice is the runaway production argument: it's cheaper to film outside of the US. Runaway productions are economically driven, rather than aesthetically or narratively driven, as Toby Miller, Nitin Govil, John McMurria and Richard Maxwell outline in detail in *Global Hollywood* (2001: 57–79).

When film producers find a script's settings too expensive for location shooting or impossible to recreate, Prague has played the role of a variety of other locations in films like *Van Helsing* (Stephen Sommers, 2004; Budapest), *Running Scared* (Wayne Kramer, 2006; New Jersey), the 1998 *Les Misérables* (Billie August; Paris), and *Casino Royale* (a host of non-Prague locations, including Miami and Montenegro). It also played itself in the first *Mission: Impossible* (Brian De Palma, 1996). But while this industrial-economic explanation can often explain why a film would be *shot* in a particular location, it cannot always explain why it would be *set* there. The economic logic of backpacker-tourism that informs the first two *Hostel* films (Eli Roth, 2005, 2007), set in eastern/central Europe, and *Turistas* (John Stockwell, 2006), set in Brazil, uses its cheap production site as its narrative setting. The New Zealand government giving Warner Bros. $25 million and friendly union laws to film *The Hobbit* (Peter Jackson, 2012–14) in New Zealand appeals to the bottom line. Beyond such brute economic concerns, Prague in *Casino Royale* and *Mission: Impossible* signifies as a former Cold War hot spot, a location of continuity, but the Prague-as-other-cities examples make no such use of the city and its history, rather using it as an architectural simulation or even as an anonymous space. A third explanation is the film tourism argument, for which the Bond films provide the template.[2] But if you want to make the tourism claim, then why does New Zealand play rural Middle Earth and Narnia, but not urban Auckland, New Zealand itself? What prevents Bond or Bourne from going to Petropavlovsk-Kamchatsky, Russia, which has abundant natural beauty close to interesting urban form, rather than the less-tourist-friendly Korean DMZ or the docks of Napoli?

The structural-industrial reasons for choosing a film's shooting locations certainly go a long way to explaining why more films might be *shot* somewhere. However, such explanations, though they recognise geopolitical-narrative concerns in their setting, do not consider formal aspects of spy thrillers, especially that formal aspect most likely to draw on the resources of a city in the developing world: the chase sequence.

THE CHASE SEQUENCE

Films like *The Great Train Robbery* (Edwin S. Porter, 1903), *The General* (Clyde Bruckman and Buster Keaton, 1926), and *Stagecoach* (John Ford, 1939) established the conventions for inventive chase sequences through the Classical era. These early chases are predominantly horizontal. While pre-war films tended to feature a number of different transportation modes in their chases – foot, horse, train, boat, cars – the car predominates after the war. Tico Romao provides the best account of the car chase sequence's history after the Classical era, and his account pays special attention to the generic identity of films that deploy chases. The principal attraction of many late-1960s and early-1970s police/crime thrillers was the elaborate chase sequence (2003: 41). If for Romao the first phase starts in 1968, the film to inaugurate the car chase cycle is *Bullitt* (Peter Yates, 1968). In the years between 1939 (*Stagecoach*) and 1968 (*Bullitt*), the US undertook a huge public works road-building program that added more than forty thousand miles of interstate highways, which not only linked the nation's major cities, but also went directly into and through them. The post-war car-centered infrastructure, cheap fuel and suburbanisation-led economic expansion both led to car ownership rates more than doubling between 1945 and 1965. They also played a key role in the social decay of cities, leading to increased poverty and crime and therefore, the kind of narratives present in police and crime thrillers.

The French Connection (William Friedkin, 1971) successfully combined drug crime and the visual equation of grittiness and realism to explore 'different varieties of moral degeneracy in the city' (Romao 2014: 136). Police/crime thrillers like *The French Connection* find solutions to the danger of criminal moral degeneracy through the narrative centrality of the chase sequence. The visible grey grime shows the effects of crime on the urban form, and in the chase sequences the physical danger of the crowded, crime-infested city becomes overwhelming, causing a man in a Santa suit chasing another man down city streets to be entirely logical (see Rotella: 2002: 112–18). But the key innovation to the chase sequence extends its realism beyond the narrative world and into the world of film production. That is to say, in addition to the film's *mise-en-scène*, the physical presence of the actors themselves in the midst of the chase – in the car, in physical danger – takes on added importance. By showing, through careful framing of both close ups and long shots, that Gene Hackman or Steve McQueen is actually driving the car, 'What is at stake then is not narrative functions but the very credibility of the stagings' (Romao 2014: 134). The realistic nature of the escalating danger of these chase sequences takes on increased narrative and stylistic prevalence.

Police thrillers tend to be set in major urban centres – New York, Los Angeles, San Francisco, Chicago – where the sorts of crime at the heart of their narratives can credibly take place. In addition, these cities offer an extensive and varied transportation infrastructure in which to stage chase sequences. By the mid-1970s, a different sort of chase film appeared, with what Romao first describes as 'a more regional complexion' (Romao 2003: 42), meaning that chases moved to the (union-free, tax incentive-offering) US South, most successfully in *Smokey and the Bandit* (Hal Needham, 1977). But Sunbelt cities did not offer the kind of urban transportation infrastructure that could support extended city chase sequences. Almost forty years after *Smokey and the Bandit* was filmed, the Google Street Views of the downtowns of Sunbelt cities like Phoenix, Arizona, Houston, Texas, Dallas, Texas and Orlando, Florida, show a number of similarities that explain why they have not been used as shooting locations for chase sequences. Like most American cities, Phoenix, Dallas, Houston and Orlando are ringed and divided by limited-access interstate highways. Their business and government district streets generally follow a grid pattern, with wide, mostly straight streets. On the streets, there are a great many cars and trucks, but few motorcycles, bicycles or pedestrians. There is also little public transit infrastructure, from buses to subways and elevated rail. While this could be a trick of the timing of Google's car driving through town, the limited street views of a number of non-US cities indicate that most of them have a greater variety of transportation modes than their American counterparts: as the volume of three-wheeled vehicles (Bangkok), motorcycles (Ho Chi Minh City), bicycles (Copenhagen) and foot traffic (Johannesburg) demonstrates.

No metropolitan region in the United States saw its percentage of car commuters decrease after 1980, which means that even if their absolute numbers increased, other modes of transport – public transit, bicycle, pedestrian – shared an increasingly smaller percentage of overall commuters (and, it would stand to reason, other trips as well). In 2000, outside of New York, Chicago, Boston, San Francisco, Philadelphia and Washington DC, almost every metropolitan region in the US saw more than 90 per cent of commuters travelling by car, an indication of the prevalence of automobile travel in general (see US Dept. of Transportation 2011). Such a proportion of a single mode of transportation makes the inclusion of other modes difficult, and often obviously manipulative rather than narratively necessary, as when an old woman using a walker magically appears to cross the street in *The Rock* (Michael Bay, 1996), which pays homage to – or rips off, depending on your feelings about Michael Bay – *Bullitt*'s chase. The realism of Steve McQueen actually driving the car and the particular topography of San Francisco generates much of the sequence's tension. The city's hills add verticality to an otherwise horizontal car-car chase, enabling not only short flights at crests, but vertical danger: what's on the other side of the hill is invisible. A few years later, *Dirty Mary Crazy Larry* (John Hough, 1974) staged an elaborate car-car-train-helicopter chase in a fairly open and flat rural setting. Paul Newland reads the chase in ideological terms:

> a phallic muscle car (signifying youth and sexual freedom) is spectacularly driven into the side of a speeding train, which (as public transport) signifies the faceless community that has held the protagonists Larry (Peter Fonda) and Mary (Susan George) down for so long. (2009: 13)

Such a reading has its appeal and force (but how does he account for the helicopter – rich elites?) but misses the formal construction of the scene. Cars share the horizontal axis with a train, but the San Joaquin valley is fairly flat, which mitigates against the vertical danger hilly streets can provide. The chase's helicopter introduces that vertical component. Combined, this multi-modal, multi-level chase makes the film's social critique possible.

In short, a chase sequence is simply a series of credible obstacles overcome. *The French Connection*'s major chase sequence involves

> placing some form of obstacle in the way of Jimmy Doyle's vehicle. Indeed, one could maintain that the main type of stunt in car chase films consists of a

vehicle either avoiding, crashing or leaping over some obstacle placed in its path. (Romao 2014: 146)

Bullitt, *Dirty Mary Crazy Larry*, *Smokey and the Bandit* and *The French Connection* all feature police, who have limited jurisdiction. The spy thriller genre expands boundaries/jurisdiction by obliging its central character to work across national boundaries. By expanding the possible locations where a spy might operate and face danger, the spy thriller genre expands the locations where chase sequences might be staged. Finding locations equal to that task requires places where horizontal and vertical obstacles can proliferate – the growing cities in the developing world most of all.

URBANISATION IN THE DEVELOPING WORLD

Since 1980, the developing world has urbanised at a pace far greater than the industrialised world. In 1980 China's population was 80 per cent rural, but in the span of thirty years, 236 cities of more than 500,000 people grew, making the country 50 per cent urban (UN News Centre 2010: np). Among those 236 cities, six – Shanghai, Beijing, Guangzhou, Shenzhen, Tianjin and Chongqing – are megacities, urban areas with more than ten million inhabitants, the most visible instance of the increasing urbanisation of the developing world. While some of the Asian megacities are in industrialised nations – Japan, South Korea – the newest megacities are all from the developing world: Kinshasa, Lagos, Jakarta, Guangzhou, Lahore, Shenzhen and Chennai (UN 2008: 6). The image frequently deployed in film to represent megacities places slums next to skyscrapers or a beautiful tourist setting, as when Jamal and Salim sit together in an unfinished skyscraper looking over Mumbai in *Slumdog Millionaire* (Danny Boyle, 2008) or the helicopter shots that place Rio de Janiero's beaches and favelas in the same image in *Fast & Furious Five* (Justin Lin, 2011). This juxtaposition contrasts the economic opportunity and power that makes megacities attractive to the dire straits of the migrants who move there.

But twenty-first century urbanisation is occurring in more than thirty-six megacities. According to the UN, '95 per cent of the world's urban population growth over the next four decades will be absorbed by cities in developing countries' (2008: 15). And while megacities will continue to grow, large cities in the developing world are growing the slowest – the cities of 100,000–500,000 are growing the most, then cities of 1–5 million, then cities of 500,000–1, and then finally cities of over 5 million. In 'The World City Hypothesis: Reflections from the Periphery', David Simon (2006) traces the growth of Nairobi, Kenya. Whereas Chinese cities like Guangzhou created special economic zones and accented manufacturing, Nairobi based its economic expansion in the services sector.

However, services made possible through the development of the communications infrastructure still require transportation infrastructure. In her extended analysis of Nairobi in *Extrastatecraft: The Power of Infrastructure Space* (2014), Keller Easterling buries the importance of the transportation infrastructure in the middle of an analysis of what Nairobi lacks:

> Just as mobile telephony is an information network, infrastructure space itself is a carrier of information, and it reciprocally shapes the resilience and robustness of all the broadband networks. The road between Mombasa and Nairobi – two lanes for some of its length and poorly maintained – is a reminder that despite the ubiquity of the cell phone, major improvements are needed in the auxiliary infrastructure. (2014: 98)

Nairobi's growth through investment in communications and information networks is one of the main approaches governments have taken to growth, but the poorly maintained road to Mombasa that physically isolates the city signifies the similar, practical importance of the 'auxiliary' transportation infrastructure. Practically speaking, 'in the absence of adequate NMT [non-motorized transport] infrastructure and strong law enforcement capability with respect to driver behaviour and vehicle roadworthiness, more heterogeneous traffic typically leads to greater vehicle conflicts and crash risks, especially for pedestrians' (Behrens 2014: 462). More heterogeneous traffic leading to greater vehicle conflicts and crash risks describes the key characteristics of a chase sequence.

BOND CHASE SEQUENCES

Bond movies all start in much the same way. We're thrown into a big action sequence *in medias res*, in some far-flung location. In their examination of geopolitics, gender and genre in Bond films, Linda Racioppi and Colleen Tremonte argue that, 'like most films in the contemporary spy genre, Bond films and their pre-title sequences frequently engage in narrativising the defense of the state and the global capitalist world order from serious threats that are increasingly transnational in scope' (2014: 16). The most recent Brosnan and Craig Bonds show a continued predilection for Cold War-identified locations, with the most European/Western locations, Bilbao and Siena, both featuring financial crimes in their openings to provide the threat. Thus while '[a]cross the series, then, the films' vitality is dependent on both generic continuity and adaptability … the global security threat that 007 must confront occurs within a dynamic restructuring of known Bondian conventions' (Racioppi and Tremonte 2014: 17). In other words, *where* can global military, political and, especially, economic threats most credibly be located?

In spy thrillers, threats motivate both chase sequences and the political ends of those chases' locations. Racioppi and Tremonte perceive the continuing influence of a Cold War vision informing Bond's travels across the globe. '[T]he geographical leap between the Eastern European and third-world locations in *Casino Royale* and *Quantum of Solace's* narrative movement through the Czech Republic, Haiti, Bolivia, Uganda and Madagascar,' in their account, 'situates global insecurity in the economically impoverished and politically unstable periphery (for example, in Madagascar and Uganda)' (2014: 18). On the one hand, this is nothing new – Bond ran off to Jamaica in the very first film in the series. Earlier Bond films show colonial connections (especially the Bahamas) and Cold War concerns (SPECTRE as a rival (Communist) spy ring) – and often place organised crime in the middle. What distinguishes the newer iterations, Racioppi and Tremonte note, is the way in which the Bond franchise

> echoes studies in contemporary international insecurity, particularly the human security literature, pointing to linkages between terrorist activity and 'legitimate' business and state interests, articulating new security threats such as water shortages and continuing concerns about oil shortages and suggesting tension between the haves and have-nots (in terms of financial, military, and natural resources), while reinforcing old Bondian notions about the Eastern Bloc and Russia. (2014: 18–19)

The change in approach seems to take off in *A View to a Kill* (John Glen, 1985), in which Bond foils Max Zorin's attempt to monopolise the microchip trade and control the future direction of the global economy. The two Timothy Dalton Bonds both hinge on the drug trade's connections to the arms trade and global destabilisation/terrorism. Among the Brosnan Bonds, *Tomorrow Never Dies*, especially its villain, the Rupert Murdoch-like media mogul Elliot Carver, makes three key replacements. First, Carver, with no more markets to conquer in the industrialised world, turns his attention to the developing world of China and Asia. Secondly, and consequently, in doing so, his business expansion replaces Cold War concerns of national spheres of influence and power with transnational corporate ones. And third, *Tomorrow Never Dies* thus treats the violence in 'exotic' locations that usually solves problems in a Bond film the same way Carver does: as content that solidifies Carver's media power. That is to say, the three changes show that Carver's expansion of his media holdings into China and Asia is not a way to reach London. Rather, China and Asia are the destination because they're the future.

The opening chases in Bond films compete with their predecessors in their spectacle: *GoldenEye* begins with Bond bungee jumping down a dam face, then travelling through a military facility's duct work, having a shootout with most of the Russian army, then chasing a taxiing plane. Bond boards and then throws himself out of the plane while it's on the runway, then chases it by motorcycle. Then, Bond skydive-chases the same plane, catches it, and pilots it to safety as the facility explodes behind him. Such a chase is possible thanks to the combination of 'Russian military installation' and the terrain near Arkhangelsk. The chase that opens *Casino*

Royale similarly combines the built environment and its surroundings. The chase begins in a village fighting pit, then runs through a market. The chase runs along a dirt road, then into a construction site in Mbale. At the building, Bond and his prey parkour-run up and around the multistory skeleton of the building, all the way out to the end of a crane boom. The proximity of nature to a city also appears in *Quantum of Solace,* which opens in Italy, *en medias* car chase. The chase goes through narrow tunnels, curving mountain roads, and a quarry before Bond arrives in Siena's narrow old world streets, tunnels and garages. The combination of vertical (bungee jumping, skydiving, flying, building frames, quarry depths) and horizontal (floors, streets, alleys) makes for exciting, if slightly ridiculous, opening chase sequences.

While the Bond series' gadget fetish makes multi-modal chases logical within the narrative, counting the ever-increasing number of horizontal and vertical dangers and obstacles in a mid-film Bond chase sequence shows the extravagance a fast-growing city's chaotic built environment can provide a chase sequence. For example, in *Tomorrow Never Dies*, megacity Bangkok, Thailand plays large city Ho Chi Minh City, Vietnam. When Bond and Wai Lin (a Chinese spy working with Bond) are captured in the South China Sea, they are taken by helicopter to Ho Chi Minh City, flying over a city with a literally fantastic CGI skyline punctuated by a fictional 'CMGN Tower' looming over the city, their destination. Their escape from CMGN and Elliot Carver takes up about seven minutes of screen time, during which they flee by foot (mode 1, horizontal danger 1) out the windows (obstacle 1) of Carver's office at CMGN Tower (level 1), using a banner on the side of the building to guide their descent (vertical danger 1). Then they re-enter the tower through windows (obstacle 2) many stories lower down (level 2). After reaching street level by foot (level 3), they steal a motorcycle (mode 2), and are chased by cars (mode 3, horizontal danger 2) through streets and alleys crammed with cars, pedestrians and cyclists (obstacles 3, mode 4). They then ride up an incline, onto the roofs of buildings (level 4). They then descend into and through a building (level 5, obstacles 4), then jump over an alley (vertical danger 2), and ride over more rooftops. At this point, a helicopter joins the chase (mode 5, vertical danger 3), and the Bond-Wai Lin motorcycle jumps over helicopter (vertical danger 4, obstacle 5), crashing through the roof (obstacle 6) of a building on the other side of the street (level 6). The motorcycle then races along the building's second-storey walkway/verandah (level 7), then down onto the roof of a passing truck (level 8) and then, finally, back onto the street (level 9). The chopper is still chasing them (continued vertical danger 4). The helicopter attacks the pedestrian-crammed street, angling so that its blades chop up everything at ground level (vertical danger 5, horizontal danger 3). The motorcycle escapes along alleys and streets (obstacles 7) and, in the end, slides under the chopper (level 10, horizontal danger 4). After slipping under the chopper, Bond throws a cable onto its rear rotor and destroys the chopper (vertical danger 6). Then Bond and Wai Lin share a shower, celebrating their achievement of overcoming more obstacles than the traditional fruit cart and mother-with-a-pram, and with a greater logic given the sequence's particular urban setting. The combination of new glass skyscrapers next to wide boulevards, second-storey verandahs in old multiuse areas filled with tightly-packed buildings with thin walls (action movies love slum and near-slum areas), narrow streets and footpaths filled with pedestrians, cyclists, motorcyclists, buses, trucks and some cars expands not only the transportation modes on offer, but also the available levels in the urban fabric through which the chase can occur.

CHASE SEQUENCES IN THE BOURNE LEGACY: EXTENDING THE GENRE FRANCHISE

The Bourne series shares an imperial vision with Bond, but while the imperial power on the surface is the United States, by *The Bourne Legacy*, multinational corporate power outside US boundaries replaces previous imperial presences. In *Action Movies: The Cinema of Striking Back,* Harvey O'Brien notes that the *Bourne* films are a bit more rooted in everyday reality than Bond films, as they

> consciously deglamorised and reactualised the espionage genre by an emphasis on defining rather than stylising physical detail in depicting the environment – places where action could occur in spaces that facilitated the dynamics of action itself rather than serve as a picturesque backdrop, an increased use of hand-held 'shaky-cam' shooting to capture dynamic motion in close-up during scenes of combat, and featured extensive chases both on foot and in vehicles that emphasised physical authenticity through explicit, visible damage and injury to property and person. (2012: 92)

Defining the physical details of the *Bourne* film environments takes the form of the streets that bookend *The Bourne Supremacy:* the crowded multimodal Goan streets at the beginning and the car-centred Moscow streets at the end. On the one hand, the scale of the Goan streets in which cars are a much less-frequently used mode, increases the odds of damage and injury to not just Bourne and Marie, but also to pedestrian-scale bystanders (who then gawk at the chase's bridge-jump final damage). On the other hand, the chase through Moscow's streets focuses its damage on vehicles and the people inside them and the infrastructure itself rather than to other modes of travel such as pedestrians and cyclists. While the Goa chase begins the movement, the *The Bourne Ultimatum* chase through Tangiers directs the *Bourne* series towards global megacities as necessary chase sequence locations.

Tangier's brief history as an international zone, from 1923 to 1956, presents a model for understanding the subsequent non-Western cities in the *Bourne* series. Established as a demilitarised international zone to placate colonial and economic powers Britain, France and Spain, Tangier bears a family resemblance to the zones that Keller Easterling identifies as among the most important organisations of space in the twenty-first century, the Export Processing Zone (EPZ). *Extrastatecraft's* first chapter writes the history of EPZ. 'With persuasive arguments about nation-building and free trade,' she writes,

> the United Nations and the World Bank promoted the EPZ as a tool that developing countries should use to enter the global marketplace and attract foreign investment with incentives like tax holidays and cheap labor. Although intended as a temporary experiment and judged to be a suboptimal economic instrument, the zone spread widely during the 1970s even as it also spread new waves of labor exploitation. There were, however, unexpected consequences: rather than dissolving into the domestic economy, as was originally intended, the EPZ absorbed more and more of that economy into the enclave. (2014: 25)

Whereas the international zone of Tangier had a beginning and an end, many EPZs and related Special Economic Zones (SEZ) seem not to be scheduled to end. Tangier itself is part of the industrial and logistics complex Atlantic Free Zone, centred in Kentira, that uses Tangier as a port (but keeps its headquarters in Murcia, Spain). Established to entice major multinationals into developing nations,

> The zone offers a clean, relaxed, air-conditioned, infrastructure-rich urbanism that is more familiar to the world that the context of its host country.... Moreover, as the entrepôt of the world's resources, the zone, despite its attempts to be apolitical, invariably ends up in the crosshairs of pirates, terrorists, and traffickers of all kinds. (2014: 67–8)

In other words, EPZs and related SEZs and the megacity regions they call home – Shenzhen, Shanghai, Bangalore, much of the island of Luzon in the Philippines, and others – represent logical locations in which to situate narratives about the maintenance of US cultural hegemony in its economic form of multinational corporate hegemony.

The Bourne films, like the Bond films, place their centres of gravity in a major city of the Western world. Bond has London. The top executives who control and manage their hunts for Bourne and Cross from New York and Washington DC (Langley, Virginia). The established old-world cities house the governmental apparatus, but the ops world is elsewhere. The same is true of multinational corporations and Hollywood. They may stash their money in the Caymans and have factories in the mega-city regions of the global south, but their headquarters are almost uniformly in the main cities of the Western world. Larry Gross, in an article titled, 'Big and Loud' identifies where action movies don't put their energies: 'since *Star Wars*, Big Loud Action Movies have managed to repress, eliminate or overcome: psychological complexity, and the registration of accurate social and historical detail' (2000: 4). Calling the Bourne films, 'unusually smart works of industrial entertainment, with action choreography that's as well considered as the direction' (Dargis 2007: np) recognises the film-historical detail of improvements to the 'what' and 'how' of the film, but still misses the 'where'.

The locations of *The Bourne Legacy* certainly register social and historical details. For instance, the Bourne series registers historical detail in the way surveillance technology seems to have achieved total saturation in major urban centres, with the frequently-invoked national security interest as the rationale for CCTV-enabled invasions of privacy. In *The Bourne Legacy* in particular, the United States' attempts to maintain its imperial reach through multinational corporate intermediaries registers in the film's Manila climax. The purpose of moving through US locations in *Bourne Legacy* – Alaska, Chicago, suburban Maryland, JFK Airport – is to arrive in Manila, where outsourced labour makes secrecy and conspiracy hard to reach and thus overcome. Which is to say, the Bourne movies, *Legacy* foremost among them, most certainly register the historical details of the twenty-first century neoliberal order in the locations of villainy and their reach into every corner of everyday life in America.

In terms of narrative, *The Bourne Legacy* roots its vision of globalisation and US empire-protection in the pharmaceutical industry, which does high-value research in the US but manufactures in cheap-labour Manila. Terry Ward, a Senior VP for the pharmaceutical firm that makes the Outcome programme's chems, describes the company's factory in Manila as 'basically a kitchen … we tweak the recipe and we bake up a batch when we need it'. But a narrative that acknowledges the importance of outsourcing is only satisfying if it addresses the generic demands of an effective (and hopefully spectacular) chase sequence. While *Tomorrow Never Dies* heads to southeast Asia to deal with a media conglomerate bent on monopolising a major market, *The Bourne Legacy* heads to East Asia to follow the production of pharmaceuticals that support the US imperial mission, both politically and militarily. In need of more the 'chems' that maintain his status as a super-soldier, Aaron Cross first goes to the US east coast, where a pharmaceutical company's headquarters and research and development work is most likely to be located (see EPA 1997: 11). Even if a US-headquartered drug company were to produce drugs like the 'chems' Aaron seeks out, the production plant would almost certainly be offshore, even if the pills were Made in America. As the EPA notes, tax incentives led to the growth of the 'Pharmaceutical Preparations and Medicinals and Botanicals sectors' in Puerto Rico throughout the 1990s. Since the mid-twentieth century, the high-value twenty-first century operations like finance and pharmaceutical and biotech research and development have replaced manufacturing as the key economic functions that US policy seeks to enable. But when it comes to manufacturing, pharmaceutical companies tend to locate production not in suburbs close to their R&D office, but in the global south.

One significant location for pharmaceutical manufacturing is the Philippines, Manila in particular. *The Bourne Legacy* accurately registers some of social and historical details of pharmaceutical research, manufacture, and mis-use, and turns them into defining physical details in the *mise-en-scène*: the workers' uniform of pink scrubs, the brightly and uniformly-lit shop floor and its symmetrical layout of the blue machines, and the bright yellow-railed mezzanine level for supervisors in the factory, contrasts with the crowded, often murky look of much of the rest of the film.

The Bourne Legacy as a narrative needs a pill factory and *The Bourne Legacy* as a genre film needs a transportation infrastructure. Manila supplies both. The twelve- and-a-half minute chase through Manila proceeds on foot over rooftops and down streets and alleys, along power lines, on a staircase to an elevated walkway, off the walkway down onto a bus roof, and back down onto street level. From there, Aaron and Marta ride on a motorbike, and the assassin LARX-3 chases them in a police car, a motorbike and a police motorcycle, sometimes shooting at them, sometimes turning the other vehicles on the highway into weapons.

The sequence begins with a horizontal chase that consistently deploys vertical movement and vertical danger. The chase begins with Marta screaming a warning to Aaron, who uses a window security grille and then exposed rebar to climb up the outside of their hotel. While Aaron runs over rooftops, none of which appear to be at exactly the same height, Marta runs through a series of streets and alleys that seem to get narrower and narrower, until police trap her in an alley barely wider than her shoulders. Aaron becomes the vertical danger to the chasing police at this point, sliding between the two walls to land on top of one policeman. After dispatching the first wave of pursuers, Aaron and Marta take off together, trying to blend in on a crowded street, the frame filled with every mode of road transport – pedestrians, rickshaws, cars, jitneys, buses, motorbikes, bicycles – many of them passing in front of the camera, obscuring Aaron and Marta, adding to the sense of crowding and chaos. Two different sets of point-of-view shots reveal the vertical danger and visual confusion that Manila's streets afford. In one set, Aaron's point of view scans the streets beneath the ferry boat walkway, revealing the police closing in from multiple directions. In a second set, the assassin LARX-3 trails Aaron and Marta, who at first do not see him. In the first POV shot, a close-up shows LARX-3 pause on a rooftop. The reverse, POV, long shot shows a street teeming with pedestrians, obstructed by power lines and poles in the foreground. In the second, after Aaron and Marta climb the ferry entrance stairs, LARX-3 again pauses, and the reverse shot of his POV, an over-the-shoulder shot, shows Aaron and Marta clearly, in the middle of the frame in a long shot, with Aaron looking directly at the camera (that is, LARX-3), stopping for a moment, and then moving quickly. A quick series of vertical-danger stunts – Aaron drops Marta onto a bus roof, LARX-3 glides down a ladder – punctuate the first, foot, portion of the chase and move it to street and highway level, where the sequence can take advantage of Manila's choked road system.

The chase shifts from frequent vertical dangers in a horizontal foot chase to near-continuous horizontal dangers in a motorbike-vehicle chase when the location moves from residential spaces to more public, business and industrial spaces.

Once *The Bourne Legacy*'s chase turns into a motorcycle-car chase on highways and streets, it uses the variety of vehicles on Manila's streets to create horizontal dangers, but re-imagines the cramped, narrow alleys as obstacles of and in motion. While Aaron needs to move around or over some obstacles on the highway, quite often the horizontal dangers are not physical obstacles but temporal windows: narrow spaces between vehicles and between vehicles and concrete dividers, are only obstacles as long as they are there; once they disappear they cease to be obstacles and become dead ends. These rapidly shrinking traversable spaces generate the chase's speed and urgency. Whereas the earlier Bourne chases were predominantly car-based (including the vehicles in the background), the Manila streets in *The Bourne Legacy*'s final chase feature pedestrians, bicycles, rickshaws, motorbikes, cars, jeepnies and large trucks. Much as Jason Bourne drove up and down stone steps in Paris, Aaron and Marta detour from the road to go up and down steps, even axle grinding down a handrail to avoid pedestrian-obstacles (LARX-3 runs over a pedestrian on the same steps). Throughout the chase Aaron and Marta change speed to use other vehicles as visual and bullet shields. For his part, LARX-3 weaponises other vehicles, ramming into a jeepny to crush Aaron and Marta into the concrete wall on the edge of the highway. But while most of the previous Bourne chase sequences take place on streets filled with driver-only cars, the vehicles on Manila's streets – especially the decorated jeepnies – are filled with passengers. And unlike the Bourne-and-pursuer focus in the earlier films, *The Bourne Legacy* even spares a moment to show the inside of a jeepny as LARX-3 rams it, making the danger to the public more than a matter of anonymous crushed fenders.

The chase changes levels about a dozen times – five up and eight down, not counting the uneven rooftops Aaron runs over – and poses five types of vertical and around fifteen types of horizontal dangers, many of which Aaron and Marta face multiple times, such as the narrow spaces between cars and pedestrians. At one point it seems that the chase will end with LARX-3 literally crashing into a Marikina Market fruit cart, but the chase ends with a final mode change: in an echo of *The Bourne Identity* (in a film and series full of repetition compulsion) a boat takes Aaron and Marta to the future anonymity of life in an island tourist town. *The Bourne Legacy* thus stages a foot-motorbike-car chase over sidewalks, pedestrian overpasses, roofs, scaffolding, streets, highways, industrial lots, a pedestrian-centred market and the South China Sea (as well as an implied Manila Bay), leaving Manila's light rail system on the table for a later film. The Bourne series moves from the US government as its antagonist to the military-industrial-pharmaceutical complex as its antagonist. Thus Jason Bourne goes to New York to free himself, but Aaron Cross goes to Manila. In both cases the location serves a narrative-ideological purpose: a knowledge-production – brain-washing – centre for Jason Bourne and an outsourced drug-production centre for Aaron Cross. The films' narrative and ideological projects, however, depend not just on the buildings where brain-washing and pill-production happen, but also on a transportation infrastructure suited to chase sequences' formal needs.

OUR MAN IN KARACHI?

In his analysis of 'James Bond and Imperial Decline', Jason Dittmer argues that 'the James Bond films can be seen as illustrating shifts in Britain's relationship to the world from colonial to imperial, while nevertheless remaining consistent in its representation of that world as exotic places in which British power remains central and British geopolitical action are to be carried out' (2010: 63). David Graeber digs slightly deeper in *The Utopia of Rules*, noting with some amusement that '*Casino Royale* gave Bond psychological depth. And by the very next movie, Bond was saving indigenous communities in Bolivia from evil transnational water privatizers' (2015: 210). For Dittmer, location choice – as national boundaries, as establishing-shot landscapes/skylines – acts as the primary ideology delivery device in Bond films. That's true, but not the whole story; how location choice takes form creates the contours of spy thriller ideology. Graeber sees a particular indigenous political movement as the narrative key to Bond's ideological shift, but recognises that shift is temporary – the Bond films remain wedded to their imperial vision. In terms of narrative-plot concerns, Dittmer and Graeber capture why mass audience entertainments like the Bond and Bourne series are important: they tell stories that make the powerful centre exerting its power and control over far-flung locations acceptable, heroic even, whether the audience is positioned to enjoy the maintenance of that power, in Bond films, or the resistance to it in the Bourne films. But such narrative-focused accounts can generate additional force (and complicate matters) when tied to film form.

Generic conventions such as chase sequences within a complex, multimodal urban transportation infrastructure put the abstraction of imperial interest in a location in concrete terms. A montage of the elimination of Outcome project agents in *The Bourne Legacy*, a chase scene of sorts, makes the importance of a multimodal infrastructure to spy thrillers clear. Agents in Karachi, Seoul and Baltimore picking up their new chems are cut against Colonel Byer and Lieutenant General Paulsen discussing terminating the project. The new chems eliminate the agents quickly, quietly, in public, and in the transportation infrastructure. The agent in Seoul walks through a crowded neon-lit street, picks up her new chems, and then dies on the subway. The agent in Karachi dies as he walks down a street crowded with pedestrians. Rather than moving around in a car, isolated from their settings the agents travel in close contact with the people they work with and against. The transportation infrastructure speaks for how deep the agents are embedded in locations key to imperial expansion: one, Paulsen claims, is an active agent in Pakistan's ISI. A similar indication of the importance of large cities in the developing world appears in the shift in the agents sent to kill Bourne/Aaron. A chase through Manila is not the sole cause of *The Bourne Legacy's* increase in international box office returns, but as the series and the genre grinds on, generic conventions demand a world beyond North America and Europe. From Cold War cities (Berlin, London, Moscow, NYC, Paris) to cities in the developing world (Tangier, Seoul, Manila, Bangkok), where long, dangerous, and testing chase-fights can credibly be staged. Here the tendency of a series to need to top its previous set pieces generates a need for chase locations that can present ever-greater obstacles for its hero to overcome.

Skyfall digs into Bond's past, and in doing so destroys parts of London. But the chase scenes at the end of *The World is Not Enough* and *The Bourne Legacy* point to likely spy thriller chases in the future. The narratives of Bond and Bourne and other spy thrillers need not only to stay current with the globalised construction of the economic and political order, but also with the genre's formal demands. By staging chase sequences in the cities in the developing world – in a multi-modal, multi-level, obstacle-heavy transportation infrastructure – future spy thrillers can keep up to date with political and ideological changes while keeping faith with the genre's form.

NOTES

1 See, for example, Frederick Wasser's mid-1990s account, in which he notes that 'The global audience's influence goes beyond the aggregate figures. If one merely looks at the returns then the only change has been quantitative, as the foreign returns increase from the 30 per cent characteristic of the twenties and thirties (Donahue 1987: 145) to the current level of 51 per cent' (Wasser 1995: 433).
2 There is an extensive literature of film tourism in journals such as *Annals of Tourism Research, Journal of Travel Research* and *Journal of Vacation Marketing*.

BIBLIOGRAPHY

Behrens, Roger (2014) 'Urban Mobilities: Innovation and Diffusion in Public Transport', in Susan Parnell and Sophie Oldfield (ed.) *The Routledge Handbook on Cities of the Global South*. London: Routledge, 459–73.

Dargis, Manohla (2007) 'The New Bourne: A Spy Gone Dark, Brooding, and Haunted', *New York Times*, 3 August; http://www.nytimes.com/2007/08/03/arts/03iht-flik4.1.6970713.html?_r=0

Dittmer, Jason (2010) *Popular Culture, Geopolitics, & Identity*. Lanham: Rowman & Littlefield.

Donahue, Suzanne Mary (1987) *American Film Distribution: The Changing Marketplace*. Ann Arbor: University of Michigan Press.

Easterling, Keller (2014) *Extrastatecraft: The Power of Infrastructure Space*. London: Verso.

Environmental Protection Agency (1997) *EPA Office of Compliance Sector Notebook Project: Profile of the Pharmaceutical Manufacturing Industry*. Washington DC: United States Environmental Protection Agency.

Graeber, David (2105) *The Utopia of Rules: On Technology, Stupidity, and the Secret*

Joys of Bureaucracy. Brooklyn: Melville House.

Gross, Larry (2000) 'Big and Loud', in Jose Arroyo (ed.) *Action/Spectacle Cinema: A Sight and Sound Reader*. London: British Film Institute, 3–9.

Miller, Toby, Nitin Govil, John McMurria and Richard Maxwell (2001) *Global Hollywood*. London: British Film Institute.

Motion Picture Association of America, *U.S. Theatrical Market: 2005 Statistics* (2005) http://stop-runaway-production.com/wp-content/uploads/2009/07/2005-MPAA-Market-Stats-26-Pages.pdf

Newland, Paul (2009) 'Look past the violence: automotive destruction in American Movies', *European Journal of American Culture*, 28, 1, 5–20.

O'Brien, Harvey (2012) *Action Movies: The Cinema of Striking Back*. London: Wallflower Press.

Racioppi, Linda and Colleen Tremonte (2014) 'Geopolitics, Gender, and Genre: The Work of Pre-Title/Title Sequences in James Bond Films', *Journal of Film and Video*, 66, 2, 15–25.

Romao, Tico (2003) 'Engines of Transformation: An Analytical History of the 1970s Car Chase Cycle', *New Review of Film and Television Studies*, 1, 1, 31–54.

____ (2014) 'Guns and Gas: Investigating the 1970s Car Chase Film', in Yvonne Tasker (ed.) *Action and Adventure Cinema*. London: Routledge, 130–52.

Rotella, Carlo (2002) *Good With Their Hands: Boxers, Bluesmen, and Other Characters from the Rust Belt*. Berkeley: University of California Press.

Simon, David (2006) 'The World City Hypothesis: Reflections from the Periphery', in Neil Brenner and Roger Keil (ed.) *The Global Cities Reader*. London: Routledge, 203–9.

Stewart, Andrew (2013) 'James Bond film picks up $5.1 million Monday from 8,079 screens', *Variety*; http://variety.com/2013/film/news/skyfall-sees-record-opening-day-in-china-1118064956/

UN (2008) *State of the World's Cities 2008/2009. Harmonious Cities*. London: Earthscan.

UN News Centre (2010) 'China now home to one quarter of world's largest cities, UN reports', *UN Daily News*, 25 March; http://www.un.org/apps/news/story.asp?NewsID=34202#.VWpGm1yqpHw

US Department of Transportation Federal Highway Administration (2011) 'Means of Travel to Work', *Census Transportation Planning Products*; http://fhwa.dot.gov/planning/census_issues/ctpp/data_products/journey_to_work/jtw4.cfm

Wasser, Frederick (1995) 'Is Hollywood America? The Trans-nationalisation of the American Film Industry', *Critical Studies in Mass Communication*, 12, 4, 423–37.

INDEX

Abdellatif, Kechiche 12, 21, 203, 208
Act of Killing, The 41
Adventures of Goopy and Bagha, The 119
aesthetic: aesthetic of decay 112; aesthetics of intermediality 10; aesthetic perception of slum 190; aesthetic practices 3; noir-esque visual aesthetics 223; Nollywood aesthetics 73; Nordic Noir aesthetic 9, 38; politicised aesthetic 208; retro aesthetics 105; vertical aesthetic 124
affinitive transnationalism 38, 40
Africa 10, 59–61, 63–5, 71, 194n.5, 202, 235; Africa Magic 65–6; French North Africa 202; neoliberalism in West Africa 9; North African diaspora 207, 211; North African immigrant 201, 211; South Africa 63, 65–6, 184; Sub-Saharan Africa 206–7
Ai Weiwei 11, 159, 170–1, 173
Ajeossi see Man from Nowhere, The
Alone Together 83
Althusser, Louis 148
Ameur-Zaimeche, Rabah 12, 204–8, 211, 216n.7
Amores perros 23

Amsterdam 21, 29
Amsterdam Global Village 21
Anderson, Benedict 37
Anderson, Wes 104
Annie Hall 97–8, 100–1
Apartment, The 100
Argentina 79–81
Audiard, Jacques 12, 204, 211–13
audience: African diasporic audiences 9, 70; Africa magic audience 65; cinephile audience 205; diasporic audiences 5, 9; domestic audiences 38; expatriate Nigerian audiences 65; global audience 12, 48, 250n.1; mass audience 249; international audiences 38, 50; middle-class audience 125, 183; Nollywood audience 62; target audience 104; urban audience 61, 137n.2; Western audiences 11
audiovisual: audiovisual aesthetics 37; audiovisual culture 3, 38–9, 42; audiovisual industry 30, 40–1; audiovisual language 10, 81; audiovisual media 1, 25, 37; audiovisual texts 37, 47; Regional audiovisual 41–3
Auf der anderen Seite 21

auteur   25, 30, 97, 122, 205; auteurial agency   158–9; auteurist cinema   27; auteur-driven   122; European auteur cinema   6; humanist auteurs   209; Parallel Cinema auteurs   10
authenticity   8, 96–8, 105–6, 111, 113, 244
Autograph   120, 126–7, 130–1, 134
avant-garde   158, 166
Avellaneda's Moon see Luna de Avellaneda

Babel   23
Baby Mama   103
Bachelard, Gaston   119, 121, 126–7, 134, 136
banlieue   12, 187, 201, 204–6, 208, 211, 213, 215n.5, 216n.7
Bar El Chino   80
Barrett, K.K.   96, 107, 111
Baudrillard, Jean   150
Beat   218, 221
Beijing   144, 159–60, 163–5, 235, 240
Bendiksen, Jonas   11, 178–80, 182, 186–93, 193-194n.3
Bend it Like Beckham   21
Bengali film   10, 119, 125, 132, 137n.8
Benjamin, Walter   22, 26, 33, 82, 110
Beomjoewaui jeonjaeng   230
Bereullin   231
Berlinale *see also* Film festival
Berlin File, The see Bereullin
Better Tomorrow, A   219, 227
beur cinema   12, 201, 209, 211
Beur sur la ville   202
Bhaumik, Mainak   10, 120
Bhooter Bhabishyat see Future of the Past, The
Big City, The see Mahanagar
Big Hero   6
Big Switch, The   184, 195n.15
Biteu see Beat
Bittersweet Life, A   219, 223, 225, 227
Biutiful   23
Biyeolhan geori see Dirty Carnival, A
Blade Runner   7, 10, 96–7, 105, 108, 110, 112–13
Bled Number One   211, 216n.5
blockbuster   12, 27, 31, 218; *see also* Hollywood
Bloody Tie   219, 223, 227, 229–30

blue wall   38
Bolivia   80
bonaerense, El   80
Bond films   235–7, 241–2, 244–5, 249–50
Borgen   49, 51
Bourne (series)   236, 244–6, 248–50
Bourne Identity, The   236, 248
Bourne Legacy, The   236, 244, 246–50
Bourne Supremacy, The   30, 236, 244
Bourne Ultimatum, The   236, 244
Breakfast at Tiffany's   100
Breathless see Ddongpari
bricoleur   164, 187–9, 193, 196n.25
Bridge, The see Bron/Broen
Bron/Broen   9, 36–52
Buenos Aires   10, 79–92
Bullitt   238–40
Busan   12, 218–21, 223, 225, 227–31
Bye-bye   202, 209–10

Café Noir see Kape neuwareu
Cahiers du cinéma   202, 209
Cairo   7, 11, 143–7, 150–3
Calcutta   121, 135, 137n.n.3,4
Calcutta 71   135
capitalism   19, 27, 67, 70, 79, 136, 150; global capitalism   59, 149, 182, 192, 194n.6, 196n.25; international capitalism   60, 63; post-Fordist capitalism   102, 113; transnational capitalism   232
Caracas   11, 178, 180, 188, 193, 193-194n.3
Caracas: Growing House   193
car chase   237, 239, 243, 248
Casino Royale   236–7, 242, 249
Challenge of Slums: Global Report on Human Settlements, The   180
China   12, 23, 110–11, 144, 148–9, 163, 165, 168, 172, 173n.6, 231–2, 235–6, 240, 242–3, 248; China as neoliberal   149
Chinese independent New Documentary Movement   165
Chingu see Friend
Chorok mulgogi see Green Fish
Chungking Express   23
ciné-club movement   121–2

cinephilia 10, 119, 120–36; cinephilia take two 120–3; cinephilia take one 120–3, 132, 135–6; post-war cinephilia 121
city: cityscape 12, 26, 68, 87, 96, 98, 111, 128, 131, 133–4, 136, 165, 191, 204, 224–5, 228; cityspace 204–5, 214; cluster city 9, 19, 26, 28–32; digital city 10, 97, 102, 105, 108, 114; generic city 7, 9, 11, 25–9, 33, 105–7, 111–12, 119, 143–54, 224; hybrid city 111, 126, 131, 202; megacities 4, 12, 178, 240, 244; post-industrial city 39, 143; Western cities 20, 244; *see also* global city
City of God 22, 185
City Stars 151–3
Classique 67
CMGN Tower 243
Code 46 111
Cold War 25, 237, 241–2, 249
colonialism 5, 20, 22, 119, 123–4, 126, 130, 135, 218, 220–1, 223, 242, 244, 249; anticolonialism 6; postcolonialism 2, 5, 10, 24, 122–3, 133, 137n.4, 201, 212–13, 232
Comme un aimant 202
Copenhagen 9, 36–8, 41–4, 46–7, 50–1, 239
Copenhagen Film Fund (CFF) 41–2, 50
Crash 22
creative class 6, 10, 81, 92-93n.2, 96, 104
cross-border 37–8, 40–2, 45, 51–2
Cruel History of Myeongdong see Myeongdongj anhoksa

Dalkomhan insaeng see Bittersweet Life, A
Danmarks Radio (DR) 40
Davis, Mike 11, 13, 112, 178, 180–2, 189, 194n.n.7,9
Ddong gae 221
Ddongpari 221
death of distance 2
death of place 120, 131
Debord, Guy 144, 150, 153, 162
Denmark 36, 38–40, 45–6, 49, 50–1, 53n.8

dérive 144
Dernier Maquis 12, 204–8, 213, 215, 216n.5
Desiring China 149
Die Another Day 236
digital cartograph 48
Dimendberg, Edward 12–13, 115n.7, 219–20, 222, 224–5, 230–1
Dirty Carnival, A 219 , 221, 223–5, 227
Dirty Mary Crazy Larry 239–40
Dirty Pretty Things 21
Doctor Who 151
Dridi, Karim 202, 209
Drôle de Félix 203, 215
Dry Toilet 193
Duchamp, Marcel 172
Dutta, Anik 10, 119
dystopia 6, 11, 27, 97, 108, 112, 150; dystopian noir 96; technodystopianism 109; utopia/dystopia 97, 112–13

East Asia 97, 110–11, 218, 246
Egypt 145, 147, 149
Electric Dreams 108
Elite Squad 22
El Khalafawi 145, 151
Elliot, Desmond 10, 66
Emelonye, Obi 10, 67, 70
Ershiyi lou you duo gao? 171
ethnicity 12, 20, 23, 33, 40, 46, 64, 71–2, 102, 200, 203–7, 209, 211, 215, 231–2; ethnic hatred 22; ethnic Other 219, 232; multi-ethnic city 202
Eurocentric 4–5, 24
European cinemas 6, 9, 24–5, 27, 30, 201
Exils 211
Ex Machina 108–9

Fast & Furious Five 240
Festac Town 71–3
(500) Days of Summer 103–4, 106
film festivals 4, 7, 9, 21, 23–33, 41, 64, 125, 205, 228
Film i Skäne 41–2
First World 21
flâneur 22, 27–8

Florida, Richard 67, 92n.2, 104, 115n.5
Forbrydelsen 49
Forrest Gump 159
44 Myeondong see *Myeongdong 44 beonji*
found footage 11, 157–73
Fourth World 81
Frances Ha 104
French cinema 201–15
French Connection, The 238–40
Friend 218–19, 227, 229
Future of the Past 10, 119–20, 134–6

Gangnam Blues see *Gangnam 1970*
Gangnam 1970 221
Gegen die Wand 21
Geimui beopchik 218
General, The 218, 237
General's Son, The 221, 223–4
generic architecture 120
Ghatak, Ritwik 10, 120–2, 133
Ghosh, Rituparno 124–5, 136
digital media 1, 3, 10, 64, 85–6, 97, 114, 179, 182; digital mediascape 99
digital production 2
digital space 2–3
Glamour Girls 67
global: global economy 29, 59, 63, 111, 242; global film 5; global markets 110–111; global urbanism 6, 105
global city 1, 4, 6–11, 20–3, 25–8, 33, 67, 81, 96–7, 111–14, 119–20, 124, 127–8, 134, 132, 143–4, 149–50, 154, 205; global city imaginary 111–12
globalisation 1, 7, 10, 79, 97, 110, 120, 122, 131–2, 136, 143–9, 180–1, 246; economic globalisation 180; neoliberal globalisation in Africa 60
global North 5, 79, 181
global South 2, 6, 12, 111, 181, 145–6
Goldeneye 236, 242
Gongdong gyeongbiguyeok 218
Good Bye Lenin! 30
Goopy Gyne Bagha Byne see *Adventures of Goopy and Bagha, The*
Gourevitch, Philip 179, 192

Graine et la mulet, La 12
Great Train Robbery, The 237
Green Fish 218, 223
guantes mágicos, Los 80
Gukjesijang 228
Gwoemul 218

Haeckel, Ernst 89
Haeundae 228
Haine, La 21, 206, 213
Hamburg 21, 235
Havre, Le 203
Hawa Bodol 120, 125–7, 129
Heap, Chad 184
Her 10, 28, 95–114
heritage 39, 106, 124
Hindi films 125
Hobbit, The 237
Hollywood 5–9, 12, 23–4, 29, 31, 33, 39, 69–70, 110–11, 115n.7, 121; Hollywood blockbusters 12, 31, 218; Hollywood noir 219, 223, 227; Hollywood romantic comedies 99–100; non-Hollywood film 25
homemade video 160, 163
homogenisation 7, 81, 96, 105–6, 114, 120, 132, 143, 146, 149
Hong Kong 7, 23, 153, 219–20, 235
Host, The see *Gwoemul*
Hostel (films) 237
How Do You Know 103
How high is the 21st floor? see *Ershiyi lou you you duo gao?*
How the Other Half Lives 11, 183, 187–8, 195n.12
human and nonhuman 10, 80–1, 87–90, 92
hybridisation 6–7, 10, 93n.5, 114, 130
hyper-modernity 23
Hwanghae see *Yellow Sea, The*

identity: generic identity 237; genre identity 108; identity creation 104; identity work 164; local identity 106; national identity 43, 232; new social identity 37, 227; regional identity 9, 37, 41–2
imagined community 37

immigration: Belgian immigrant 212; Danish immigrant 183; in France 12, 201–15, 215–216n.4; immigrants and slum 186, 195n.17; Maghrebi immigrants 203; militant immigrant cinema 201; non-European immigrants 202, 212; North African immigrant 201, 206; post-colonial immigrant 201, 212
independent cinema 104, 116n.11
Indian cinema 122
In Search of a Midnight Kiss 103, 106
In the Mood for Love 23
Invisible City 26–7
iROKO 65–7, 70–2
Istanbul 21, 153, 235

Jakarta 11, 178, 180, 187–8, 193-194n.3, 240
Jameson, Fredric 7, 20, 102, 108, 150
Janggunui adeul see General's Son, The
Japan 110, 227–8, 240
Jonze, Spike 10, 28, 95–101, 107–8
JSA see Gongdong gyeongbiguyeok

Kant, Immanuel 9, 27–8, 32
Kape neuwareu 220
Kawauchi, Rinko 107
Kechiche, Abdellatif 12, 21, 203, 208–9, 211
Killing, The see Forbrydelsen
Killing Only Took Seven Seconds, The 171–2
Kolkata 10, 119–20, 122–5, 126–36, 137n.9; global Kolkata 124; Kolkata eye 123; Kolkata as generic city 119; Kolkata one 123, 128–9; Kolkata take two 123, 128–9, 134–6; postcolonial transformation 10, 133
Koolhaas, Rem 7, 9, 20–1, 26, 33, 34n.3, 106, 112, 144, 149–50
Korean War 221, 228
Kosslick, Dieter 31
Koven, Seth 184
Kracauer, Siegfried 8

Lagos 9–10, 33, 59–73, 194-195n.10, 240

Lagos Cougars 10, 63, 66–7
Last Flight to Abuja 10, 67–9
Latin America 79–80, 90
Latour, Bruno 26–7, 29, 92, 93n.5
Lefebvre, Henri 219
Li Juchuan 11, 159, 170–3
Line of Passage 22
Little Yueyue 166, 168–70, 173n.6
Living in Bondage 62
London 21, 33, 34n.3, 65, 70–1, 111, 123–4, 147, 153, 154n.1, 184, 194-195n.10, 195n.13, 235, 242, 245, 249–50
Looper 110–11
Los Angeles (LA) 6–7, 10, 20, 22–3, 28, 95–7, 100–3, 110–13, 115n.8, 219, 238
Los Angeles Times 95, 102, 114n.1
Love, A 227
Luna de Avellaneda 80

Maach, Mishti and More 10, 120, 127–8
Maghreb 201–3, 206–7, 209–11
Magic Gloves, The see guantes mágicos, Los
Magnolia 22, 100
Mahanagar 129–30, 133, 137n.4
Malafouris, Lambros 87
Maljukgeori janhoksa 221
Malmö 9, 36, 38–9, 43–4, 47, 50, 53n.5
Man from Nowhere, The 219, 228–9
Manhattan 98
Manila 12, 21, 33, 184, 246–50
Marseilles 12, 202–5, 209, 215, 215-216n.4
Marxism 136, 181–2; Marxist urban geography 2; neo-Marxism 194n.7
Ma 6-T va crack-er 206
Masquerade 72
mass culture 61, 73, 183
Mauvaise foi 202
McQueen, Steve 238–9
media capitals 7
media ecology 11, 86, 158, 161, 170, 173
Medianeras 10, 80–92
Neombeo sseuri 218
Metropolis 3, 7, 10, 97, 108–10, 112–13

INDEX 257

middle class: global middle class 124; middle class immigrant 202; upper-middle-class Lagos 61–3; upper middle class in Cairo 150–1; urban middle-class 6, 19, 125, 184
middle of the road cinema 10, 120, 123, 125, 128, 130–1, 133–7, 137n.n.n.2,8,10
mise-en-scène 8, 105, 107, 110, 112, 206–7, 238, 247
Misérables, Les 237
Mission: Impossible (series) 236–7
Mission: Impossible III 110
movie theatre 1, 143
moving image 1, 3–4, 8, 11, 41, 115n.7, 120, 143, 157, 168–9
Mrinal, Sen 120, 135, 137n.4
Mujeokja see Better Tomorrow, A
Mukerjee, Srijit 120, 130–1
MultiChoice 65–6
multiculturalism 23; Multicultural Cinema 24; multicultural communities 21; multicultural representation 51
multi-lingual television 51
Mulvey, Laura 143
Mumbai 11, 22, 124, 129, 178, 180, 184, 187–8, 193-194n.3, 195n.15, 240
Mumbai cinema 124
Murdering six people in seven seconds see Sharen guocheng jin qi miaozhong
Mutt Boy see Ddong gae
Myeongdong Blues see Myeongdong bureuseu
Myeongdong bureuseu 220
Myeongdong chulsin 220
Myeongdong 44 beonji 220
Myeongdong janhoksa 220
Myeongdong nosinsa 220
My Sassy Girl 228–9

Naficy, Hamid 12, 204–5
Nahan zixu see Outcry
Nairobi 11, 178, 180, 187, 189–90, 192, 193n.3, 240–1
Nameless Gangster: Rules of the Game see Beomjoewaui jeonjaeng
narrative: crime narratives 43; fictional narrative 48; gangster narrative 222; geopolitical-narrative 237; immigrant narratives 202, 204–8, 211–12, 214, 215-216n.4; low carbon narratives 103; multiple narratives 46; multi-vocal narrative structure 46; narrative fiction 48; narrative films 22; narrative-ideological purpose 248; narrative landscape 4; narrative location 235; narrative logic 85; narrative space 97; narrative topographies 11; narrative universe 50; narratives of timespace 23; network narrative 189; positive counter-narratives 11
national cinema 1, 5, 25, 39, 209
Native of Myeongdong, A see Myeongdong chulsin
Nayak/The Hero see Today's Hero
neoliberalism: in Argentina 79; in West Africa 9, 59–73; in China 144, 149–54; neoliberal capitalist system 180–1; neoliberal culture of globalisation 144; neoliberal ethos 136; neoliberal penumbra 59; neoliberal screen culture 11
Netflix 9; Netflix of Africa 65–6
new media 2, 11, 81, 92, 173, 179–80, 185-7, 192, 194n.4
New World 219, 231
New York 7, 21, 33, 100, 105, 107, 121, 128, 137n.9, 173n.6, 183–4, 186, 195n.12, 219, 238–9, 245, 248
Nigerian film 9, 59, 71, 73
Nilsson, Thomas 50
Njoku, Jason 65, 71
Njoku, Mary Remmy 71–2
Noah 99
noir: dystopian noir 96; gangster noir 218–32, 220, 231; Hollywood noir 223, 227; Korean noir 220, 223; noir-esque visual aesthetics 223; post-war Hollywood noir 219; South Korean noir films 230; *see also* Nordic Noir
Nollywood 9–19, 59–73, 73n.n.1,2; New Nollywood 64, 67, 70, 73
Nordic Noir 9, 37–8, 44–8, 52, 52-53n.4
nostalgia 114, 121, 128, 134, 136, 218

No. 3 see Neombeo sseuri
nouvelle vague   209

objet trouvé see found footage
Ode to My Father see Gukjesijang
Old Gentleman in Myeongdong see
    Myeongdong nosinsa
Olins, Wolff   36
Once Upon a Time in High School see
    Maljukgeori janhoksa
One Wilshire   102
On Photography   185
Øresund   9, 36–52, 52n.n.1,2, 53n.9
Øresundsbron   36, 38
oso rojo, Un   80
Outcry   172
Overexposed City   26

pan-European television   51
pan-Nordic   40
Parallel Cinema   10, 120–2, 125, 134–5, 137n.1
Paris   6, 12, 21, 26, 33–4, 110, 121, 183, 187, 195, 120–5, 209, 211, 215, 215-216n.4, 237, 248–9
People's Republic of China   11, 159
pharmaceutical industry   246–8
photographic imagery   178
Pizza, Beer, and Cigarettes see Pizza, birra, faso
Pizza, birra, faso   80
Places We Live, The   11, 178–9, 182–3, 185–93, 193-194n.3, 194n.4
planetary urbanisation   2
Plunder Road   231
Pointe courte, La   209
Poisoned Bait   67
Police thrillers   238
post-anthropocentric   80;
post-cinematic   2, 11, 85, 143, 150, 153–4
post-classical comedies   98
post-colonialism   24, 122–3, 133, 201, 212, 216n.8; post-colonial Calcutta 137n.4
post-Fordist   31, 102, 113
post-gender   109
post-human   80, 97, 109; post-human romance   95, 114; post-human subjectivity   10, 99, 106

post-industrialism   9, 20, 23, 30, 37, 39, 44, 79, 81, 112, 143; post-industrial decline   3, 39, 113, 215-216n.4; post-industrial ecology   30
postmodernism   20–1, 25, 90–2, 95, 150; postmodern cinema   7; postmodern city   20; postmodern metropolis   21; postmodern urbanism   13
post-nationality   20, 23
post-panopticism   164, 166
post-war   121; post-war cinephilia   121; post-war Hollywood   219; Post-war Seoul   220–3
Potrč, Marjetica   193, 196n.25
poverty   6, 102, 123, 178, 183, 185, 192, 204, 224, 238; in Africa   60; in Buenos Aires   10, 79; childhood poverty   222; poverty porn   185; urban poverty   11, 130, 180–2, 185, 195n.13
Prague   235, 237
pre-war films   237
Progressive Era   183, 195n.13
public space   3, 11, 28, 31, 81, 96, 99, 101–2, 143, 146, 148, 150, 157, 159–62, 165–6, 168–9, 170, 172–3, 219

Quantum of Solace   236, 242–3

Raï   213
Ray, Satyajit   10, 119–22, 129–30, 132–3, 135–6, 137n.4
realism   8, 72, 201, 238–9; inadvertent realism   62
Red Bear, A see oso rojo, Un
remediation   5, 11, 85–6, 114, 148, 179, 186–7, 190–2
Results   103
retroactive temporalities   121
Riis, Jacob   11, 182–90, 193, 195n.n.12,16, 196n.n.19,20
Rio de Janeiro   21, 184, 240
Rock, The   239
romantic comedies   66, 84, 104, 202; Hollywood romantic comedies   99–100
Romao, Tico   237–8, 240

rouille et d'os, De   12, 204, 211–15
Rules of the Game see Geimui beopchik
Run Lola Run   30
Running Scared   237
Rust and Bone see rouille et d'os, De

Salut cousin!   202
Samba   202
Samia   202
Sarang see Love, A
Sasaeng gyeoldan see Bloody Tie
Sassen, Saskia   6–7, 20, 67
Saturday Night Live   95
Scandinavian television   37
science fiction   10, 96–7, 99, 108–13
Scott, Ridley   7, 27, 32, 96
screen cultures   3, 11, 143–154
screen media   1
selfies   11, 159–66, 170, 172
Sen, Aparna   125
Seoul   12, 21, 218–32, 232n.2, 249–50
Sète   208–11, 213, 215
Sex and the City   67
Shanghai   10–11, 28, 95, 97, 110–11, 115n.9, 143–54, 171, 225, 235–6, 240, 245
Sharen guocheng jin qi miaozhong   159
She's Out of My League   103
Shiri see Swiri
Short Cuts   22, 100
Shouf, Shouf Habibi   21
Shui de yanjing   159
Sidewalls see Medianeras
Silrok Kim Du-han   221
Silver Linings Playbook   103
Silvia Prieto   80
S1m0ne   108
Sinsegye see New World
Skäne   37, 41–2, 50, 52n.1, 53n.5
Skyfall   110, 236, 250
slum   178–93; diegetic slum worlds   189; slum-dwellers   179–80, 182–3, 186–9, 191–2, 194.n.n.5,6,8, 195n.15; slum imagery   11, 192; slum show   195n.12; slum tourism   11, 179, 184; 192; planet of slums   11, 178, 180–1; Victorian slums   194-195n.10
Slum, The   184
Slumdog Millionaire   22, 185, 240

Slum-TV   192–3, 196n.23
Smokey and the Bandit   238, 240
social documentary photography   179, 185, 189, 192–3
social media   99, 157, 160–7, 172
social voyeurism   184
Sontag, Susan   121, 185
Southern California   12, 110
South Korea   12, 218–23, 230–2, 240–1, 249–50
South Korean cinema   218, 221–2
South Korean gangster cinema/films   12, 219–21, 223–4; Korean gangster noir   223
Southland Tales   85
spy thriller   12, 235–7, 40
Stagecoach   237–8
Still Life   22
Straight Outta Compton   102
surveillance :   Surveillance Cameras   166, 172; surveillance video   11, 157–9, 166–9, 171–2; fake surveillance video   169
Suspect, The   219, 231
Sveriges Television (SVT)   40
Sweden   36, 38–41, 45, 48–50, 53.n.n.5,8
Swiri   218

Taegukgi hwinallimyeo   218
Taegukgi: The Brotherhood of War see Taegukgi hwinallimyeo
Tan Tan   11, 159, 168–70, 172–3
Taretto, Gustavo   10, 80–1, 85, 87, 92
Tatort/Standort   29–31
Team, The   51
Ten'ja   211
Terminator, The   110
terrain vague   210, 212
Thé à la menthe, Le   202
theatrical exhibition   1, 3
Third World   21, 181, 242; Third World urbanization   182
Thirst   228–9
Thy Will Be Done   70
Tidal Wave, The see Haeundae
Timecode   22
Tinsel   66
Today's Hero   130–1
Tokyo   6–7, 20–1, 33, 110, 112, 220

Tomorrow Never Dies   236, 242–3, 246
topoanalysis   121
topophilia   10, 120–9, 134, 136; topophobic discourse   123, 133
Tout ce qui brille   202
Transformers 4: Age of Extinction   110
Transformers: Revenge of the Fallen   110–11
transnational imaginary   9, 52, 231
transnational urban region   36–52
transnational urban space   37
True Story of Kim Du-han, A see Silrok Kim Du-han
Turistas   237
Turning Torso   39, 44
21 Grams   23
2001: A Space Odyssey   108, 110

Uniqlo   107, 160–6, 170, 172–3, 173n.3; Uniqlo incident   160–6, 169, 172, 173n.4; Uniqlo sex video   161–3
Up in the Air   26
urban: anti-urban   181; contemporary urbanism   102; hegemonic global urbanism   105; intra-urban class   6; Marxist urban geography   2; urban areas   2, 194n.5, 240; urban centres   104–5, 238, 246; urban cinema   5, 13, 81; urban citizenship   11; urban culture   7, 97, 107, 107n.5; urban economies   1; urban environment   1, 3–4, 10–11, 20, 22, 26, 28, 92, 104, 157, 164, 173, 214; urban failure   123; urban growth   2, 89, 181; urban hybridity   7; urban imaginaries   5; urban landscape   45, 62, 128, 182; urban life   2, 4, 19, 162; urban living   2–3, 28; urban space   1, 4, 7, 11–12, 21, 37, 43–4, 48, 96, 100, 101, 104, 160, 164–5, 181, 203–5, 219–20, 223, 226–7, 230, 232; urban past   11, 119–20, 136, 224; urban planning   60, 90, 171, 193; urban poverty   11, 130, 180–1, 185, 195n.13; urban representation   97, 114; urban romance   98; urban/rural   2, 181; urban underworld   183, 187

Van Helsing   237
van Hoytema, Hoyte   107–8
video art/artwork   11, 159, 168–71
View to a Kill, A   242
Village Headmaster   72
Virilio, Paul   26–7
virtual spaces   11, 159
visual agency   158, 160
visual ecosystem   11, 159
vital materialism   88

Xiao Wu   172
Xiao Yueyue shijian   166

walking word   144, 148–9, 152
Web documentaries   189, 196n.21
Weird Science   108
WeiweiCam   159, 171–2
Welcome   203, 215-216n.4
Welcome to Lagos   184
Western   203
Western media   161
Westworld   108
When Harry Met Sally   100
When Night Falls see Wo hai you hua yao shuo
Whose Eyes see Shui de yanjing   159, 168–70, 172
Wings of Desire   30
Wo hai you hua yao shuo   171
working-class: democratic working-class   208; militancy of the working class   19; working-class in Antibes   214; working-class decline   209, 214; working class community   208–11, 215; working class immigrant   202; working class in South Korean cinema   221; *see also* neoliberalism
world cinema   4–10, 24–5, 192–3
world citizenship   9, 27
World Is Not Enough, The   236, 250
World War II   30
Wujiaochang   145–6, 150–3

Yellow Sea, The   219, 229, 231–2
Ying hung boon sik   227
Yonguija see Suspect, The
YouTube   32, 47, 65, 84–5, 158, 172, 174n.8
You've Got Mail   99, 100